D1524885

Gateways to the Global Economy

Edited by

Åke E. Andersson
Professor in the department of Infrastructure and Planning
Royal Institute of Technology
Stockholm, Sweden

David E. Andersson
Research Fellow in the Institute of Economics
Academia Sinica
Taipei, Taiwan

Edward Elgar
Cheltenham, UK • Northampton, MA, USA

Published by
Edward Elgar Publishing Limited
Glensanda House
Montpellier Parade
Cheltenham
Glos GL50 1UA
UK

Edward Elgar Publishing, Inc.
136 West Street
Suite 202
Northampton
Massachusetts 01060
USA

A catalogue record for this book
is available from the British Library

Library of Congress Cataloguing in Publication Data

Gateways to the global economy / edited by Åke E. Andersson, David
  E. Andersson.
      Includes bibliographical references and index.
      1. Regional economics. 2. Urban economics. 3. Computer networks.
  4. Communication and traffic. I. Andersson, Åke E., 1936– II. Andersson,
  David E., 1966–

  HT388.G38 2000
  382'63—dc21   00–037619

ISBN 1 84064 389 7

Printed and bound in Great Britain by MPG Books Ltd, Bodmin, Cornwall

Contents

PART THREE
Asia-Pacific Gateway Regions

PART FOUR
European Gateway Regions

Contributors

Åke E. Andersson, Professor, Royal Institute of Technology, Sweden

David E. Andersson, Dr, Research Fellow, Academia Sinica, Taiwan

Lata Chatterjee, Professor, Boston University, USA

Søren Find, Section Leader, Technical Knowledge Center of Denmark

Michael A. Goldberg, Professor, University of British Columbia, Canada

Niles Hansen, Professor, University of Texas, USA

Börje Johansson, Professor, Jönköping International Business School, Sweden

Wolfgang Kasper, Professor, University of New South Wales, Australia

Kiyoshi Kobayashi, Professor, Kyoto University, Japan

Knut Koschatzky, Dr, Hanover University, Germany

T. R. Lakshmanan, Professor, Boston University, USA

Stefano Magrini, Professor, Università Ca'Foscari di Venezia, Italy

Dino Martellato, Professor, Università Ca'Foscari di Venezia, Italy

Jessie P. H. Poon, Professor, University of Buffalo, USA

Javier Revilla Diez, Dr, University of Hanover, Germany

Komei Sasaki, Professor, Sendai University, Japan

Folke Snickars, Professor, Royal Institute of Technology, Sweden

Roger R. Stough, Professor, George Mason University, USA

Luis Suarez-Villa, Professor, University of California, USA

Mikio Takebayashi, Research Associate, Kobe University, Japan

Edmund R. Thompson, Professor, University of Hong Kong

Christian Wichmann Matthiessen, Professor, University of Copenhagen, Denmark

Annette Winkel Schwarz, Director, Technical Knowledge Center of Denmark

Wei-Bin Zhang, Professor, National University of Singapore, Singapore

Preface

Globalization of the economy is now a fact. The improvement of networks for communication and transport has improved the conditions for global corporate strategies. The increasingly dense transport and communication networks and the regional equalization of education have at the same time improved the possibilities of planning and policy making at the regional level.

The consequence of this simultaneous globalization and regionalization processes is declining potentials of policy making by the territorial national governments. Not all regions are equally capable of exploiting the new opportunities provided by the emerging new globalized economy with its rapid expansion of communicative and creative possibilities. Large economic size of a region is a necessary but not a sufficient condition for a region to develop into a gateway to the new global economy. New infrastructural strategies are also required in order to generate a transformation into a sustainable gateway to the global economy.

The Stockholm County Council has taken the initiative to open up for a theoretical and empirical inquiry into the causes and consequences for metropolitan regions of the globalization process. This book is the primary outcome of the analysis of the position of metropolitan regions in the new globalized economy. The focus of the case studies presented in the book is on the experiences of different, highly developed metropolitan regions of policy making and planning, for positioning themselves as gateways to the new global economy. In this sense this is a benchmarking study, useful to metropolitan policy makers and planners. The contributors to this volume are all well-known experts on the dynamics of metropolitan regions.

This volume could never have been completed successfully without the coordinating activities of Jan Linzie, the stringent editorial work by David E Andersson and the cooperation between Gunvor Albihn and the editorial staff of Edward Elgar Publishing Company in the process of transforming the manuscripts into a printed book.

Åke E. Andersson
Professor of Infrastructural Economics
Royal Institute of Technology
Stockholm, Sweden

Bo Malmsten
Director, Office of Regional
Planning and Urban Transportation
Stockholm County Council
Stockholm, Sweden

PART ONE

Gateways to the Continents and the World

1. Gateway Regions of the World – an Introduction

Åke E. Andersson

THE CONCEPT OF A GATEWAY

Networks for transport, communication and other forms of interaction consist of links and nodes. In the economic context a *node* is often rather pragmatically defined as a city or a city region, homogeneous enough to be seen as an economic entity that interacts with other nodes. The interaction between the nodes is channeled through *links*. A link can be a telephone line, a pipeline, an air corridor or a road. In this context we make a fundamental distinction between networks and *networking*. The network is the channel through which interaction occurs, while networking is the process of interaction. A network is in almost all cases the result of a very time-consuming investment process. Networks are mostly highly durable, while networking can have a durability of days, hours or even seconds. Networks are public goods to the extent that they can be of simultaneous use to many without any necessity for rationing. The high degree of durability and publicness is the reason for classifying networks as *infrastructure*.

HIERARCHICAL NETWORKS

Networks are by geometrical necessity almost always hierarchical in the sense that some nodes are considered better than others. If a network is placed on a land formation of almost any geometrical shape, there will be some node at the center of gravity of the geometrical shape that will have a better than average access to all the other nodes. If, for instance, the land formation resembles a circular plane, the midpoint of the circle will be the center of gravity if transport is possible in all directions at a cost or economic friction proportional to the Euclidean distance between the points. It can easily be shown that the potential average cost of connecting with all points on this circular plane will increase monotonously with increasing radial

3

distance from the center of the circle. Defining *accessibility* as the inverse of the potential cost, the average accessibility on this circular plane is monotonously decreasing from the center to any point on the periphery. If we transform the circular plane into an ellipse of the same size, the difference in average accessibility between the center and the periphery will increase. This is one reason why oblong countries such as Norway, Sweden, Chile or Japan tend to have greater differences in economic conditions between the center and the periphery compared with countries of a more circular or quadratic shape.

Would it be possible to generate a geometric shape that would equalize the accessibility of all nodes? The answer is yes. An atoll, i.e. a hollow circular disc, would not give an accessibility advantage to any specific point. All nodes would have the same average potential cost and accessibility to all other points. Thus, there would be no natural center. But this is a highly exceptional case, if we look at subsets of the globe. Any region, nation or continent tends to have a hierarchical potential cost of interaction and accessibility distribution. And the networks placed upon these geometrical areas tend not to counteract these hierarchical tendencies. Networks of transport and communication are generically hierarchical at the sub-global level.

SOURCES, SINKS AND SADDLES

The networks for trade flows (the networks for flows of goods and services) are traditionally perceived as the most important economic networks. However, there is additionally a subset of important specialized networks that are designed to carry only one type of flow. One example from this subset is the electricity transmission network. Another is the network of natural gas pipelines. When we look at such a specialized network it is often advantageous to specify some of the nodes as *sources*, other nodes as *sinks* and a third type of nodes as *saddles*. The three types of nodes perform different roles in the network. The source nodes of an electricity network are the locations of the electricity sources such as nuclear reactors and hydroelectric generators. The sinks are the locations of electricity-using production units and households. Between the sources and the sinks there are saddle nodes, which are nodes where different types and flows of electricity are brought together, transformed and redirected to different sinks. These nodes are called saddle nodes because the incoming flows are not used in the node but sent out in other directions than the incoming flow directions. In short: flows originate in sources, are transformed in saddles and terminate in sinks.

The clear-cut properties of sources, saddles and sinks do not pertain to road networks and other *multi-purpose* networks, which together carry most of the economically important flows of any developed node.

HUBS AND GATEWAYS

Modern airline systems have developed into *hub-and-spoke* structures. This means that airlines tend to select one or a few nodes to have a more important role than the other nodes in the network. In a way these more important nodes or hubs function as saddle-point nodes through which much of an airline's traffic is channeled. One example is Copenhagen Airport, which is a hub for the Scandinavian Airlines System. Much of the traffic from Sweden and Norway is channeled through this hub airport. In many cases passengers from the Stockholm region traveling to airports in Asia or North America have to change planes at the Copenhagen hub airport. Similarly, Lufthansa uses Frankfurt as a hub airport through which most of the intercontinental German traffic is channeled. In the United States, American Airlines currently uses O'Hare Airport in Chicago as the main hub.

Large seaports have also had a (slightly different) role as hubs in the sea transport network. Southampton harbor once channeled most of the transatlantic passenger traffic from Britain. The Cunard Shipping Company used to have scheduled passenger sailings to and from New York, and these two big ports were the hubs to which passengers had to travel by train and other means of land transport before the transatlantic link could be used. But the seaports were hubs in a different way than airports. While the passengers using a hub airport enter and leave the hub by the same mode of transport, there is a modal change in most large seaports. The institutional conditions for creating an airline hub are also different when compared with the creation of a hub seaport. A decision-making process that is internal to an airline or a cartel of airlines primarily determines the creation of an airline hub. The Port of New York became a hub for transatlantic shipping of passengers and goods by a much more spontaneous evolutionary market process, without much of the centralized strategic planning typical of airline hubbing decisions.

How can we distinguish a gateway node from a hub? Is a distinction really necessary? I think a distinction ought to be made that is analytically and strategically meaningful. A hub can be analytically defined to be a node in which incoming flows of passengers, goods and other objects are reallocated to other links for onward transport to other destinations. A gateway can then be defined as a *multi-hub node*.

Hubs, as well as gateways, can have different geographical extensions. For example, Moscow is a very large gateway in terms of the volume and multitude of flows being channeled through that region. But the geographical extension is generally quite limited. Most of the traffic going through the gateway region of Moscow has the origin as well as the destination within the borders of Russia. The same is true of the gateways of Beijing and even of Shanghai, sometimes claimed to be the new gateway to Asia. On the other hand, there are examples of regions of rather limited size, such as Amsterdam or Frankfurt, which would qualify as global gateways in spite of their much more limited size in terms of population or gross regional product.

WHY GATEWAYS?

The creation of a hub is a necessary but not a sufficient condition for the emergence of a gateway region, according to our definition of the two concepts. A hub is created because of economies of scale and economies of scope within individual transport firms. To clarify the issues involved it is fruitful to concentrate on the example of airline hubs. Theoretically, an airline corporation could decide to use all nodes of a given airline network in a completely symmetric way. The planes could be serviced to the same extent at all the airports of the network. Administration could be equally large everywhere. Training, re-training, medical check-ups and personnel could also be spread equally between all airports and tactical and strategic personnel could be completely decentralized in space. But all of these functions require large and indivisible equipment and a multitude of highly specialized personnel who generate additional unavoidable fixed costs. If all planes are channeled through one airport, equipped with all the indivisible capital and specialized labor, there can be a much higher degree of average capacity utilization of capital and specialists. A concentration of indivisible capital and specialized labor therefore leads to a substantially lowered cost per passenger mile (or freight unit mile). To the airline company there is of course always a trade-off against the passengers' valuation of their loss of time and comfort when traffic is being hubbed. Excessive hubbing could lead to a loss of revenues that would outweigh the gains in terms of cost reductions. This is the reason why the largest airlines have a number of hubs in their networks, while smaller airlines are forced to limit the number of hubs to only one.

In the formation of financial hubs the comparative transaction-cost level has always been of great importance. Transaction costs are closely related to risks associated with transactions, especially those risks that are a necessary part of credit arrangements. Banking has always been a highly clustered economic activity and the same is true of stock, bond and option exchanges. Financial law-making as well as the reliability of public and private institutions in the financial market is crucial to the build-up of trust, which is a precondition for lowered transaction costs. Empirical studies have shown that a long financial history is of crucial importance to the perception of the quality of a financial market like London or Amsterdam. The same studies also indicate that the size and the scope of the market are essential determinants of which regions become financial gateways.

THE HISTORY OF GATEWAY FORMATION

Gateway cities and regions have a long history. Over the past millennium the role of accessibility by waterways has been crucial. Venice and Lübeck are two examples of medieval gateways. The independent city state of Venice became the most important gateway to the Mediterranean, where it connected the regions to the east and west as well as to the north and south of the sea. It was not only a hub for trade but also for the flows of cultural, artistic, religious and scientific ideas. Moreover, Venice gained in importance from the political unrest in the late middle ages. During the crusades to the Holy Lands the importance of Venice increased considerably and Venice became the undisputed gateway to the East.

However, during the fourteenth century Florence increased in relative importance, further increasing the role of northern Italy as a gateway region. With the expansion of trade, banking became crucial and the Medici family provided much of the financial resources needed for the risky and time-consuming trading expeditions. In the fifteenth century the importance of the Medicis steadily increased and Florence became a leading trading, financial, artistic and scientific gateway city, increasingly oriented to interacting with northern Europe.

Meanwhile, the late middle ages saw the development of a powerful network economy of the north – the Hanseatic League. The Hansa system consisted of trading towns around the Baltic Sea and the North Sea with extensions to towns along the big rivers of northern Europe. Each trading town was dependent upon agricultural and handicraft production in the surrounding *hinterland*.

In Northern Europe, with its weak connection to Southern Europe, Lübeck was the primary gateway to the Hanseatic League. The Hanseatic League had a complex combination of financial laws and regulations, trading houses, shipping and political conflicts with the emerging north European nation states. But with the opening up of routes for increased trade between the Mediterranean economic system and Northern Europe, financial and trading activities as well as artistic interchange moved to Bruges in Flanders, the new primary gateway to the European economy. In Bruges, the important trading towns in different parts of Europe had their own trading houses and representatives.

At the time of the integration of the Venetian and the Hanseatic trading systems three major gateway regions had emerged. Northern Italy was one such region with its focal points in the cities of Venice, Florence and Genoa. The second region was northern Germany with Lübeck as the major city. In the Low Countries, Bruges was the major city both of that region as well as in the European network as a whole. By the end of the fifteenth century, however, the role of these gateway regions was steadily diminishing. There has been some dispute about the reasons for the decline of northern Germany, Bruges and its surrounding region and the cities of northern Italy. Some have focused on local factors within the Hanseatic League or even siltation in the port of Bruges. But such explanations seem to be much too local to provide a general explanation.

More reasonable from a system-wide point of view are the rather dramatic changes that occurred in the transport and transaction systems by the end of the fifteenth century. In the earlier period, sea technology was dominated by the Hanseatic cog and similar small ships in the south of Europe. These ships could only safely be used for transport in waters protected from heavy winds. Most of the shipping of these times was thus confined to coastal stretches and rivers. For journeys between Northern and Southern Europe, land routes – often in the hands of 'robber barons' – had to be used.

Meanwhile, sea trade and other risky transactions had been increasing to a point where the primitive banking system and the reliance on scarce precious metals as mediums of exchange had become a constraint on the further expansion of trade.

With the invention and innovation of a new type of ship – the *caravelle* – both of these trading constraints slowly but steadily became less important and a new pattern of location and trade flows could emerge. With the caravelle it was possible to sail around the Pyrenean peninsula, which put Portugal and the city of Lisbon into focus as a new potential gateway for trade, financial and cultural exchange between the north and the south of Europe. But even more importantly, Lisbon became a natural terminus for trans-oceanic trade and colonial expeditions. The caravelle was capable of regular expeditions between Europe and the Americas, which opened up Europe both for new goods and, crucially, a steadily increasing flow of precious metals, which was necessary for a renewed expansion of trade transactions.

The role of Lisbon as a major gateway city turned out to be transitory. In the long run, accessibility to the tradable goods of Europe and the Americas was much better in the Low Countries. Two expanding cities were to become important gateways in that part of Europe. These two major gateway cities were Antwerp and Amsterdam. Amsterdam eventually became the most successful of the two in the sixteenth- and seventeenth-century economy. Again, the key to success for Amsterdam and the northern Low Countries was major inventions and innovations in transportation and transaction technologies.

The caravelle had opened the oceans for combined military and trading expeditions, but at a high cost of manpower and other necessary resources on long and dangerous voyages. After the initial stage of colonization there was a need for more efficient and less labor-intensive shipping. The Dutch provided the new means of transportation when they invented the *flute*, an ocean-going but much more cost-efficient ship. The Dutch superiority in ship-building was so widely recognized that it induced Tzar Peter the Great to travel incognito to Holland in order to personally learn the science and art of ship-building – a remarkable early case of systematic 'benchmarking'.

The other important invention was a new organization of banking. Earlier banking had been based on guarantees provided by private banker-traders. These combined bankers and traders sometimes provided high-risk credit to kings and the church. The mixing of purposes among the banker-traders tended to increase the cost of borrowing to high levels, which were further increased by the inherently risky nature of long-distance, time-consuming, international trade. Consequently, there was a need for some reform that would secure better means of payment for internal and external trade, more reliable stores of value and less costly forms of credit in association with commercial activities.

The rulers of the city of Amsterdam were the first to realize that these needs could only be satisfied by a bank with some form of public guarantees. The first public central bank useful for all these purposes was therefore established by the city of Amsterdam. It rapidly made Amsterdam a preferred place for all types of commercial, industrial, political and cultural transactions. The growth of Amsterdam's population was a reflection of its growing importance as the most important European gateway of the seventeenth century (Braudel, 1979).

In the seventeenth century, the population quadrupled, reaching 200,000 by the end of the century. The growth of income and wealth was of course highly skewed in favor of the expanding class of commercial capitalists, who dominated the economic, political and cultural life of Amsterdam (seen by Fernand Braudel as the capital city of the world economy of those days).

During the first logistical revolution, which ended during the Renaissance, creativity in the arts and sciences blossomed in the major gateway regions of Flanders and northern Italy with the cities of Bruges and Florence as major nodes for the interchange of new ideas. History repeated itself during the second logistical revolution when the Netherlands and Amsterdam as the point of interchange became one of the major centers of artistic and scientific creativity. The general inflow of different ideas and the amassment of wealth in the commercial capital of Amsterdam seem to have triggered the financial means for creativity in the arts and sciences.

In the eighteenth century the relative role of Holland and Amsterdam started to decline in favor of England and London. The idea of a publicly supported central bank as a key to lowered transaction costs was too good not to be imitated by others. In England the concept of the central bank was taken up, gradually refined and put into a new and more important form, when the Bank of England and the stable currency were created and supported by parliamentary guarantees.

The new, increasingly powerful, Bank of England became one of the preconditions for the expansion of the North Atlantic economic system that emerged in the eighteenth century and which grew in scope and size during the third logistical or industrial revolution of the nineteenth and early twentieth centuries. The third logistical revolution proceeded in distinct spatial and temporal stages. In the first stage, England and the newly established state of Belgium, with London, Manchester–Liverpool and Antwerp, became major gateway regions on the European side of the Atlantic, while Philadelphia, New York and Boston became major gateways to the American economy.

The possibility of becoming a gateway in the industrial economy was closely related to the building of a new transport infrastructure. In the earliest stage of industrialization this implied the availability of a big harbor suitable for intercontinental transport and trade in industrially produced goods, combined with being connected to a large hinterland by canals and river networks. This double dependence on waterways constrained industrialization to take place only on low-lying plains.

Further industrialization in a second stage required a new transportation technology and a new transportation network. The railroad networks of Europe and the United States became the precondition for the second stage of industrialization in Europe and North America. During the first stage of the industrial revolution the major gateways were London, Manchester, Antwerp, New York and Boston, with an absolute and lasting dominance of New York and London. And London and New York never lost their primary gateway positions in the world economy thereafter. A combination of dynamic economies of scale and path dependence have reinforced the advantages of such successful global gateway cities and their surrounding regions.

On both sides of the North Atlantic, the nineteenth century became the century of railroad network construction. By the early twentieth century the transportation infrastructure of the industrialized world had established a structure (topologically) that would determine the comparative advantages and disadvantages of different regions into the second half of the twentieth century. Favored by this new infrastructure were those regions that were located at points with simultaneously (relatively) excellent potential accessibility by sea and the new rail network. The railroads linked up to the rich deposits of natural resources in the interior of the continents.

A further precondition of rapid industrialization was the establishment of new and liberal economic laws. In all the successful industrialization processes, freedom of trade, property rights and the creation of a (British) banking system have been necessary conditions for the take-off into sustained industrialization. The building of an industrial infrastructure required enormous investment funds that could rarely be found by standard credit financing.

In most countries a combination of political propaganda supporting railroad and other infrastructural projects, government guarantees for loans from foreign countries and increasing rates of taxation were used to gather the necessary funds for massive investments in industrial infrastructures. All of this, together with the increasing use of national natural resources, became important factors behind the general rise in nationalism in the industrializing countries.

It thus became increasingly important to establish commercial and industrial activities close to the centers of political decision-making in the national capitals. Some of these capitals were conveniently located with the necessary accessibility by sea and rail. Others, such as Paris or Berlin, lacked efficient harbors and were consequently somewhat disadvantaged in global relations. These regions could only grow by strengthening their role in a hierarchically organized national, industrial, economy governed by state initiatives, rules and regulations. In Germany, Hamburg and the Ruhr region became important hubs of industrial trade and transport, without ever being transformed into generalized gateways.

The same separation of gateway functions between the political capital and the industrial districts on the Atlantic coast was also typical of French industrialization. Paris grew into the most important domestic gateway, but never became a global gateway during the third logistical or industrial revolution. The French economic historian Fernand Braudel has expressed his wonder over the remarkable capacity of Paris to grow by coordination of national economic interaction while at the same time managing to avoid interaction forces working at a continental, intercontinental and global level.

By the end of the 1960s, industrialization had reached the final decade of the third stage. During this third stage that part of Europe that had remained within the capitalist market economy (and belonged to the international

Organization for Economic Cooperation and Development (OECD)) had become industrialized. In the third stage, Scandinavia, Italy, Spain and Japan industrialized at a much higher rate of change than had been recorded during the first and second stages of industrialization. This is reflected by the steadily increasing rate of growth of real per capita income of countries belonging to later stages of industrialization. While Britain recorded a rate of real per capita income growth of close to 1 percent per year, Germany experienced a growth rate of almost 2 percent and the countries on the periphery of the then industrialized world grew at rates of between 2.5 and 3.5 percent (Maddison, 1982).

There was an 'economic advantage of backwardness' during the industrialization process. This is not as paradoxical as it may seem. The industrialization process gained in speed when countries had the opportunity of learning from other, earlier industrialized countries, rather than when they had to make all the mistakes themselves and engage in costly creative activities. And here the interaction by trade and other forms of economic exchange played an enormous role as a device for imitation, learning and other different forms of benchmarking. There was a steady flow of ideas from the early to the late industrializers, a process that is still under way in the non-OECD countries that are currently being industrialized in Asia and Latin America.

It is highly probable that the former communist economies will see similar gains from benchmarking, when their infrastructure of common values and laws and rules of economic behavior have converged sufficiently to allow for a speedy transformation into industrialized market economies.

THE TRANSFORMATION INTO THE NETWORKING C-SOCIETY

Much of the clustering of industrial companies and their major plants and control units at the ocean coasts was a direct consequence of the industrial transport and communication infrastructures. Only at a few nodes could the simultaneous demand for efficient international trade and inbound commodity freight be realized at reasonable cost. Likewise, the knowledge infrastructure was concentrated at these points of industrial agglomeration, because of a combination of economies of scale of teaching at higher levels and the high costs of personal transport of students and teachers.

As a result, technological institutes as well as business schools were established in the vicinity of industrial and trading hubs. Higher education contributed to the gateway function since it supplied people trained for the internationalization of production, commerce and technological development.

In the early stages of industrialization, educated people were extremely scarce and the average level of education was low. It has been estimated that around 1900 in the OECD countries the average level of formal education amounted to less than three years per capita while engineers, managers, lawyers and members of the bureaucracy had education levels of 15 years or more. It was therefore economically advantageous to adopt the hierarchical organization principles of the church and the military in industrial organization within plants and companies as well.

Extensive division of labor was applied at the bottom level, while coordination and creative activities was reserved for a small, well-educated managerial and technological élite. The majority of the population of the industrial countries accepted a spatial and organizational hierarchy, because it seemed the most efficient way of organizing society.

This acceptance was reinforced by educational programs that stressed not only reading, writing and arithmetic but also disciplined behavior for materialistic gains (Inglehart, 1977). All of the infrastructural preconditions for industrial organization have now changed. Table 1.1 summarizes the transformation of the infrastructure.

The infrastructural preconditions for the transformation of most advanced market economies was completed by the 1980s. It required equally dramatic transformations of economic organization, logistical behavior and locational patterns. The reorganization and relocation process is currently well under way. The changes have been most profound in the new reliance upon communications, creative activities and financial services. In all of these three cases globalization is the dominant tendency.

The reason for the new creativity orientation is quite consistent with the classical theory of comparative advantages. Most of the advanced market economies and especially those regions endowed with high-quality educational institutions have seen their relative supply of natural resources, energy and unskilled labor reduced, while the relative availability of skilled labor at a high level of education has been steadily increasing.

Meanwhile, the comparative advantage of production of simpler commodities has been expanding in the newly industrialized countries with growth rates of more than 5 percent annually. Increasingly complex products, research and development and the design of products have thus become major comparative advantages and a competitive strategy of industries in the scientifically advanced regions of the economically advanced countries. But this is not a stable strategy for the classical industrial firm.

New knowledge will in the long run become a public good, while most of the cost of creative investments is borne by firms and other economic agents in the creative region. The most efficient way of protecting the right to the revenues is by creating a global sales organization and by transnational investments, mergers and acquisitions. This process has also been beneficial for the creative process itself.

Table 1.1 The infrastructural transformation from industrial to C-society

	From	To
TRANSPORT	Low capacity for transportation	High capacity for continental or global personal and goods transport
	Sparse and rigid networks	Multi-layered dense and flexible networks
	Large scale of vehicles	Small scale of vehicles
	Hierarchical and monopolized	Non-hierarchical and competitive
COMMUNI-CATION	Low capacity of communication networks	High capacity for global communication
	Intra-national structure of nodes and links	Dematerialized information transfer
	National monopolies	Competitive entry and exit of continental or global communication firms
EDUCATION	Average schooling: 3 years	Average schooling: 12–14 years
	Large differences	Small differences
RULES OF ECONOMIC CONDUCT	National efficient controls	Continental, inefficient controls
	Effective taxation of firms and households	Ineffective taxation
COMMON VALUE	Materialistic: Nationalistic, Hierarchical, Productivity-oriented	Post-materialistic: Cosmopolitan, Non-hierarchical, Creativity-oriented

As has been shown by Edwin Mansfield (1977, 1995), the co-location of marketing units and research and development activities tends to be efficient for creative activities. This is probably one of the reasons why so many research, development and design activities are concentrated in large city regions with good connections to a local, dynamic market as well as being centers of transnational marketing, exports and imports.

Regions with agglomerations of higher learning and basic research have become increasingly attractive for producers of knowledge and information-intensive products. It is not an unreasonable forecast that such regions will be *the* global gateways of the future. The new information and knowledge infrastructures are creating gateway advantages for these C-regions, richly endowed with capacities for communication, cognitive activities and creativity.

At the same time the increasing capacity for transporting goods and people, which is necessary for service production, has come to imply completely new opportunities for building logistical networks based on outsourcing to small production or distribution units according to the comparative advantages of often distant regions.

One example is the Ikea corporation, a major interior decoration company with a steadily increasing number of production and distribution units around the world and a highly concentrated location of design, financial and information technology units.

Other examples can be found in the pharmaceutical, software and entertainment industries. The entertainment industry is especially interesting from a locational point of view.

In this industry economies of scale in the creative activities are extremely pronounced while, at the same time, the cost of transportation and distribution of the end products is decreasing over time. Still, a quarter of a century ago many entertainment services were dependent upon live performances in large concert halls or theaters, primarily located in metropolitan areas. This has been changing rapidly.

The increasing reliance on electronic media and the possibility of consuming these services at home or in a scattered and flexible pattern of festivals has led to an increasing dominance of a few regions. Gateways such as London, New York, Chicago and Los Angeles are the locations for producing an increasing number of different cultural products. These products can easily be distributed through the modern communication networks to a steadily increasing number of distribution nodes.

For some products we are already at a point where southern California, with Los Angeles as its core, is the gateway region for entertainment products to be consumed at home, all over the world, through a truly multi-domestic network.

GLOBAL GATEWAYS OF THE FUTURE

With the globalization of transport communication networks, the leading market economies are no longer concentrated on the Western hemisphere but are spread around the globe. Countries like South Korea, Japan, Taiwan and cities like Hong Kong and Singapore as well as Australia and New Zealand are similar to the advanced economies of Europe and North America in terms of per capita incomes, infrastructural and other capital resources and accessibility to import markets. The world economy is now placed on a global disc that allows for the emergence of important gateways almost anywhere. Before, the trade in goods and raw materials dominated economic interaction. This is not the case any longer and will probably be so even less in the future. Trade in services is growing rapidly, financial flows are increasingly important and the exchange of information, knowledge and artistic ideas is an increasingly important aspect of global interaction. Today, and even more in the future, a region can be a major gateway without even having its own shipping facilities.

This does not mean that city regions like New York or London will lose their positions as the super-gateway regions of the world. The internal and external economies of scale that have already been achieved and the accessibility advantages that have developed over long periods of investment in the transport and communication infrastructures have brought these regions lasting locational advantages. These advantages are likely to remain, even if other regions will rise to become continental or global gateways.

REFERENCES

Braudel, F. (1979), *Le Temps du Monde*, Paris: Libraire Armand Colin.
Inglehart, R. (1977), *The Silent Revolution: Changing Values and Political Styles among Western Publics*, Princeton, NJ: Princeton University Press.
Maddison, A. (1982), *Phases of Capitalist Development*, Oxford and New York: Oxford University Press.
Mansfield, E. (1977), *The Production and Application of New Industrial Technology*, New York: Norton.
Mansfield, E. (1995), *Innovation, Technology and the Economy*, Aldershot, UK and Brookfield, US: Edward Elgar.

2. Research Gateways of the World: an Analysis of Networks Based on Bibliometric Indicators

Christian Wichmann Matthiessen, Annette Winkel Schwarz and Søren Find

INTRODUCTION

Universities, research institutions, firms and leaders of (large) urban agglomerations interact at a growing rate in creating a solid knowledge base for their city. They do so because they share the view that the local knowledge base is of increasing importance for urban economic growth and change. They also do so because a high and growing level of investments in research and development is worthwhile for activating the region. And they do so in spite of their belief that distance plays a less and less important role and that access to information is almost universal in the 'information society'.

There has indeed been a remarkable decrease in communication and transportation costs over the past few decades, giving rise to networking over long distances. And if one asks scientists about their individual pattern of contacts they will often point out that it is international or even global. But when summarized for scientists of a given region, it turns out that the 'gravity model' offers the best explanation of contacts with other regions. This implies that a short physical distance between scientists is still an important criterion for cooperation. Synergies between ideas and direct face-to-face communication between scientists still are major factors of productivity (Andersson and Persson, 1993). So are economies of scale in the successful development of ideas (Zhang, 1994). In their book on technopoles of the world, Castells and Hall (1994) write:

> Cities and regions are being profoundly modified in their structure, and conditioned in their growth dynamics, by the interplay of three major interrelated, historic processes: a technological revolution based on information technologies, the formation of a global economy that works as a unit in a worldwide space for capital, management, labor, technology and markets, and the emergence of a new form of

economic production and management characterized by the fact that productivity and competitiveness are increasingly based on the generation and distribution of new knowledge.

In their Swedish study on urban growth, Andersson, Anderstig and Hårsman (1990) link innovation capacity with a high economic growth rate at the municipal level and find a clear positive relation. We assume that a solid knowledge base is reflected in the economic life of a given city, and the assumption is founded on examples such as the location pattern of the pharmaceutical industry, the Cambridge Phenomenon (Wickstead, 1985; Keeble, 1989) and the Silicon Valley experience (Hall, 1997).

Castells and Hall (1994) remark that no region can prosper without linkages to sources of innovation and production, and that a new industrial geography with different levels of specialization and a diversity of markets is advancing rapidly. In a world economy whose productive is infrastructure more and more made up of information flows, cities and regions are increasingly becoming critical agents of economic development. Cities and regions thus throw themselves into the roles of entrepreneurs. Their leaders want to engage their local area in competition by attracting new activities in the form of investments and visitors (Berg et al., 1998). They also want to establish the best framework for local firms, which are the real competitors. The strengths and structural characteristics of individual regions are often grouped in broad themes under different headings. One of these groups is inevitably marked as creativity or categorized under related headings such as knowledge, innovation or research and development.

Scientific wealth can be analyzed in terms of the rapidly growing number of research papers and documents. Nations are often taken as the units of analysis since statistics are presented on a national scale and can be used as input data. Another reason is that many quantitative studies of research production use the large bibliometric data banks directly. When doing so, the obvious registration unit is again the nation, because it is easy to identify the nation in the address of the author of a given publication. May (1997) presented an overview of the scientific wealth of nations and pointed out that productivity levels were different as well as the specialization profiles. But in a world where the importance of regions and cities as sites of competition and as producers of strategic plans is rising, it is also of interest – especially for investors, local planners and people 'selling' cities – to identify comparative positions in scientific strength. The university as a knowledge source for local or regional spin-off has rarely been investigated empirically, write Geenhuizen et al., (1997), but evidence based on an analysis of co-authorships (Andersson and Persson, 1993) suggests that local and regional spin-offs are an important factor for economic development.

Figure 2.1 Top 40 research centers of the world. Ranking based on number of papers produced by authors located in city

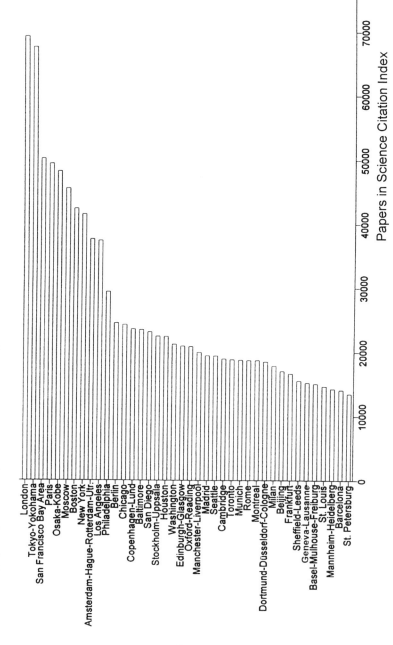

The recent shifts in industrial geography combined with the increasing importance of regional and urban competition may lead one to focus on different factors. In this chapter research strength of the major research metropoles of the world is analyzed in general terms because the importance of this factor in regional and urban competition is generally recognized, although relations between urban and regional economic growth and knowledge levels, as mentioned above, are far from clear. The present chapter analyzes scientific volume and interrelations between centers using indicators such as co-authorship and citations. The aim is to identify the research gateways of the world. These gateways are defined as nodal cities with access to large research networks, and which play important roles in the research community of the world. A spatial geographical urban delimitation is combined with the systematic use of the Science Citation Index (SCI)[1] to elaborate a reasonably significant list of important research centers as measured by research output registered under the address of the authors' institutions. Data compilation on research is discussed in reports from EUROSTAT and the OECD and the method used here is related to this work.[2] The analysis covers the urban units presented in Figure 2.1. They represent the largest scientific centers of the world, measured by output of SCI-registered papers between 1996 and 1998 in science, medicine and engineering, with all the biases and problems inherent in this type of data. International bibliographic databases are useful tools for studying many aspects of the international research system, but the data are not unproblematic, due to various biases of coverage, to different publication patterns in different disciplines and to technical intricacies, like multiple authorships[3] (Schwarz et al., 1998). Some analysts find it impossible to evaluate scientific productivity on the basis of publication and citation data. We obviously do not share such an opinion. Our conclusion is that analyses based on bibliographic data can give indications (but indications only) of a quantitative nature, but that interpretations must be seen in the light of the shortcomings and biases inherent in the data.

DELIMITATION OF URBAN UNITS

There exists no easy way to obtain comparable data on large cities. National statistical offices delimit urban units by different philosophies and postal services do not provide lists of place names or postal numbers that are clustered to comparable functional urban units. Series of attempts at constructing a European counterpart to the metropolitan region concept of the United States are still short of results that can be used for the purpose of comparing the scientific volume of large cities. NUREC (1994) is working on this, and so are other organizations, like the RECLUS–DATAR group (RECLUS–DATAR, 1989;

Cattan et al., 1994). This French group has done original work on categorizing and analyzing the urban system of the European Union. In general the closest one comes to a generally accepted definition of the urban unit is the United Nations *urban area concept*, but it is purely physical and based on distance between buildings. This widely used definition is actually an anachronistic delimitation of greater urban units, especially when it comes to comparative studies, because distance between buildings does not determine function, although distances influence function. Extension and density in urban regions differ due to tradition, legal factors, physical layout, and development stage.

Lacking a general formal or functional definition, we have used a spatial physical concept as the basis for identifying a borderline for each large agglomeration conceptualized as a 'greater' urban region. We have used the NUREC concept and thus added neighboring local units to the urban area defined by the UN method, and further added additional local units if densities of urbanized areas on detailed topographical maps indicated suburbanization. We additionally checked this with population figures to find an acceptable extension of a single agglomeration. Outside the NUREC atlas area delimitations are estimates. Homogeneity of estimates has been given priority but no precise method has been used. We have further included neighboring agglomerations in a single regional unit if the travel time between city centers is less than 45 minutes. This way of spatially delimiting urban regions using a strict rule to aggregate the units thus established combines similar cities with high levels of interactivity (for example the units of the Rhine–Ruhr area), but also puts together dissimilar cities with few interactions (for example Oxford and Reading). We have been careful not to let our varying knowledge about the cities influence the exercise.

RESEARCH OUTPUT: MEGACITIES OF THE WORLD

The top 40 research centers are listed and ranked in Figure 2.1. Concentrations of research output form a distinct pattern, with North America, the northwestern part of Europe, and Japan in dominant positions. Ten urban regions constitute the top level in terms of research output. London and Tokyo–Yokohama are the outstanding centers. They are followed by the San Francisco Bay Area, Paris, Osaka–Kobe, Moscow and Boston. Additionally, New York, Randstad (Amsterdam–Hague–Rotterdam–Utrecht) and Los Angeles join this super-league (to use terminology from sports). The next group of eight metropoles is led by Philadelphia and Berlin followed by Chicago, Copenhagen–Lund, Baltimore and San Diego. Stockholm–Uppsala and Houston also belong to this first division. The rest of the cities on the list form a second division (to stay with sports language) with 22 participants. This group is dominated by

European cities. Also, three United States centers and two Canadian cities are found here, together with Beijing and St Petersburg.

National patterns of concentration are obvious, relating to differences in policy over centuries. Nations with a tradition of urban concentration, like France and Russia, demonstrate a very centralized pattern of research output, and nations with a tradition of deconcentration such as Germany, Britain and the United States also demonstrate a decentralized pattern for the production of research results. There are also clear differences that derive from university location policy, ranging from the university-town or campus philosophy, with Cambridge as an example, to the capital-city university structure with Washington, Rome and Madrid as examples. The research output of a city, measured as the number of papers produced by scientists located in the greater urban area, clearly demonstrates a pattern that deviates fundamentally from the way the large cities of the world are generally conceptualized. Even relatively small cities like Cambridge or Stockholm–Uppsala present themselves as megacities when it comes to research output. Clearly a pattern of economic development stage is also reflected in the ranking of the centers. What must be remarked too is the very high number of large research centers located in Britain and the United States.

To obtain this list of the top 40 cities in the world measured by research output we have tested many other cities in order to do justice to all. For the European centers we have registered the output of 1996–98 for the 39 centers which ranked highest in 1994–96 (Matthiessen and Schwarz, 1999), measured by methods similar to the one presented here. The European cities are ranked almost identically in 1994–96 and 1996–98, and the list in Figure 2.1 excludes cities such as Zürich, Brussels–Antwerp, Vienna, Helsinki, Lyon and a series of East European metropoles. They are simply not large enough in research output to find their way into the global top 40 list. For the rest of the world, 31 centers have been measured, but only 18 found their way into the top 40 list. Centers like Auckland, Dallas, Denver, Detroit, New Delhi, Singapore, Sydney and Tel Aviv are not large enough to enter this list.

For the years 1996–98, the Science Citation Index registers 2,768,615 papers on a worldwide basis. Out of this large number of papers the 40 largest centers account for 1,071,716.[4] The data set used for analysis comprises these 40 cities. It registers output measured as papers, co-authorship between authors from each pair of cities and citations from authors in each city to authors in the other cities.

RESEARCH COOPERATION: CO-AUTHORSHIP PATTERNS

The interaction pattern of researchers mirrors the flows of ideas and reflects attraction patterns and traditions of cooperation. It is influenced by similarities and differences of many types and also reflects different kinds of barriers against contacts. Research cooperation contributes to the status of a given city and demonstrates the nodal position of the center in question. The geography of co-authorships is indicated on two similar map-type diagrams.[5] Observed co-authorships are linked to the expected level of co-authorships between scientists in two cities estimated from statistical averages across the intercity links considered.[6]

Total intercity co-authorships number 186,445 cases and the major links are given in Figure 2.2, where links of 200 percent or more of the expected co-authorships between two cities are indicated. The diagram is dominated by national intercity links within the United States with major nodes being Boston, Los Angeles, the San Francisco Bay Area, New York, Philadelphia and Baltimore. National patterns for Britain and Germany are also evident and some additional strong urban interrelations within nations are present in Canada, Japan, Russia, Spain, Italy and Switzerland. The number of international links within Europe implies a more international perspective than the American one except for Britain, whose scientists are as nationally focused as in the United States.

Important European nodes are cities like London, Geneva–Lausanne, Mannheim–Heidelberg, Basel–Mulhouse–Freiburg, Munich and Berlin. Only two intercontinental links are strong enough to be indicated on the diagram. The 12 centers mentioned above represent the top tier of intercity co-authorship relations and are thereby characterized as major gateways in terms of the total (national plus international) research network.

LEADERS AND FOLLOWERS: CITATION PATTERNS

Researchers cite other researchers when they use results, discuss papers, reflect on or criticize methods and findings. Many motivations lie behind the way people cite other people. We assume that the overall citation pattern reflects or indicates mutual respect for the cited paper, although there are other motives for citing. The citation pattern reflects many underlying factors like language, nationality, religion, culture, economic blocks and even friendship (there are notorious examples of 'mutual citation clubs'). Citation traditions vary between disciplines, universities and between the university world and other producers of research output, like private firms and public organizations. An idea or result might be so advanced or untraditional that it is not immediately or generally understood as a breakthrough, and thus nobody cites the paper presenting the idea. The profile of citation patterns is very complicated but in our opinion an analysis of citation patterns nevertheless yields a meaningful indication of leaders and followers.

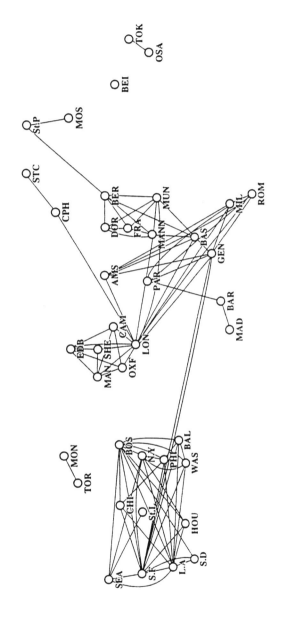

Figure 2.2 Intercity c-oauthorship. Total of national and international links larger than 200 percent of the expected volume indicated

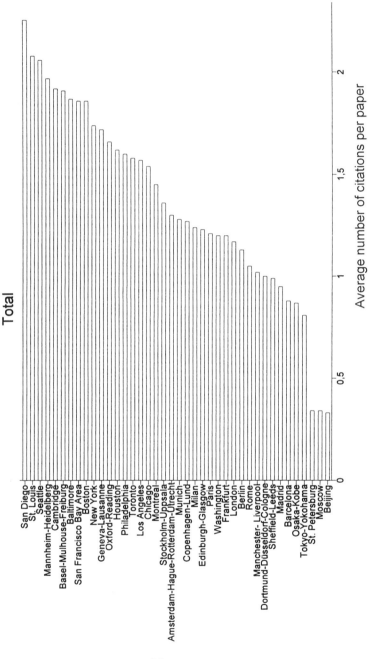

Figure 2.3 Ranking of cities by leadership. National plus international citations

Figure 2.4 Level and impact of leadership. National plus international citations

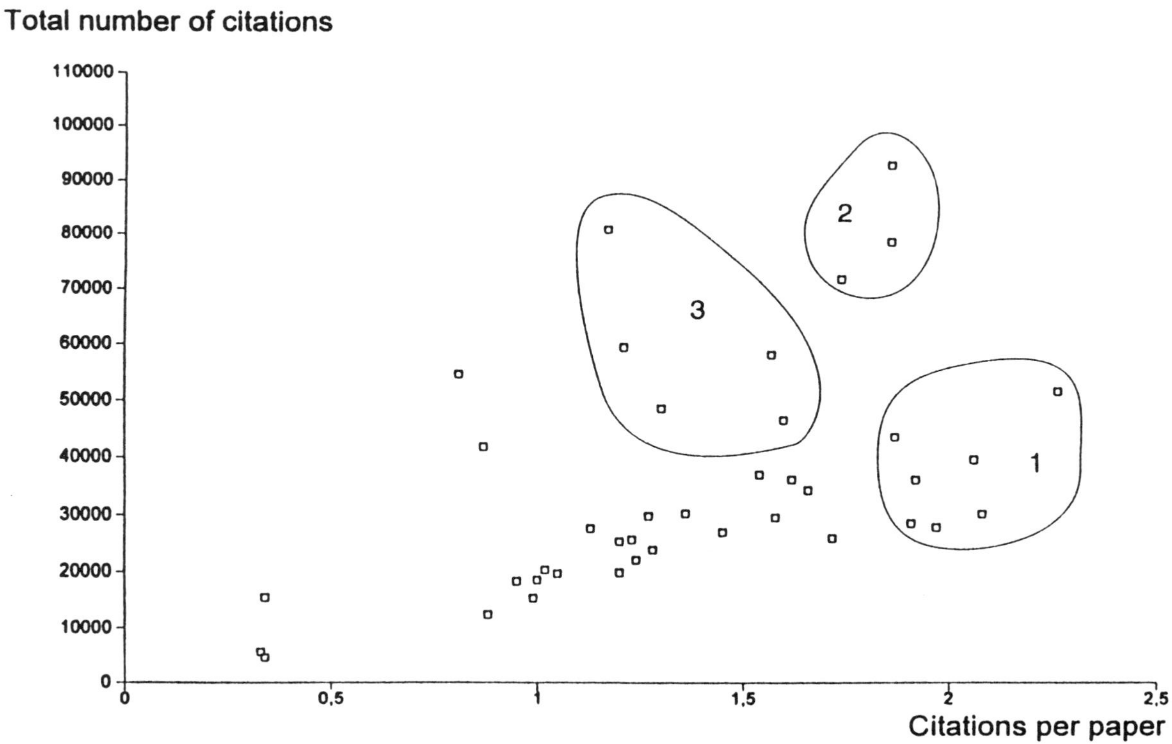

The mere number of citations in the data set is so large that it may include a lot of 'noise'. We find a total of 1,425,779 cross-citations in the data set, of which 1,000,985 are international.[7] The total number of papers in the same data set is 1,071,716 and on average each paper is cited 1.36 times by authors from other cities and 0.98 times by authors from other cities located in other nations. The period of publication and citation is 1996 to 1998, which implies that citations can be expected to be fewer for the newer papers than for the older ones. The analysis of citation links aims of identifying leading cities to give an additional characterization of the research gateway pattern.

In Figure 2.3, average citations by authors from all other cities to papers from the cities indicated are ranked by citation-receiving cities. The variation in the citation rate is large. Papers from the most cited unit, San Diego, are on the average cited 2.3 times while papers from the least cited city, Beijing, are cited 0.3 times. The leading citation-receiving cities are mostly located in the United States and also in the northwestern part of Europe. The very top level consists of three US cities: San Diego, St Louis and Seattle. They are closely followed by the European centers of Mannheim–Heidelberg, Cambridge and Basel–Mulhouse–Fribourg. The top level also includes Baltimore, the San Francisco Bay Area and Boston. The mid level includes cities located all over the world, and the bottom level of low-ranking cities includes units from Spain, Japan, Russia and China. Close to the bottom end of the list we also find three declining European manufacturing centers.

The next analytical step is to incorporate the volume of citations and combine it with the average number of citations per paper. The way research centers draw attention from other researchers is, as mentioned, influenced by many factors, one being the quality profile of research. A specific city can have a uniform quality level for all disciplines or it may have disciplines of both high and low quality represented in its profile. The latter combination is probably normal although some centers have general patterns of high-quality research while others only have a few core high-quality disciplines. Because of these differences, the total volume of citations is assumed also to provide meaningful information about the pattern of mutual respect and links of innovation and thus to indicate the level of research leadership and gateway position. This is demonstrated in two diagrams; one with national plus international intercity citations; the other with intercity citations only from researchers in other countries.

City-to-city pattern is presented in Figure 2.4, showing the gateway cities (in terms of total citations). Three clusters of leaders can be identified. Group 1 is composed of 7 cities of very high impact (measured as the average citation rate of their publications) and of a medium level in their total number of citations. This group comprises San Diego, Seattle, Baltimore, St Louis, Cambridge, Mannheim–Heidelberg and Basel–Mulhouse–Fribourg. Group 2 combines high impact and a very high total volume of citation and includes the San Francisco Bay Area, Boston and New York. Group 3 combines moderate impact with a high total volume. The five members of group 3 are Los Angeles, Philadelphia, Paris, London and Randstad. The United States dominance in these three leading categories of cities reflects the pattern of a very large volume of citations within the US. This pattern is also present within Germany and Britain, but not at the intense American level.

RESEARCH GATEWAYS OF THE WORLD

In this chapter we have identified the 40 largest research centers of the world measured in general terms of research output. Synthesizing the analysis to a simple picture of the major global system and identifying nodes and gateways of research is as complicated as all summaries of categories are.

Gateway functions of the large research centers have not been directly linked to their economic performance in this paper, but the structure of – and the links within – the network of research represent important aspects of contemporary economic geography and give rise to some additional observations. The picture demonstrated in this paper confirms that economic and political connections, language and distance play roles in the pattern of research networks. By analyzing the data set we further find that even for the major research centers, national links in general outweigh international links.

NOTES

1. The Science Citation Index (SCI) is a database produced by the Institute for Scientific Information (ISI, Philadelphia, PA) along with a number of related products. It records, for over 5600 journals leading in their field, and for a large number of conference proceedings and other research publications, all contributions with full bibliographic description, all authors with affiliations, subject codes for journals and all references (citations) to the research literature. The on-line version is available as 'SciSearch' in major hosts, e.g. DIALOG and STN. Details are given on *http://www.isinet.com/products/citation/citsci.html*. Recently, a version with extended search facilities has been launched as 'Web of Science'. Details are given on *http://www.isinet.com/prodserv/citation/wosprev.html*. There is a large literature on applications of these databases. A number of indicators useful for comparative analysis of R&D productivity, and of problems related to data analysis, are discussed in Schwarz et al. (1998).
2. Several publications contain definitions and recommendations concerning data compilation with a view to establishing indicators for uniform and internationally comparable measures of input, processes and output of regional R&D and innovation. Starting from OECD handbooks on national indicators, in particular the 'Frascati Manual' (OECD, 1974), and the 'Oslo Manual' (OECD, 1992), the reports extend the scope to cover regional aspects (EUROSTAT, 1996 and 1997).
3. Multiple authorship is registered so that each author carries one bibliographic unit. This implies that papers with several authors count once for each author in the statistics. While distorting

the actual count of papers produced, it accounts for the collaboration links in terms of persons involved.

4. The two figures cannot be compared as papers with authors from more than one city are registered for each relevant city.

5. The position of the cities on these maps is not in any way precise. Latitude and altitude, scale and direction differ throughout. Distances between cities of different nations are as a rule of thumb indicated larger than distances between cities of the same nation. The maps only give primitive but recognizable crude pictures of the world.

6. For a set of city pairs (e.g., London and Paris or Berlin and the San Francisco Bay Area) an average co-authorship factor is defined as: (sum of all intercity co-author papers in all city pairs) divided by (sum of all papers published in the smallest city of each pair). The expected number of co-authorships for a given pair of cities is then defined as the co-authorship factor multiplied by (number of papers published in the smallest city of that pair).

REFERENCES

Andersson, Å.E. and O. Persson (1993), 'Networking scientists', *Annals of Regional Science*, **27**, 11–21.

Andersson, Å.E., C. Anderstig and B. Hårsman (1990), 'Knowledge and communications infrastructure and regional economic change', *Regional Science & Urban Economics*, **20**, 359–376.

Berg, L. van den, E. Braun and J. van der Meer (eds) (1998), *National Urban Policies in the European Union: Responses to Urban Issues in the Fifteen Member States*, Aldershot: Ashgate.

Castells, M. and P. Hall (1994), *Technopoles of the World*, London and New York: Routledge.

Cattan, N., D. Pumain, C. Rozenblat and T. Saint-Julien (1994), *Le système des villes européennes*, Anthropos.

EUROSTAT (1996), *F&U- og Innovationsstatistik. Set i Regionalt Perspektiv. Regionalhåndbog.*

EUROSTAT (1997), *Research and Development in Europe.*

Geenhuizen, M. van, P. Nijkamp and H. Rijckenberg (1997), 'Universities and know-ledge based economic growth: the case of Delft (NL)', *GeoJournal*, **41**, 369–377.

Hall, P. (1997), *The University and the City*, The Hague: Kluwer Academic Publishers.

Keeble, D.E. (1989), 'High-technology industry and regional development in Britain: The case of the Cambridge Phenomenon', *Environment and Planning C: Government and Policy*, **7**, 153–172.

Matthiessen, C.W. and A.W. Schwarz (1999), 'Scientific centres in Europe: An analysis of research strength and patterns of specialisation based on bibliometric indicators', *Urban Studies*, **36**(3), 453–477.

May, R.M. (1997), 'The scientific wealth of nations', *Science*, **275**, 793–796.

NUREC: Network on Urban Research in the European Union (1994), *Atlas of Agglomerations in the European Union*, vol. I–III, Duisburg.

OECD (1974), *Proposed Standard Practice for Surveys of Research and Experimental Development.*

OECD (1992), *Proposed Guidelines for Collecting and Interpreting Technological Innovation Data.*

RECLUS–DATAR (1989), *Groupement d'Intérêt Public RECLUS: Les villes 'Européennes'*, Montpellier.

Schwarz, A.W. et al. (1998), 'Research and research impact of a technical university – a bibliometric study', *Scientometrics*, **41**(3), 371–88.

Wickstead, S.Q. (1985), *The Cambridge Phenomenon. The Growth of High Technology Industry in a University Town*, Cambridge: Segal Quince.

Zhang, W.B. (1994), 'Knowledge, growth and patterns of trade', *Annals of Regional Science*, **28**, 285–303.

3. Financial Gateways

Åke E. Andersson

INTRODUCTION

Financial activities have always been concentrated in major cities. The first bankers in the late middle ages had their offices in the major trading centers of Europe. The commercial rise of a city tended to go hand in hand with a rising importance as a center of banking, insurance and other financial services. Amsterdam would never have become the most important gateway for trade in the seventeenth century if it had not had the most trusted financial services.

The industrial revolution was not only caused by the increasing division of labor or the use of machinery for producing and transporting goods. It was also caused by financial inventions and innovations, where new markets for stocks, bonds and insurance provided investment resources at levels never before recorded in economic history. It was a combination of growing industrial production, its spatial concentration at the crossroads of sea and rail transportation, and the agglomeration of financial activities that brought London, New York and Tokyo to their respective positions as the most important gateways of the industrial era.

FINANCIAL GLOBALIZATION – CAUSES AND CONSEQUENCES

During the 1980s, the world's international trade in goods and services underwent a phase-transition, in the sense that the annual growth rate went up from 3.5 percent to more than 6 percent (the average growth rate from 1987 to 1994). Thereafter the growth rates have reached even higher values. At the same time there has been a similar phase-transition for transnational direct investments. As a share of GNP, foreign direct investments accounted for about 2 percent in the OECD countries during the 1970s. By the late 1980s, direct investments as a share of GNP had risen to close to 7 percent, and in the 1990s they grew even further. The only major economy to experience a decrease in the share of foreign direct investment is Japan.

However, the most radical transformation of the global economy is the growth of foreign ownership and international transactions in bonds and securities. As late as in 1980 most of the large financial markets were national. In the United States, cross-border transactions of bonds and shares accounted for less than one tenth of GNP. By 1995 that share had risen to 135 percent. Table 3.1 illustrates the internationalization of trade in bonds and securities.

Table 3.1 Transactions of bonds and securities across country borders as a percentage of gross national product

	1980	1985	1990	1996
USA	9	35	89	152
Japan	8	63	120	83
Germany	8	33	57	197
France	8	21	54	229
Italy	1	4	27	435
Canada	10	27	64	235

Source: IMF (1997).

The extent of the financial globalization is also mirrored by the growth of trade in the global currency market. In 1986 the *daily* trade in the currency market was approximately 7 percent of the value of the global exports of goods and services *per year*. By 1995 this share had grown to close to 20 percent.

The strong globalizing tendencies of trade in goods and services and real transnational investments have a mirror image in the globalization of the financial markets. Tangible and financial globalization must go hand in hand in the long run.

THE REASONS FOR GLOBALIZATION

During the 1980s, a structural change occurred in the global economy. Global trade doubled its annual growth rate and foreign direct investments grew at an increasing rate. These tendencies are similar in most countries and the explanations must therefore be found at the global level.

The most important reason for globalization is the slow but steady expansion of the capacity and density of the transport and communication networks. Communication networks have been expanding to ever-increasing capacities through digitalization and computerization, and have provided increasingly efficient connections within and between different countries. The development efforts by the US military that finally led to the creation of *Arpanet* amounted to the necessary experimental foundation for the civilian Internet (see Roger Stough's contribution to this book – chapter 6). The availability of a fully computerized telecommunication system, based on inexpensive personal computers around the world, resulted in the final push for massive global interactions in the markets for goods, financial products and services. The improvements to the communication networks have also led to reduced communication costs, illustrated in Table 3.2.

Table 3.2 Prices of standardized air travel, telephone calls and computer power (index 1990 = 100)

	Air travel	Telephone calls	Computers
1960	218	1 381	12 500
1970	145	951	1 947
1980	91	145	362
1990	100	100	100

Source: IMF (1997).

From the late 1980s onwards, the interregional and international trade in goods, services and different financial products has increased drastically. Such a generally observed rapid transformation must be caused by system-wide changes to interaction possibilities and interaction costs. It is a highly reasonable hypothesis that the degree of connectivity of the computerized telecommunications network suddenly increased in the 1980s, paving the way for the remarkably rapid expansion of networking and trade. It has often been believed that such a massive change to a system has to be preceded by some grand, global infrastructural plan. But recent research in the dynamics of network formation into large clusters of interaction possibilities shows that system-wide phase transitions do not require any system-wide planning. The following example should clarify the reasons for non-linear responses to link investments.

Gateways to the Continents and the World

Figure 3.1 Evolutionary networks

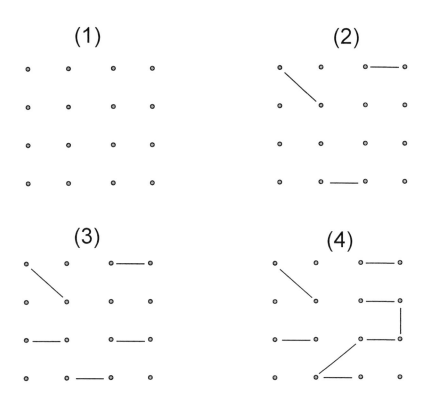

and so on...

Although only pair-wise nodes are connected at the early stages of such a process, at later stages there will be a high probability that large clusters will emerge. An ongoing process of such link creation will at some stage, with an extremely high probability, lead to the generation of a very large cluster of nodes, which are directly or indirectly connected with each other. The biologist Stuart Kauffman (1995) has shown, by using simulation techniques, that a phase transition from small clusters to an almost global clustering can be expected. This is illustrated by Figure 3.2, a computer simulation graph for a spatial system consisting of 400 equally spaced nodes, which are successively and randomly connected by links.

Figure 3.2. Network integration as a function of the ratio between the number of links and the number of nodes in a random network formation computer simulation

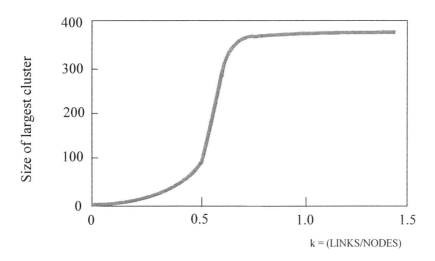

Source: Kauffman (1995).

When the number of links exceeds half the number of nodes, random forces will create a global cluster. But this clustering does not imply that all points of the globally connected network will be equally accessible. Some of the nodes will have an accessibility structure *vis-à-vis* other nodes that will provide opportunities for achieving a hub or gateway role.

It is thus probable that the rapid growth of the stock of personal computers in old developed economies, in combination with the introduction of Internet software and inexpensive telecommunication services, triggered (almost randomly) new Internet links between nodes that within a short period of time created large transnational Internet clusters. The globalization of the Internet in its turn generated new opportunities for low transaction cost interactions expanding at a disequilibrium rate of growth.

FINANCIAL GLOBALIZATION BY TRANSNATIONAL CLUSTERING

The increasing accessibility to different financial markets for households, pension funds and other financial investors has been coupled with economic efficiency and generally lower transaction costs. Already in the 1980s it could be shown that international diversification of portfolios would be highly efficient for US investors. In one of these studies, it was shown that an American fund manager could raise the expected return on a portfolio from approximately 8 to 13 percent, and still keep the expected risk (measured as the standard deviation of returns) at a constant level of 14 percent. But this diversification would have to be thorough. It would require a switch from US bonds and securities to a diversified global portfolio.

The correlation between different markets determines the gains to be made from diversification. Recent studies of the correlations of returns on equities in different markets have shown that higher correlations result from the globalization process. But the correlation coefficient, seen as an average of all correlations between stock markets, is still well below 50 percent. This implies that there are still large gains to be made from global diversification. A crucial question is then why the rapid increase in foreign ownership of capital has not led to a better synchronization of returns at the global level. Increasing ease of transactions combined with unexpected and almost unlimited access to information would presumably make it possible for anyone to own an optimal portfolio.

This is, however, probably a misconceived view of portfolio allocation strategy. For the speculative short-term investor, ease of transactions and rapid availability of information are crucial. The story is quite different for the strategic long-term investor, who is uninterested in risk on a daily basis and instead focuses on long-term returns and risks. Such return and risk calculations require much more knowledgeable analyses of long-term invention and innovation prospects, the political orientation of regions and countries, as well as social stability and international security and similar epistemic risk and return factors.

Epistemic risk and return calculations are dependent upon the geographical, social and cultural distance between the financial investor and different financial centers. There is an obvious difference in the long-term return assessment on stocks in the Malaysian car industry between a fund manager in Bangkok or Singapore and a manager of a pension fund in Cincinnati or Bremen. Differences in the perception of epistemic risks and returns tend to lead to a clustering of different financial markets in patterns which are determined by psychological, social, cultural and geographical distance.

One way of judging the degree of clustering is by looking at the interdependency of stock market returns over a recent but extended period of time. I have chosen to use the price movement correlations, measured by quarterly data in the 1990s, for all stock markets covered by the *Wall Street Journal* statistical series. These have then been clustered with the help of factor analysis. The clustering results are given in Figure 3.3.

Figure 3.3

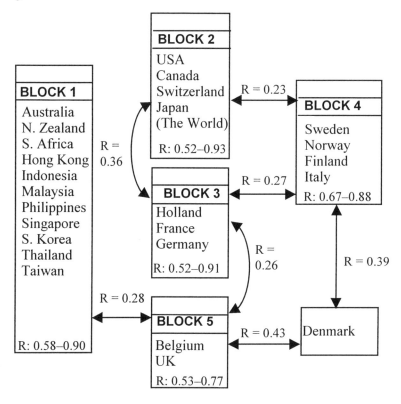

Source: *Wall Street Journal* data (own compilation).

The first cluster is clearly oriented to Asia, Australia, New Zealand and South Africa. This is clearly a Pacific cluster within which different countries tend to be highly correlated with each other regarding the behavior of investors in the stock markets. Within Europe there are three clearly distinguishable clusters. France and Germany dominate one of these, the second one is dominated by the UK and Belgium, and the third consists of the Nordic countries. Recent mergers within the financial sector would indicate that Denmark is becoming fully integrated into the Nordic cluster, and in the long run there would be an augmentation of this cluster by the financial integration of states and regions around the Baltic Sea. There is also a set of Southern European financial markets that remain quite unclustered. These countries would presumably be integrated into the French and German cluster, when the Euro has become the dominant European currency. According to the correlation data, the United States, Japan, Canada and

Switzerland are highly correlated with the index on global stock market price movements. The United States is the single most financially globalized economy, measured both absolutely and relatively.

WHITHER SMALLER FINANCIAL GATEWAYS?

In the early 1990s, the Harvard futurist Daniel Bell (1997) claimed that in the future marketplaces would collapse and 'the network will be the market'. Thus, there would be no need for financial marketplaces or gateways, with the possible exception of one global center such as Wall Street. The reasons for such a development would, according to Bell, be the increasing ease of communicating information, lowered transaction costs due to increasing global competition, and the general availability of personal computers hooked up to the Internet.

According to this hypothesis, information is the crucial factor determining payoffs in the stock market. This is obviously the case for short-term investors who buy and sell low-technology stocks. For these stocks, quick and reliable information about transnational mergers, order movements, unemployment and inflation figures, as well as shifts in different stock indices, significantly influence decisions to buy and sell. But for long-term investors focusing on high technology and other research-and-development-dependent companies, rapid information is not central, but rather the availability of deeper analytical knowledge. Such knowledge tends to be available in research-and-development-intensive regions, where specialized financial analysts can regularly interact with scientists and R&D engineers and other members of the high-technology business community. This knowledge is distance-sensitive.

Bell's scenario will probably be correct for stocks and other financial instruments associated with homogeneous products with little or no technological development potential. There is probably going to be a reduction in the total number of marketplaces and an increase in the size of the largest ones, especially for trade in currencies, oil and other bulk commodities. But for stocks in firms that specialize in complex products and services that are dependent upon a steady inflow of new scientific and engineering ideas, much of the trade will have to be located in marketplaces where relevant knowledge can be assembled and critically scrutinized. Before industrialization, financial centers were also centers of interregional and international trade. Today and increasingly in the future, there will be a similar synergy between science, high-technology innovations and financial activities. The supply of risk capital will be crucial to the innovation and growth of high-technology production and the reduction of epistemic risks will be the central factor determining the size and growth of regional financial markets. Financial markets like Zürich, Amsterdam, Stockholm or Helsinki depend on the quality and potential applicability of research in medicine and the other pharmaceutical sciences, biotechnology, chemistry, electrical engineering and computer science. Small financial markets with their own stock exchange do have a future, but only if surrounded by research-and-development-dependent and innovation-prone industries.

THE FINANCIAL GATEWAY HIERARCHY

Stock exchanges are the clearest indicators of a financial gateway region. And the regional stock exchanges of the world follow a rank size distribution. This is illustrated by Figure 3.4, which shows how the size decreases with increasing rank number. The largest stock exchange, whether measured by market capitalization or turnover, is much larger than the exchanges in second or third place. The rank size distribution of the 40 largest stock markets is given in Figures 3.4 and 3.5.

Figure 3.4 Rank and stock market turnover, 1993

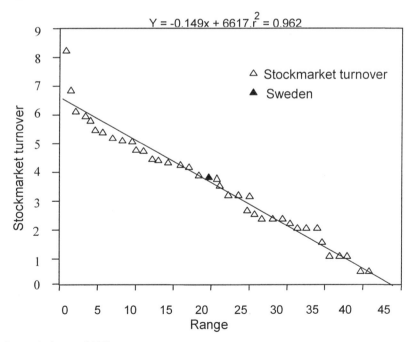

*Source:*Andersson (1998).

Figure 3.5 Rank and market capitalization, 1993

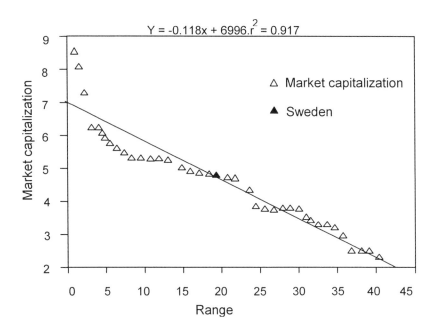

Source: Andersson (1998).

Both in terms of turnover and capitalization there are three global financial gateway regions – New York, London and Tokyo. An analysis of stock exchange data before and after the 'Big Bang' deregulation and the large-scale introduction of efficient global telecommunications can test Daniel Bell's scenario or hypothesis.

It is convenient to represent the degree of concentration with the aid of rank size distributions. A comparison of the slope of the rank size distribution equation before and after the globalization of the financial markets enables us to determine whether the world's financial markets have become more concentrated.

Using data on the hierarchical structure of the financial markets in 1976 and 1993 leads to the surprising result that concentration has decreased between 1976 and 1993. The smaller stock markets have grown more than the larger ones and the slope of the curve has decreased by 25 percent! There is thus no tendency of concentration in the global financial markets in accordance with Bell's hypothesis. The network is becoming the market, but financial hubs and gateways seem to be important anyhow.

THE ATTRACTIVENESS OF FINANCIAL GATEWAYS

The most important part of the financial market after the 'Big Bang' and the following internationalization are the exchanges for stocks, bonds and futures. In general, these exchanges form the core of the financial market of a country and the economically dominant metropolitan region. Around this core there is a network of financial consultants and other advisors, business journalists, rating offices, analysts, traders, corporate financial officers, bankers and financial regulators. The internal connectivity, the capacity to communicate internally and globally and the knowledge base of the regional financial network determine the efficiency of the market. On the other hand, the external economies of scale of the financial market explain the agglomeration of financial activities in the cores of large metropolitan regions. In most countries there are only one or two financial centers. Even in the largest countries the number of financial centers is only a handful.

The core concept in financial markets is *risk*. Some of this risk can be reduced by portfolio diversification. But the increasing emphasis on creativity rather than productivity has induced firms to focus on research and development to an extent not even considered by corporations before the 1970s. Research and development projects are generically uncertain. According to studies by Edwin Mansfield and others, only one out of five industrial research and development projects eventually becomes successful in the marketplace. Many of these uncertain research and development projects involve fundamental research of considerable depth and complexity. Any high-tech portfolio will thus not only have a diversifiable risk but also a much more substantial *epistemic risk*. It is only by a thorough understanding of what is happening in the R&D laboratories that the financial investor can reduce this kind of epistemic risk. It is of course completely impossible for most individual financial investors to gather and properly analyze scientific information. There are substantial economies of scale in such information gathering and analysis. As a consequence there has been a steady growth of consultants and divisions of high-tech analysis in banks and other financial institutions. These analytical groups are dependent upon frequent participation in scientific seminars, informal discussions with scientists, patent engineers and other experts on the implementation and innovation of newly developed technologies. Economies of scale in the use and development of knowledge are becoming an increasingly important factor determining the efficiency of the financial market.

How then should the efficiency of a financial market be measured and evaluated? The two measures generally used are returns and risk (as measured by the standard deviation of the returns over time). A financial portfolio could be said to be more efficient than another one if it has a higher expected return but the same expected risk. Conversely, a portfolio that combines a lower risk with an equal or higher expected return is also more efficient. In other words, higher expected returns and lower expected risks make for better portfolios.

The Nobel laureate Sharpe (1991) has proposed a simple measure of the efficiency of a financial market (i.e., the securities and bond markets). This efficiency measure is the ratio of returns to risk, as measured over a given time period. Such a measure would of course disregard the possible differences in risk aversion between investors in different financial markets. It is not a meaningful measure for people having extremely low or extremely high risk aversion. It is a good measure only for 'balanced' investors. The Sharpe measure as calculated by Kwok (in Solnik, 1996) and based on Morgan Stanley's data sets is presented in Table 3.3.

Table 3.3 Efficiency of different financial markets, as measured by the Sharpe measure, 1977–1996 (the ratio of expected return and standard deviation)

	M	Index	Corruption index 1996
Netherlands	0.197	184	8.71
UK	0.162	151	8.44
Sweden	0.143	134	9.08
USA	0.143	134	7.66
Belgium	0.141	132	6.84
Switzerland	0.127	119	8.76
France	0.113	106	6.96
Hong Kong	0.113	106	7.01
Average	**0.107**	**100**	
Japan	0.099	93	7.05
Denmark	0.092	86	9.33
Singapore	0.090	84	8.80
Germany	0.089	83	8.27
Australia	0.078	73	8.60
Canada	0.076	71	8.96
Norway	0.073	68	8.87
Italy	0.071	66	3.42
Spain	0.060	56	4.31
Austria	0.055	51	7.59

Source: Data from Morgan Stanley's Capital International Perspective. Compiled by Kwok.

As can be seen from this rank ordering of efficiencies, there is no evidence of efficiency equalization between different markets. The average Sharpe-value is 0.107 and there is a substantial spread about this value. At the top we find the Netherlands (Amsterdam), Britain (London), Sweden (Stockholm), the United States (New York) and Belgium (Brussels). At the bottom we find Austria (Vienna), Spain (Barcelona and Madrid), Italy (Milan and Rome) and Norway (Oslo). There is no obvious correlation between the size of the country and the efficiency of the dominant financial market. Amsterdam and Stockholm are, despite their smaller size, on a par with London and New York. However, there seems to be a positive relation between the efficiency of the financial market and the relative importance of large, multinational corporations in the trading volume of the stock market.

THE INCENTIVES FOR FINANCIAL GLOBALIZATION

Anyone engaging in purchases of equities, bonds or currencies has to consider the trade-off between expected returns and the risk associated with the different financial products. In most theorizing around the optimal composition of portfolios since the path-breaking article by Markowitz (1952), risk has been represented by the standard deviation of the portfolio. An investment in a financial product, for example an equity, implies a certain combination of the risk (measured in percentages) and expected return (also measured in percentages over the given time period). Let us assume that the expected return would be approximately 16.5 percent at the risk of approximately 18.5 percent for a specific share. Let us further assume that we could diversify the portfolio by allocating half of it to another share with approximately the same expected return but at an expected risk of approximately 22 percent. The counterintuitive result is that such a diversification could be highly beneficial even if there is a positive correlation between the returns on the two equities. For instance, a correlation of +0.4 implies that the diversification would be highly desirable. The total return from the portfolio would just be the average of the two expected returns, i.e. it would remain at the same level, while the risk would be reduced by approximately 7 percentage points to 11 percent.

It is clear that such advantages of risk spreading *within nations* had already been achieved in the early 1980s. However, most countries had laws and regulations against diversification at the international level. With the massive deregulation of capital flows ('Big Bangs') in the 1980s, the opportunities for risk-reducing transnational capital movements were exploited in country after country. Initially, the advantages of international diversification were very large, as the international correlations of returns were often very low. Because of the increasing mobility of financial capital these correlations have been increasing, but not as much as could have been hypothesized at the onset of international capital market liberalization.

ATTRACTIVENESS DETERMINANTS

Empirical studies of the location of different types of economic activities have shown that financial services of different kinds, including consulting firms, tend to be among the most over-represented activities in large metropolitan regions.[1] The concentration of financial services in metropolitan regions is generally more pronounced than the concentration of different types of high-tech and other knowledge and creativity-based activities.

J.P. Abraham (1994) of the Institute of European Finance recently evaluated the most important regional attractiveness factors for financial firms. The study was based on interviews with executives and 47 different questions were asked, relating to larger issues such as:

Capitalization
Accessibility to knowledge and skills
The capacity of the infrastructure
Macroeconomic conditions
The technological development of the financial market
The size and scope of the market
Capacity of financial innovations
Financial tradition
Political organization and tradition
Rules and regulations
Taxation
Costs of transactions

This investigation showed that the efficient but small financial center of Amsterdam was considered quite superior to both Frankfurt and Paris. The study showed that Amsterdam was evaluated as 'excellent to rather good' according to 70 percent of all criteria. The comparative advantages of Amsterdam were primarily in terms of:

Freedom from capital controls
Stability of the currency
Low and steady rate of inflation
Presence of multinational corporations
Positive attitudes to innovations
Political stability (predictability)
Access to sophisticated financial instruments
A functioning futures market

In 1996, Karen Bindemann (1997) of the University of Bristol performed a similar study based on questions to representatives of stock exchanges, commercial banks, investment and other consulting firms, central banks and financial journals and newspapers in five to seven countries.

Also in this study a large number of different factors (23) were used to rank the role of different factors in determining the attractiveness of different financial centers. In order to summarize these rankings into a total ranking, different methods can be used, where each one of the methods has certain advantages and disadvantages.

Kenneth Arrow (1963) has shown that there is no self-evident criterion for the aggregation of rankings. There is certainly no indisputable and consistent method for aggregating partly or totally different rankings.

The mathematical economist Donald Saari (1994) has, however, shown that aggregation according to Borda's method is the best method in terms of a number of different criteria.

Borda's method means that in a ranking of 23 factors the factor that is in the first position will be given 23 points, the one in the second place will get 22 points and so on, down to 1 point for the factor in 23rd place. Using this method we can aggregate the rankings of the different actors in the financial markets; see Table 3.4.

It is quite clear from this study that information technology is not of overriding importance, as has been presumed by many observers, including Daniel Bell. The modern financial market is much more dependent upon the availability of knowledge and skills as well as its creative and innovative capacities.

This gives an advantage to regions rich in science and technology, such as London and New York, but also to similar medium-sized regions such as Randstad (Amsterdam) or the Stockholm–Uppsala corridor. By contrast, the Rhine–Ruhr region of western Germany, with its enormous production capacity and a greater regional product than London, would not be a preferred location for financial activities due to its relatively low accessibility to advanced knowledge.

Another example of an economically powerful region – Hamburg – which not only lacks a large international airport but also a developed research and development network, would also not qualify to become a financial center. The study also shows that there is a large element of self-perpetuating economies of scale and scope in a region that has already become a financial center.

Factors associated with information technology tend to be rated at lower positions, e.g. cost and speed of transactions, the accessibility to information and the availability of an automatic and continuous system of transactions.

Table 3.4 The total Borda-aggregated rank ordering of factors determining the attractiveness of an international financial center

Rank	Factor	Borda points	Coefficient of variation, %
1	Access to knowledge and skills	85	9
2	Number of different financial products available	76	5
3	Size and scope of the market	74	33
4	Presence of international banks	73	4
5	Volume of transactions	71	19
6	Infrastructure	65	23
7	Market regulations	62	29
8	Cost of transactions	55	49
9	Capitalization	55	43
10	Political stability	48	59
11	Capacity of the banking system	43	33
12	Transaction speed	43	49
13	Accessibility to information	42	52
14	Financial tradition	39	46
15	Innovation frequency	37	25
16	Strength of the currency	34	67
17	Language	31	44
18	Cost of courts	31	52
19	Automatic and continuous transactions	26	61
20	Banking secrecy	23	87
21	Economic growth of the country	21	121
22	Independence of the central bank	20	108
23	Taxation rules	18	60

Source: Andersson (1998), based on Bindemann (1997).

There is a remarkably small variance in the responses to some of these factors. The uniformity of opinion is especially evident regarding the presence of international banks, the availability of a large number of different financial products and the access to knowledge and skills. The evaluation of the importance of different macroeconomic factors gives a completely different picture. The representatives of different actors in the financial markets differ widely on the importance of the economic growth of the host country of the financial market. On the whole, and quite predictably, the representatives of the central banks put macroeconomic and political factors among the highest ranked, while representatives of private banks and investment companies put these macroeconomic and political factors at the lowest levels.

THE INCREASING DEPENDENCE ON KNOWLEDGE

For rapidly expanding industries, dynamic competition by investments in research and development has become the predominant strategy. This kind of dynamic competitive strategy is inherently long-term. Edwin Mansfield (1979) has estimated that R&D-intensive projects need a maturation time of more than ten years before a meaningful evaluation of the returns to such investments is feasible. Since the 1970s the relation between technological development and fundamental research has been strengthened. Innovation is no longer based on activities among 'tinkerers' with limited formal education. Especially in the pharmaceutical industry and the telecommunication and software industries, research and development budgets are large in relation to total value added. Many of the research executives in such corporations maintain strong ties with academic institutions. In these research-based industries there is often a symbiotic relationship with the scientific community.

The same is increasingly true for the financial services. They are increasingly becoming as innovative as high-tech manufacturing industries. Also within the more strictly delimited financial economics area there is a growing interdependency between universities, research institutes and financial innovators. This research field is now highly established with a number of refereed journals such as the *Journal of Finance*, the *Journal of Portfolio Management*, the *Journal of Banking and Finance* and *Financial Management*. Statistics on the twelve most important financial economics journals indicate that New England has the largest concentration of research within this field. More than 30 percent of the total production of refereed articles on financial issues originated in New England during the 1990s. Financial economists in the New York region contributed close to 12 percent of the world's production of refereed scientific articles. This implies that the northeastern region of the US is the pre-eminent environment for financial research, development and higher education. Not only does this provide an explanation for the stability of New York as a center of the most advanced activities for large financial corporations. It also indicates that New York will remain the global financial gateway long into the future. The two other American centers are California with approximately 8 percent of the world production of scientific articles, and Illinois, with Chicago as its gateway region, accounting for approximately 6 percent.

remain the global financial gateway long into the future. The two other American centers are California with approximately 8 percent of the world production of scientific articles, and Illinois, with Chicago as its gateway region, accounting for approximately 6 percent.

In Europe, London is the leading scientific center in the financial area. But the fact remains that, although large by European standards, it lags far behind New York, accounting for less than 2 percent of world production during the 1990s.

My main conclusion of this analysis is that the fate of financial centers will be determined by the knowledge infrastructure in the regions where the financial activities are located.

NOTE

1. Report No. 6, 1998, Regionplan- och trafikkontoret, *Regioner, handel och tillväxt*, Stockholm 1998.

REFERENCES

Abraham, J.P. (1994), Working paper from the Institute of European Finance.

Andersson, Å.E. (1998), *Finansplats Stockholm – En Tillväxtmotor*, Stockholm: SNS Förlag.

Arrow, K. (1963), *Social Choice and Individual Values*, New York: Wiley and Sons.

Bell, D. (1992), 'The breakdown of time, space and society', *Framtider International*, **92** (3), 9–13.

Bindemann, K. (1997), *On the Optimal Design of an International Financial Center*, Dept of Economics, Bristol: Bristol University.

IMF (1997), *World Economic Outlook* (May), Washington, DC.

Kauffman, S. (1995), *At Home in the Universe: The Search for Laws of Complexity*, London: Penguin Books.

Mansfield, E. (1979), *The Production and Application of New Industrial Technology*, New York: Norton.

Markowitz, H.M. (1952), 'Portfolio selections', *Journal of Finance* (March).

Saari, D. (1994), *Geometry of Voting*, Berlin and Heidelberg: Springer-Verlag.

Sharpe, W.F. (1991), *Investments*, Englewood Cliffs, NJ: Prentice Hall.

Solnik, B. (1996), *International Investments*, Reading, MA: Addison-Wesley.

4. Three Global Cities: New York, London and Tokyo

**T.R. Lakshmanan, David E. Andersson,
Lata Chatterjee and Komei Sasaki**

INTRODUCTION

This chapter is concerned with the three largest conurbations in the developed world: New York, London and Tokyo. These three regions are the focal points of economic activity in the world's three most advanced regions: North America, Western Europe and Japan. In this chapter we analyze to what extent these regions also qualify as global economic capitals in the sense of Braudel (1979).

Our focus is on four gateway properties. First, we look at the positioning of these regions as financial centers as measured by the relative size of their stock exchanges. Second, their roles as centers of scientific and cultural creativity are discussed. Third, we draw attention to the importance of these regions as innovation centers. Fourth, the innovative capacity is strongly related to the diversity of their populations. Diversity is understood as giving rise to synergies of ideas.

The rise of these large agglomerations to their current size and importance cannot be understood without some reference to the economic history of the past three centuries. The growth of these regions has paralleled the industrialization of the world from the eighteenth to the twentieth century. Although London was already a major economic center in the seventeenth century, the growth of its population accelerated with the massive industrial expansion of the North Atlantic basin, which began in the early nineteenth century.

In 1820, London's population size amounted to about 1.2 million, a figure that grew by 2.1 percent annually until 1900, when the population was estimated to have reached 6.5 million. In the same period the population growth of New York was even more spectacular, at 3.9 percent annually. The growth of Japan into an industrial nation is more recent. There, industriali-

49

zation started with the Meiji restoration in 1868, although the extremely rapid growth phase of the Tokyo region did not occur until Japan's reindustrialization after the Second World War.

The reader might wonder why we have refrained from discussing the role of the Paris region as a major global gateway on a par with London. One of the reasons for disregarding Paris is historical. For a very long time after London had become a global gateway, France was under the influence of the centralizing principles of mercantilism, which centralized the organization of economic life according to statist principles. The other reason, which is closely related to the first one, was the priority given to Paris as the hierarchical, nationalistic focus of all interregional infrastructural investments. Even today, practically all railroads, airline links and roads are centered on Paris. Paris is undoubtedly a thriving city region with the best accessibility to the global economy of all French regions, but it is a French gateway to Europe rather than a European gateway to the world.

NEW YORK: AMERICA'S GATEWAY TO THE GLOBAL ECONOMY

What is barely hinted in other cities is condensed and enlarged in New York.
                                                                    Saul Bellow

New York is the global gateway city *par excellence*. Since around 1810, New York has risen rapidly to its incomparable position as America's gateway, playing an increasingly important role in national economic growth, and social and cultural evolution. By 1850, it was leading the nation in every major type of economic activity save agriculture and mining (Lichtenberg, 1960).

Thanks to the natural advantages of the port, and the strategic actions and social innovations of its business and political communities (and a little luck), in the nineteenth century the city emerged dominant nationally in foreign trade, wholesaling, and in financial and related services. In the century following the Civil War, the New York Metropolitan Region has served as a powerful magnet for many of the nation's market activities – relating to strategic positioning, management, control and financing – in the form of central offices, money-market specialists, manufactured goods sold to the nation, and some highly specialized services.

Again in the last three decades or so, the city is reinventing itself in the emerging era of 'knowledge societies', characterized by the complex economic, political and cultural dimensions of globalization. Engaging in social learning, adaptation and strategic activities, New York has emerged –

primus inter pares – at the head of a set of major international financial and business centers or 'global cities'. These global cities form a new geography of centrality and agglomeration in today's distributed global economy and culture (Sassen, 1997, 1998; Crahan and Vourvoulias-Bush, 1997; Castells, 1996).

This recurrent ability of New York to remain an economic leader over two centuries reflects both its capacity to exploit technological advances and its social capability, comprising its capacity to create the institutions, the policy-making and the incentives that promote continual learning and adaptation in a rapidly evolving context. Such a combination of technological know-how and organizational knowledge and creativity is successful in New York by embracing the diverse networks through which the world economy is constituted.

Such (global city) networks of economic globalization owe to several factors. These factors include, but are not limited to, the internationalization of capital and the organization of command and control centers that are able to innovate, manage and coordinate the linked activities of multinational firms.

Other important factors are the innovation and production of urban activities, which not only promote the emerging dynamic sectors (of finance, information technologies and advanced business services), but also facilitate social learning and adaptation in the city, as well as the acquisition and maintenance of the diverse urban human capital that the new global cities require. New York has indeed developed these dense multifaceted networks which underlie its current dynamism and its strategic role in the global economy and the international social and cultural realms (Sassen, 1998; Drennen, 1991; Castells, 1996).

This chapter surveys broadly the recent transformation of New York into a strategic pole of the international economic system, marked by the new mobility of money, people and production. It focuses in particular on one less noted aspect of the many rich networks mentioned above, namely the new diverse workforce that has facilitated the ongoing structural change in New York.

The region has managed to transform itself from a declining actor in managing national economic production to a booming presence in managing international production. We will argue that the diverse migrants (domestic and foreign), whom the city has attracted in the last two decades have endowed it with not only the economic flexibility and rapid adaptation to the flexible mode of production characteristic of knowledge economies; they have also provided the human capital resources to continue to operate as a learning environment locale for the creation of the technical and social innovations that facilitate New York's command and control of the world economy.

GLOBALIZATION, MOBILITY OF CAPITAL AND LABOR, AND THE CENTRALITY OF PLACE

The contemporary phase of the world economy is characterized by the ascendancy of knowledge technologies, the accompanying increase of mobility and liquidity of capital, and the associated deregulation of large economic sectors that have dynamic international markets, in particular in finance, in advanced business services and in information industries. In the new economy, technological advances and institutional innovations in transport and communications are shrinking distance, eroding time and borders, and creating a knowledge-rich global production system. Global markets with extensive outsourcing and 'just-in-time' deliveries are requiring ever-increasing on-time shipments of semi-manufactured products, components, spare parts and final goods between production and assembly centers scattered all over the globe. As the life span of many new products in this knowledge economy becomes shorter and shorter, and as the spatial distribution of supply and demand points is changing rapidly in such a system, *what* is transported, *how* it is transported, and *to where* and *from where*, are all rapidly changing.

This emerging global knowledge economy is thus a distributed system with a vast array of geographically dispersed economic operations. All the value-adding components of a global corporation's activities (e.g., R&D, strategic control, production, post-sale services) can be and are globally located (Porter, 1990). People, capital, goods and services are increasingly mobile, and powerful trends of decentralization are afoot. Decentralization and denationalization are radically altering the way business gets done. Ideas, goods and services, and people from 'elsewhere' are clearly now more evident than they have been at any time in the past. There is increasingly in this economy a wide variety in the types of firms, workers, work cultures and residential milieux for the mobile transnational workers.

The enhanced mobility of capital, goods and production, and the new mobility of people and their efficient fusion into a dynamic global economy are enabled by two types of innovative processes and human capital. First, there are the innovations associated with the *technical infrastructure* of globalization – embodied for example in the transport and complementary information technologies – which permit this globally distributed economic system to function at its current fast and increasing pace and efficiency. Second, there are innovations associated with the *social infrastructure* of globalization, as embodied in an organizational structure that creates dynamic *learning environments* (Lakshmanan, 1989, 1993). Such learning environments provide two critical functions: they are locales for the innovation and production of new activities necessary for the control, management and coordination of the spatially far-flung activities of the global economy. New activities are being spawned continually in the dynamic finance, advanced business services and information industries. The other function is that they create the milieux for continual adaptation to changing circumstances (Aydalot, 1985), and a locale for social learning and evolution in the economic, social and cultural realms.

The creation, application and diffusion of these two types of innovations undergirding the global economy require a workforce that has the requisite technical knowledge and organizational knowledge as well as creativity. This workforce must also be able to continually monitor, analyze, report on and act to sustain the efficient performance of the various dimensions of the rapidly evolving economy. Such attributes in the workforce – high levels of knowledge, a willingness to experiment and flexibility – and the learning environments where innovations are produced, are not ubiquitous. Indeed they are limited to a few large cities.

Thus these few large cities (described as global gateways or the geographic foci of the spatially dispersed global economy) serve as locales for creating and sustaining new ideas, relationships, conventions and other social innovations which motivate these cities' activities pertaining to financial control, management, and strategic positioning and coordination of the global economy. The essential feature of the global economy is thus an ever-growing economic concentration and differentiation between financial control, strategic planning and information management on the one hand and manufacturing and service delivery on the other. In this scheme the global gateway cities represent the new geography of centrality, which complements the oft-noted geography of the distributed global production system.

The extensive literature on the economic, political and cultural dimensions of globalization views a few large global gateway cities, such as New York, London and Tokyo, as dominating a larger set of international financial and business centers, which are sites for large concentrations of economic power and command and control centers in a global economy (Sassen, 1998, 1999; Castells, 1996). The larger network of these financial and gateway centers includes not only cities such as Frankfurt, Los Angeles and Hong Kong, but also Sao Paulo, Taipei, Bombay and Mexico City (Sassen, 1998). This is a new global network of strategic places which amounts to a new cross-border geography of economic centrality. This new geography also cuts across the old North–South divide. Indeed, in an economy where there is rapidly increasing production of cultural goods and services, the new centrality is economic and cultural.

The scope and intensity of transactions – through investments, financial markets and services trade – among these cities have grown explosively. At the same time, the strategic resources and activities are becoming disproportionately concentrated in the relatively larger global cities. Sassen (1999) notes that in 1997 in the financial industry, 25 cities controlled 83 percent of the world's equities under institutional management and accounted for approximately half of the world's market capitalization ($20.9 trillion). London, New York and Tokyo together account for 58 percent of the global foreign exchange market. Again, among the 50 biggest financial service firms in the world in 1997, the top ten carried out 72 percent of all transactions. Eight of these were American. New York with its continual market innovations and new financial products dominates this field (Sassen, 1999).

The notion of a strategic place as central to a global market system and spatial division of labor is not new. It is a critical part of Braudel's (1973) conception of the three facets to a world economy: a given geographic space with limits to mark it off, a pole or a center represented by one dominant city and a world economy which is divided into successive zones. The contemporary variation of the Braudel view is that not one central place (e.g., Amsterdam, London or New York, as in the past), but a small number of gateway cities jointly play the strategic pole role in today's world economy.

However, there are different theoretical conceptions of how and why these cities function as geographical foci of global economic activity at a time when the constraints of what Braudel called the 'tyranny of distance' seem to be disappearing. One view holds that global cities are agglomerations of those internationally oriented financial and business services which are critical to the governance of the global economy (Sassen, 1998). These cities concentrate command functions in the global economy. They are also production sites for leading financial and business services firms as well as transnational marketplaces where firms and governments can buy financial instruments and specialized services (Sassen, 1997). A second idea is that in an economy where all activities can be reduced to knowledge generation and information flows regarding ever-changing linkages, these cities are the poles of the 'Informational Economy' (Castells, 1989). A third approach is to think of these cities as locales offering a flexible pool of labor and industries in an era of moving away from economies of scale to economies of scope. This flexibility is then achieved through agglomeration (Scott, 1988). Krugman's work (1991) is reviving this emphasis on urban agglomeration economies that was evident in the much richer and earlier (1950s) analyses of the economic role of large cities, in particular New

York's economic governance role in an earlier time (Lichtenberg, 1960; Vernon, 1960; Hoover and Vernon, 1959).

While these alternative explanations account for many observed activities of global gateway cities, they do not offer any clues to the urban processes underlying global economic governance. Our view of these processes and their dynamics, as noted above, derives from the notion of urban learning environments that continually incubate the innovative activities which enable a city like New York to continue to serve as a strategic pole of economic governance. A dynamic social entity such as New York not only acquires and deploys the knowledge necessary for its development but also the social capacity to monitor, analyze and guide the efficient performance of various dimensions of the global economy. These activities constitute social learning and require the creation of institutions, policy-making and incentives for continual learning and adaptation to changing circumstances. The delineation of the social learning activities is clearly a large project and we limit ourselves in the rest of the paper to exploring one critical aspect of New York's ability in this regard. We focus on the new migrants in New York, outlining the multiplicity of the economies and work cultures they represent, the flexibility and adaptability they provide to a restructuring economy, the endogenous urban growth the application of their physical and human capital generates, and the multiple networks and institutions they develop and adapt in New York. We precede this discussion by a brief profile of New York and its recent evolution as a global gateway.

A PROFILE OF NEW YORK AS A GLOBAL CITY

New York is a metaphor for the ongoing vast and rich post-industrial transformation and is an epicenter of global trends. The contemporary experience of New York illuminates not just one global city or all global cities but the various forces that drive this transformation. These forces may include a major technological revolution, the emergence of a new international division of labor, the growing relative power of finance over production and migration from the industrializing Third World countries to the core cities of the affluent North.

Over the last two decades, New York has been central to these transformation processes. New York has redefined international trade, global financial markets and patterns of global investment in production and in information technologies, marketing and media. It has also served as the primary destination of immigrants in the United States. Between 1980 and 1992, sales of the multinational corporations (MNCs) more than doubled from $2.4 trillion to $5.5 trillion (Crahan and Vourvoulias-Bush, 1997). By the mid-1990s, these MNCs controlled 33 percent of the world's productive assets, integrating the production of goods and services, and deploying an increasingly dispersed and mobile workforce. As the major commercial and financial city in the world's largest national economy, New York has been well positioned to benefit from this global interdependence.

The city (which accounts for 3 percent of the nation's non-farm employment, 4.5 percent of its output, and 5 percent of payrolls) has a disproportionate share of US finance, insurance and real estate (FIRE) as well as business services employment. New York accounts for 43 percent of the national payroll in the securities industry, 24 percent in advertising, 14 percent in banking, 10 percent in legal services, and 5 percent in accounting and managerial consulting (O'Cleireacain, 1997). New York's financial institutions are dominant globally, offering unparalleled depth, with twice London's number of financial specialists and related business professionals, and dwarfing Tokyo in the expertise in Anglo-Saxon law under which most international transactions are negotiated (Rosen and Murray, 1997).

The FIRE sector, business and professional services, culture and media production, tourism and most manufacturing comprise New York's export sector. The business services sector is now larger than manufacturing, which employed four times as many people in 1950. While new information technologies have moved backroom activities in the FIRE sector out of New York, the city plays host to a new high-tech sector: Silicon Alley, a collection of firms that develop multimedia software, web sites, on-line entertainment, and related goods and services (Roche, 1997). In this new sector, employment rose in Metropolitan New York from 28,500 in 1992 to 71,500 in 1995, with income estimated at $3.8 billion (Crahan and Vourvoulias-Bush, 1997).

Table 4.1 Total and foreign revenues of US multinational corporations, 1986

Headquarters location	Number of firms	Foreign reve-nues	Total reve-nues	Foreign revenues as percentage of total
Greater New York Area	40	$212	$515	41.2
New York City	24	$137	$293	46.8
New York City Suburbs	16	$75	$222	33.8
Elsewhere US	60	$172	$704	24.4
Total	100	$384	$1,219	31.5

Source: Drennen 1991.

The above activities exhibit an increasing degree of internationalization. Of the 100 largest multinational corporations in New York in 1986, 24 had their headquarters in New York City. Almost half their revenues derived from foreign operations. The 16 MNCs with headquarters in New York's suburbs derived a third of their revenues from abroad. The region's share of foreign revenues of its MNCs' total revenues is 41 percent (Table 4.1). Six of the ten largest US banks with foreign deposits are in New York, and together they had 85 percent of these foreign deposits (Drennen, 1991). Six of the 'Big 8' accounting firms (which have twice as many branch offices abroad as they have in the US) are headquartered in New York. While the service sectors dominate the region's economy and manufacturing has declined sharply in employment, it is worth noting that New York Metropolitan Area currently leads all US metro areas in merchandise exports to the World (Table 4.2).

Table 4.2 Merchandise exports to the world by the top 12 metropolitan areas

Metropolitan area	Merchandise exports to the world 1997 (in billions of $)
1. New York, NY	29.083
2. San Jose, CA	29.057
3. Seattle–Bellevue–Everett, WA	27.006
4. Detroit, MI	25.967
5. L.A.–Long Beach, CA	25.816
6. Chicago, IL	23.210
7. Houston, TX	18.596
8. Miami, FL	12.692
9. Minneapolis–St. Paul, MI–WI	12.007
10. Phoenix–Mesa, AZ	11.108
11. San Francisco, CA	9.979
12. Boston, MA–NH	9.571

Source: Bureau of the Census.

THE NEW IMMIGRATION: MIRROR AND SHAPER OF NEW YORK CITY'S EVOLUTION

Demographic Dimensions of the New Immigration

The vast flow of migrants has shaped New York City throughout its history, in terms of its demography, economy, politics and culture. The geographic sources and the ethnic composition of this migration into New York have changed over time, yielding a diverse demographic and economic mosaic. For much of the city's history, people of European and African origin dominated these immigrant streams. Recently, Third World migration has made the city's population truly global in character, with persons of European background becoming a minority. These migrants, drawn largely from Latin America, the Caribbean Basin and Asia, are described as constituting the new immigration.

In every era over the last two centuries, new groups of people have brought new competencies and entrepreneurial energy to the city, helping it to reinvent itself economically, socially and culturally. In the process they have periodically reoriented the city to the nation and the world.

The ethnic diversity of New York was first evident in the bustling vitality of the founding Dutch settlement (Binder and Reimers, 1995). While the British guided the city's rise as a commercial hub, the big push for the city's growth came in the early nineteenth century. The deep port provided the great stimulus, which was exploited by many bold city business and political initiatives. In short order, the city achieved dominance in textile imports, and in Southern plantation cotton exports. The launch of the first transatlantic packet ships, and the building of the Erie Canal to reach out to the Great Lakes made New York the main American gateway (eclipsing Boston and Philadelphia). By the Civil War, New York accounted for over half the nation's foreign trade (Lichtenberg, 1960).

The relationship between the growth of the New York region and the flow of migrants was strong in this era. Two types of migrants shaped this stage of New York's evolution (Lichtenberg, 1960): those that arrived with capital and knowledge, principally from New England, and those that came just with their labor power. The former, sensing the greater opportunities in New York's port, took over much of the commercial activity. Other New Englanders came to invest in the better opportunities New York offered, or to work as clerks in the mercantile houses. The second group of immigrants – Irish, Germans and Scandinavians – from the 1830s onwards, gave rise to the manufacturing establishments and also created various craft guilds.

The volume of immigration has varied considerably, but the pattern has been adjusted upwards since 1970, following the liberalization of the 1965 Immigration Act. Since the majority of the nation's immigrants entered through the port of New York (many of them establishing initial residence) until recently, the city continued to grow well into this century, becoming the country's premier city. The internal migration from other states and Puerto Rico to New York City in the 1930s and 1940s was a growth factor as foreign immigration cooled. The suburbanization of New York's population since the 1950s would have depleted the city's population seriously, but for the immigrant flows into New York.

The recent immigration flows set in motion by the 1965 Immigration Act have led to a marked increase in the number of immigrants entering the US in general and New York in particular. Average annual migration to the city climbed from 47,000 in the 1950s to 85,600 in the 1980s, and to 112,598 during 1990–94. This increasing immigration has offset the population losses due to suburban out-migration. The city's population grew 4 percent in the 1980s largely due to the 85,600 immigrants in that decade. Fifty-five percent of New Yorkers are now first- or second-generation immigrants.

Another aspect of the post-1965 immigration is the difference from earlier immigrant streams in geographical origins and ethnic composition. Immigrants from Latin America, the Caribbean and Asia dominate the flow. The city's non-Hispanic whites are expected to drop from 5 million (63 percent of total population) in 1970 to 2.6 million (35 percent of total population) by the year 2000. In the same period, Hispanics would increase their share of the total population from 16 percent to 29 percent Asians from 2 percent to 10 percent and Non-Hispanic Blacks from 19 percent to 26 percent (Salvo and Lobo, 1997).

The New Immigrants and New York's Economic Evolution

Today's immigrants into New York City have a comparable role in shaping the city's economy, polity and culture as their counterparts had a century and a half ago, as noted earlier. This role is best described in the context of the emerging patterns of labor demand in the global economy as a whole and in its strategic gateway cities like New York.

The major reason for the continuation in the last quarter-century of large inflows of immigrants from Asia and the Caribbean basin into New York City (at a time of sharp losses in manufacturing and goods-handling jobs) lies in the rapid expansion of the supply of low-wage jobs and the casualization of the labor market associated with the new growth industries (Sassen, 1998). Sassen persuasively argues that the globalization of the economy has contributed to the *initiation* of the labor migration to New York and other cities, while its *continuation* at high and growing levels is traceable to the economic restructuring in the US and other advanced industrial economies.

The growth of low-wage jobs in New York and other cities is partly the result of the global organization that has channeled investments and manufacturing jobs to low-wage countries. Cities like New York also have a rapidly growing number of low-wage service sector jobs (in addition to the well-known high-income jobs in the financial services and management sectors). Sassen (1998) notes that in addition to using such low-wage workers directly, the service sector indirectly generates demand for workers for servicing the lifestyles and consumption patterns of the growing affluent managerial and financial class in New York. The demand created by this affluent class for residential and commercial gentrification leads to an army of low-wage workers in occupations such as building attendants, child care providers, food preparation and restaurant workers. These are the kinds of jobs that immigrants rather than US citizens take and where the informal economy grows. Thus it is at this intersection of the ongoing internationalization of economic processes and a bimodal labor market evolution in advanced industrial economies that immigrants from low-wage countries to New York and other cities play a key *economic facilitative role*.

The New Immigrants and Cultural Production in New York

New York City has for a long time been dominant in the national production of cultural goods and services. It built its primacy as a cultural center on its position as the most important port linking Europe and North America and as a transshipment point between Europe and the Caribbean. The interaction in a commercial city between diverse people and ideas, and the hybrid ambience were powerful sources of creativity. Kaplan (1997) notes that the ideas, values and creativity of New York's diverse residents found expression in cultural production for the market as well as for non-commercial channels in clubs, lyceums and cafés. New York's ideas, popular entertainment and high culture, reflecting the vibrant connections among its people, led in turn to cultural tourism and a cultural export economy (the vaudeville circuit, theater tours, etc. (Kaplan, 1997)). The market position that New York enjoyed in cultural products derived from the strong local relationship between cultural production and consumption.

Recent technologies (e.g., films, audio and video recordings, jet travel) have undermined the geographical and temporal linkages between cultural production and consumption, making possible the assembling, financing and marketing of performances (the Three Tenors, rock bands, etc.) to global audiences. Kaplan notes that in this era of broad cultural diffusion, New York is reinventing itself so as to retain its cultural hegemony. While New York remains powerful as a cultural producer and a center of consumption, it provides direction to the cultural enterprise in two ways. First, by establishing aesthetic standards, offering criticism and consumer advice and by launching styles through media, marketing, journalism and advertising. Second, by the exercise of cultural control by New York persons and institutions that affect cultural market decisions (e.g., which books, plays, and films to back) or what non-profit cultural activities to support (Kaplan, 1997).

New York also plays an important role in the cultural dimension of globalization. The frequent observation that New York, with its rich and complex cultural infrastructure, has a central role in directing cultural globalization and that this is *unidirectional* (only center to periphery cultural flows) is only part of the story.

New York's large and only partially assimilated foreign-born residents today have as rich and vibrant interactions and as hybrid an ambience as earlier groups and are creating cultural crossover products. Orlando Patterson (1994) notes that reggae, drawing upon indigenous Jamaican musical traditions, evolved into an original form in response to American rhythm-and-blues, bluegrass and cowboy music. This musical genre, brought to New York by poor Kingston immigrants, stimulated in turn the development of African-American rap. Patterson's example illustrates the contributions of today's immigrant groups in New York to the cultural life and to the production of cultural goods and services.

The Role of Immigrant Institutions and Social Networks in New York

Social networks, and institutions fostering these networks, affect the economic productivity of immigrants in a variety of ways. They play crucial roles in the assimilation process and in immigrants' labor market absorption. They also foster entrepreneurial development, provide access to legal, capital and other financial services and contribute to their identity formation through cultural production. These institutions and networks have played formative roles in the continual evolution of New York as a gateway city since the seventeenth century. As successive new immigrant groups entered New York's economy, institutions that had their roots in the culture of the originating country were initially transplanted, and eventually transformed, to address the social and economic needs of the new group in the host city.

New York, relative to most other gateway regions in the world, has a long history of fostering institutions that improve the productivity of immigrants. Helped by commercially minded social leaders, New York became a multi-ethnic city because these social networks aided the assimilation of the immigrants and enriched the culture and economic productivity of the city they settled in. For example, the recent resurgence of New York after its fiscal crisis in the 1970s, was partly fueled by the attractiveness of an increasingly cosmopolitan city with new immigrants from the various countries of Asia, Africa, the Caribbean, the Mideast and Latin America (Berrol, 1997). The cosmopolitan atmosphere added to the vibrancy of urban life which then attracted the younger, upwardly mobile professional classes to the city. Both groups – the immigrants and the migrants – invested their capital and labor, thereby turning around the fortunes of a declining urban fabric. The ability of the immigrants to contribute to the cultural and economic life of the city depends on a number of institutions, whose cultural forms may vary with the migrant group, which perform these essential socio-economic functions.

While the importance of social institutions in fostering the economic development of an immigrant community has not declined in the last one hundred years, the character of these institutions appears to be changing. We can broadly identify two types of community institutions that influence immigrant economic welfare: the traditional and the emergent. The traditional ethnic associations are based on sub-regional identities and are characterized by strong patron–client relations. They provide employment opportunities, business capital and overall protection in return for political and social loyalty to key members and leaders. The Italian and Irish bosses, the Chinese and Japanese clans, and the more contemporary Russian associations are examples of this type. While some may have criminal and illegal elements, the majority are legal, socially conscious and philanthropic entities. A prime example is the Chinese Consolidated Benevolent Association (CCBA). Its pattern of social organization, transplanted from mainland China, is hierarchial and includes district and clan organizations at lower tiers.

While dominant politically in the Chinese community, it is declining in importance relative to the Chinatown Planning Council (CPC), which also runs various programs to help the social and economic assimilation of new Chinese immigrants. In the Korean community the emergent institutions are based in churches and the media. In the Indian community, they are the business and professional institutions. These newer institutions, of which the CCP is but one example, act as bridges between the ethnic enclave culture and the larger society in which the immigrants are embedded. Thus they can be contrasted to the traditional ones that draw their base from segregating the community.

The newer forms provide information on public assistance and help the immigrant community to access public funds and laws, to learn the languages, customs, mores of the host society, and thus to integrate with the host community more efficiently. These two forms reflect, to a large extent, the changing nature of the immigrants and the maturation of the immigration process. In fact, there appears to be competition between the earlier, traditional form and the emergent, modern form.

Both types perform useful roles in assimilating and enhancing the economic productivity of immigrants. Given the foreign sociocultural milieu of the host country, many, if not most, migrants need assistance in being incorporated into the new society. New York, as an important initial entry point into the United States, has had to develop appropriate institutions to address the needs of newcomers. These institutions, both the traditional and the emergent, address the non-material needs – such as information requirements about the unfamiliar host environment – as well as material needs such as the supply of temporary housing, food, clothing and other forms of private economic assistance.

For example, 20,000 Vietnamese, Laotian and Cambodian refugees settled in New York after the Vietnam War. These groups had a difficult adjustment period, as the majority had been farmers and the adjustment to urban life was difficult. Often they were powerful élites in their country of origin but were reduced to penury and powerlessness in the host country. Several voluntary organizations helped through English-language classes, provision of economic aid and like support. The traditional ones have drawn people solely from a specific ethnic group while the more modern forms like churches have drawn on the support of both US and ethnic groups.

Social networks and support institutions reinforce a migrant's sense of ethnic distinctiveness and provide emotional support systems. For example, Foner (1987), in her analysis of Jamaican immigrants, found that 80 percent of her respondents saw or phoned relatives in New York at least once a week and that 69 percent had relatives living in the same neighborhood. Seventy percent of her sample gave only the names of other Jamaicans as friends. Cultural institutions among the Indian, Polish, Irish, Italian and Greek, to name a few, perform similar roles in fostering group pride and identity. Such close ties within the community have important economic spillovers.

Close community ties facilitate the job search through personal networks and provide employment opportunities in immigrant enterprises. For example, 75 percent of Koreans in the New York metropolitan area are employed in Korean-owned businesses. Waldinger (1989) found that relatives and friends made up the entire labor force of several Dominican garment factories. Similar patterns exist in the Chinese community.

The majority of immigrants have a high rate of savings and many immigrants become small entrepreneurs, developing businesses that hire family and friends as employees. Korean greengrocers accounted for 90 percent of the greengrocers in the city. By 1990, Dominicans controlled more than 70 percent of Hispanic businesses, such as Bodegas catering to the Hispanic population. A few Indians controlled the newspaper kiosks. The Chinese and Dominicans controlled the garment industry, replacing the earlier control by Jewish immigrants. The diamond and precious gem industry is still controlled by the Jewish jewelers, but with Asian Indians as new entrants. All ethnic groups are in the restaurant and ethnic craft industries. The new immigrants, like the Italians and Jews of a previous immigration phase, operate these small businesses.

Consequently, these start-up or expanding enterprises need access to capital. Social networks aid in capital generation and access through savings associations, rotating credit societies and ethnic banks – some federally chartered. For example, in the 1990s scholars noticed that West Indians were economically more successful than African-Americans. The West Indians from Trinidad, Jamaica, Barbados and Haiti financed their upward mobility through rotating credit unions, which provided funds for homeownership, business enterprises and education. These immigrants, in turn, rescued decaying neighborhoods in Brooklyn and the Bronx (Berrol, 1997). There are numerous examples of self-help or community-based institutions among immigrants where capital access and know-how is transmitted through personal connections, guarantees and peer counseling. These informal institutions have different eligibility standards, which make access to capital possible for groups with weak formal forms of collateral.

The newspapers and ethnic media are also important institutions for disseminating business, political and cultural information. Nearly 50 percent of the city's 80 foreign-language and ethnic newspapers were established between 1970 and 1990. There are nine dailies in Chinese alone. The circulation of *Carib News*, founded by West Indian immigrants in the 1980s, increased its circulation to more than 60,000 within a few years (Kaisinetz, 1992).

These newspapers not only provide networking services in the city, they assure a cultural, economic and political continuity with the homeland. Indian English-language newspapers have advertisements for brides and grooms available from India and brokerage service for the Bombay Stock Exchange. They also permit intervention in the political events in the country of origin. The Haitians were influential in the removal of Duvalier, the Chinese in securing US support in favor of the democracy movement.

Approximately 50 percent of the foreign-born population of New York in 1980 has arrived only since 1965. Ethnic absorption has gone smoothly because of the cultural and religious institutions. Churches and cultural institutions play critical roles in forming these personal networks where the boundaries between what is economic, social and personal become blurred. Religious and cultural institutions provide for identity formation: these institutions are familiar and are easily transplanted into ethnic neighborhoods.

However, different immigrant groups cluster around various cultural institutions, the roots of which lie in their homelands. The Jamaicans cluster around sports and music associations. The Irish use the bars and the parish church to foster a Gaelic revival. The Protestant Church is very influential in the Korean community, even though there are a large number of Buddhists in the congregation. Kim (1987) notes that the Korean Protestant churches in

New York increased from 6 to 285 in a 15-year period. Churches provide a large variety of secular functions such as the sharing of job and business information. They also assist in forming new contacts, savings clubs and like efforts of mutual assistance. The Filipinos formed political associations to foster democracy in the Philippines. These cultural institutions, through network formation, aid the economic welfare of the migrant and the community. The modern forms show the adaptability of the religious and cultural institutions as they reach beyond the ethnic enclave and yet retain the ethnic base. For example, the same Methodist church in Queens offers services in Korean, Chinese, Spanish and English (Berrol, 1997). When East Harlem began to lose its Italian population, the Haitians breathed life into Mt Carmel Church and both ethnic groups share the same Roman Catholic church, even though services are now offered in Creole as well as in the Italian and English languages.

Currently, there are also inter-ethnic contacts through sports. For example, the expanding Cosmopolitan Soccer League, founded by Germans in 1923, did not have a single German team in the 1980s. There were, however, Polish, Italian, Turkish, Yugoslavian, Irish and Ukrainian teams, just to mention a few. The Albanians fielded five teams. Such inter-ethnic contacts through cultural festivals and parades add to the vibrant recovery of the city and its inhabitants. Ethnic and US social networks play a vital role in the expanding economic growth and attractiveness of New York.

LONDON: EUROPE'S WORLD CITY

London's rise to become Europe's global gateway region depends on a number of institutional inventions and innovations that can be traced back to the eighteenth century. Its inventions included a new optimizing approach to production and a systematic use of the division of labor. The city's innovations were modeled on Amsterdam's central bank and financial markets. Taken together, the inventions and innovations allowed London to surpass Amsterdam as Europe's financial and trading center. It has remained Europe's economic focal point ever since.

Today, the London region has the world's largest foreign exchange market and its second-largest stock market. It has the world's largest production of scientific papers. In addition, London's airports have the world's greatest number of international passengers. Culturally, London is home to Europe's greatest concentration of artists and musicians and its West End theatre scene is the European counterpart to New York's Broadway. This section will in turn look at the following factors: institutional quality, agglomerations of knowledge and immigration.

London's Institutional Quality

England's legal and political institutions have from the Middle Ages onward developed characteristics which set them apart from continental Europe. Whereas France, Germany and Italy share a 'civil law' tradition derived from Roman law, England developed its own tradition known as 'common law'. The common law offers an evolutionary framework of judge-made law, where informal habits and conventions are gradually formalized within the rule of law. The common law system has also proved to have greater evolutionary capacity than the civil law system, and has been more responsive to institutional innovations. England's political development has also differed from continental developments. Whereas the rise of the nation state and democracy were accompanied by conflicts and revolutions in France, Germany and Italy, Britain exhibited a more evolutionary process of gradual democratization and decentralization of sovereign power.

Amsterdam, not London, was the center of the world economy in the sixteenth and seventeenth centuries. This focal point of the Low Countries had reached this position after a transition period with Lisbon and Antwerp as consecutive global economic gateways. The reasons for the relocation of centrality were revolutionary inventions in sailing technology and financial innovations. In the sixteenth century, Amsterdam was the city where these trade-enhancing transitions took place. Amsterdam's dominant position in the world economy caused the North Atlantic basin to become the most important part of the emerging world economy. A side effect of this geographical shift was that London's accessibility to the world market also improved.

At the beginning of this North Atlantic era, Amsterdam remained the most important city for financial middlemen, bankers, borrowers and lenders. Uncertainty was the unavoidable consequence of trade in objects of credit, which made it possible to engage in speculative activities. People of means thus became involved as speculators in the financial and commodity markets of Amsterdam. The most infamous of the speculative dramas of Amsterdam was the 'Tulipmania' around 1634, when it is recorded that at the peak a covered wagon and two accompanying horses could be given in exchange for one tulip bulb (Braudel, 1979). Financial speculation had also become common in London, but on a much smaller scale. The Royal Exchange, which was reopened after the fire of 1666, experienced a large speculative wave in government bonds and in stocks of the Bank of England and the East India Company. During the sixteenth century and the two centuries thereafter, London became the great financial imitator city, closely following the creations and innovations of Amsterdam.

In the eighteenth century, several events acted in tandem to ensure London's lasting position as a global gateway. At the beginning of the century, Amsterdam was still the center of the world economy, owing to a number of innovations that the English successfully copied. Crucial among these were Amsterdam's central bank, which the Bank of England was modeled on, and Dutch shipbuilding technology. By the end of the century, London had overtaken Amsterdam as the world's largest seaport and its largest financial center.

These 'benchmarking' efforts were accompanied by institutional and technological innovations. England became the first country where a new approach to production was put into effect. The new approach focused on optimizing production techniques and the division of labor, rather than on taking advantage of differential natural resource endowments. This approach was also reflected in the new economic theory that emerged in Britain among classical economists such as Adam Smith and David Ricardo. And new technological inventions such as the steam engine amplified the usefulness of the division of labor. The new approach to production, new technology and new financial institutions were all contributing factors behind the industrial revolution and London's emergence as the world's most important financial center. London's position was reinforced by Britain's colonization of the world economy in the eighteenth and nineteenth centuries. The British legal system became the standard for international transactions, since it was shared by its erstwhile colony, America, and became the dominant system in Asia, Africa and Australia, including the emerging gateways to the Far East: Shanghai, Hong Kong and Singapore.

Central to the workings of the City of London as a global financial center was the Exchange, where both financial and real products were traded. A purely financial exchange, the London Stock Exchange, was established in 1801, nine years after the establishment of the New York Stock Exchange. These stock exchanges (and in later years Tokyo) have ever since been the leading stock exchanges in the world in terms of capitalization or turnover. Around these stock exchanges there has been a continuing growth of a multitude of financial services, such as trade in derivatives, insurance (with Lloyds as a prime example), legal and other financial advice and financial news reporting.

Still, the world economy in the nineteenth and the first half of the twentieth centuries was centered on nation states. With the industrialization of the much larger United States in the second half of the nineteenth century, it is not surprising that the center of gravity of the world economy started to shift toward New York. This shift was accelerated by the world wars, especially the Second World War and the attendant flight of Jewish industrialists and scientists from Vienna, Berlin, Amsterdam and Paris to

New York. In parallel, the New York Stock Exchange became an innovation center in its own right, an example being J.P. Morgan's introduction of acquisition financing in the 1880s (Drucker, 1999). While London experienced a slow decline in its relative importance in the world's financial network from the late nineteenth century, the globalization of the world economy from the 1960s onwards created new opportunities for London, which reversed London's decline. One opportunity was the result of a short-sighted American policy initiative. The Kennedy administration imposed a punitive tax on interest payments to foreigners, which led to the collapse of the American foreign-bond market. As a result, the Eurobond and the Eurodollar were created in London, leading to an inflow of international investors to London at the expense of New York (Drucker, 1999).

An even more important development was the rise of the multinational firm, which created a new need for regional headquarters. With its time-tested financial institutions, its free-trade orientation and its use of English, London became the logical European operations center for North American and Japanese multinationals. Today London is the second largest global financial center, and it is yet again dependent upon another center for creative and innovative financial ideas. New York is the contemporary financial innovation center and the spatially contiguous New York and New England regions are the centers of financial creativity and research in financial economics.

Table 4.3 European stock markets, rank ordered according to turnover of securities

City region	Securities, turnover	Capitalization	Air transportation	Science
London	100	100	100	100
Paris	41	40	49	64
Frankfurt	40	72	33	18
Zürich	40	24	20	9
Amsterdam	17	16	29	32
Milan	16	2	11	13
Stockholm	10	9	11	21
Madrid	6	14	11	11
Barcelona	5	11	4	2
Copenhagen	3	4	16	22
Brussels	3	7	13	21

Sources: Andersson and Wichmann Matthiessen (1993) and Andersson (1998).

For financial bench-marking, the Londoner rarely has to travel to any other city than New York, however. Today, London is by far the most important financial gateway of Europe, vastly surpassing city-regions like Amsterdam (or Randstad), Paris and Frankfurt. It is doubtful if Frankfurt could ever catch up, in spite of hosting the central bank of the Euro area. The dominance of London is illustrated by Table 4.3. As shown by this table, London was in the 1990s 2.5 times greater than the second largest securities market in Europe. Today it is more than five times the size of its former competitor Amsterdam.

Why is London so superior to other European financial centers? An answer to this question has been provided by Bindemann (1997), based on interviews with representatives of actors in other financial market places. This is illustrated by Table 4.4.

Table 4.4 Rank ordered reasons given for the leadership of London as a European financial center

1	The availability of knowledge and skills
2	Financial traditions
3	Size and scope of the market
4	Accessibility to international banking
5	Number of financial products available
6	Rules and regulations
7	Capacity of the banking sector
8	Capitalization
9	English as the language of operations
10	Transaction volumes and costs
11	Economic and financial politics
12	Political stability

Source: Bindemann (1997) (with some minor modification of wording).

A reflection of the quality of the financial institutions is the efficiency of the stock market. The ratio of expected return to expected risk is a measure of this efficiency (see Chapter 3 by Andersson).

On this measure, London is the second most efficient stock market in the world, after Amsterdam (which is, perhaps, an illustration of the durability of institutional quality).

The increasing agglomeration of financial services firms and multinational corporations, together with the quality of the (internal and external) institutions related to financial services, has reinforced London's position as Europe's premier financial center.

The Role of Knowledge

Although London already had a number of academic institutions in the eighteenth century, such as the Inns of Court and a number of teaching hospitals and learned societies, it was not until 1826 that the first university was founded in London. University College was founded as a reaction against the universities at Oxford and Cambridge, which required of their lecturers and students that they belonged to the Church of England. Jeremy Bentham and James Mill were among those who were instrumental in achieving a separation of church and academia, and University College became the first English university without any religious ties (Tames, 1998). The opponents of a non-denominational university soon also wanted their own London university, however, and this led to the establishment of the Anglican King's College in 1828. In 1836, the Parliament created an umbrella organization called the University of London, which standardized the examinations at the two colleges (Tames, 1998). Over the next 150 years, the University of London absorbed about 30 additional colleges, schools and hospitals, all of which have retained a substantial degree of autonomy. Among London's population of working age,[1] 27.5 percent have a tertiary degree, compared with 20.5 percent for Britain as a whole (Office for National Statistics, 1998).

While Oxford and Cambridge could hardly be considered part of the London region in the eighteenth century, they gradually became more accessible over the following two centuries. This increased accessibility was first the result of the investments in railways in the nineteenth century, investments that were later dwarfed by the new roads and the rise of the car in the twentieth century. At present, the universities at Cambridge, Oxford and Reading are all within one to one-and-a-half hours from central London, depending on congestion levels.

Currently, London has the greatest concentration of scientific production of any region in the world, if scientific production is measured as the output of refereed papers in recognized journals (see Chapter 2 by Wichmann Matthiessen et al.). The London–Oxford–Cambridge region produces almost 70 percent more published scientific papers per year than the second largest research region, Tokyo–Yokohama. This is even the case if the London region is defined as the area within the Green Belt, which excludes Cambridge, Oxford and Reading. According to this rather narrow regional delimitation, London produces 50 percent more scientific output than Paris, and three times as much as Europe's third-ranking region, Holland's Randstad (i.e., Amsterdam, The Hague, Rotterdam and Utrecht). London is especially over-represented in medicine and the life sciences (see Chapter 19 by Andersson and Johansson). Thus, it has a research profile that is similar to the Scandinavian countries and the Netherlands. London's central position among Europe's regions becomes even more evident if knowledge is understood in a wider sense than academic research. This is especially true of the arts. More artists reside in the Borough of Hackney than in Paris (Tames, 1998), and almost half of all theatre tickets are sold to tourists. London is also the center of the British film and music industries. Both are industries where Britain exports more than any other country except for the US.

London's Immigrants

London's role as an immigration hub can be traced back to the sixteenth century. In the beginning, London was a gateway for immigrants mainly by virtue of being a seaport, so that many of London's foreigners were either seamen or former seamen. Most early immigrants were Dutch, which was a precursor of the close commercial ties between London and Amsterdam that were to develop in the seventeenth and eighteenth centuries. By the end of the sixteenth century there were about 4,000 foreign residents in London, of which almost 3,000 were Dutch (Tames, 1998). From the seventeenth century onward, London has attracted a large number of immigrants involved in financial services. Most of these were continental Europeans who were attracted by the sheer volume of opportunities created by London's large financial services sector. England's lack of deeply rooted anti-Semitism was an added attraction for those among them who were Jewish. Many of the firms that one associates with the City were founded by eighteenth, nineteenth and early twentieth century immigrants such as Baring, Rothschild, Schroder, Warburg (all from Germany), Hambros (Norway), Lazard (France) and Morgan (America) (Drucker, 1999).

With London's emergence as a global financial center and as a center of regional headquarters of MNCs in the 1960s, large numbers of immigrants from rich countries started arriving for the first time. This is reflected in the number of people born in countries with a higher per capita GDP than Britain. In 1991, there were as many as 150,000 Londoners who were born in the European Union outside of Britain and Ireland (Office of Population Censuses and Surveys, 1993). Germany was the single largest source of continental European immigrants, followed by Italy. In addition, there were 45,000 and 17,000 residents who were born in North America and Japan, respectively. At present, the number of European immigrants is probably greater still, but this is now more difficult to estimate, since work permits have not been required of EU nationals since 1992.

Although immigrants had an impact on the financial services sector at an early stage, London was not an American-style city of immigrants in the nineteenth or early twentieth centuries. On the eve of the Second World War,

London's population was still overwhelmingly of British ancestry. The only source of mass immigration in the first half of the century was Ireland. But the early post-war period transformed London into a truly global city. This period of massive immigration occurred in the 1950s and early 1960s. There were two causes for the increase in immigration.

Most importantly, the new availability of affordable air travel made it possible for large numbers of non-European Commonwealth citizens to take advantage of their right of abode in Britain. Second, the more restrictive American immigration policy that was promulgated in 1952 had the effect of making Britain rather than America the destination of choice for prospective emigrants, especially in the Caribbean. Most of the immigrants were either from the Caribbean islands or from Asia. This immigration period came to an abrupt halt in the early 1960s, when new immigration regulations made it more difficult for non-European immigrants to obtain residency rights. Even so, London's non-white population accounts for 24.3 percent of the total (Office for National Statistics, 1998).

West Indian immigration
The first arrival of black immigrants from the Caribbean to London dates back to 1948, when about five hundred Jamaican veterans from the Second World War decided to settle in or near London's Brixton area. These first settlers were followed by about one thousand West Indian immigrants per year between 1948 and 1952, and about twenty thousand per year for the following ten years. The much greater figure for the period after 1952 was due to the US policy shift in 1952.

The West Indians were not only from Jamaica, however, but also from countries such as Trinidad, Barbados and Guyana. From early on, West Indian immigrants moved in disproportionate numbers to certain areas in London. Jamaicans have for example been heavily over-represented in Brixton and Stockwell, whereas immigrants from Trinidad have tended to settle in Notting Hill. Many of the immigrants were recruited in their countries of origin by large London employers, such as London Transport and various hospitals (Tames, 1998). In the 1960s, the Caribbean immigrants started to impart their character on, in particular, London's cultural life. The Caribbean Notting Hill Carnival, for example, has now become Europe's most well-attended carnival. In music, first- and second-generation immigrants have become influential in shaping both contemporary British rock music as well as the more experimental 'world music' genre.

In 1997, there were almost 680,000 black Londoners, of whom most hailed from the Caribbean (Office for National Statistics, 1998). This amounts to 9.7 percent of London's total population, which means that the proportion of blacks is almost five times higher than in Britain generally. In addition, many of London's 405,000 'mixed-race or other' inhabitants are probably part Caribbean, since inter-racial marriage and cohabitation rates are much higher among blacks than among other minorities (which is, interestingly, the reverse of the American case). The average educational attainment of black Londoners is now similar to white levels, although blacks still differ from whites in having a smaller share of home owners and a greater share of out-of-wedlock births (Office for National Statistics, 1999).

Asian immigration
The other main source of non-European immigration was Asia, especially the Indian subcontinent, as well as ethnic Indians from Kenya and Uganda. In descending order, the three largest Asian ethnic groups are Indian Hindus, Pakistani/Bangladeshi Muslims and Chinese. Although both the Indian and the Pakistani/Bangladeshi communities hail from the Indian subcontinent, the two communities have markedly different socioeconomic characteristics.

Indians constitute London's most highly educated ethnic group, with the highest proportion of degree-holders. Indians are especially well represented in the medical and legal professions. Less educated Indians are notable for a high proportion of self-employed, especially as owners of small family businesses. Types of business that are especially favored by Indians include restaurants, convenience stores, newspaper kiosks and *bureaux de change.* In 1997, there were more than 380,000 Indian Londoners, equaling 5.6 percent of the total population (Office for National Statistics, 1998; 1999).

Conversely, South Asian Muslims are the least educated of London's ethnic groups, and are much more likely to have unskilled occupations. They are more geographically concentrated than Indians, which accounts for Muslim neighborhoods such as 'Banglatown' in Tower Hamlets. Moreover, Pakistanis and Bangladeshis are less likely to marry outside their ethnic group than any other minority. There is also, however, a large group of self-employed people in this group, and they resemble Indians in their preferred lines of business.

About 3.1 percent of London's population is accounted for by Pakistanis and Bangladeshis, compared with slightly more than 1.5 percent of Britain's total population, of which 51 percent are Pakistanis and 49 percent Bangladeshis. They are thus less over-represented in London than any other ethnic minority (Office for National Statistics, 1998).

The Chinese, finally, have educational and economic features that resemble Indians. Most of London's Chinese are not from Mainland China, however. More than two-thirds of London's Chinese population were born in Hong Kong, Malaysia or Singapore. They amount to about 1 percent of London's population, which is almost five times their share in the rest of Britain.

London – a Gateway to Three Global Communities

London is Europe's world city by virtue of being a focal point in three communities: the Anglo-American community, the Commonwealth and the European Union. Its ethnic composition partially overlaps several other gateways in all three communities such as New York and other North American gateways (English-speaking whites, blacks and Asians), Singapore (Chinese and Indians), Hong Kong (Chinese and British expatriates), Frankfurt (Germans) and Milan (Italians). Consequently, London has Europe's greatest agglomeration of expertise in non-European cultures, languages and institutions. But London is also closer – geographically, politically, economically and culturally – to continental Europe than any other English-speaking metropolis. In addition, English common law has become the legal system for international transactions. Eight of the 12 non-European gateways presented in this book use the common law, whereas London is the only European gateway with an English legal system. London is therefore a good location for international transactions involving one or more European firms. The use of the English language further enhances its institutional attractiveness as a preferred location for North American and Asian firms. London's nodal functions reflect its institutional quality, ethnic diversity and agglomeration of scientific and cultural knowledge. As a first example, London's airports offer more non-stop intercontinental flights than any other city. A second example is that London is the only European region with higher than expected scientific cooperation with several Asia-Pacific countries such as India, Hong Kong, Singapore and Australia (Andersson, forthcoming). Most importantly, London is the preferred European headquarters location for most non-European firms and organizations, regardless of whether they are American, Japanese, Overseas Chinese, Middle Eastern, Caribbean or Indian.

GATEWAY FUNCTIONS OF TOKYO

Although Tokyo is normally counted as one of the three global cities, along with New York and London, its function is more limited than that of the other two cities. While New York is a gateway to North America and London a gateway to Europe, Tokyo is a gateway to Japan rather than Asia. In this way it is more similar to Paris than London. It is only the size of the Japanese economy that renders Tokyo a global city, not the internal internationalization of the region. Combining the world's greatest agglomeration of wealth with a national orientation yields some unexpected results. While Tokyo has Asia's largest stock market and its largest agglomeration of scientific knowledge, Hong Kong has more international flights and a greater number of regional headquarters of American and European MNCs. Tokyo not only has a much smaller share of foreign-born residents and ethnic minorities than New York and London, but a smaller share than Hong Kong and Singapore as well. In addition, Tokyo, like Paris and Frankfurt, relies on the civil law tradition rather than on British common law, which is the international standard used in the other major Asia-Pacific gateways: Hong Kong, Singapore and Sydney. Altogether this means that Tokyo is a global city by the force of its size rather than by being a microcosm of the world. Below, we discuss the various 'gateway' functions of Tokyo, particularly the flow of information, production agglomerations, and the accumulation of human capital.

An Information Gateway

It is said that we live in an 'information society'. Information is sent to us personally as well as through the mass media. Measuring the amount of information in terms of the number of 'words' sent, data on information flow via personal media within Japan (Ministry of National Land Planning, 1987) reveal that 19 percent of telephone calls, 47 percent of computer network flows, 35 percent of facsimile transmissions and 31 percent of postal mail, originated in Tokyo. For the mass media, 78 percent of TV broadcasting, 40 percent of newspapers by volume, and 90 percent of other publications originated in Tokyo. More than three quarters of the total information flow via the mass media in Japan thus originates in Tokyo. Since the annual amount of information flow conveyed by the mass media is 1.5 times the amount conveyed through personal communications, about 62 percent of the entire information flow in Japan originated in Tokyo. This is a tremendous share: the second largest origin of information flow, Osaka, has a share of 12 percent. The information gateway function of Tokyo becomes clear when we survey the data on information flow destinations. Only 23 percent and 12 percent of total information flows through personal media and mass media, respectively, are destined for Tokyo. This implies that only 16 percent of all information is sent to Tokyo, a ratio which is not much larger than Osaka's share, at 10 percent.

The ratio of the information quantity originating in Tokyo to that destined for Tokyo is 1.62 for personal-media-information, 6.46 for mass-media information, and 3.75 for the entire information flow. These ratios are 1.01, 1.36, and 1.17, respectively in Osaka, and are less than unity in all other regions. That is, in all regions except for Tokyo and Osaka, the inflow of information is greater than the outflow.

Agglomeration Economies

Table 4.5 shows the national population shares over time of the Tokyo Metropolitan Area, Tokyo City (Tokyo-to), and Central Tokyo (ku-bu). The share of the Tokyo Metropolitan Area has been increasing monotonously, and consequently more than a quarter of the total national population now live in the Tokyo Metropolitan Area. The share of Tokyo has been slightly decreasing over time, and there is also a trend toward a decreasing relative population in central Tokyo (ku-bu). Migration into the Tokyo Metropolitan Area has increased, and is mostly accommodated by the outer area. Therefore, the Tokyo Metropolitan Area is undergoing population decentralization.

Table 4.5. Share in the national population (%)

Year Area	1970	1975	1980	1985	1990	1993
DID in Tokyo (ku-bu)	8.4	7.7	7.1	6.9	6.6	N.A.
Tokyo-to	10.9	10.4	9.9	9.8	9.6	9.5
Tokyo Metro-politan Area	23.0	24.2	24.5	25.0	25.7	25.9

Population concentration in terms of the population share of the central area (ku-bu) in the total population of Tokyo has been declining (77 percent in 1970; 69 percent in 1993). But this concentration is very high in comparison with the primacy rate (defined as the ratio of population of the capital city to the total population in a prefecture) in other regions, whose mean is 29 percent The population density in central Tokyo (i.e., the ku-bu) is 12,897/km^2, almost 40 times the national average density of 328/km^2. These statistics imply that the space in inner Tokyo is used intensively, generating agglomeration economies (as well as diseconomies, due to congestion). In 1993, 2,017 Japanese firms were listed in the first-class section of the Tokyo Stock Exchange. Because of agglomeration economies, more than half (1,018) of these firms have their headquarters in Tokyo, and 493 of them are concentrated in the central business district (CBD) of Tokyo (i.e., in two ku's, Chiyoda-ku and Chuo-ku, which together comprise the core area of central Tokyo). Agglomeration economies emerge in the form of easier exchange of information, better access to customers, and a lower search cost for obtaining labor. The tremendously high land prices and office-space rents in the Tokyo CBD are notorious. Nevertheless, the headquarters of many firms are located there because, in addition to the agglomeration economies, locating the headquarters in the Tokyo CBD has become the 'status symbol' of an enterprise.

As far as manufacturing industry is concerned, 8.7 percent of the total number of establishments and 6.2 percent of the total workforce were concentrated in Tokyo in 1993. In the service sector, 11.3 percent of total establishments and 15.8 percent of the total workforce are in Tokyo. As is well known, Tokyo is one of the major international centers of financial trade. In 1994, the total value of stocks traded in Japan (mainly in Tokyo) accounted for about 30 percent of the total stock value in the world, so Tokyo is also a gateway in the international financial network.

It might seem that Tokyo is a city of the tertiary sector (including finance, insurance, real estate and commerce, but it should be noted that Tokyo, unlike London and New York, has large agglomerations of the manufacturing sector as well (Sassen, 1991)). Among the manufacturing industries, Tokyo is especially over-represented in printing and publishing, the location quotient (calculated by gross output) of which is 3.2: that is, the share of the printing and publishing sector in the total output of manufacturing industries in Tokyo is 3.2 times the corresponding national average share. It is noteworthy that the output of the printing and publishing sector supports a large amount of the information flow originating in Tokyo, as described above. The concentration of the electrical and general machinery sectors is also high: the location quotients are, respectively, 2.27 and 1.14. The highest shipment value is recorded in the electrical machinery sector.

Not only large firms operate in Tokyo, but also small and medium-sized firms, which are densely located in a specific district (Ohta-ku in southern Tokyo and the Tama district area in Kawasaki city). Most of them operate in the high-technology sector as subcontractors to large firms. It has long been argued that the agglomeration of these small high-technology firms in Tokyo has been a supporting factor in the growth of Japanese manufacturing industries (Imai, 1984).

The reason why the small firms are agglomerated in a specific district is that each firm receives various orders for products, and so that it can make special products to order within a given time period, each firm must cooperate with different specialists. In such circumstances, they need to be located in proximity to each other so that meetings, communications and transportation among them are highly efficient. Face-to-face meetings have proved to be essential for this cooperation and cannot be replaced by telecommunications or the like. In addition, the residence of a company's owner and the factory building need to be adjacent to each other so that business meetings with customers and others in the trade can be held even at night. Reflecting the agglomeration economies in both the manufacturing and tertiary sectors, the per capita income in Tokyo is as high as 4.42 million yen (in 1993), which is 1.46 times the national average of 3.02 million yen.

Tokyo's Educational Resources

Institutions of higher education are concentrated in Tokyo-to. The numbers of universities and colleges per 100,000 inhabitants are 0.92 and 0.62, respectively, in Tokyo, compared with a national average of 0.46 and 0.47: that is, universities are located in Tokyo twice as densely as they are in other regions. The discrepancy in the admission capacity of universities between Tokyo and other regions is almost the same as the discrepancy in the number of universities. Such a concentration of tertiary education generates a large influx of young people (new undergraduate students) to Tokyo from other regions. The share of university graduates among total residents in Tokyo-to is 21 percent, which is nearly twice the national average (12 percent). Since Tokyo has more highly educated people than elsewhere in Japan, the average labor productivity is correspondingly higher. The Tokyo region also has the world's second largest concentration of scientific production, after London. The high ratio of highly educated people is also reflected in per capita retail sales of books and magazines, which in Tokyo is nearly twice the national average.

This section has attempted to identify the gateway functions of the Tokyo region (Tokyo-to), sometimes with reference to the wider Tokyo Metropolitan Area and sometimes to the more localized Tokyo 'ku-bu'. The focus has been on the information flows, agglomeration economies, and human capital stock associated with this region in comparison with other regions of Japan. Tokyo sends a large amount of information all over Japan: 62 percent of the total information flow in Japan originates in Tokyo. Outflow of information overwhelmingly exceeds inflow of information in Tokyo by a factor of 3.75, which illustrates Tokyo's function as an information gateway. More than half of the firms listed on the first-class section of the Tokyo Stock Exchange have their headquarters in Tokyo, and more than half of these are located in the Tokyo CBD. Such a concentration in inner Tokyo has arisen because of agglomeration economies, such as easier access to information, easier communication with customers and lower search costs for labor.

Many small to medium-sized manufacturing firms are concentrated in a specific area in Tokyo. They are predominantly high-technology firms that operate as subcontractors to large firms. This unique agglomeration of small to medium-sized firms in Tokyo has supported the growth of manufacturing industries in Japan. Institutions of higher education (universities and colleges) are heavily concentrated in Tokyo. This has caused a recurring annual in-migration of young people from other regions to Tokyo. Also, people in Tokyo have a higher average educational background than outside Tokyo, which contributes to above-average regional labor productivity.

NOTE

1. 16–64 years for men and 16–59 years for women.

REFERENCES

Andersson, Å.E. (1998), *Finansplats Stockholm – en tillväxtmotor*, Stockholm: SNS.

Andersson, Å.E. and C. Wichmann Matthiessen (1993), *Øresundsregionen: Kreativitet, Integration, Vækst*, Copenhagen: Munksgaard/Rosinante.

Andersson, D.E. (forthcoming 2000), 'Scientific cooperation networks in Eastern Asia', in D.E. Andersson and J.P.H. Poon (eds), *Asia-Pacific Transitions*, London: Macmillan.

Aydalot, Philippe (1985), 'L'aptitude des milieux locaux a promouvoir innovation technologique', Paper presented in *A Symposium on New Technologies and Regions in crisis* , Brussels, 22–23 April.

Berrol, S. (1997), *The Empire City: New York and Its People: 1624–1996*,New York: Praeger.

Bindemann, K. (1997), *On the Optimal Design of an International Financial Center*, Department of Economics, Bristol: Bristol University.

Binder, F.M. and D.M. Reimers (1995), *All the Nations under Heaven*, New York: Columbia University Press.

Braudel, F. (1973), *Civilization and Capitalism 15–18th century,* vols 1–3, New York: Harper and Row.

Braudel, F. (1979), *Les Jeux de L'Échange*, Paris: Librarie Armand Colin.

Castells, M. (1996), *The Rise of the Network Society*, London: Basil Blackwell.

Crahan, M.E. and A. Vourvoulias-Bush (eds) (1997), *The City and the World*, New York: The Council on Foreign Relations.

Drennen, M. (1991), 'The decline and rise of the New York economy', in J. Mallenkoff and M. Castells (eds), *Dual City: Restructuring New York*, New York: Russell Sage, pp. 25–41.

Drucker, P. (1999), 'Innovate or die', *The Economist*, 25 September, pp. 27–34.

Foner, N. (ed.) (1987), *New Immigrants in New York*, N. Y: Columbia Univ. Press.

Hoover, E. and R. Vernon (1959), *Anatomy of a Metropolis*, Cambridge: Harvard University Press.

Imai, K. (1984), *The Society of Information Networks*, Iwanami Shoten (in Japanese).

Kaisinetz, P. (1992), *Caribbean New York*, Ithaca: Cornell University Press.

Kaplan, J. (1997), 'Rooting for a logo: culture, identity, and civic experience in the global city', in M.E. Crahan and A. Vourvoulias-Bush (eds), *The City and the World*, New York: The Council on Foreign Relations, pp. 159–170.

Kim, I. (1987), 'The Koreans: small business in an urban frontier', in N. Foner (ed.) (1987), *New Immigrants in New York*, New York: Columbia University Press.

Krugman, P. (1991), *Geography and Trade*, Cambridge, MA: MIT Press.

Lakshmanan, T.R. (1989), 'Technological and institutional innovations in the service sector', in Å.E. Andersson, D.F. Batten and C. Karlsson (eds), *Knowledge and Industrial Organization*, New York: Springer-Verlag, pp. 63–80.

Lakshmanan, T.R. (1993) 'Social change induced by technology: promotion and resistance', in N. Åkerman (ed.), *The Necessity of Friction*, Boulder, CO: Westview, pp. 75–97.

Lichtenberg, R.M. (1960), *One Tenth of a Nation*, Cambridge: Harvard Univ. Press.

Ministry of National Land Planning (1987), *Interregional Information Flow* (in Japanese), Tokyo.

O'Cleireacain C. (1997), 'The private economy and public budget of New York City', in M.E. Crahan and A. Vourvoulias-Bush (eds), *The City and the World*, New York: The Council on Foreign Relations, pp. 22–38.

Office for National Statistics (1998), *Regional Trends*, 33, London: The Stationery Office.

Office for National Statistics (1999), *Social Trends*, 29, London: The Stationery Office.

Office for Population Censuses and Surveys (1993), *1991 Census*, London: HMSO.

Patterson, O. (1994), 'Ecumenical America: global culture and American cosmos', *World Policy Journal*, **11** (2), 103–17.

Porter, M. (1990), *The Competitive Advantage of Nations*, New York: The Free Press.

Roche, E.M. (1997), 'Cyberopolis: the cybernetic city faces the global economy', in M.E. Crahan and A. Vourvoulias-Bush (eds), *The City and the World*, New York: The Council on Foreign Relations, pp. 51–69.

Rosen, R.D. and R. Murray (1997), 'Opening doors: access to the global market for financial sectors', in M.E. Crahan and A. Vourvoulias-Bush (eds), *The City and the World*, New York: The Council on Foreign Relations, pp. 39–50.

Salvo, J. and A.P. Lobo (1997) 'Immigration and the changing demographic profile of New York', in M. Crahan and A. Vourvoulias-Bush (eds), *The City and the Word*, New York: The Council on Foreign Relations.

Sassen, S. (1991), *The Global City: New York, London, Tokyo*, Princeton: Princeton University Press.

Sassen, S. (1997), 'Cities, foreign policy, and the global economy', in M.E. Crahan and A. Vourvoulias-Bush (eds), *The City and the World*, New York: Council on Foreign Relations, pp.171–187.

Sassen, S. (1998), *Globalization and Its Discontents*, New York: New Press.

Sassen, S. (1999), 'Global financial centers', *Foreign Affairs*, **78** (1), 75–87.

Scott, A.J. (1988), *Metropolis: From the Division of Labor to Urban Form*, Berkeley: University of California Press.

Tames, R. (1998), *A Traveller's History of London*, London: The Windrush Press.

Vernon, R. (1960), *Metropolis 1985*, Cambridge: Harvard University Press.

Waldinger, R. (1989), 'Structural opportunities or ethnic advantage: immigrant business development in New York', *International Migration Review*, **23**.

PART TWO

North American Gateway Regions

5. Southern California as a Global Gateway Region: Polycentricity and Network Segmentation as Competitive Advantages

Luis Suarez-Villa

Southern California is one of the most interesting global metropolitan regions to be found today. It is the world's best example of polycentric metropolitan form, with a vast mosaic of municipalities sprawling over 11,000 square kilometers of very diverse terrain. Southern California is also the only binational megalopolis in the Americas, and the only in the world to comprise both First and Third World national contexts within its functional boundaries.

The Southern California conurbation is about to become the most populated urban region in the United States, passing the New York–Philadelphia metropolitan corridor as the country's largest demographic agglomeration. Southern California has the world's eleventh largest economy today, on its own, and it is the United States' most important foreign trade center, with the largest volume of exports and imports. The region is also a major transport node, with the world's fourth busiest air cargo and shipping port facilities. It is the United States' most important industrial region, with one of the most diverse production structures in the world, comprising every imaginable product, from textiles and furniture manufacturing to biotechnology, advanced electronics, aerospace and computer software.

Southern California has one of the largest concentrations of high-technology industries in the world, comprising about one-quarter of United States' employment and almost one-seventh of the world's production capacity in those industries. It is also one of the world's largest sources of research and development (R&D) work in technology, and it concentrates the largest number of inventors in the United States. The region's technological creativity is complemented by an enormous variety of service activities, among which the entertainment sector and Hollywood are probably the best known.

As a fairly new metropolitan region that grew large with the automobile, Southern California's structure and form had much to do with the transport infrastructure. Southern California has possibly the most extensive road infrastructure of any metropolitan region in the world. Over 95 percent of all human movement within the region occurs by road, with private automotive travel accounting for almost all such movement. Almost all shipments of goods also occur by road, relying on a hierarchy of freeways and local roads for access to port, air cargo and external rail shipping. Probably no other global metropolis has accumulated so much physical capital in as short a period of time as Southern California.

Complementing all these features is the region's unique binational context. No other international border area has such deep and numerous contrasts as those found between the American and the Mexican sides of the metropolitan region. In no other part of the world can one find an advanced country sharing one of its largest conurbations with a Third World nation. As a result, for example, labor costs can drop as much as 85 percent simply by crossing to the less developed part of the metropolitan region. A substantial flow of labor migration from the poorer part of the metropolitan region has also created an underground economy of its own, the magnitude of which is difficult to find in any other advanced metropolitan area of the world.

To a great extent, Southern California's current standing as a globally connected region is derived from its metropolitan form and the kinds of network structures that have developed within its boundaries. Its polycentric metropolitan structure has fostered a great deal of segmentation, in virtually every sector or activity. As a result, vastly different activities, disparities and standards have been able to coexist within this region. The high level of segmentation found within the region has also provided it with many competitive advantages, by allowing firms and institutions to connect with the vast spectrum of opportunities and resources that are available in the sprawling metropolitan mosaic.

This contribution will provide an overview of the most significant internal aspects that have promoted Southern California's rise as a global metropolis. A central argument of this chapter is that Southern California's rising importance has been largely supported by its polycentric metropolitan structure, and by the multifaceted segmentation and flexibility that it has fostered in almost every aspect of its economic and social life. Although the perspective of this contribution will be general in scope, much of the discussion will be concerned with labor and employment. The following section will provide a brief overview of Southern California's history, its rapid urban growth, and its polycentric character. That will be followed up by a brief discussion of its global relevance and the two main characteristics, segmentation and flexibility, which have helped it become a world-class metropolis. A final section will then consider the segmentation of networks, with particular attention being given to the proliferation of *barrier* network structures within the region, and their impact on labor flows and employment. In general, the approach taken by this contribution will be macro-level, providing broad overviews rather than focusing on micro-analytic details.

SOUTHERN CALIFORNIA'S POLYCENTRIC METROPOLITAN STRUCTURE

One hundred years ago, the two most important cities in Southern California, Los Angeles and San Diego, were peripheral outposts to the American urban system. Both cities were founded through the missionary settlement efforts of Spanish colonization, starting in the seventeenth century. After Mexico's independence from Spain in the early nineteenth century, the region became a part of its territory until 1848, when it was ceded to the United States at the end of the Mexican–American War. Both cities were sparsely populated until the late nineteenth century. Until the 1910s, Los Angeles and San Diego were both devoid of industry and of the kinds of infrastructure that were common in such places as New York City or Chicago. By the 1930s, San Diego was mainly a Navy port, servicing the US Pacific fleet, while Los Angeles comprised a relatively compact central business district, with a growing Hollywood film industry employment. Tijuana, on the Mexican side, was little more than a border village, subsisting on local cross-border trade and the limited agricultural capabilities of its immediate area (see, for example, Starr, 1990; Profitt, 1994; Arreola and Curtis, 1993; Rolle, 1981; Nadeau, 1960).

San Francisco, in northern California, concentrated most of the state's urban population up to the 1920s, wielding enormous political and economic power. San Francisco had urbanized much earlier than Los Angeles, growing rapidly after the Gold Rush years and the Mexican–American War of 1848, and it became the main destination of the transcontinental railroad when it reached the Pacific coast. Los Angeles, in contrast, did not have a direct transcontinental rail link until the late nineteenth century, leaving it dependent on the San Francisco rail hub for shipments to the rest of the United States. The construction of the first direct rail link and roads across the desert helped increase Los Angeles' population substantially, reaching over 300,000 by 1910 (see Starr, 1990).

The end of the Second World War then marked the start of a major and sustained construction boom in Southern California. Between the late 1940s and 1980s Southern California developed into a vast continuous metropolitan mosaic of over 160 municipalities and 25 major business centers, spread over 6 contiguous counties (see Figure 5.1 and Table 5.1). Today, most of the business centers are individually comparable to the downtown areas of many large American cities, concentrating highly diverse service and industrial activities that are made accessible through the region's system of freeways and roads. The vast mosaic of disparate communities fostered much spatial segregation by income or wealth, with more than 300 gated neighborhoods providing the most obvious examples of social and economic separation that one can probably find in the United States. As a result, Southern California became the quintessential example of polycentricity, with an extremely diverse agglomeration of communities, activities and population (see, for example, Gordon et al., 1986; Giuliano and Small, 1991; Gordon and Richardson, 1996; Suarez-Villa and Walrod, 1997).

Figure 5.1 The Southern California metropolitan region

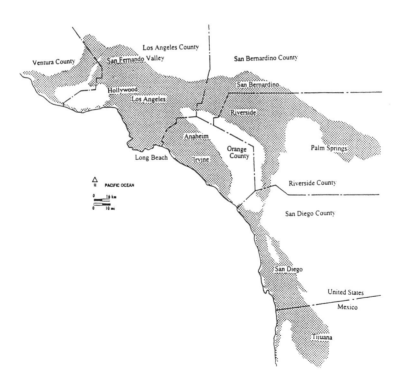

Source: US Bureau of the Census (1993, 1999).

Two very important elements supported Southern California's polycentric growth, and catapulted it to its current status as a major metropolitan region. One of them was water. The region's arid terrain could not have supported much urban growth without the massive imports of water from such far away sources as the Colorado and Sacramento rivers (in Arizona and Northern california, respectively). Starting in the 1920s, massive construction programs of canals and tunnels, and a vast system of reservoirs, underpinned Southern California's urbanization. Enormous imports of water from other regions of the American west supported both sprawling urbanization and a change of the very landscape of the region, in ways that would be hard to imagine anywhere else in the world. Almost all of Southern California's current urban vegetation, for example, is not indigenous to the region and would not exist today without the vast irrigation networks supplied with imported water.

Table 5.1. Southern California metropolitan population

	Population (millions)		
	1980	1990	projected 2000
Southern California totals	15.802	19.679	23.657
US side total	15.340	18.932	22.457
Counties:			
Los Angeles	7.478	8.863	10.724
Orange	1.933	2.411	3.375
Riverside	0.663	1.170	2.059
San Bernardino	0.895	1.418	2.269
San Diego	1.862	2.498	3.372
Ventura	0.529	0.582	0.658
Mexico side total	0.462	0.747	1.200
Tijuana municipality	0.462	0.747	1.200

Source: US and Mexican censuses, 1980 and 1990.

The second element supporting Southern California's growth was the automobile. As early as 1915, Los Angeles led the nation's cities, with the largest number (55,000) of privately owned cars in the United States. As they became a mass consumption good, automobiles provided the basic technology of movement for the region and its sprawling settlements (see Wachs, 1984). A streetcar network operating in various parts of Los Angeles was dismantled by the late 1950s, leaving the automobile as the only transport mode available to most residents. Southern California therefore grew to its present size with the automobile, with most residents having used no other form of transportation to any significant extent.

Unlike most other major cities around the world, rail technology never gave much support to needed goods or shipments, and even today public transit, whether through buses or commuter rail, is largely ineffective, because of low population densities and the long-standing reliance on the automobile. Recent efforts to establish light rail lines in the central areas of Los Angeles and San Diego have been very disappointing, with very low ridership and high operating losses. Much the same can be said for the recently opened subway line linking downtown Los Angeles with parts of the San Fernando Valley in Los Angeles County. If long-standing habits are difficult to break with, it is therefore not surprising that many Southern Californians cherish the individual mobility and routing flexibility provided by the automobile, despite the congestion and expenses involved. To a great extent, therefore, the region's polycentric structure owes its existence to the automobile and the vast road and freeway networks that were developed over the past six decades.

POLYCENTRICITY AND THE GATEWAY FUNCTION

Polycentricity is possibly the most distinctive metropolitan characteristic of Southern California. Southern California's gateway function has been greatly conditioned by its polycentric structure. In many ways, therefore, the region's polycentricity has set the spatial context in which flows, network structures, transactions and location decisions occur. Beyond the region's specific context, it can be argued that polycentricity has also affected the functional relationships involved in many economic activities, including those which provide it with its globally competitive base.

Among the various factors which make up Southern California's global gateway function, labor is one of the most important. A unique aspect of the region, which is also linked to its polycentricity, is the binational First World/Third World context, which has made labor extremely important for production. The sort of binational polycentricity which marks Southern California's economy and society has, for example, turned part of the metropolitan region (on the Mexican side) into a major 'offshore' production center in electronics, rivaling the most successful Asian enclaves to be found today. But labor flows and networks have also have also become extremely important for almost every economic activity found in the region, from Hollywood to the furniture and textile manufacturers of Los Angeles, to the advanced high-tech, aerospace and biotechnology complexes that have proliferated throughout the coastal counties. Thus, almost every other activity that has attained importance in the region's gateway function depends on the labor flows which are structured and conditioned by its polycentricity.

It may be difficult for anyone who has not lived in Southern California to understand the extent to which polycentricity can influence such seemingly 'non-spatial' aspects as labor flows, employment networks or even labor demand. In many respects, the predominance of the monocentric model of urban form has made it difficult for us to understand how polycentric structure can condition activities, flows and transactions differently from those of almost every other global metropolis. Urban economists have not yet devised an adequate model of polycentric structure, and so our conception of how cities work tends to be limited by the monocentric model's baggage (see, for example, Richardson, 1988; Berry and Kim, 1993). Until the time when a working model of polycentric metropolitan structure can be devised, we may have to rely on evidence from isolated factors, historical accounts or case studies of specific areas.

Two important characteristics distinguish metropolitan Southern California from the monocentric structures of almost every other global metropolis, and help condition its gateway function. These characteristics are vital for structuring labor flows and production within, from and to the metropolitan region. This is especially important for the location of workplaces, residences and the commuting flows involved in all activities. The most important characteristic is segmentation. Segmentation is exemplified by the very diverse mosaic of communities, the multiple commercial and industrial centers, and the lack of dominant central areas or downtowns in the older major cities of the region (Los Angeles, San Diego). In the context of Southern California's segmentation, the downtown or central business areas of Los Angeles or San Diego, for example, vie with the numerous other centers found throughout the region for businesses and customers. In many respects, the old centers are disadvantaged compared with the newer commercial centers, because of their older infrastructure, congestion, limited and costly parking, higher crime, or distance from the rapidly growing residential areas of the region (see, for example, Clark, 1981; Light, 1988; Davis, 1990; Garreau, 1991).

The kind of segmentation fostered by Southern California's polycentric structure allows the most valuable places or communities to abstract themselves from their local context, and to project themselves nationally and globally. The lack of strong or dominant older central cities no doubt facilitates this process, by eliminating the need to bypass or offset entrenched interests and their influence. This condition renders the process of abstraction all the more dynamic, since the places with global potential have mostly to look to their own resources and advantages to project themselves, wasting little effort in overcoming opposition from external interests and powers within the metropolitan region.

This phenomenon partly explains why regional governance or coordination have never existed in Southern California to any influential extent. The Southern California Association of Governments (SCAG), a regional planning agency, has always been basically toothless, with virtually no powers to make municipalities and counties comply with any of its recommendations. Even in the City of Los Angeles, the most influential urban area in the region, a weak mayor–strong council form of government empowers council members with extraordinary influence within the districts they represent, often at the expense of the City's larger interests. This atomization of metropolitan power works to the advantage of the most valuable communities within the region, by practically eliminating the need to comply with the dictates of a regional government or suprametropolitan authority. It is difficult indeed to find any other global metropolis where communities and municipalities act solely on the basis of their own interests, even in such areas as public finance or international contacts, and often at the expense of the larger metropolitan polity (see, for example, Baldassare, 1998).

Segmentation affects the less valuable places or communities, comprising poorer populations with lower labor skills and incomes, by embedding them in the local context and tying them to the needs of the more valuable communities. It is not surprising, therefore, that the less valuable communities are the main destinations of poor immigrants, who provide the cheap labor required by the higher-value activities of the region. This sort of embedded coexistence between low and high-value communities, resulting from polycentric segmentation, is very important for the region's global competitiveness. Without it, the higher-value communities would find it much more difficult to project themselves nationally and globally, facing manpower shortfalls, higher labor costs, and eventually capital flight to less costly locations elsewhere.

Segmentation, as it embeds the lower-value communities economically, can also make it easier to isolate them in a social and political sense. In Southern California's polycentric structure, economic embeddedness can coexist with isolation remarkably well. Lower-value communities can be isolated through specialization, as embedded suppliers of cheap and compliant immigrant labor, with little or no possibility of projecting themselves beyond this narrow functional role. It is therefore not surprising that such communities do not partake in the most significant technological advances found within the metropolitan region. While many places in Southern California have, for example, been wired for the latest technologies, lower-value communities such as South Central Los Angeles had no fiber-optic connections whatsoever as of late 1998. Also, the use of electronic communications in that community was virtually non-existent, with extremely low computer literacy rates among its residents.

Another important characteristic of Southern California's polycentric structure, which is partly a result of segmentation, is flexibility. The vast mosaic of communities and business centers provides greater locational flexibility than would occur in older, monocentric metropolises, or in cities with less well-defined polycentric structures. Southern California's polycentricity makes it possible for a large number of disparate activities to be found in relatively close proximity, often straddling municipal boundaries. The high reliance on individual transportation adds to this flexibility, through the sheer number of routing choices and the redundancies of the road networks. It is not uncommon, for example, for a commuter to take a different route to work every day of the week, with little or no impact on travel time. As a result, a slight routing adjustment in almost any commute-to-work trip can provide a very different constellation of choices in many shopping or service activities. Similarly, the diversity of routing possibilities also makes it easier for those activities to gain access to the region's vast segmented labor market.

The large number of locational alternatives within the metropolitan region also provides most businesses with a great deal of flexibility. Firms searching for a location may have a diverse number of business clusters or districts to choose from, in contrast with the more limited range of possibilities found in monocentric cities (see, for example, Gordon et al., 1986; Sivitanidou and Sivitanides, 1995; Suarez-Villa and Walrod, 1997). Thus, some businesses may select locations with strong access to low-wage labor, while others may choose places with better access to highly skilled labor, in clusters or districts that may even be contiguous or relatively close to each other (see Wartzman, 1999). Similarly, firms targeting customers in certain income groups may find a multiplicity of favorable locations within a given area. Thus, the question of choice becomes a more important aspect of business location in Southern California, because of the greater locational flexibility provided by its polycentric structure.

The greater segmentation and flexibility fostered by Southern California's polycentricity are also a source of competition. Business districts or centers, of which there are at least 25 major ones in Southern California, compete with each other for customers and businesses to attract. By inference, the communities or municipalities in which they are located also compete with each other, since success in attracting new businesses can be a major source of new sales and property tax revenues. Such revenues help support municipal governments and their local projects, including the provision of local infrastructure and various services, such as police, fire-fighting, libraries and community parks. Increasing sales and property tax revenues may also help municipalities to reduce property taxes on their residents and local businesses, thereby enhancing their own locational advantages.

The sort of competition fostered by segmentation can be found in almost any economic activity. In high technology, for example, industrial parks compete with one another to attract new firms. A recent study of advanced electronics production in the Los Angeles basin, for example, found 12 major geographical clusters in Los Angeles, Ventura and Orange counties, employing over 40,000 workers (see Suarez-Villa and Walrod, 1997). Most of the clusters competed with each other for the larger plants, which tend to have higher revenues and employment. Municipalities prize such clusters as sources of local employment and higher incomes which, in turn, also enlarge their tax revenues. Competition between municipalities has promoted a great deal of boosterism, with some local governments providing the larger firms with such incentives as free infrastructural or land improvements on their sites, in order to attract or keep them.

Polycentric segmentation has also fostered much diversity among the various communities and municipalities of Southern California. Enormous ethnic, racial, religious and cultural diversity is a component of life in the region. Such diversity tends to be closely related to labor or employment segments in the region's economy. Over 60 ethnic groups have significant communities in Southern California, connecting the region and its economy with their counterparts throughout the world. They enhance Southern California's global standing, by providing access to networks in a wide range of markets abroad, and by minimizing the language and cultural barriers for economic exchange.

The diversity of the region also encompasses small businesses and almost every economic sector. Small businesses have benefited greatly from Southern California's polycentric segmentation. Localized booms of small business activity have sustained the region's economic vitality and account for much of its employment today. Firms employing less than 100 workers, for example, are responsible for more than half of the existing jobs in Los Angeles County (see *The Economist*, 1997). Small businesses in old traditional sectors have also become locally embedded in the region's diverse polycentric structure. Los Angeles, for example, now has the largest garment and textiles industry in the United States, employing over 100,000 workers with annual sales of over 10 billion dollars.

An area of central Los Angeles now known as Toytown has more than 100 businesses, mostly owned by Chinese immigrants, that link local designers and marketers with toy production in Asia. Those businesses accounted for almost two-thirds of all the toys sold to American retail shops in 1995. Los Angeles alone has more than 1,100 food processing firms employing over 50,000 workers, with annual sales of over 12 billion dollars. The Los Angeles area is also the second largest furniture producer in the United States, with over 600 firms employing more than 30,000 people.

All of these traditional firms and sectors coexist with high-tech or well-paid professional activities in the region's vast mosaic of communities and business districts. Los Angeles alone has over 800 biomedical firms, generating annual sales of over 5 billion dollars. Multimedia firms employ over 150,000 people in Los Angeles County, a level higher than that of similar businesses in both New York and San Francisco added together. The Los Angeles area also has over 4,400 firms and 100,000 freelance professionals or individuals in activities related to the film industry, many of them based in the Hollywood district (see Kotkin and Levy, 1996). Over 20 percent of Orange County's labor force is employed in high-technology activities, such as electronics, software production, biotechnology or aerospace (Flanigan, 1997; Miller, 1997). San Diego County has one of the largest concentrations of biotechnology firms in the United States, producing annual sales of over 7 billion dollars. Southern California's polycentric structure has been a major factor for embedding such an enormous and disparate range of economic activities.

The diversity of economic activities also provides much resilience for the region in difficult times. Economic diversity, for example, was thought to be largely responsible for Southern California's rapid recovery from the massive federal defense cutbacks of the late 1980s and early 1990s (see Suarez-Villa, 1997; Kotkin and Levy, 1996; Dertouzos and Dardia, 1993). After losing nearly 500,000 jobs between the late 1980s and 1993, employment within the region rose sharply, recovering all the job losses within four years (see Figure 5.2). The recovery was by far the most impressive of any region in the United States affected by defense cuts or recession in modern times.

The embedding and coexistence of disparate communities, economic activities, income levels and population made possible by Southern California's polycentric structure have been very important for the region's development as a world-class metropolis. Seven decades ago, few people could have foreseen that the region would become the United States' most important conurbation. Today, Southern California ranks with New York City as one of the nation's two major metropolitan gateways to the world. Over the coming decades, Southern California's global standing may be enhanced further, perhaps allowing it to become the most important node in the Americas for east–west and north–south trade and population flows.

Figure 5.2 Southern California non-agricultural employment, 1990–98
(Los Angeles, Orange, Riverside, San Bernardino, San Diego and
Ventura counties)

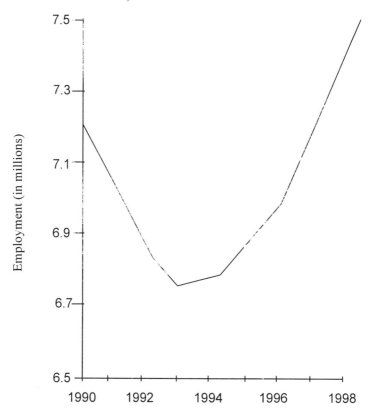

Source: California Employment Development Department (unpublished estimates); Suarez-Villa (1997).

NETWORK SEGMENTATION AND COMPETITIVENESS

The definition of networks used in this paper refers to a group or system of interconnected entities, such as employment sources or communities, within the metropolitan region. The connections are achieved by means of flows (or links) and control points (or nodes). Flows can be materially oriented, as in the case of labor or manufactured goods, or they can be intangible, as with information. The control points have an important role to play in segmentation, since they help structure parts or subsystems of a network in unequal ways, either by isolating some parts or by providing better access to others. The context of networks can be formal or informal. Formal network flows are those officially sanctioned or regulated by existing legal structures. The informal flows, on the other hand, can be either unregulated, as in the case of social contact, or they can be basically illegal, as in the case of undocumented labor flows. The latter are particularly important in Southern California, since they involve substantial cross-border movements or migration that are fundamentally illegal but which nevertheless occur in response to labor demand or economic need.

The segmentation of networks is a natural outcome of Southern California's polycentricity. It is possible to see that the vast mosaic of communities, populations and activities, along with the binational context of the region, involves both a territorial and a functional separation of networks, which can either facilitate or impede access, depending on the kinds of network structures and flows that are involved. Network structures, access and flows can therefore be selectively linked up with sources of competitive advantage, based on local needs and resources.

Segmentation can occur in two different ways. One way is to separate networks of different flows or activities. In this case, segmentation will be functional, and it can be due to a lack of shared interests with the flows or activities of other networks, or it may be mandated through regulation. Examples of functionally segmented networks are quite common. Markets for unskilled labor are often segmented from those of skilled labor, because they involve very different activities and products. Commercial air routing networks have little to do with road networks, because they have different purposes. Networks of contraband or illegal activities typically try to isolate themselves from law enforcement networks, in order to avoid detection. Defense projects often require networks of suppliers to be isolated from one another, in order to maintain secrecy and prevent most participating firms from acquiring complete knowledge about the final product.

The second way of segmentation is to isolate parts of a network's structure territorially or within the same function or activity. Territorial segmentation of networks may, for example, be mandated by national sovereignty. This typically occurs along international borders, and it applies to interaction between the US and Mexican sides of the Southern California conurbation. Such territorially sensitive segmentation introduces a unique dimension in the case of Southern California, because of the vast disparities found between the US and Mexico, and the controls it places on cross-border flows within the region.

The segmentation of networks within the same function or activity also occurs in Southern California, and is supported by the region's polycentricity. Such segmentation can be found, for example, between different communities that are linked by the same network flows. Lower-income communities tend to have less valuable flows, and are therefore more isolated, even though they may be well embedded in the region's economic and social structure.

Higher-income communities, on the other hand, have more valuable flows and tend to be globally connected, regardless of how well embedded they are in the region's productive structure. This situation can be found both within the US and Mexican sides of the conurbation, but more frequently in the former.

Southern California's polycentric structure makes it easy for such communities or areas to coexist, sometimes even contiguously, despite their contrasts in flow value and access. An example of this condition can be found in the connection of high- and low-income communities to the employment markets of the region. High-value (or high-income) communities, for example, may be strongly linked to high-technology and financial clusters, providing highly skilled expertise. Low-value communities will also be linked to the same clusters, but providing instead the less skilled labor needed to staff janitorial services, low-wage production tasks, security guards, and similar occupations.

The labor and income flows of the low-value communities will keep them relatively isolated within the region's larger employment market, as providers of manpower for the less skilled occupations or menial jobs. Both communities may therefore be linked to the local employment market networks, but with vast differences in the flows of income and skills that they receive or provide.

Network nodes play a major role in such segmentation. Nodes are the control points for flows, and they articulate the structure of a network. In Southern California, such nodal functions are typically taken by the multiple business and industrial clusters in the region's polycentric structure. Through their nodal position, those clusters serve as important control points for labor demand, and they help articulate the segmentation of networks within the region.

Network segmentation in Southern California typically occurs through what may be referred to as *barrier* network structures. Barrier structures impede or resist flows to certain areas or components of their networks (see Suarez-Villa et al., 1992; Suarez-Villa, 1998). Closure of a part (or parts) of their network is therefore a major characteristic of this kind of structure. Partially isolating loops, nodes or flows from the larger network is the usual way of achieving segmentation in barrier networks (see Figure 5.3).

Figure 5.3 Barrier network typologies

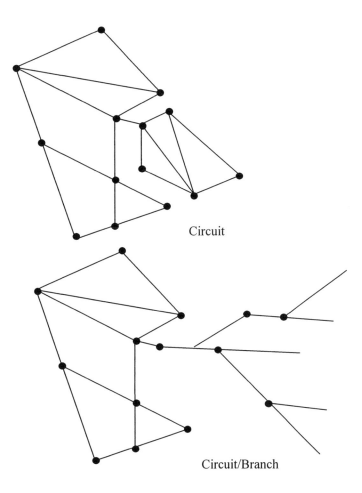

Circuit

Circuit/Branch

Barrier network structures are commonly found in international border regions. They are therefore typical of most network flows involving the US and Mexican sides of the Southern California region. However, polycentricity has also fostered the growth of barrier networks within the US side of the region. Barrier structures within the US side may be referred to as 'value barriers' and are based mostly on income levels, but also more subtly on ethnicity or race. Such barriers allow a selective segmentation of areas, with higher-income locales having better access to farther-ranging network flows, while poorer districts are mostly limited to subsidiary flows.

The subsidiary flows may be made up of low-skilled labor, for example. Within the US side of the region, subsidiary flows of less skilled labor support virtually every kind of economic activity. It is therefore not surprising that many such activities achieve lower-cost advantages which are unknown to most metropolises in other advanced nations. In a way, therefore, the barrier network structures fostered by polycentricity allow aspects of third-world contexts, such as access to plentiful low-cost labor, to coexist with high-value skills and activities in the same geographical area. Within the US side of the Southern California conurbation, this sort of 'barriered' coexistence is possibly the most extreme of any major metropolitan area in the United States, because of its direct connection with the Mexican side of the region.

Although barrier networks are common in the US side of the region, they are most noticeable in the kinds of flows that occur between the US and Mexican parts of the conurbation. Segmentation or partial closure of some network flows, such as labor or transportation, result from 'sovereignty barriers' along the US–Mexico border. Such barriers typically aim to control cross-border flows, but in the case of Southern California they are quite permeable, especially for undocumented labor migration (see, for example, Cornelius, 1998; Bustamante et al., 1992; Weeks, 1993; Chavez, 1992; Ham-Chande and Weeks, 1992; Herzog, 1990; Hansen, 1981). The sovereignty barriers resulting from the US–Mexico border in Southern California have therefore been largely adapted, formally and informally, to support the region's competitiveness in many economic activities.

An example of this condition can be found in the rapid growth of 'twin' manufacturing plants on the US and Mexican sides of the region. Such plants, usually belonging to the same firm, have their internal organization structured to take advantage of the very low labor costs available on the Mexican side, which can be as much as 85 percent lower than those found on the US side (see, for example, Hansen, 1981; Suarez-Villa, 1985; Echeverri-Carroll, 1989; South, 1990; Szekely, 1991). Thus, the labor-intensive components of a production process are located on the Mexican side of the region, in Tijuana, while the capital- or technology-intensive operations are kept on the US side. Because of the close geographical proximity, management of the twin plants is fairly simple, compared to what would be involved if the labor-intensive component were located in far-away locations, such as China or Southeast Asia. In many cases, the savings on shipping, management or coordination can offset the lower labor costs found in some Asian nations. Formal arrangements, such as the creation of the Mexican

Border Industrialization Program in the 1960s, and the implementation of the North American. Free Trade Agreement (NAFTA) in the 1990s, have facilitated those cross-border production links over the years (see, for example, Hansen, 1981; Suarez-Villa, 1985; South, 1990; Krugman and Hanson, 1993; Compa, 1997).

Twin plants and cross-border production subcontracting are found today in various industrial activities, and especially in electronics production, but they are also becoming more common in such high-tech sectors as medical equipment, aerospace and instruments manufacturing. Electronics assembly has so far been predominant in Tijuana's manufacturing base, however, making the city one of the largest agglomerations of electronics plants in Latin America. Such arrangements are part of a cross-border network that uses and transcends the sovereignty barrier to great advantage, because of the substantially lower industrial wages found on the Mexican side. Activities that cannot engage in those arrangements, such as the vast range of service businesses found on the US side of the region, also transcend the sovereignty barrier, albeit informally, by employing the vast underground pool of undocumented Mexican labor that find its way across the border. Thus, the presence of a sovereignty barrier along the border has been considerably neutralized in Southern California, to benefit the vast number of businesses on the US side and their national and international competitiveness.

A subsystem of the region's labor networks can therefore be found on the Mexican side, which is largely a source of very low-cost labor for the US side of the conurbation. The very large and rich markets on the US side of the region ensure that such labor will be used, either by the enormously diverse industrial and service activities found on the US side, or by the assembl plants (or the labor-intensive component of the twin plants) on the Mexican side, which export most of their production to the US. The subsystem on the Mexican side can be visualized as the isolated component of the circuit or circuit/branch networks shown in Figure 5.3. That subsystem is compartmentalized by the sovereignty barrier (which can be visualized as a control node), that regulates labor flows from the Mexican to the US side of the metropolitan region. Even though such formal controls do manage to compartmentalize or isolate that subsystem from the US side of the region, they cannot control labor flows completely. Thus, significant labor flows from the Mexican to the US side of the metropolitan region occur informally, evading the control node imposed by the sovereignty barrier, which also has a territorial dimension. Such flows are illegal, but they serve the very important function of supplying the US side of the region with very low-cost labor, which is essential for many industries and services to survive or remain competitive.

Informal flows of labor across the sovereignty barrier also benefit the Mexican side, by providing additional income to families and households through remittances. Undocumented Mexican workers on the US side send home a large amount of their wages, boosting local income on the Mexican side of the conurbation (see Bustamante et al., 1992; Cornelius and Martin, 1993). It is not surprising to find, therefore, that Tijuana has had the highest per capita income in Mexico for many years, with levels that are well above those of Mexico City, the country's capital and core metropolitan region.

The neutralization of the sovereignty barrier for labor flows is in sharp contrast with the rigid barriers that have been erected and maintained to prevent access to public services by undocumented Mexican labor on the US side. Barriers to such service networks prevent much additional public expenditure for municipalities on the US side of the region, and for the State of California, by making many potential claimants ineligible. Such barriers also help maintain the low cost of undocumented labor on the US side of the region, by avoiding higher taxes to businesses that would eventually be required to pay for those services, if they were provided. Thus, the sovereignty barriers have been selectively adjusted to help the region's business climate.

Segmentation through barrier networks has therefore become a selective mechanism for supporting Southern California's economic competitiveness. A virtually inexhaustible pool of low-cost labor, either on the US or (at much lower cost) the Mexican side, flows through the segmented networks and polycentric cities of the region, supporting a vast range of economic activities. The main beneficiaries of the region's segmented networks and their labor flows are export firms. Such firms can take advantage of labor costs that rival those of many third-world nations, while at the same time maintaining immediate access to one of the world's most technically skilled labor pools, all within the same metropolitan region.

Ready access to both skilled and low-cost (or less-skilled) labor also provides much flexibility to many firms. Structuring production processes, supply networks and service delivery to take advantage of both the highly skilled and less-skilled labor markets has become a routine managerial practice in most of Southern California's businesses. In many ways, the dualism rooted in the segmented labor markets of the region has been internalized as an integral part of production and service delivery. Dualism has become synonymous with greater flexibility. Such flexibility is an important competitive advantage in today's global economy. This situation contradicts the assumptions of many economic development specialists over the past five decades, who typically assumed dualism to be synonymous with competitive disadvantages or backwardness.

Network segmentation has also supported the anchoring and embedding of many firms in the region's productive structure. There is little doubt that the advantages provided by Southern California's dual labor market have kept many firms from moving all or part of their operations elsewhere. Polycentricity has also helped to anchor firms locally by providing a vast range of location alternatives within the region, with very diverse characteristics. Thus, firms contemplating a relocation to places outside the region have often found it more advantageous to remain, but at a different location within the conurbation, where they can gain better access to their support networks. Such possibilities are at the core of Southern California's resilience and competitiveness in the global economy.

CONCLUSIONS

This contribution has provided an overview of several aspects that have supported Southern California's rise as a global metropolis. The region's polycentric diversity, its high growth rate, and its binational context are about to turn it into the United States' largest metropolis. Southern California is already the United States' most important economic region, and its single most important source of new technologies, industries and market trends. This region has also become the nation's most important window on the Pacific Rim, and its largest export center.

Few, if any, studies on the rise of global metropolises have considered urban form to be a significant factor. More often than not, such studies turn to exogenous influences or circumstances, ignoring how internal organization can condition a metropolis' competitive advantages. In Southern California's case, its polycentric structure fostered patterns of segmentation that have provided much flexibility and resilience to the region's economy. It is revealing that, far from being a handicap, such segmentation can become a source of economic advantage in the new global economy.

The segmentation of networks in Southern California occurs at all levels of the region's social and economic fabric. Such segmentation is not only functionally driven but, in contrast with most other global metropolises, it is also territorially based, because of the region's polycentric organization. Southern California's binational territorial context has furthered and deepened the region's segmentation, by selectively fragmenting networks to provide competitive advantages. Barriers to labor flows along the US–Mexico border, for example, have been greatly neutralized to allow both formal and informal arrangements that use low-cost labor on both sides of the border. Barriers to access to public social services by undocumented labor, on the other hand, have been rigidly maintained, thereby preventing greater public expenditures on the US side of the region and, eventually, higher taxes that would diminish local competitiveness.

In an era where segmentation can be turned into an advantage, such barriers are bound to enhance Southern California's competitive position in the new global economy. Industries have gained access to low-cost labor to an extent unknown in most any other advanced global metropolis. Network barriers have also allowed many firms to segment production, by restructuring their operations and locating their labor-intensive components on the Mexican side of the region. Such examples of segmentation are becoming ever more common in Southern California, attesting to the region's capacity for adjustment.

In the coming decades, Southern California's profile as a global gateway region is bound to rise considerably. It is perhaps a reflection of Southern California's rapid emergence that hardly any studies of globalization consider the region to be a top-tier global metropolis today. This perception is bound to change, as the region's polycentric structure, its highly segmented networks, and its binational territorial context become recognized as important competitive advantages in the twenty-first century's global economy.

REFERENCES

Arreola, D.D. and J.S. Curtis (1993), *The Mexican Border Cities*, Tucson: University of Arizona Press.

Baldassare, M. (1998), *When Government Fails*, Berkeley: University of California Press.

Berry, B.J.L. and H.-M. Kim (1993), 'Challenges to the monocentric model', *Geographical Analysis*, **25**, 1–4.

Bustamante, J.A., C.W. Reynolds and R.A. Hinojosa-Ojeda (eds) (1992), *U.S.– Mexico Relations: Labor Market Interdependence*, Stanford: Stanford University Press.

Chavez, L.R. (1992), *Shadowed Lives*, New York: Harcourt Brace Jovanovich.

Clark, D.L. (1981), *Los Angeles: A City Apart*, Woodland Hills, CA: Windsor.

Compa, L. (1997), 'NAFTA's labor side accord: a three-year accounting', *NAFTA: Law and Business Review of the Americas*, Summer, pp. 6–23.

Cornelius, W. (1998), 'The structural embeddedness of demand for Mexican immigrant labor: new evidence from California', in M.M. Suarez-Orozco (ed.), *Crossings: Mexican Immigration in Interdisciplinary Perspectives*, Cambridge: Harvard University Press.

Cornelius, W. and P.L. Martin (1993), *Controlling Immigration*, San Diego: Center for U.S.–Mexican Studies, University of California.

Davis, M. (1990), *City of Quartz*, London: Verso.

Dertouzos, J. and M. Dardia (1993), *Defense Spending, Aerospace and the California Economy*, Santa Monica, CA: Rand Corporation.

Direccion General de Estadística (1993), *Censo General de Población, 1990*, Ciudad de Mexico: DGE.

Echeverri-Carroll, E. (1989), *Economic Impacts and Foreign Investment Opportunities, Japanese Maquilas: A Special Case*, Austin: Bureau of Business Research, University of Texas.

The Economist (1997), 'How to remake a city', 31 May, pp. 25–6.

Flanigan, J. (1997), 'A reinvented O.C.: self-billed 'technology coast' has a vision for its future', *Los Angeles Times*, 14 May, p. D-1.

Garreau, J. (1991), *Edge City*, New York: Doubleday.

Giuliano, G. and K. Small (1991), 'Subcenters in the Los Angeles region', *Regional Science and Urban Economics*, **21**, 163–82.

Gordon, P., H.W. Richardson and H.L. Wong (1986), 'The distribution of population and employment in a polycentric city: the case of Los Angeles', *Environment and Planning A*, **18**, 161–73.

Gordon, P. and Richardson, H.W. (1996), 'Beyond polycentricity: the dispersed metropolis, Los Angeles, 1970–1990', *Journal of the American Planning Association*, **62**, 289–95.

Ham-Chande, R. and J. Weeks (eds) (1992), *Demographic Dynamics of the U.S.– Mexico Border*, El Paso: Texas Western Press.

Hansen, N.M. (1981), *The Border Economy*, Austin: University of Texas Press.

Herzog, L.A. (1990), *Where North Meets South*, Austin: Center for Mexican– American Studies and University of Texas Press.

Kotkin, J. and S. Levy (1996), *California: A Twenty-first Century Prospectus*, Ontario, CA: Center for the New West.

Krugman, P. and G. Hanson (1993), 'Mexico–U.S. free trade and the location of production', in P.M. Garber (ed.), *The Mexico–U.S. Free Trade Agreement*, Cambridge: MIT Press.

Light, I. (1988), 'Los Angeles', in M. Dogan and J. Kasarda (eds), *The Metropolis Era: Mega-cities*, Newbury Park, CA: Sage.

Miller, G. (1997), 'Irvine declared high-tech hub of the Southland', *Los Angeles Times*, 7 April, p. D-1.

Nadeau, R. (1960), *Los Angeles: From Mission to Modern City*, New York: Longman.

Profitt, T.D. (1994), *Tijuana: The History of a Mexican Metropolis*, San Diego: San Diego State University Press.

Richardson, H.W. (1988), 'Monocentric vs. polycentric models: the future of urban economics in regional science', *Annals of Regional Science*, **22**, 1–12.

Rolle, A.F. (1981), *Los Angeles: From Pueblo to City of the Future*, San Francisco: Boyd and Fraser.

Sivitanidou, R. and Sivitanides, P. (1995). 'The intra-metropolitan distribution of R&D activities: theory and empirical evidence', *Journal of Regional Science*, **35**, 391–415.

South, R. (1990), 'Transnational "maquiladora" location', *Annals of the Association of American Geographers*, **80**, 549–70.

Starr, K. (1990), *Material Dreams: Southern California through the 1920s*, New York: Oxford University Press.

Suarez-Villa, L. (1985), 'Urban growth and manufacturing change in the United States–Mexico borderlands: a conceptual framework and an empirical analysis', *Annals of Regional Science*, **19**, 54–108.

Suarez-Villa, L. (1997), 'California's recovery and the restructuring of the defense industries', in R.D. Norton (ed.), *Regional Resilience and Defense Conversion in the United States*, Greenwich, CT: JAI Press.

Suarez-Villa, L. (1998), 'The structures of cooperation: downscaling, outsourcing and the networked alliance', *Small Business Economics*, **10**, 5–16.

Suarez-Villa, L., M. Giaoutzi and A. Stratigea (1992), 'Territorial and border barriers in information and communication networks: a conceptual exploration', *Tijdschrift voor Economische en Sociale Geografie*, **83**, 93–104.

Suarez-Villa, L. and W. Walrod (1997), 'Operational strategy, R&D and intra-metropolitan clustering in a polycentric structure: the advanced electronics industries of the Los Angeles basin', *Urban Studies*, **34**, 1343–80.

Szekely, G. (ed.) (1991), *Manufacturing across borders and oceans: Japan, the United States and Mexico*, San Diego: Center for U.S.–Mexican Studies, University of California.

US Bureau of the Census (1992), *Census of Population, 1990*, Washington, DC: US Government Printing Office.

US Bureau of the Census (1993), *Census Tracts: Census of Population and Housing, 1990*, Washington, DC: US Government Printing Office.

US Bureau of the Census (1999), *Statistical Abstract of the United States, 1998*, Washington, DC: US Government Printing Office.

Wachs, M. (1984), 'Autos, transit, and the sprawl of Los Angeles: the 1920s', *Journal of the American Planning Association*, **50**, 297–310.

Wartzman, R. (1999), 'Southern California sees a low-tech boom', *Wall Street Journal*, 25 January, p. A-1.

Weeks, J. (1993), 'The changing demographic structure of the San Diego region', in: N.C. Clement and E. Zepeda Miramontes (eds), *San Diego–Tijuana in Transition: A Regional Analysis*, San Diego: Institute for Regional Studies of the Californias, San Diego State University.

6. The Greater Washington Region: a Global Gateway Region

Roger R. Stough

INTRODUCTION

The origin of the gateway concept is uncertain but easy to grasp when one thinks of the international migration waves that have occurred. Increasingly, and in particular with the rise of globalism, other less well-developed flow networks have emerged (e.g., industrial, business, government, policy, touristic and hospitality related, cultural and artistic, to name a few), thereby broadening the concept of a gateway region. Thus, today, regions serve as gateways for multiple network functions. For example, London is a gateway in the global policy, finance, population migration and information networks while the New York City gateway is a node in the financial, population migration and fashion networks.

The purpose of this chapter is to describe the gateway functions and supporting networks of the Washington, DC region. The chapter also examines the factors that will constrain or influence the sustainability and growth of these functions relative to other US and global centers.

The gateway region concept has been the focus of recent analyses including work focusing on international migration (Aboud and Freeman, 1990), demand estimation between gateways (Ghobrial, 1993), intra-urban distribution of immigrants in gateway cities (Rydin, 1998) and as the source of US producer service exports (Drennan, 1992). In this chapter, as in the referenced articles, the investigation is directed to the types of networks for which the Washington Metropolitan Region is a gateway. These include immigration, public policy-making, hospitality, the arts, visitation and business. The infrastructure that supports the gateway function is also examined.

The chapter begins with a brief background statement that identifies critical historical, geographical and institutional issues. It moves on to a discussion of the region's primary gateway function as a global policy-making center. Its role as an immigration gateway is discussed within the context of the analysis of its policy-making function because a significant

105

proportion of migration to the Washington region is tied to policy. The analysis then moves to an examination of the region as a gateway for visitors and the amenity base that supports and attracts visitors including the recent recognition of the region as a center for the arts. This is followed by an assessment of the air transportation infrastructure, the arrival and departure mode for most of the region's international visitors.

Over the past two decades the region has become a gateway for commercial business largely centered on the technology business services sector. This development has propelled the region into a new role as a business gateway. The final part of the chapter examines the barriers and constraints the region faces as it strives to sustain and expand its gateway functions.

BACKGROUND

Washington, DC was established several centuries ago at the upper part of the navigable Potomac River on the east coast of the United States. It, like numerous other fall-line cities, e.g., Boston, Philadelphia, Baltimore, Richmond, Charlotte (NC), is located where the coastal plains make the transition into the more rugged Piedmont region of the United States. Early in its development, Washington, like other fall-line cities, exhibited a pattern of wealthier residents locating on the Piedmont side of the region and those of less fortune settling in the Upper Coastal Plains to the east where geographic conditions were more demanding. There, drainage problems created marshlands and thus less attractive living conditions. Vestiges of this pattern may still be observed in many of the fall-line cities and in the Washington region. The sector to the west along the Potomac River, as it winds its way up onto the Piedmont, is home to those who have greater wealth and education. It is also the area where the region's recent technically driven commercial development is concentrated.

Today the Greater Washington Metropolitan Region is a three-state, federal district, region. It is composed of the District of Columbia which forms the historic, geographic core of the region and two major suburban parts: one in the Commonwealth of Virginia and one in the State of Maryland (Map 6.1). The metropolitan region also has two counties located in the state of West Virginia. This multi-state governance context gives the region a special character under the federalist structure of the US political system where states are constitutionally responsible for the health, welfare and education of their constituents. Thus, it is not surprising that institutions with a cross-region-integrated perspective and agenda have been slow to form.

Map 6.1 The national capital region

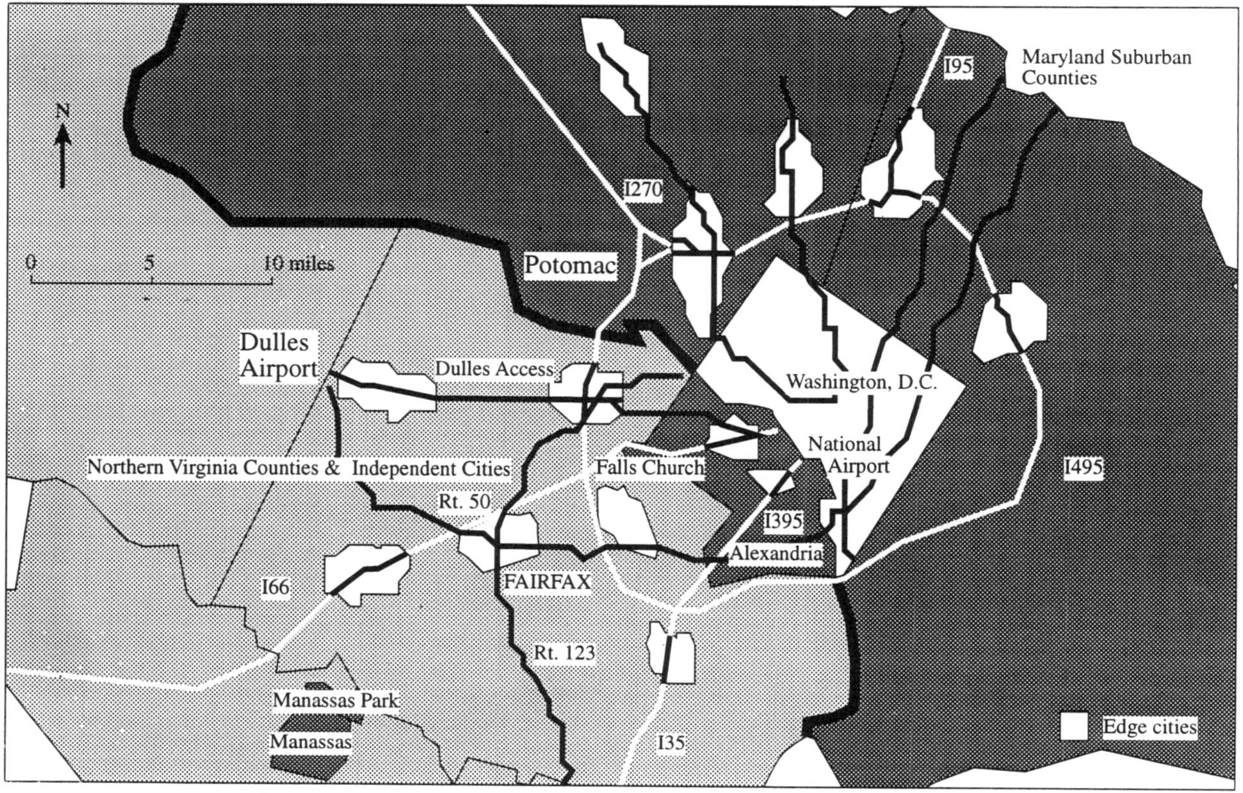

Maryland Suburban Counties

I95

I495

I270

Potomac

Washington, D.C.

National Airport

I395

Alexandria

Falls Church

I35

Dulles Access

Dulles Airport

Northern Virginia Counties & Independent Cities

Rt. 50

FAIRFAX

Rt. 123

I66

Manassas Park

Manassas

Edge cities

N

0   5   10 miles

This, coupled with a 30-year growth rate that surpassed nearly all US metropolitan regions, results in fragmented regional leadership. Rapid growth coupled with fragmented governance means that leadership for cohesive regionwide development and management is a – if not the – fundamental problem the region faces as it enters the twenty-first century.

A GLOBAL POLICY-MAKING CENTER

Washington has for most of the twentieth century been a major global policy-making center. This function was increasingly recognized following the First World War and then mushroomed in the Second World War and cold war eras. As one of the several major centers of global policy influence in the world, Washington became a policy-making gateway with advisors and those wishing to peddle influence attracted to the region and those charged with influencing outcomes going to other parts of the world. The policy-making function attracts a wide and diverse population from places within the US and from abroad. Policy-making is the historical signature function of the region and, therefore, defines its primary gateway function. Most if not all other gateway functions are tied either directly or indirectly to policy-making.

Like most national capitals, Washington attracts a disproportionately large number of young and well-educated people from the US and abroad. Thus it is not surprising that the region boasts the second highest average individual and household incomes of all US metropolitan regions and much higher than average education levels (Northern Virginia Economic Development Coalition, 1999 and US Bureau of the Census, 1991). It also has the highest percentage of adults with graduate and professional degrees. In short, the region's high income and education levels stem directly and historically from its national policy-making function. Similar patterns persist in many other national capital regions of the world for similar reasons.

As interesting and important as the region's domestic attraction for the 'best and the brightest' through its policy-making function is, its role as an international migration destination is even more so. Consequently, it has produced an ethnically and culturally diverse population.

Other activities (e.g., business and cultural groups) have, however, attracted and contributed to the formation of an even more diverse population. Perhaps the greatest source of population diversification (other than the sheer size of the region) stems from the US Amnesty program whereby foreigners from strife-torn situations are allowed (due to military or natural disasters) to more freely immigrate to the US. A large number come to the Washington area because they have direct or indirect ties to US officials or agencies, i.e., to the policy-making function. This has led to the formation of ethnic concentrations in the region, especially over the past 30 years (see Lin, 1998). For example, following the Vietnam War a large number of pro-American Vietnamese immigrated to the US and, in particular, to the Washington region. Soon numerous Vietnamese establishments were created, including restaurants, barber salons, cleaning and repair establishments, and so on. At the same time Vietnamese children populated the school system. Many of these second-generation Vietnamese have created a more diverse range of establishments (including advanced technology), with some entering politics, the professions and rising to other visible leadership positions. Similar stories have unfolded or are unfolding around other groups such as Taiwanese, Chinese, Lebanese, Turks, Ethiopians, Guatemalans, Ecuadorians, Central Europeans, Koreans, and so on. In short, the region's ethnic diversity is extensive and its growth over the past three decades has contributed to the development of a more cosmopolitan regional character.

The US Immigration and Naturalization Service (1997) recognizes the Washington region as the fifth largest destination of immigrants over the recent past with 34,327 immigrants in 1996 and, between 1990 and 95, more than 140,000. The regions that attracted larger numbers of immigrants were New York, Los Angeles, Chicago and Miami.

TOURIST AND BUSINESS ATTRACTION

Like most national capitals the Washington region is a major destination for visitors. In 1997 it had 22 million visitors who generated nearly $6 billion in direct spending in the region (Fuller, 1998a). More than half of this was in the District of Columbia, showing that the primary focus of hospitality expenditures is located in the region's historic core. However, more than 25 percent of these expenditures was by business visitors who spent an average of 4.2 days in the region.

Business visits are more heavily concentrated in suburban parts of the region, the locus of the large majority of the region's business activity. Ten percent of visitors are from international destinations. More important, the rate of growth of international visitation has been 5 percent per year since 1994, while domestic visitation grew at 2.5 percent per year (US Immigration and Naturalization Service, 1997).

International and domestic visitors come for a variety of reasons. Some arrive merely to sightsee or visit museums, monuments and other historic sites. Others visit to observe or participate in the public policy-making process. Still others come for the region's performing arts programs which include 19 symphony orchestras including the renowned Washington

Philharmonic Symphony, 9 opera companies including such well-known ones as the National Lyric Opera, the Washington Opera and the Wolf Trap Opera. The Washington region had the highest score for the arts among all metropolitan areas in the US in 1998 (*Places Rated Almanac*, 1998). Visitors also come for business, as indicated above. Some of the reasons for business visits include influencing the policy process, attending conferences and trade shows, meeting with business suppliers or consultants and accessing the region's rapidly growing technology services sector. Finally, it offers ready access to amenities such as the Appalachian Mountains to the interior, and the sea (the Chesapeake Bay) to the east and south, all within an hour's drive.

TRANSPORT INFRASTRUCTURE AND NETWORKS

One of the strongest indicators of a region's global gateway function, other than its population size, is its air transport network (O'Connor, 1998) and support operations. The Washington region has three major airports, two of which have significant international linkages. These are Dulles International and Ronald Reagan National Airports (both located in Virginia) and Baltimore–Washington International Airport (BWI) located on the Maryland side of the region (Map 6.1). Of these, Reagan National is located across the Potomac River from the District of Columbia near the Pentagon and serves mostly domestic passengers. Dulles is located about twenty miles to the interior and is the region's primary international airport. In 1997 it had 15.1 million passengers, of which 3.2 million were international, although Reagan had 207,359 Canadian travelers (Federal Aviation Administration, 1998). In that year Reagan National had nearly 16 million passengers (most were domestic) and BWI, located some fifty miles to the north, had a passenger volume similar to Dulles but with fewer international and business travelers. With these three airports serving the region, it has an infrastructure capacity comparable to Atlanta, Chicago, Los Angeles or New York.

About 10 percent of the region's 22 million annual visitors are international and nearly all of these arrive via air transportation, with the large majority coming through Dulles. Dulles currently ranks eighth nationally among airports in terms of the international passenger gateway function and is well positioned to increase its ranking. About fifteen years ago Dulles was not ranked as an international passenger gateway. The relative importance of the re-gion's international passenger gateway activity is illustrated in the following citation from the Washington Airports Task Force *Report* (1998, p. 2).

As a transatlantic gateway, the combined Washington/Baltimore region now is behind only the New York/Newark and Chicago areas in terms of weekly flight activity and well ahead of traditional sea gateways such as Boston, Philadelphia, Miami, Los Angeles and San Francisco. Atlanta is just ahead of Washington Dulles but behind Dulles and BWI combined. Dulles has 135 weekly flights to 10 European cities. BWI adds 14 weekly flights in two additional markets.

The major international markets served by the region's airports are Europe (with more than half of the traffic), Asia, Canada, Latin America and Oceania, in order of importance.

THE WASHINGTON REGION AS A BUSINESS GATEWAY

Unlike most national capital regions, Washington has, until quite recently, been little more than a government services center. Even today government is responsible for about half of the region's economic activity, with 54 percent of its gross regional product produced either directly or indirectly by government spending. This is considerably higher than any other US metropolitan area, as 33 percent alone comes from direct federal spending in the region. Thus the region's economy is highly dependent on the federal sector (Fuller, 1998b; Stough et al., 1999). This dependency includes salary and wages, payments (e.g., social security) and contracts.

Figure 6.1 Main sector incomes (1996)

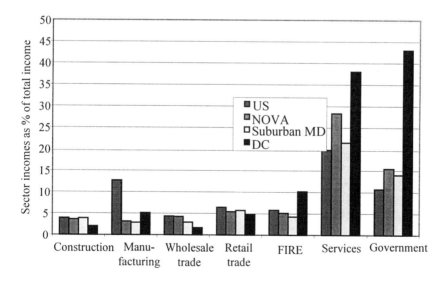

Figure 6.1 shows that the region has little manufacturing, with less than 4 percent of earnings in that sector. However, the government and service sectors are most important both in absolute terms and structurally (i.e., they are relatively more important to Washington's regional economy than to the nation as a whole). Thus the region has and continues to be viewed by many outsiders as little more than a government services center, with the federal government providing the economic base and the non-basic services supporting the needs of government workers. This was a defensible description of the economy 20 and perhaps even 15 years ago. However, this view fails to recognize that much of the recent growth in services has been in the technology sector (i.e., export base services) rather than just concentrated in non-basic retail or support services such as warehousing.

Figure 6.2 Detailed service sector incomes (1996)

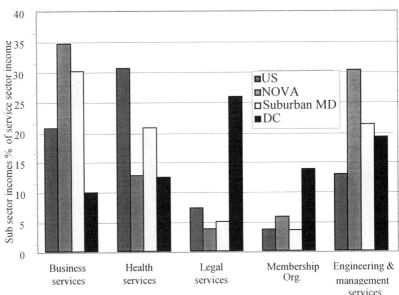

It is largely in technology services that the region has become a business and entrepreneurial gateway. Much of its new role stems from the concentration of considerable information technology and Internet-related business. An analysis of the region's private sector economy shows that dominant industries, i.e., ones that are more important to the Washington region than they are nationally, are primarily in the technology sector (Stough et al., 1998a and 1996). These include systems integration and architecture, information and Internet technology, software engineering, space and aerospace technology, and biotechnology.

Association headquarters, policy-related sectors, and tourist and travel-related functions are also structurally important (Figure 6.2), but secondary to technology.

Unlike tourism and associations, technology is a large sector that has more than 300,000 employees (Potomac KnowledgeWay, 1998) estimates more than 400,000), thus making it one of the largest technology regions in the US. Its level of technology employment equals or surpasses that of the Silicon Valley, Orange County (Los Angeles) and the Boston 128 regions, all of which have more than 300,000 employees in their technology sectors (Table 6.1).

Table 6.1 Technology employment change between 1988 and 1997 by region

Region	1988	1995	1997	% change 88–97
Austin–San Marcos (TX)[a]	41,243	78,532	72,693	76.26
Rt. 128 (MA)[b]	283,746	285,825	272,098	-4.11
Greater Washington region[c]	188,172	281,980	284,724	51.31
San Jose (CA)[d]	306,982	313,953	300,409	-2.14

Notes:
a Bastrop, Caldwell, Hays, Travis, Williamson
b Arlington, Fairfax, Loudon, Pr. William, Alexandria, Fairfax City, Falls
  Church, Manassas Park, Manassas, Pr. George's, Montgomery, Washington.DC
c Essex, Middlesex, Norfolk, Suffolk
d Alameda, Santa Clara

Source: Employment estimates are derived by aggregating technology-intense 3- and 4-digit SIC data for technology-intense categories as defined in Appendix A of Technology Region Report to CIT, 1998.

The technology sector has emerged in the Washington region over the past decade or two and in so doing has created, for the first time in its history, a commercial and industrial economic base. This sector is concentrated in the Maryland and Virginia suburban parts of the region (Map 6.2) with a greater concentration on the Virginia side (Stough et al., 1998b; Stough et al., 1997b; and Stough et.al., 1996).

Map 6.2 Greater Washington region. Technology firms by location

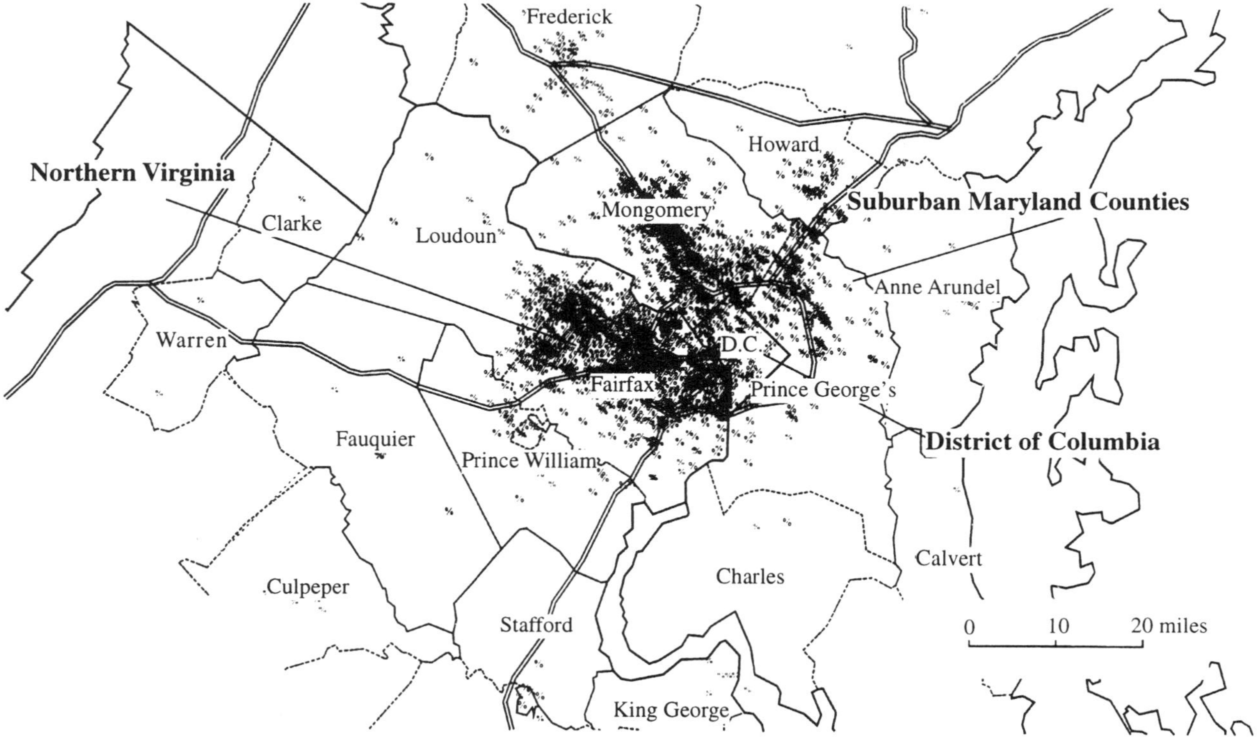

Figure 6.3 shows growth in total private sector and technology employment in the Virginia part of the region from 1969.[i] The aggregate private sector and technology sector data generally mirror each other's growth profile. However, early in the 1980s, technology employment growth accelerated relative to total private sector employment. The 1980s, as illustrated in Figure 6.3, were years where the technology sector emerged as a foundation component of the region's economic base.

Figure 6.3 Technology and private sector in northern Virginia

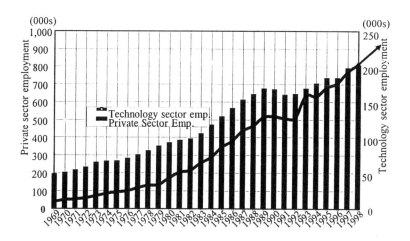

Source: Mason Enterprise Center, Northern Virginia Technology Survey, 1993–94 used to estimate the technology sector employment from 1969 through 1992.

At the start of the Reagan administration in 1980 a defense build-up policy was adopted (Stough et al., 1997a). Significant growth in federal spending stimulated growth throughout the US, which of course included the national capital region as one of the major impact areas. This was also a stimulus to local growth in the technology sector. From that time on, defense spending focused increasingly on the technical and software attributes of arms and arms systems (electronics, design, systems management) rather than on the armaments themselves (e.g., aircraft carriers, airplanes, guns and tanks). Thus, some of the region's 1980s technical growth and related economic acceleration can be attributed to the defense build-up.

Many have forgotten another policy of the Reagan administration that contributed even more to the expansion of the region's technology sector. This was the policy of federal outsourcing adopted early in the Reagan years (Stough et al., 1998b). Federal outsourcing flowed from President Reagan's belief that the role of government had become too pervasive. With the formal pronouncement of a policy aimed at increasing the outsourcing of federal goods and services production to the private sector, the growth of the technology services in the region accelerated. While outsourcing impacted all parts of the US economy, the kinds of contracts successfully procured in the capital focused largely on the design and management of large and complex systems, and projects closely tied to national security (such as the design of new arms and delivery systems). The reason for this was that senior management, e.g., the Joint Chiefs of Staff of the US Department of Defense, did not wish to be geographically separated from the development of these systems for both security and control purposes. Similarly, the procurement of design services for most large, complex non-defense government systems, e.g., personnel system reconfiguration, redesign of government payment and distribution systems like social security, were also let to contractors in the capital region. Thus grew a large technical capacity in systems design, integration and architecture and related capability in software engineering. Much of the growth in the 1980s was focused on the further development and expansion of these industry components. However, this began to change in the late 1980s and 1990s with the rise and concentration of Internet services in the region.

The Army Research Programs Administration (ARPA) and the National Science Foundation (NSF) supported the development of several electronic networks (e.g., ARPANET, BITNET and NSFNet) in the late 1960s, 1970s and 1980s (see Zakon, 1999; Leiner et al., 1998 and Howe, 1999 for more information on the history of the development of these networks and the Internet). These functioned much as today's Internet but were more limited in scope as they served primarily the needs of military and research groups rather than everyone. These earlier networks and supporting infrastructure may be viewed as the incubators of today's Internet.

The emergence of the Internet, with significant parts of the soft infrastructure established in the national capital region (e.g., backbone development supported by NSF and its role of creating a registration system for the Internet through a contract provided to Network Solutions, Inc.), created a local comparative advantage. This led to the creation of new industries, for example, network products and services, and to the transformation and expansion of more traditional ones like telecommunications. Building from this comparative advantage, the region grew a large cluster of Internet and related enterprises, of which several have become Fortune 1000 companies, e.g., America on Line (AOL) and MCI WorldCom. The emergence of this Internet-related sector, while stimulated by government action, has, unlike the systems integration sector, evolved as a commercially dominated sector, i.e., a large part of the market for Internet-related services is commercial. This has, for the first time in the history of the region, spawned an entrepreneurial culture. The related entrepreneurial and innovative activity has begun to attract investors and has created local investor networks that are accelerating the growth of this industry. Today more than half of all of the global Internet volume is handled or managed by companies in the national capital region (Potomac KnowledgeWay, 1998).

Before concluding this section it is important to recognize the primacy of the role federal government policy played in the development of the technical services industry in the region, although not an intended one. The decision to expand the defense capabilities of the US and the adoption of an outsourcing policy in the 1980s were driven by much larger macro and ideological forces than those targeted to regional economic and industry development. Likewise the development of the Internet was not a conscious outcome of policies adopted by the US Department of Defense or the National Science Foundation. Thus the rise of the technology services industry in the region, making it a major national and global player in this industry, may be viewed as one consequence of these policies and decisions. This outcome is a good example of how government policy may impact a region – albeit in this case a positive impact.

GATEWAY GROWTH AND SUSTAINABILITY ISSUES

The enormous growth that the region has experienced over the past two to three decades is unprecedented. Further, not only has this growth been large in an absolute sense, it has also been large compared to other US metropolitan areas. The Washington region has, in a matter of 30 years, grown from a center that was known only for its role as the nation's policy-making center with a limited gateway function to one of the largest metropolitan gateways in the US. However, it is a region that is still facing considerable institutional turbulence. All of this reflects on its ability to function as a global gateway.

As mentioned in the introduction, the region has had difficulty guiding and managing itself at the region-wide level (Stough, 1994). Consequently, its institutions and organizations, which were designed for a metropolitan region with, at best, a limited gateway function, have experienced difficulty adjusting to the hard and soft infrastructure demands associated with significant and sustained development. While much of this is due to rapid growth, it is also due to the fragmented multi-state/federal district nature of its local government. This has slowed the formation of effective region-wide organizations that can build agreement on what to do and how to act upon the region's major problems.

The Washington region is the second most congested metropolitan area in the US and has the highest costs associated with congestion (Schrank and Lomax, 1998). A thorough study of the history of surface transportation planning in the region shows that fundamental links in the road infrastructure that were planned in the 1960s for the region were never built. Further, the region, which is split by the Potomac River, has many fewer bridges linking residents and businesses than the other major cities in the U.S that are divided by rivers (Greater Washington Board of Trade, 1997). This problem, while due in part to rapid growth, is also due to the region's inability to create a region-wide transportation organization to assume responsibility for the construction, operation and management of the transport system.

The point of this discussion is to illustrate the difficulty the region has had in forming region-wide leadership necessary to address the demands of growth and its changing role as a national and global gateway. Thus a major issue the region faces at the turn of the century is how to develop effective leadership to guide its development and to ensure sustainability of its emerging commercial base (DeSantis and Stough, 1999). Maintaining and improving environmental quality and its amenity base, and further developing its emergent economic base in the technology services in general, and its Internet businesses in particular, are also important issues.

The quality of life in the Washington Metropolitan Region is exceptional on many dimensions, as described earlier. But quality of life is often increasingly impacted by sustained and rapid growth. Because much of the growth has been fueled by development of so-called 'clean industry', air quality impacts and other negative physical environmental effects have been less than many expected. It is largely in the areas of decentralized land-use impacts that quality of life seems to be most affected.

The region's growth in the 1980s and more recently was driven by the development of the technology services sector. Nearly all of the activity in this sector demanded campus-like commercial space to support the largely human-capital-intensive nature of this industry. This, together with the residential concentration of the more qualified workers in bedroom suburban communities, has led to the development of so-called edge cities (Garreau, 1991). These concentrations, with more than 5 million square feet of commercial floor space and 1 million square feet of retail space, have become the new work centers of the region (see Map 6.1 and Map 6.3). They are located, as indicated by their name, on the edge of the region. Places such as Tysons Corner, Rockville, Bethesda and Fair Lakes are the new commercial and work centers of the region. This has changed the character of the geography of the region which had always been a hub and spoke urban region with the central geographic core, the District of Columbia, lying at the heart of the region.

The region has become a polynuclear city with several edge-city concentrations rivaling if not surpassing (e.g., Tysons Corner) the scale and future capacity of the historic geographic core, i.e., the District of Columbia. The Washington Metropolitan Region now has at least 12 edge cities by Garreau's definition (1991) and it is composed of 23 counties in three states. The region has grown in diameter from about forty miles to more than 100 miles in 30 years (that is, the developed area of the region expanded almost seven times). It now threatens to expand well beyond this to as much as 130 or 140 miles in the next decade, which is where the highest rate of growth is occurring today, as illustrated in Map 6.3 (Stough, 1995). As a consequence, the region's congestion level has risen to nearly the highest in the country (Schrank and Lomax, 1998).

Map 6.3 Percentage population change by jurisdiction: 1990–1998

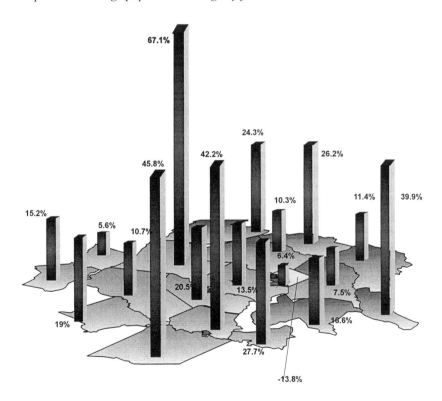

Proposals for smart growth and other infill concepts are increasingly promoted by growing growth control interests in the region as a way to turn the clock back to a simpler and less congested time. However, the region continues to be attractive to Internet and information technology companies as it provides one of the best sites in the world (Potomac Knowledgeway, 1998). Smart growth or infill sites are not sufficiently large or numerous for ventures such as MCI WorldCom or AOL which are in need of large new campus-like facilities to house their growing global headquarters and production activities. One estimate is that MCI WorldCom will need space to house a workforce of more than 30,000. Such a development can only be located on the edge, where space sufficiently large to house such a facility exists. Moreover, application of information technology to support telework, electronic commerce, telebanking and so on makes it possible to shrink relatively long commutes when workers need only travel to their workplace two or three days of the week (Stough and Paelinck, forthcoming; Stough, 1995). This in turn creates further demand for residential relocation further to the periphery in order to access a more rural setting while still capturing urban employment and amenity benefits. As a consequence of these combined forces, continued decentralization is the probable future development trajectory for the region (Stough, 1995). Without enhanced regional leadership this issue will be very difficult to manage. As such it could sow the seeds of decreasing returns that could eventually result in a failure to sustain current growth and development.

The region has recently experienced a large increase in demand for technical workers, not unlike that which has occurred in other regions. While this demand is outstripping supply nationally and globally, the supply shortfall is particularly acute in regions where technical production is concentrated, like the national capital region (Stough and Trice, 1998c), and where competition for technical workers is heavy. As a consequence, regions have adopted both attraction and training strategies to compete better for technically skilled personnel. In the national capital region efforts to address this issue have expanded considerably. The Greater Washington Initiative of the Greater Washington Board of Trade, various regional economic development agencies and many companies have initiated major attraction efforts. The Northern Virginia Regional Partnership for Economic Development, area universities and community colleges as well as private sector initiatives have taken the lead in training. While the workforce supply problem has not disappeared, regional leadership through these efforts has been strengthened somewhat. This is a very important by-product of the workforce crisis in the national capital region.

A final issue concerns the national capital region's role as a gateway for trade. In 1997, the region was ranked seventeenth nationally for the value of its manufacturing exports and 220th in terms of percentage change in the value of exports (Office of Trade and Economic Analysis, 1999). The region's role as a gateway for trade thus appears to be quite modest given that it is one of the largest market areas in the US. These data are, however, misleading. The region, as noted above, has a very small manufacturing sector and consequently would not be expected to generate large-scale trade of manufactured goods. Further, it is a technical-service economy and anecdotal evidence suggests that exports are increasingly concentrated in these services, e.g., electronic transmission of computer code and other electronic transactions. Unfortunately there is little reliable data on the volume of tradable services, let alone tradable electronic services. At the same time a recent study by Deloitte & Touche (1998) found a sizeable internationally oriented sector in the national capital region with 700 foreign firms employing more than 50,000. Thus, while the trade of manufactured goods is quite modest, it is likely that there is considerable trade in the producer and technical service categories.

CONCLUSIONS

The paper has identified and described a series of gateway functions associated with the US national capital region. These include policy-making, immigration, hospitality, the arts, and technology business. While policy-making was seen to be the traditional and strongest gateway function, the emergence of a new technology services sector in the regional economy has became a significant business gateway activity. Rapid population growth and immigration have been driven by the growth of this technology services sector. This growth is the source of many of the region's management problems, including extensive population decentralization and commercial activity, surface transport congestion, governance fragmentation and the lack of regional leadership, and a very tight and competitive technical workforce. Traditional measures show the region to be lagging in international trade although anecdotal evidence suggests that it is exporting and importing considerably more than is being measured because much of the trade is not recorded, e.g., electronic transfer of services. As the technical services sector continues to grow, the national capital region will increase the range and scope of its gateway functions, thereby possibly becoming one of the super-gateways of the next century.

Finally, it is important to note again that the rise of the technical services sector in the region's economy occurred largely because of federal policy. However, this outcome was not an intended consequence of polices such as defense build-up, outsourcing or the Internet spin-off. Rather, it was an unintended consequence and, therefore, a windfall for the development of the region's gateway status.

NOTE

1. Data for the other parts of the region are not available in the same form as for the Virginia part.

REFERENCES

Aboud, J.M. and R.B. Freeman (1990), 'The internationalization of the U.S. labor market', *National Bureau of Economic Research Working Paper 3321*, Cambridge, MA.

Deloitte & Touche LLP and S. Fuller (1998), 'International business in the Greater Washington region', *The Greater Washington Initiative of the Greater Washington Board of Trade.*

DeSantis, M. and R.R. Stough (1999 forthcoming), 'Fast adjusting urban regions, leadership and regional economic development', *Regions et Development.*

Drennan, M.P (1992), 'Gateway cities: the metropolitan sources of US producer service exports', *Urban Studies*, **29** (2), 217–36.

Federal Aviation Administration (1998), 'Passenger traffic in Washington Metropolitan Region Airports: 1987–2011', Airports Council International.

Fuller, S. (1998a), 'The contribution of nonprofit organizations to economic development in Washington, DC', working paper, Center for Regional Analysis, The Institute of Public Policy, George Mason University, Fairfax, VA.

Fuller, S. (1998b), 'The Washington, DC economy: Its evolution, performance and outlook', working paper, Center for Regional Analysis, The Institute of Public Policy, George Mason University, Fairfax, VA.

Garreau, J. (1991), *Edge Cities: Life on the New Frontier*, New York

Ghobrial, A. (1993), 'A model to estimate the demand between U.S. and foreign gateways', *International Journal of Transport Economics*, **20** (3), 271–83.

Greater Washington Board of Trade (1997), *Board of Trade Transportation Report Series* (Nos 1–5 and Executive Summary), Washington, DC: Greater Washington Board of Trade.

Howe, W. (1999), 'A brief history of the Internet' [http://www.O.delphi.com/navnet/faq/history.html]

Leiner, B.M. et al. (1998), 'A brief history of the Internet' [http://www.isoc.org/internet-history/brief.html]

Lin, J. (1998), 'Globalization and the revalorizing of ethnic places in immigration gateway cities', *Urban Affairs Review*, **34** (2), 313–40.

Northern Virginia Economic Development Coalition (1999), *Economic Profile*, Northern Virginia Economic Development Coalition, www.northernvirginia.org.

O'Connor, K.B. (1998), 'The international air linkages of Australian cities 1985–1996', *Australian Geographical Studies*, **36** (2), 143–56.

Office of Trade and Economic Analysis (1999), Washington, DC: US Department of Commerce [http://www.ita.doc.gov/cgi-bin/otea_ctr?task-otea]

Places Rated Almanac (1998), Comparison of top 10 metropolitan areas in the US', *Places Rated Almanac.*

Potomac KnowledgeWay (1998), *Toward a New Economy: Merging Heritage with Vision in the Greater Washington Region*, The Potomac KnowledgeWay Project.

Rydin, Y. (1998), 'The enabling of local state and urban development: Resources, rhetoric and planning in East London', *Urban Studies*, **35** (2), 175–91.

Schrank, D.L. and T.J. Lomax (1998), *Urban Roadway Congestion: Annual Report 1998*, College Station, TX: Texas Transportation Institute.

Stough, R.R. (ed.) (1994), *Proceedings of the 1st Annual Conference on the Future of the Northern Virginia Economy*, Fairfax, VA: The Center for Regional Analysis, The Institute of Public Policy, George Mason University.

Stough, R.R. (1995), 'Technology will spur satellite cities, more sprawl', *The Edge City News*, **3** (4).

Stough, R.R., H. Campbell and J. Popino (1996), *Technology in the Greater Washington Region*, Washington, DC: The Greater Washington Board of Trade.

Stough, R.R., H. Campbell and K.E. Haynes (1997a), 'Small business entrepreneurship in the high technology services sector: An assessment of edge cities of the US National Capital Region', *Small Business Economics*, **9**, 1–14.

Stough, R.R., R. Kulkarni and J. Riggle (1997b), *Technology in Virginia's Regions*, Fairfax, VA: Center for Innovative Technology.

Stough, R.R. (ed.) (1998a) *Proceedings of the 5th Annual Conference on the Future of the Northern Virginia Economy*, Fairfax, VA: The Center for Regional Analysis, The Institute of Public Policy, George Mason University.

Stough, R.R., R. Kulkarni, J. Riggle (1998b), *Technology in Virginia's Regions*, Fairfax, VA: Center for Innovative Technology.

Stough, R.R. and M. Trice (1998c), *Regional Information Technology Workforce Survey: 1998 Annual Survey*, Fairfax, VA: Northern Virginia Regional Partnership.

Stough, R.R. (ed.) (1999a), *Proceedings of the 7th Annual Conference on the Future of the Northern Virginia Economy*, Fairfax, VA: The Center for Regional Analysis, The Institute of Public Policy, George Mason University.

Stough, R.R. and J. Paelinck (Forthcoming), *Papers in Regional Science*.

US Immigration and Naturalization Service (1997), 'Immigration by selected metropolitan areas of residence', Washington, DC: US Immigration and Naturalization Service.

US Bureau of the Census (1991), 'Washington DC Metropolitan Area: Population Distribution by Ethnic Group in 1990', Washington, DC: US Bureau of the Census.

Washington Airports Task Force (1998), *1998 Annual Report*, Herndon, VA: Washington Airports Task Force.

Zakon, R. H. (1999), 'Hobbes' Internet Timeline', 4.1, Washington, DC: The Mitre Corporation [http://isoc.org/guest/zakon/internet/history/HIT.html]

7. Miami: Multicultural Gateway of the Americas

Niles Hansen

INTRODUCTION

This chapter chronicles the evolution of a city that came into existence only a century ago but now is an undisputed international gateway metropolis, especially with respect to the United States and Latin America. The first section presents an overview of Miami's historical development. The next three sections give more specific consideration to the nature of the city's population, employment and income characteristics. In the fifth and sixth sections the trade and tourism gateway roles of Miami International Airport and the Port of Miami are discussed in some detail. The seventh section examines the tourist industry and tourists' perceptions of Miami. The eighth section highlights the gateway activities of multinational firms and international banking in Miami. The ninth section deals with the important contributions that Cuban immigrants have made in Miami's development process, as well as with the impacts of more general Hispanic immigration. The concluding section considers the many current challenges confronting a city that has been evolving from sometimes chaotic frontier conditions toward greater maturity.

It should be remarked at the outset that unless otherwise stated 'Miami' will be understood in this chapter to mean metropolitan Miami. In keeping with the federal government's definition of Metropolitan Statistical Areas (MSAs) in the United States, the Miami MSA is Dade County, sometimes also referred to as Greater Miami. Almost 82 percent of the population of the Miami MSA resides outside of the City of Miami.

MIAMI'S DEVELOPMENT: A PRELIMINARY OVERVIEW

A little over one hundred years ago, what is today Miami consisted of a few plantations, a small trading post and the ruins of an army camp that had been

Fort Davis. Although South Florida's mild winters had been attracting visitors from the north for some decades, the area around the Miami River was cut off by the Everglades and largely regarded as an uninhabitable wilderness. In 1891, Julia Tuttle, the widow of a wealthy Cleveland industrialist, purchased 40 acres on the north side of the Miami River and began a campaign to transform the outpost into a real city. Realizing that easier access was the key to her ambitions, she attempted without success to persuade railroad barons to extend lines to Miami. One of these, Henry Flagler, had built his Florida East Coast Railway as far as Palm Beach by 1893, but he was not interested in adding another 66 miles of track to tiny Miami.

The turning point came when freezes in the winter of 1894–95 ruined citrus groves in northern and central Florida, but did not affect the south. According to tradition, Tuttle sent Flagler orange blossoms to demonstrate that the area had great agricultural potential. The message had its effect, though Tuttle also offered Flagler half of her land as well as waterfront rights. In April 1896, a rail line to Miami was finished and the 300 residents of the village, which then officially became a city, greeted the first locomotive. The following year Flagler opened a grand hotel. Soon tourists were arriving and wealthy northerners began building elaborate winter retreats overlooking Biscayne Bay. By 1900, Miami's population had risen to 5,000.

During the early years of the twentieth century a modest boom took place as swamps were drained (marking the beginning of the threat to the Everglades), access to Miami's harbor was improved, and Carl Fisher began dredging operations to create a beach for Miami Beach. Meanwhile, national advertising attracted thousands of tourists as well as permanent residents to the perpetual warmth and sunshine of Miami.

Following the First World War, widespread middle-class interest in Miami prompted a period of spectacular growth. In just five years the population increased from 30,000 to 100,000, and over 300,000 vacationers visited the area in the winter of 1924–25 alone. Real-estate speculation was rampant. Property often changed hands many times sight-unseen with an inflated profit attached to each new sale. Dozens of new communities appeared, often featuring exotic architecture. George Merrick's Coral Gables, the single largest real-estate venture of the time, also became one of the most beautiful and exclusive residential areas.

But by the mid-1920s the boom began to unravel. The realization that many land buyers had purchased worthless plots resulted in a chaotic financial environment and numerous bank failures. In 1925, sales at Coral Gables began to decline. Anti-Florida sentiment, tax investigations and a freight embargo put a damper on new investment. In 1926 a deadly hurricane devastated tropical vegetation and destroyed or damaged nearly every downtown building. The tropical paradise had become a place to be avoided. By the end of 1927, Coral Gables mansions that had survived the hurricane without serious damage could not be sold at any price. George Merrick lost everything, and Carl Fisher, who made $50 million out of Miami Beach, would eventually die drunk with less than $50,000 in assets. Bank clearings in Miami dropped from over $1 billion in 1925 to $260 million by the end of 1927. To make matters still worse, in 1928 a hurricane even more lethal than that of 1926 struck Miami.

If Miami's troubles preceded the stock market crash of 1929 and the subsequent Great Depression, the area's economy was among the first in the country to revive. Tourism and even permanent settlement increased as northerners sought to escape cold winters. Jewish migrants were particularly in evidence. The welcome prospect of accompanying money inflows constrained any latent anti-Semitism within the local Protestant establishment. Hundreds of Art Deco hotels and apartments were built in Miami Beach to provide for the needs of newcomers. In 1934, Pan American Airlines began passenger flights between Latin America and Miami, now presented as the Gateway to the Americas.

National prohibition of alcoholic beverage sales also provided an economic stimulus. Local officials largely turned a blind eye not only to illegal gambling, but also to the smuggling of rum and Scotch whisky from Cuba and the Bahamas. By the end of the 1930s, organized crime dominated the gambling scene as well as other nominally illegal activities, as it would for some decades. When the notorious mobster Al Capone moved from Chicago to Miami and openly suggested that his friends should join him there were objections that this would create an image harmful to real-estate sales in Miami. But, as Allman (1987, p.230) points out

> It was a brave but pathetic gesture: The Chicago Mafia was as welcome in Miami in the thirties, in spite of the ritual lamentations of 'respectable' Miamians, as the cocaine Mafia would be in the eighties, and for the same reason.
> Al Capone was great for business.
> In the thirties, as in the eighties, no Miami bank was ever recorded as having turned down suspicious deposits, scrupulous though it might have been to report them to the competent authorities. No realtor – or car dealer or yacht broker or jeweler or haberdasher – raised moral objections to a 100 percent down payment, paid for goods sight unseen.
> Miami has always been capable of pharisaical niceness when it comes to distinguishing between the fruit and the tree that bore it.

The advent of the Second World War virtually destroyed Miami's tourist industry, but officials persuaded the government to use Miami and Miami Beach as major military training centers. By the end of 1942, 147 hotels had been transformed into military barracks, and still others were used as temporary hospitals for wounded soldiers. Formerly expensive restaurants and élite social clubs were now used to feed the troops.

Following the war, many ex-soldiers returned to Miami to take advantage of inexpensive housing and many studied at the University of Miami under the GI Bill, which subsidized their education. A new development boom ensued. Again entire communities were built and sold. During the 1950s large, glamorous hotels sprouted along the Miami Beach coast. By the end of the 1950s, thanks in part to the benefits of air conditioning, the population of Greater Miami was nearly one million.

In 1959, Fidel Castro deposed the Cuban dictatorship and subsequently installed a socialist regime with strong ties to the Soviet Union. It was a revolution that eventually revolutionized Miami. Thousands of Cubans left Havana, most going to Miami. Entire neighborhoods became filled with persons speaking only Spanish. A failed US invasion of Cuba in 1961 and the Cuban missile crisis in 1962, in which the United States promised not to invade Cuba and the Soviet Union promised to remove its missiles, meant that Cuban refugees were in Miami to stay. Over a seven-year period beginning in 1965, some 230,000 Cuban political refugees fled to Miami on 'freedom flights'. By 1973, the Cuban population of Miami was estimated to be 350,000. Between 1960 and 1970, the population of metropolitan Miami grew by 323,000. Three-quarters of the growth was due to net migration; about 70 percent of the net migration was accounted for by Cuban refugees (Longbrake and Nichols, 1976).

Although a recession in the early 1970s was a setback, Miami was prospering again by the end of the decade. America's demand for illegal drugs poured large amounts of money into the city, but the legitimate business community also thrived. The downtown area was being revitalized. Innovative office towers and high-rise condominiums went up and construction was under way for a $1 billion futuristic Metrorail System. With money flowing in from Latin America, Miami became an international banking center.

In the 1980s Miami was to emerge as a truly major international metropolis, but the decade was nevertheless marked by considerable turbulence. In 1980, growing anti-Hispanic sentiment resulting from large inflows of Latin American immigrants caused the city to rescind a 1973 bilingual ordinance. Meanwhile 'boat people' from Haiti were landing almost daily on South Florida beaches. Then Fidel Castro allowed anyone who wanted to leave Cuba to do so. Miami Cubans who sailed to Mariel Harbor in Cuba to pick up those who were departing were forced to include some criminals and inmates of Cuban prisons and mental institutions. Many among the 125,000 Cubans brought to Miami by the Mariel boatlift settled in South

Beach; the Art Deco neighborhood of the 1930s was now regarded as a run-down area to be avoided, especially at night.

Meanwhile tensions were rising in the African-American community due to the perception that their workers were being displaced by the immigrants. In 1980, a three-day riot in the Liberty City neighborhood left 19 persons dead and caused more than $50 million in damages. Many Anglos began leaving Miami, often heading northward to Broward County and beyond. And many vehicles had a bumper sticker requesting 'Will the last American leaving Miami please bring the flag?'

In 1981, 621 persons met violent deaths in Dade County and Miami gained a national reputation as Murder Capital USA. By the mid-1980s, a national economic recession hit Miami hard. The newest downtown office tower went bankrupt, banks foreclosed on unfinished condominiums, shopping malls stood half empty and the Metrorail had few riders. For a time it appeared that Miami was a fading resort where the only gainers were the 'cocaine cowboys' who generated an estimated $10 billion a year in the illegal drug trade. If crime had given Miami a bad image, *Miami Vice*, a highly successful national television program that ran from 1984 to 1989, gave the city's underworld an air of alluring glamour. But the series also highlighted Miami's warm climate, tropical vegetation and best architecture, thereby promoting an attractive image in the national consciousness.

Despite the problems of the 1980s, the decade was also marked by many positive developments. A major building boom produced yet more beautiful and unique skyscrapers, especially in and around Brickell Avenue, making the Miami skyline one of the most memorable anywhere. Many of the designs came from Miami's own highly innovative Arquitectonica International. In the late 1980s, once blighted South Beach experienced a remarkable renaissance as millions of dollars were poured into the renovation of Art Deco structures and it became trendy for both ordinary tourists and the jet-set elite to frequent its restaurants, cafés, theaters and art galleries. Miami International Airport became America's second busiest international gateway and the seaport became the largest cruise ship port in the world. Hundreds of multinational corporations, banks and insurance companies established offices in the area. Miami's evolution into a world commercial center drew millions of business visitors, many attending conventions and international trade shows.

During the 1990s, Miami continued to enhance its status as an international gateway city. The only major interruption occurred in 1993, when tourism declined as a result of a series of robberies and murders of foreign tourists. Increased police patrols around the international airport, improved directional signs along the roads, and the elimination of markings identifying rental cars all served to reduce sharply crimes against tourists.

Personal safety is no longer perceived to be a significant problem by tourists in Miami.

While Miami remains a place with abundant opportunities, it also must cope with challenges posed by a multicultural and multi-ethnic society. Because this is increasingly the case in the United States as a whole, Miami's efforts to deal with change should prove instructive for other communities.

POPULATION CHARACTERISTICS

Between 1970 and 1997, the population of the Miami MSA grew from 1,268,000 to 2,045,000. However, the pace of growth declined from an annual average rate of 2.8 percent during the 1970s, to 1.9 percent during the 1980s, to 0.8 percent between 1990 and 1997. Between 1990 and 1997, the Miami MSA population increased by 107,406, the excess of births over deaths amounted to 107,005, and net international migration added 162,617 to the population (US Bureau of the Census, 1998). This implies that net out-migration to other US destinations was approximately 162,000, or 8.4 percent of the 1990 population. Neighboring Broward County probably absorbed a significant portion of the out-migrants. During the 1980s, when the US population grew by 9.8 percent, the population of the Miami MSA increased by 19.2 percent and that of Broward County increased by 23.3 percent. Between 1990 and 1997, when the US population grew by 7.6 percent, the population of the Miami MSA increased by only 5.5 percent, while that in Broward County increased by 17.1 percent, suggesting a continuation of 'white flight' from the Miami MSA.

By 1997, the population composition of the Miami MSA was 54.4 percent Hispanic, 21.1 percent African-American, 1.8 percent Asian and 22.7 percent non-Hispanic white. In Broward County, the population composition was 10.9 percent Hispanic, 17.5 percent African-American, 1.9 percent Asian and 69.7 percent non-Hispanic white (US Bureau of the Census, 1998).

Between 1980 and 1996, the average annual rate of population growth in the City of Miami was only 0.3 percent, whereas it was 1.5 percent for the Miami MSA. In 1996, the population of the City of Miami was 365,000, which accounted for only 18 percent of the Miami MSA population (US Bureau of the Census, 1998). Since the early 1960s, the City of Miami has been the location of choice for immigrants to South Florida, but since the 1970s the city has also experienced an out-migration of its middle class. The city is probably unique in the United States with respect to ethnic and racial diversity. Over 90 percent of its population is composed of minorities, over 60 percent is foreign-born, and nearly 50 percent of its residents are not US citizens (Greater Miami Chamber of Commerce, 1997).

EMPLOYMENT CHARACTERISTICS

Between 1970 and 1993, total employment in the Miami MSA rose from 645,200 to 1,088,200 (Table 7.1). In keeping with the pattern of population growth, the largest gains were made earlier in this period. Between 1970 and 1985, employment increased at an average annual rate of 3.3 percent, but between 1985 and 1993 the corresponding rate was only 1.6 percent.

Table 7.1 Employment by place of work and economic sector in the Miami Metropolitan Area, 1970–93

Year	1970	1975	1980	1985	1990	1993
Construction	38,700	34,200	48,300	48,800	50,000	51,200
Manu-facturing	78,000	83,000	100,800	96,200	90,600	84,300
Retail trade	112,400	123,400	152,200	164,100	181,500	181,100
Wholesale trade	39,800	50,700	66,300	68,500	78,900	79,000
FIRE*	54,300	73,300	88,400	94,700	102,500	92,900
Transpor-tation	59,300	62,200	78,500	75,000	80,800	81,300
Services	179.700	207,500	257,300	301,800	354,200	376,900
Government	79,400	99,700	107,400	110,700	133,900	134,200
Agriculture	3,600	4,000	5,800	5,400	6,000	6,300
Total	645,200	738,000	905,000	965,200	1,078,400	1,088,200

Note:
* Finance, insurance and real estate

Source: Greater Miami Chamber of Commerce (1997)

In the construction and transportation sectors there was rapid growth in the 1970s, followed by a relatively stable level afterward. Employment in retail and wholesale trade as well as in government increased substantially between 1970 and 1990, but then became stable in the early 1990s. Employment in the finance, insurance and real-estate (FIRE) sector almost doubled between 1970 and 1990, but then declined by about 10,000 between 1990 and 1993. Manufacturing employment declined from a peak of 100,800 in 1980 to 84,300 in 1993.

The stellar performer with respect to employment creation has been the services sector, which enjoyed rapid growth throughout the 1970–93 period. During this time, it increased by 110 percent and was the only sector to show a significant increase between 1990 and 1993, rising by 22,700, or by 6.4 percent.

Miami's relatively great orientation toward the services sector is evident from the fact that in 1993 services accounted for 34.6 percent of total employment, whereas nationwide services accounted for 24.2 percent of total employment (US Bureau of the Census, 1998, p. 416). The unemployment rate in the Miami MSA fell from 8.4 percent to 7.3 percent between 1994 and 1996, but this was still well above the corresponding national rate of 5.4 percent (US Bureau of the Census, 1998).

INCOME AND POVERTY CONDITIONS

In a study of 74 large MSAs, Wyly et al. (1998) found that the average annual increase in per capita income in Miami between 1969 and 1995 was 2.3 percent, which placed it in the 44th rank. In 1995, per capita income was $21,058 in the Miami MSA and $24,233 in southern MSAs. Between 1970 and 1990, housing in Miami became less affordable in terms of the relationship between median gross rent and median household income. Over this period, Miami ranked 60th out of 74 MSAs with respect to change in housing affordability.

In 1993, an estimated 25.4 percent of all persons in the Miami MSA were living in poverty conditions, as were 34.8 percent of children aged 5 to 17 years (US Bureau of the Census, 1998). In 1990, the poverty rate for individuals living in the City of Miami was 31.2 percent. Among 77 large US central cities, only New Orleans (31.6 percent) and Detroit (32.4 percent) had higher poverty rates (Gyourko, 1998). According to the Greater Miami Chamber of Commerce (1997), the City of Miami has the lowest median household income among the nation's cities with populations exceeding 100,000.

Inner-city residents are largely the working poor, deriving only 4.5 percent of their income from public assistance. Low levels of educational achievement and poor English-language skills contribute to low wages and earning capacity.

MIAMI INTERNATIONAL AIRPORT

Glenn Curtiss, 'arguably the greatest aviator of all time', flew 'into the small resort city of Miami in 1919 and proceeded to change aviation history forever' (Arend, 1997, p. 8). Curtiss, who invented the aileron, the movable part on an airplane wing providing lateral control in flight, opened a flying school on Miami Beach that over the years taught thousands of people how to fly. Curtiss also formed companies in Miami that operated airports and manufactured airplanes, and he founded the town of Miami Springs, which borders the present Miami International Airport (MIA).

When Pan American Field, the predecessor of MIA, opened in 1928, at a time when other airport passenger facilities were only small rooms attached to the sides of airplane maintenance hangars, it had the first separate waiting rooms for arriving and departing passengers, a restaurant, and offices for customs, immigration and public health officials. In the same year the first direct flight from Miami to Havana, Cuba took place. In 1929, Charles Lindbergh, who two years earlier had flown non-stop from New York to Paris, inaugurated the first regular service between Miami and San Juan, Puerto Rico (Metro-Dade Aviation Department, no date). The birth of US scheduled international air cargo took place in Miami in 1931, when Pan American World Airways began regular service to Havana. By 1933, Pan Am was operating scheduled cargo flights to several destinations in South America.

The air cargo business flourished in Latin America in the 1930s because railroads and highways were often few and far between, and the airplane was frequently the only means for getting freight to isolated locations. Pan Am's business strategy was to develop global routes relying on air cargo to provide revenues because passengers were slow to respond to early flights.

This approach, first undertaken successfully between Miami and Latin America and later extended to transatlantic and transpacific services, made Pan Am the world's largest carrier of cargo and mail, a position it held until airline deregulation in the late 1970s. When time ran out for the original Pan Am in 1991, its flights between Miami and South America were still profitable when all else was gone (Arend, 1997)

MIA has evolved from a small 116-acre facility that handled 8,600 passengers and 20 tons of cargo in 1930 to today's 3,230-acre giant that has become a multi-billion-dollar industry. Between 1940 and 1950, Miami's airline passenger traffic increased from 140,000 to 1,400,000, and freight tonnage rose from 350 to 51,100 (Metro-Dade Aviation Department, no date).

Between 1955 and 1997, international passenger traffic grew from 783,351 to 15,507,272, and domestic passenger traffic went from 2,275,791 to 19,025,996. During the same period, international freight traffic rose from 53,208 tons to 1,552,101 tons, while domestic freight traffic increased from 15,300 tons to 303,821 tons (Table 7.2).

Between 1985 and 1997, international passenger traffic grew by 123 percent, while domestic traffic rose by 48 percent; international freight tonnage increased by 288 percent and domestic tonnage grew by 120 percent.

Table 7.2 Miami International Airport passenger and freight traffic, 1955–97

	Passengers			Freight (US tons)		
Year	Domestic	Inter-national	Total	Domestic	Inter-national	Total
1955	2,275,791	783,351	3,059,142	15,300	53,208	68,508
1965	4,574,508	1,619,473	6,193,981	52,071	93,579	145,650
1975	7,873,930	4,194,188	12,068,118	112,867	259,860	372,727
1985	12,895,695	6,957,657	19,853,352	168,511	405,819	574,330
1995	18,792,626	14,443,032	33,235,658	334,923	1,412,247	1,747,170
1997	19,025,996	15,507,272	34,533,268	370,592	1,576,301	1,946,893

Source: Metro-Dade County Aviation Department, Miami International Airport.

At present MIA is served by 16 US scheduled passenger/cargo carriers, 45 foreign scheduled passenger/cargo carriers, 15 US scheduled all-cargo carriers, 14 foreign scheduled all-cargo carriers, and 29 charter carriers. MIA ranks first among US airports with respect to international air freight handled, and second with respect to number of international passengers, behind New York's John F. Kennedy Airport.

In terms of total freight handled, MIA ranks second in the United States, behind Memphis, which is a special case because it is a hub for Federal Express. MIA ranks fourth in the world with respect to total freight handled, behind Memphis, Hong Kong, and Tokyo's Narita Airport. MIA is the third busiest airport in the world for international freight, behind Hong Kong and Tokyo Narita. It ranks seventh with respect to total passengers among US airports, and twelfth in the world in this regard (Miami-Dade Aviation Department, 1998b).

MIA has direct air services to over 75 cities in South and Central America and the Caribbean. One can get to more cities in Latin America by traveling through Miami than by traveling within the region. Fully 81 percent of all airborne export trade from the United States to Latin America and the Caribbean departs via MIA, and 84 percent of goods imported into the United States from these areas arrives via MIA.

In terms of weight, the leading countries in share of MIA's total 1996 trade were Colombia (27.1 percent), Brazil (10.3 percent), Chile (10.0 percent), and Costa Rica (6.1 percent). In terms of value, the leading countries were Brazil (19.1 percent), Colombia (12.7 percent), Argentina (6.6 percent), and Venezuela (5.1 percent) (Metro-Dade County Aviation Department, 1997a).

THE PORT OF MIAMI

The Port of Miami is a two-island complex adjacent to downtown Miami, with gantry-crane berths just three-and-a-half nautical miles from ocean shipping lanes. It is the southernmost deepwater container port in North America and the busiest passenger cruise port in the world.

During the 1990s, the number of cruise ship passengers passing through Miami has fluctuated around 3 million annually (Table 7.3). Nevertheless, the 3.2 million passengers transiting Miami in 1997 set a new world record. In that year, one-third of North American cruise passengers sailed from Miami (Port of Miami, 1998a). The cruises offer a wide range of vacation options, including the Bahamas, the Caribbean, and longer itineraries to the world's most popular cruise destinations.

In November 1997, Cunard officially relocated its headquarters from New York to Miami, bringing some of the most famous luxury ships in the world, including the *Queen Elizabeth 2*. With the addition of Cunard and the introduction of other new ships in 1998, the number of cruise ships with a Miami home port rose from 13 in 1997 to 20 in 1998.

The Port of Miami has also recently become the home of a new 3,600-passenger cruise ship. A $60 million redevelopment program is under way at the port to accommodate the new and anticipated growth in cruise passenger traffic.

Table 7.3 Port of Miami cargo tonnage and passenger traffic, 1991–97

Year	Cargo Tonnage Total	Exports	Imports	Passengers
1991	3,882,284	1,886,942	1,995,342	2,928,532
1992	4,596,481	2,332,873	2,263,608	3,095,487
1993	5,198,292	2,568,576	2,629,716	3,157,130
1994	5,574,252	2,775,575	2,798,677	2,967,081
1995	5,840,815	2,778,765	3,062,447	2,974,703
1996	6,002,744	3,079,043	2,923,701	3,052,450
1997	6,735,388	3,371,264	3,364,124	3,191,885

Source: Port of Miami (1998a).

Cargo tonnage moving through the Port of Miami has increased steadily during the 1990s, reaching 6,735,388 tons in 1997, a 12.2 percent increase over the previous year (Table 7.3). The port has 40 shipping lines calling on 132 countries and 362 ports around the world. Of these, 26 carriers serve 33 countries and 101 ports in Latin America and the Caribbean. In 1997, the Port of Miami ranked eighth among US ports in general cargo tonnage, with an almost equal division between exports and imports. The leading exported commodities were textiles (332,000 tons), food (294,000 tons), paper (213,000 tons), and fruits and vegetables (204,000 tons). The leading imported commodities were fruits and vegetables (615,000 tons), tiles and related products (496,000 tons), textiles (459,000 tons), and coffee, tea and spices (177,000 tons) (Port of Miami, 1998b).

In 1997, the Port of Miami was the transit point for more than 42 percent of all international commerce between the United States and the Latin American–Caribbean region, which accounted for 67 percent of total cargo, 83 percent of exports and 53 percent of imports passing through the port (Port of Miami, 1998b). Of the total tonnage exported through the port of Miami, South America received 43 percent, the Caribbean 22 percent, and Central America 18 percent. Of the total tonnage imported, South America accounted for 24 percent, Central America 20 percent, and the Caribbean 9 percent.

THE TOURISM INDUSTRY

In 1997, interviews were carried out with over 3,600 overnight visitors to Greater Miami to establish a profile of a number of characteristics of such visitors, and to analyze their economic impact on the Dade County economy (Strategy Research Corporation, 1998). The results indicated that overnight visitors reached an all-time high of 9,843,300, of whom 54 percent were of foreign origin. Among all international visitors, Latin America accounted for 3.2 million, or about 61 percent. Europe accounted for 25 percent and Canada for about 12 percent.

Pleasure/vacation was the main purpose of 70.1 percent of international visitors and 39.8 percent of domestic visitors (Table 7.4). Business and convention meetings ranked second in importance for both domestic visitors (27.5 percent) and international visitors (14.1 percent). However, pleasure/vacation was at least a secondary purpose for many domestic and international visitors.

Thus, 64.8 percent of domestic visitors and 90.3 percent of international visitors stated that this objective was among the reasons for their being in

Miami. Cruises were the principal purpose for 18.3 percent of domestic visitors, but only 2.6 percent of international visitors.

Table 7.4. Purposes of visits to greater Miami in 1997, percentages by domestic and international visitors

	Main purpose			Total purposes		
	Total	Domestic	Inter-national	Total	Domestic	Inter-national
Pleasure/ vacation	52.5	39.8	70.1	75.4	64.8	90.3
Business/ convention	22.0	27.5	14.1	25.2	31.1	16.8
Friends/ relatives	11.7	11.9	11.5	15.5	17.0	13.3
Cruise	11.7	18.3	2.6	12.7	19.0	3.8
Special events	1.1	1.5	0.6	4.2	5.6	2.3
Personal/ medical	1.0	1.0	1.1	2.4	2.5	2.6

Source: Strategy Research Corporation (1998).

Fully 96 percent of all overnight visitors to Greater Miami were either extremely or very satisfied with their experiences in the area. Among domestic visitors, 51 percent were extremely satisfied and 44 percent were very satisfied. Among international visitors, 21 percent were extremely satisfied and 77 percent were very satisfied. Eighty-eight percent of domestic visitors and 82 percent of international visitors indicated that they were definitely or very likely to return.

Domestic and international visitors differed in the attractions they liked most. Allowing for multiple responses, the features most liked by domestic visitors were the weather (67 percent), sun bathing and beach activities (31 percent), Ocean Drive (23 percent), and night life (14 percent). International visitors most liked shopping (52 percent), the weather (36 percent), restaurants (32 percent), and Ocean Drive (28 percent). Crime and personal safety concerns were the least-liked aspect for 17 percent of the domestic visitors and for 10 percent of the international visitors, nearly all of whom were European. Two-thirds of the domestic visitors and three-fourths of the international visitors found nothing to dislike about their experiences in Greater Miami.

International visitors spent $6.68 billion and domestic visitors spent $4.95 billion in Greater Miami in 1997. The total impact of overnight visitors on the economy was estimated to be $16.83 billion, which includes a multiplier effect calculated from an input–output analysis. This can be translated into an impact of $8,183 per person in Dade County. Overnight visitors generated $718 million in sales taxes, which represented about half of the total collected in Dade County in 1997.

Total employment generated by overnight visitors was estimated to be 372,050 in 1997, up from 352,520 in 1996 (Strategy Research Corporation, 1998).

In evaluating the prospects for Miami's tourist industry in 1998, the Greater Miami Convention and Visitors Bureau (1998) expected the European demand to remain strong, through tempered by the strength of the US dollar, which may have a more adverse effect on Canadian tourism. Visitation from Brazil, which has been important in the past, may decline due to financial turmoil in that country. Moderate growth is anticipated with respect to domestic visitations.

MULTINATIONAL FIRMS AND INTERNATIONAL BANKING

In 1997, $47 billion of US merchandise trade was processed through the Miami Customs District, an increase of 172 percent over 1989. Export trade accounted for $29 billion and import trade for $18 billion. Although the Miami Customs District includes the southern half of Florida, these values essentially reflect activity in Miami. South and Central America and the Caribbean accounted for 88 percent of the value of exports and for 60 percent of the value of imports. Western Europe and Asia accounted for 16 percent and 19 percent, respectively, of the total value of imports (Donath, 1998).

Although many firms in Miami conduct business internationally without owning or operating an overseas office, and many firms overseas conduct business in or through Miami without having a physical presence there, the activities of multinational corporations have played a large role in making Miami an international gateway city. A 1993 survey of 332 multinationals in the Miami MSA indicated that they employed 45,000 persons, or approximately 5 percent of direct employment in the area.

One-third of the firms were based in North America, but they accounted for 70 percent of total employment in Miami multinationals. European firms accounted for 31 percent of total firms and for 22 percent of total employment. Latin American firms were only 16 percent of the total firms and they had only 3 percent of total employment, but it was thought that they were under-represented in the survey due to fears of disclosure concerning past capital flight from Latin America (Jainarain and Donath, 1994). Almost half of the multinationals were established in Miami between 1986 and June 1993. The leading types of business were banking, airlines and electronics. Over half of the firms were responsible for sales and distribution of products and services in Latin America and the Caribbean.

Miami is home to the largest concentration of domestic and international banks on the U.S east coast south of New York City. With respect to international banking, Miami ranks second in the United States to New York in terms of assets and deposits, but Miami ranks first in trade services to Latin America (Florida International Bankers Association, 1996).

In 1997, Miami financial institutions registered $50 billion in deposits. Foreign bank agencies, which act much like domestic banks with the exception that they cannot take deposits from US residents, accounted for 21.2 percent of this total. Edge Act banks, which can only serve foreign customers for international trade purposes, accounted for another 9.6 percent (Beacon Council, 1998).

The most significant change in the nature of Miami international banking has taken place with respect to lending. During the developing-country debt crisis in the middle 1980s, traditional New York banks greatly reduced their Latin American activities and in some cases closed their Miami branches. Between 1987 and 1990, when deposits in Miami international agency banks increased from $6.2 billion to $9.6 billion, loans remained virtually unchanged at about $2.8 billion.

In 1991, Miami international banks came into the trade finance market in a major way after a banking regulatory arrangement ceased classifying the trade credits of numerous South American countries as substandard and requiring a reserve against loans. Between 1991 and 1996, deposits with international agency banks increased by 13 percent but the loans rose by 261 percent. Between 1990 and 1996, the loan-to-deposit ratio for these banks went from 29 percent to 94 percent. Between 1989 and 1996, lending increased from $358 million to $879 million by South American banks; from $374 million to $1.1 billion by Spanish banks; from $569 million to $5.3 billion by United Kingdom banks; and from $778 million to $1.9 billion by continental European banks.

In 1996, the combined loan volume of international agency banks and Edge Act banks was $11.8 billion. Since trade lending ranges from 30 days to a maximum of 360 days, the $11.8 billion figure on a 180-day or 120-day turnover basis reflects the financing of an estimated $23.6–$35.4 billion in Latin American trade in 1996 (Florida International Bankers Association, 1997).

THE CUBAN FACTOR AND THE HISPANICIZATION OF MIAMI

Geography has certainly given Miami an advantage with respect to economic interactions with Latin America. South America is not only south of Miami, but most of it is also east of Miami. There are still those who maintain that owing to geography it was Miami's inevitable destiny to become the US gateway to and from Latin America, yet as recently as 1960 Miami's trade with Latin America was well behind that of such cities as New York, Los Angeles and New Orleans (Boswell, 1998). It was at this time that the influx of Cubans began, and there can be little doubt that Cuban immigrants played a key role in the transformation of Miami from an inward-looking southern resort community to a metropolis of international status.

The Cubans who arrived in Miami after Fidel Castro assumed power in Cuba in 1959 contained a disproportionate number of refugees from the middle and upper strata of pre-Revolutionary society (Fagen et al., 1968). During the 1960s they faced numerous obstacles. Most did not speak English. Those who were doctors, lawyers, engineers and teachers had to pass certification examinations before they could practice their professions. Others were discriminated against by unions. In response, the Cubans developed their own economy in Miami (Boswell, 1998).

Although a few early arrivers from Cuba brought some capital with them, most did not. Instead Cubans received financial capital from banks that were owned by Latin Americans but managed by Cubans who had banking experience before leaving Cuba. These managers made loans to other Cubans whom they had known earlier in Cuba. The loans were often made on the basis of knowledge of the borrower's character, without the usual collateral guarantees. Most of these loans were repaid.

A reliable labor force was provided by friends and relatives of Cuban entrepreneurs. These workers often accepted lower wages and longer working hours than the norm, and they were less likely to join unions. On the other hand, they learned the business and were taken care of in emergencies. Once the Cuban population reached the threshold size needed to support Cuban businesses, the success of the ethnic enclave was assured, since Cubans typically bought from other Cubans, who would also frequently extend credit when necessary. Each new wave of immigrants from Cuba and other Latin America countries expanded the development of the enclave economy (Boswell, 1998).

Allman (1987) points out that one reason why Miami became such an important gateway for international trade, communications and finance is that so many Cubans did not settle there. With the Castro diaspora, Cuban communities appeared in Paris, London and Spanish cities, especially

Madrid. Soon there was hardly a Spanish-speaking country anywhere that did not have its nucleus of Cuban immigrants. Major US commercial centers also contained important Cuban communities.

US government policies inadvertently helped to create a widespread network for Cubans. More Cubans would have stayed in Miami if given the choice, but instead US officials sent many off to various parts of the United States.

Those who refused to go were denied further federal government assistance. Moreover, the trade embargo against Cuba meant that no Cubans in Miami could survive through trade with Havana, as earlier Cuban settlers in Miami had. Because they could not go home again, Cuban exiles were obliged to become participants in a vaster, more lucrative international capitalism with Miami as its nexus. Thus Miami's Cuban community was not an isolated ghetto in a foreign land. On the contrary, the Cuban exodus created a complex international network of personal, professional and financial relations.

By the mid-1980s, the population of the Miami MSA was 43 percent Hispanic, most of whom were Cuban. The presence of large numbers of non-Cuban Hispanics in Miami suggests that the Hispanicization of Miami may have been geographically inevitable, but the difference between Miami and other US cities with large Latino populations has not been the presence of Latinos but rather the presence of a particular people, the Cubans. Without the Cubans, Miami may well have become a poor, heavily Hispanic southern city rather than a major international city (Rieff, 1987).

In the mid-1980s, Cubans could be found in the board rooms of major banks and in private clubs that did not admit Jews or African-Americans. The Miami skyline was being transformed by the Cuban firm of Arquitectonica, and the city had a Cuban mayor. Although the Cuban population was anything but invisible, 'there had come to exist in South Florida two parallel cultures, separate but not exactly equal, a key distinction being that only one of the two, the Cuban, exhibited even a remote interest in the activities of the other' (Didion, 1987, p. 56).

In fact, the growing strength of the Hispanic community and Miami's transformation from a locally focused city into a cosmopolitan center occurred in large part through the use of Spanish. Contributing to this process was the departure of large numbers of non-Hispanic whites who were uncomfortable with the increasing use of Spanish and the shift from a local to an international community (Fradd, 1996). It was indeed a different world from 1940, when 40 percent of Miami's males had been born in Georgia (Allman, 1987).

From the moment that US tourists arrive at Miami International Airport it is evident that they are not in Kansas, largely because of the ubiquitous sounds of Spanish. Because Spanish is used almost as easily as English in conducting both domestic and international business in Miami, the city has an environment favoring its position as an international center of trade and commerce.

Latin American businesses often come to Miami to finalize agreements with firms in other Latin American countries. Latin American and European investors control as much as 10 percent of real-estate sales, with a high proportion in the upper-price range. In addition to being the Gateway to the Americas, Miami also serves as the Mall of the Americas. Miami has more Hispanic-owned businesses than any other US metropolitan area, and Latin Americans account for a significant portion of the sales of top-of-the-line retail items in Miami.

International Spanish-language television networks (Univision, Telemundo, MTV Latin America) have their headquarters in Miami. Hispanic singers and other media personalities popular in Miami are also known throughout Latin America, creating and sustaining international cultural bonds (Fradd, 1996).

Nevertheless, in recent years there has been a shift from Spanish toward English as the language of general communication and business in Miami. For many acculturated Hispanics, English is the language of preference. As Hispanics have become more fluent in English, the readership of Hispanic-oriented English-language magazines has increased at the expense of Spanish-language publications, especially among the more affluent and established Hispanics.

The primary audience for Spanish-language television tends to be newly arrived and older immigrants, especially those who learned Spanish well before they learned English or who have never learned English. A study of bilingual persons indicated that those who learned Spanish first watch Spanish-language television 70 percent of the time, whereas those who learned English first watch it only 22 percent of the time (Fradd, 1996).

There is solid evidence that there are economic advantages in Miami for persons who are bilingual in Spanish and English, especially if English is spoken very well (Boswell, 1998). Among persons who spoke Spanish at home in 1990, those who spoke English 'very well' had a median income of $12,294 and a mean income of $17,711, whereas for those who spoke English 'well' the corresponding values were $11,000 and $14,703. Hispanics who spoke only English fared less well, with a median income of $8,200 and a mean income of $14,548.

However, Hispanics who spoke Spanish at home but who spoke English 'not well' had a median income of $6,874 and a mean income of $9,511, while those who spoke English 'not at all' had corresponding values of only $4,560 and $6,285. Hispanics who spoke only English had a higher poverty rate (17.2 percent) than Hispanics who spoke Spanish at home and spoke English 'very well' (13.1 percent) or 'well' (16.7 percent). However, for Hispanics who spoke Spanish at home but spoke English 'not well' the poverty rate was 22.8 percent, while those who spoke English 'not at all' had a rate of 32.0 percent. Thus there are strong economic incentives for becoming fluent in English despite the presence of a majority Hispanic population.

The policy implication is that a strong effort should be made to teach English to residents who do not speak English well, and to provide a second language to English-speaking students who want to learn one, especially if it is Spanish. A problem arises because of the different backgrounds of immigrant families (Boswell, 1998). Children of upper-class families typically attend private academies that use English and prepare them for success in the United States environment. In contrast, the public school system that serves the poor majority struggles to keep students in school at all. Developing programs that address the needs of students from such differing backgrounds poses a formidable challenge to Miami's school system.

THE CHALLENGES AHEAD

Geography and the Cuban presence have been presented as key factors in the evolution of Miami from a southern resort to an international gateway. But technological developments have also made their contribution. For example, air conditioning made it possible to enjoy the benefits of a southern climate without having to endure its disadvantages. And Miami's transformation not only coincided with the growth of the Cuban population, but also with the large-scale introduction of commercial jet airplanes, which greatly expanded opportunities for international trade, commerce and tourism. Later, the globalization of economic activity was accelerated by the advent of such innovations as computers, e-mail, fax machines, and communication via space satellites, all of which further extended Miami's possibilities to exploit its initial geographic advantage. However, by reducing the frictions of distance, these innovations have probably also increased the degree of international competition that Miami must confront.

Public policy has also encouraged inter-gateway competition. The US Department of Transportation recently awarded new Latin American air service to several US airports other than Miami. As a result, Miami's overall share of air service to and from Latin America will probably decline, though the absolute volume of both cargo and passenger traffic is expected to continue to increase because Miami 'possesses unique advantages–

geographic location, a multi-lingual and multi-cultural workforce and a reputation as an attractive business and tourism destination' (Metro-Dade Aviation Department, 1998a, p. 3). If one grants that Miami still has a geographical advantage, questions have nevertheless been raised concerning both Miami's attractiveness as an international business center and the quality of its workforce.

As indicated previously, Miami is perceived to be an attractive place by tourists. They generally have positive experiences, although 17 percent of domestic visitors and 10 percent of foreign visitors, nearly all European, express some concern about crime. On the other hand, it has been remarked that 'Viewed from corporate boardrooms in Tokyo, London or Montreal, Miami is an exotic, dangerous and corrupt city. Finding an up-and-coming regional manager to accept a job in South Florida can be more difficult than, say, filling a post in Siberia' (Westlund, 1998, p. 32). Lars Hummerhielm, the Swedish President of the Association of Bi-National Chambers of Commerce in South Florida, maintains that 'We have miserably failed in creating a favorable perception of Miami', and that 'Few people from outside our borders would contemplate moving to Miami'. He concludes that 'If we can resolve the international perception of Miami, we will have solved our biggest problem'. A prominent Miami civic organization also finds that while strides have been made against crime, there is still a public safety problem. Moreover, 'Continued public denial or minimization of the problem is not sound communications policy. Businesses and employees considering relocation to or from Greater Miami have their own perceptions. We must accept their perceptions as reality, and progress from there' (One Community One Goal, 1997b, p. 6).

With a county budget of $4.2 billion, Greater Miami is an area where a great deal of economic activity flows through government. This has been a common thread in public sector corruption scandals that have persisted for so long that corruption became the norm. In the past five years, at least 270 public employees have been charged with crimes ranging from embezzlement to falsification of records to ripping off drug dealers. The problems have been attributed to the growing pains of a place that has experienced massive immigration and is still too young to have the civic pride and established institutions that could counterbalance a frontier mentality.

While Miami's multi-ethnic population is often a gateway advantage, ethnic allegiances also seem to have led to a high tolerance among voters for transgression by public officials. When charges of corruption have involved African-American and Hispanic politicians, cries of racism are often raised in the ethnic press, with supporters often giving accused public officials the benefit of the doubt (Navarro, 1998; *New York Times*, 1998). Although public corruption seems to have little direct impact on most businesses (Westlund, 1998), for Miami residents 'it all adds up to a disappointment that some say is comparable to the recent decimation of their world champion baseball team' (Navarro, 1998, p. A1).

In more strictly economic terms, Miami faces significant difficulties related to the labor force. Miami's recent 7.3 percent unemployment rate was the highest among major US MSAs and twice that of other comparable areas in the Southeast United States. At a time when even highly qualified Miami workers cannot always find jobs, about one out of every three adults has not completed secondary school. Moreover, population growth in Miami is largely due to continuing immigration. Whereas earlier immigrants brought skills to create new businesses and jobs, today's immigrants typically do not have the skills necessary to compete in an increasingly technology-driven world. To further complicate matters, recent welfare-to-work legislation requires that the more than 20,000 local public assistance recipients find work (Fields, 1998b; One Community One Goal, 1997b).

In response to Miami's labor market problems and the need to retain and attract more advanced types of economic activity to the area, a large-scale effort has been initiated to create more than 100,000 jobs in the Miami MSA over the next ten years. This undertaking, known as One Community One Goal, relies heavily on the nurturing of seven sectors: international commerce, biomedicine, film and entertainment, tourism, financial services, telecommunications, and information technology. However, the original strategy has been modified to address also such quality-of-life issues as housing costs, crime, Miami's image, and problems concerning public education. Two years into the process it is still too early to evaluate the economic results obtained. However, it has made civic leaders more aware of the enormity of the problems and it has managed to build a consensus in a community that has often broken down into conflicts linked to ethnicity or intra-MSA geography (Fields, 1998a, 1998b; One Community One Goal, 1997a, 1997b).

Early in 1998, the head of One Community One Goal and the mayor hosted a 'summit meeting' to develop means to deal with Miami's problems and to build on potential opportunities. Nearly 3,000 persons attended, representing every segment of the community. In his report on the meeting, the mayor reminded the participants that this was merely a start, and he cautioned the various working groups that if money was required to realize recommendations, then they had to identify funding sources that would not require an increase in taxes (Office of the Mayor, 1998).

Miami is a relatively young city and in many respects has had the attributes of a frontier. However, its transformation from an inward-looking southern resort to an international gateway metropolis has clearly demonstrated that in an often chaotic environment there has still been thriving entrepreneurship, much of it the consequence of innovative immigrants. Despite the problems facing Miami, its established successes with respect to international trade, commerce and tourism, especially in relation to Latin America, have created a strong platform for future development in these areas. Miami's leaders are now beginning seriously to address the question of how to create more opportunities for those segments of the population that have not shared in the growth of overall prosperity, so that they can both enjoy a better quality of life and contribute to Miami's future development. The task may be difficult, but it does appear that the frontier has matured.

REFERENCES

Allman, T.D. (1987), *Miami: City of the Future*, New York: Atlantic Monthly Press.

Arend, G. (1997), *Pioneer: A Pictorial History of Miami International Airport Cargo*, Jamaica, New York: Air Cargo News, Great Airports.

Beacon Council (1998), *Miami Business Profile*, Miami: Beacon Council.

Boswell, T.D. (1998), 'Implications of demographic changes in Florida's public school population', in S.H. Fradd and O. Lee (eds), *Creating Florida's Multilingual Global Workforce*, Tallahassee, FL: Florida Department of Education.

Didion, J. (1987), *Miami*, New York: Simon and Schuster.

Donath, J. (1998), *Miami Customs District 1997 International Trade: Trends and Analysis*, Miami: The Beacon Council.

Fagen, R.R., R.A. Brody and T.J. O'Leary (1968), *Cubans in Exile*, Stanford, CA.: Stanford University Press.

Fields, G. (1998a), 'Jay Malina: The man behind the plan to grow Miami's economy', *Miami Herald*, Business Section, 23 March, pp. 12–13.

Fields, G. (1998b), 'One Community One Goal: A view so far of the effort', *Miami Herald*, Business Section, 23 March, pp. 13–14.

Florida International Bankers Association (1996), *The History of International Banking in Florida*, Miami: FIBA.

Florida International Bankers Association (1997), *1997–1998 Membership Directory*, Miami: FIBA.

Fradd, S.H. (1996), *The Economic Impact of Spanish-Language Proficiency in Metropolitan Miami*, Miami: Greater Miami Chamber of Commerce and the Policy Center of the Cuban American National Council.

Greater Miami Chamber of Commerce (1997), *Greater Miami Economic Report 1997*, Miami: GMCC.

Greater Miami Convention and Visitors Bureau (1998), *1997 Visitor Industry Statistical Highlights*, Miami: GMCVB.

Gyourko, J. (1998), 'Place-based aid versus people-based aid and the role of an urban audit in a new urban strategy', *Cityscape* **3** (3), 205–29.

Jainarain, C.I. and J. Donath (1994), *Miami's Multinational Business Community*, Miami: The Beacon Council.

Longbrake, D. B. and W.W. Nichols, Jr (1976), *Sunshine and Shadows in Metropolitan Miami*, Cambridge, MA: Ballinger.

Metro-Dade Aviation Department (no date), *The History of Miami International Airport*, Miami: MDAD.

Metro-Dade County Aviation Department (1997a), *Miami International Airport Top Trade Partners*, Miami: MDCAD.

Metro-Dade Aviation Department (1997b), *Miami International Airport: 1997–98 Directory*, Miami: MDAD.

Metro-Dade Aviation Department (1998a), *Miami International Airport: Competitor Airport Series 1998*, Miami: MDAD.

Miami-Dade Aviation Department (1998b), *Miami International Airport: U.S. and Worldwide Airport Rankings*, Miami: MDAD.

Navarro, M. (1998), Miami Grappling with Corruption', *New York Times*, 2 June, p. A1.

New York Times (1998), 28 August, p. A17.

Office of the Mayor, Miami-Dade County (1998), *Creating a Blueprint for Miami-Dade's Economic Future*, Miami: Office of the Mayor.

One Community One Goal (1997a) *Industries Blueprint*, Miami: OCOG.

One Community One Goal (1997b), *Report to the Community: Executive Summary,* Miami: OCOG.

Port of Miami (1998a), *Port of Miami 1998 Official Directory*, Miami: Port of Miami.

Port of Miami (1998b), *State of the Port*, Miami: Port of Miami.

Rieff, D. (1987), *Going to Miami*, Boston: Little, Brown and Company.

Strategy Research Corporation (1998), *Visitor Profile and Tourism Impact, Greater Miami and the Beaches: 1997 Annual Report*, Miami: SRC, p. 16.

US Bureau of the Census (1991), *State and Metropolitan Area Data Book 1991*, Washington, DC: US Government Printing Office.

US Bureau of the Census (1998), *State and Metropolitan Area Data Book 1997–98*, Washington, DC: US Government Printing Office.

Westlund, R. (1998), 'Hands Across The Water', *Miami Business*, July–August, p.32.

Wyly, E.K., N.J. Glickman and M.L. Lahr (1998), 'A top 10 list of things to know about American cities', *Cityscape*, **3** (3), 7–32.

8. Vancouver: a Multifunctional North American Gateway Region Linking Three Continents

Michael A. Goldberg

INTRODUCTION

Since its inception in 1886, Vancouver has been Canada's Pacific gateway, a function it has augmented significantly during the past century. For example, in the first quarter of 1989, for the first time in its history, British Columbia (BC) exported more goods and services to Asia than it did to the United States (41 percent to Asia-Pacific versus 40 percent to the US). That same year Macmillan Bloedel, the province's largest company, announced it would sell more lumber to Japan than to the US, also a first. Lastly, until May 1995 when the Canada–US 'Open Skies Agreement' came into effect, there were more Asian cities served by non-stop flights from Vancouver (8) than continental US cities (7).

This paper details Vancouver's multifunctional gateway role linking three continents, Asia, Europe and North America, through trade, travel and immigration. Below, we explore Vancouver's evolution as a diverse multifunctional gateway and speculate on its future role in the growing network of global cities.

GEOGRAPHIC AND HISTORICAL CONTEXT

Vancouver is located just north of the US border at 49° north latitude and 123° west longitude. It is blessed with a mild climate ranging from lows of roughly 0°C in the winter and infrequent snow, to summer highs in the high 20s°C. The city lies on the great circle route between the west coast of North America and Asia, giving both the port and the airport a major competitive edge. It is equidistant from Western Europe and East Asia, with excellent daily non-stop flights to major European and Asian centers and with easy telecommunication access in a normal working day, in the morning to Europe and in the afternoon to Asia.

The Pacific Rim has always been central to the city. The Canadian Pacific Railroad linked Atlantic Canada to the Pacific in 1886 (Morley, 1974). A century later Vancouver emerged globally with the city's 100th birthday and EXPO '86, an international transportation and telecommunications fair. Since then, Vancouver has developed a global outlook and verges on becoming a truly global city, largely arising from the gateway functions focused on here.

VANCOUVER'S ECONOMIC CONTEXT AND CHALLENGES

Before exploring Vancouver as a multifunctional gateway, it is important to examine its economic context, which is both a driver and outcome of its diversifying gateway roles. The 'old' Vancouver economy has historically been linked to the province's resource-based commodity economy, producing homogeneous products at world market prices. This commodity price-taking setting focused attention on engineering, cost and production issues and was very volatile. The economy was based on relatively few commodities, yielded abundant rents for government, labor and capital, was largely dependent on a few export markets (the US, Japan and Korea), and pursued a low-cost commodity production strategy.

The emerging 'new' economy is very different, if poorly understood, being entrepreneurial and niche-focused, and built on differentiated and branded products and services which allow greater control of pricing than under the commodity strategy. A number of sectors have been outstanding performers and exemplars of this new economy.

While the exemplary sectors of the 'new' economy can only be touched upon here, they do represent a major shift from commodities. To begin with, tourism is one of the major economic accomplishments of the past decade: a diversified $8.5 billion industry catering to business travelers, conventions and vacationers enjoying cruise ships, golf and skiing, entertainment, and increasingly nature and adventure tourism. Technology-based sectors have also grown dramatically to the point where they are important elements of the Vancouver economy, so that by the end of 1997 technology employment had grown to 57,000, with revenue generated by the technology sector reaching $7.6 billion, both growing by 22 percent per year compounded since 1995.

An array of knowledge-based services underpins the Vancouver economy today, including: software and information technology; consulting engineering; architecture and design; finance, insurance and real estate; health and education (especially post-secondary schooling); transportation and communication services; cultural industries and entertainment including theatre, music and film. On the manufacturing side, new sectors include: biotechnology; software, systems engineering and electronics; high-value food products such as wines, hot-house vegetables and berries; and most recently aerospace. Together, these sectors point to a very different kind of economy and are solid building blocks for a competitive future global economy.

Despite the successful transformation of the regional economy and its diversification into new activities, there are significant challenges facing the region and the provincial hinterland. First, there is still a large cyclical resource-based element in the provincial economy. Second, the province and the region are high-tax jurisdictions with rigid rent-seeking labor laws hindering the transition to a knowledge-based competitive economy. The political polarization that typifies provincial and regional politics between pro-labor and pro-business factions shows no sign of abating, which severely retards the continued evolution of the regional economy.

VANCOUVER'S STRENGTHS AS A GATEWAY AND INTERNATIONAL BUSINESS CENTER

Before reviewing Vancouver's current gateway functions, it is useful to review briefly some of the general strengths that it possesses to serve all of these functions.

Service activities in general have accounted for the major share of employment growth in the Vancouver economy over the recent past. The head office complex in downtown Vancouver, a strong public sector presence, and a regional population of 2.9 million people have encouraged the rise of a vigorous producer service sector (Hutton, 1998). Services to business management, in particular, may well be a sector in which the Vancouver economy is developing a comparative advantage. This is enhanced by the known economic linkages of this sector with the service sectors in which the Vancouver economy has been estimated to possess comparative advantages, i.e. trade, finance and commerce (Davis and Goldberg, 1988; Hutton and Davis, 1985). It is also enhanced by Vancouver's locational attributes *vis-à-vis* Asia.

Vancouver's location on the 'Great Circle Route' to Asia places the city strategically on major air and sea routes from Western North America to Tokyo, Seoul, Hong Kong, Taiwan, Shanghai and Singapore. The city thus should be a major hub for travel to Asia from North America, and even from Western Europe. The Pacific time zone allows a normal working day to bridge working hours in London, New York and Asia – of particular interest to financial firms, but advantageous to services generally. Telecommunications are also essential. Again, the metropolitan area is extremely well served.

The city's Pacific Rim location has also meant development, as noted above, of long-term broad commercial and trading ties with the Asia-Pacific region. Given this set of cultural, historical and economic linkages with the region, it is clear why Vancouver is the site of Canada's Asia-Pacific Founda-tion and the UBC Institute of Asian Research, which are matched by complementary units at Simon Fraser University and the University of Victoria. Add in diverse Asian ethnic, social and cultural institutions, a bevy of Asian restaurants, and numerous Asian language and cultural programs, and a very significant advantage emerges for understanding and dealing with the Asia-Pacific area.

From the above discussion, Vancouver clearly possesses attributes of an international service center, particularly for the Pacific Rim. It may also have a special role as an international 'honest broker', simultaneously being on the Pacific Rim, but not in Asia, and being in North America, but not in the United States, consistent with the thesis put forward by MacLeod et al. (1993) that Vancouver lies on the edge of the Pacific, of North America, of the resource frontier wilderness and of the western US. Vancouver can capitalize on Canada's lack of geopolitical aspirations to become a Pacific Rim service and management center without the high costs of such Asian centers as Tokyo, Taipei and Hong Kong, and without some of the racial and public safety problems in US west coast cities.

THE DIVERSE GATEWAY FUNCTIONS SERVED BY THE GREATER VANCOUVER REGION

Given the foregoing background, we explore the diverse gateway roles that the Vancouver region performs and is positioning itself to perform in the future. The theme of this paper is that Vancouver serves many gateway functions at once. Below we document Vancouver's gateway roles in: transportation; tourism and travel; immigration; education; government; and business, trade, finance and investment. These are key elements of the emerging 'new' economy just cited.

Transportation Gateway (and Hub) Functions

International ports and airports have always been a Canadian federal responsibility. This has in the past hampered Vancouver's port and airport development because of the distance from Ottawa, the national capital, and the control exercised by federal bureaucrats. However, the situation has changed significantly in the past decade with the devolution of power to the quasi-autonomous Vancouver Port Corporation (VPC) and the Vancouver International Airport Authority (VIAA or YVR in code letters) which have allowed both to obtain needed capital for infrastructural improvements and modernization.

Two significant events in the past seven years have led to the rapid evolution of YVR to its current status as a major North American international gateway. The first was its devolution as a local authority in July 1992, which allowed it to invest in a spectacular and efficient new international terminal and a second runway.

The second was the signing of the 'Open Skies Agreement' with the United States which more than tripled the number of US cities which could be reached by non-stop flights from Vancouver. Table 8.1 sets out the dramatic growth of Vancouver International Airport between 1992 and 1997. Some two dozen major airlines (and another two dozen regional and local airlines) provide non-stop service from Vancouver to six cities in Europe, nine cities in Asia, more than two dozen cities in the United States, and a dozen cities in Canada.

Table 8.1 YVR aircraft movements and passenger and cargo volume, 1992–97

Year	Aircraft movements	Passenge volumer	Cargo volume
1992	290,297	9,935,285	144,405
1997	343,068	14,818,564	260,773

Source: Vancouver International Airport Authority, YVR Vistas (Vancouver: Vancouver International Airport Authority), www.yvr.ca/general info/facts, various years.

The Port of Vancouver is by far the largest in Canada, and the largest on the west coast of the Americas by tonnage. It is emerging as a powerful container port with the recent doubling in container capacity from the creation of a new state-of-the-art container terminal.

Table 8.2 depicts the rapid growth of the Port's diverse international focus. These tables (Table 8.1 and 8.2) illustrate two aspects of the Port: first, its diversity as a gateway for bulk cargo, containers and passengers; second, its rapid growth, especially in containers and cruise ships.

One last transportation gateway function that needs to be noted is the increasingly important 'land bridge' function which links rail, road and air cargo modes. This multi-modal interface is of growing importance in providing North American gateways with a competitive edge, wherein cargoes, especially containers, can be off-loaded from planes and ships and trucked to destinations in the interior of North America more quickly and cheaply than if they had to be moved either by air or through the Panama Canal.

Table 8.2 Port of Vancouver tonnage handled and country of origin/destination, 1997

Country	Total tonnage ('000 metric tonnes)	Country	Container tonnage ('000 metric tonnes)
Japan	22,683	Japan	1,719
South Korea	8,190	Taiwan	862
China	4,004	Hong Kong	860
Brazil	3,092	China	631
United States	2,999	South Korea	450
Taiwan	2,446	Thailand	258
Mexico	1,601	Indonesia	157
Great Britain	1,595	Philippines	152
Italy	1,535	Malaysia	133
Indonesia	1,504	India	124

Source: Vancouver Port Corporation, Planning and Statistics, 1997 Statistics Overview, www.portvancouver.com

Vancouver's DeltaPort container facility and the larger YVR cargo operations both have superb access to US interstate highways. Combined with Vancouver's Great Circle Route location this creates a major cost advantage for cargo shipped through either VPC or YVR. Some 22 shipping and 13 bulk lines connect Vancouver globally.

Tourism and Travel Gateway Functions

Tourism is one of the major economic successes of the last decade: it is an $8.5 billion industry and the second largest employer in the province, and the largest industry in the Vancouver region. The 'products' offered range from urban Victoria and Vancouver, to cruise ships, golf and skiing, entertainment, winery visits, and nature and adventure tourism. The median location between Europe and Asia again gives easy air access to these continents and all of North America.

Table 8.3 Visitors to Greater Vancouver selected country of origin, 1993, 1995 and 1997

Origin	1993	1995	1997
Canada	3,821,531	4,224,657	4,571,678
USA	1,528,016	1,724,921	1,874,883
Japan	196,780	277,036	284,273
Hong Kong	60,107	94,206	85,175
South Korea	13,852	68,840	75,066
Taiwan	27,748	51,437	110,247
UK	113,868	145,787	155,221
Germany	92,764	118,793	108,649
Other	265,506	347,795	495,802
Total visitors	6,120,172	7,053,472	7,760,994

Source: Business in Vancouver, Market Facts Book 1998, Issue 459A–1998, www.bic.com/marketfacts

Sophisticated tourism promotion, new product development, and the expansion of Vancouver's convention center should make tourism more important in the future, aided by the low Canadian dollar, which discourages Canadian travel abroad and encourages foreign tourism in Canada. The rapid growth of the industry and its composition can be gleaned from Table 8.3. Interestingly, Japan has supplanted the United Kingdom as the largest source of non-North American visitors, which together with Taiwan and Korea outpaces all other source countries.

As with the port and airport, we can trace recent tourism development to a key event: the 1986 transportation and communications EXPO held in Vancouver. Before 1986, tourism was very much aimed at the lower end of the market such as camping and budget motels. Post-EXPO '86 this changed and the concerted efforts of Tourism Vancouver, Tourism BC, and the tourist industry have repositioned tourism at the higher-priced end of the tourism market, while greatly diversifying the visitor base, adding Asian visitors to those from the US, the UK and Germany.

Immigration Gateway Functions

Vancouver has always served as a major immigration gateway due to its port and airport. The nature of immigration has changed dramatically during the past quarter century, however, as can be seen from the data in Tables 8.4 through 8.6. First, looking at Table 8.4, we see the significant variation in total immigration over the 1990s both from the rest of Canada and internationally.

Table 8.4 Population change for British Columbia, 1991–97

Year	Net inter-provincial migration	Net international migration	Total net migration	Natural increase	Total increase
1991	34,572	25,130	59,702	21,635	75,673
1992	39,578	29,994	69,572	21,541	93,779
1993	37,595	38,883	76,478	20,262	95,795
1994	34,449	41,978	76,427	21,059	100,862
1995	23,414	37,078	60,492	20,445	89,114
1996	20,665	43,142	63,807	18,715	85,213
1997	7,094	40,202	47,296	18,675	64,594

Source: Ministry of Finance and Corporate Relations, BC Stats, 'Migration Highlights' (Victoria: Ministry of Finance and Corporate Relations), March 1998, www.bcstats.gov.bc.ca

Inter-provincial migration is particularly volatile, being very sensitive to BC's economy relative to neighboring Alberta and Ontario. Alberta's and Ontario's fortunes improved dramatically relative to British Columbia during the 1990s, with a dramatic decline in net inter-provincial migration as a result. International migration has held up, though, in the 40,000 range.

Another important facet of the changing pattern of immigration is source countries. Comparing Tables 8.5 and 8.6 is instructive in this vein. Table 8.5 shows ethnic origins from the censuses of 1996 and 1991.

Even over this five-year period one can see a significant decline in the proportion of people claiming European ethnic origins, with 'French' being the only exception, reflecting the growing French Canadian population in BC.

Table 8.6 shows recent immigrant landings for 1997 and a very different picture emerges. There were 37,562 immigrants from Asia or 74 percent of BC's total that year. European immigrants numbered a mere 5,200 or 11 percent, one-seventh of the total in 1997.

Taken together, these tables demonstrate the dramatic change in immigration that has occurred since the late 1960s. The first 25 years following the Second World War led to significant immigration from Western Europe. Indeed, only in 1991 did people claiming Chinese ethnic origin outnumber those claiming German ethnic origin for the first time.

Table 8.5 Top 10 single response ethnic origins for BC, 1996 (1991 in parentheses)

Ethnic origin	Number	% of total pop.	% of single
British	515,000 (812,470)	14 (25)	25 (42)
Canadian	357,280 (303,200)	10 (9)	17 (15)
Chinese	280,585 (181,185)	8 (6)	14 (9)
German	130,330 (156,635)	4 (5)	6 (8)
East Indian	120,645 (89,265)	3 (3)	6 (5)
Aboriginal	76,430 (74,420)	2 (2)	4 (4)
Dutch	60,765 (66,525)	2 (2)	3 (3)
French	47,910 (68,795)	1 (2)	2 (4)
Italian	46,525 (49,265)	1 (2)	2 (3)
Ukranian	40,650 (52,760)	1 (2)	2 (3)
Total single	2,064,200 (1,952,855)	56 (60)	100
Total pop.	3689755 (3,247505)	100	

Source: Ministry of Finance and Corporate Relations, BC Stats, '1996 Census Fast Facts: Focus on Ethnicity of BC Population' (Victoria: Ministry of Finance and Corporate Relations), March 1998, www.bcstats.gov.bc.ca

Table 8.6 Immigrant landings to BC and Canada, 1997

Source	Vancouver area	Total BC	Canada	Canada: BC as %
Europe	3,734	5,200	38,840	13.4
Africa	1,339	1,533	14,498	10.6
Asia	33,770	37,562	138,148	27.2
Hong Kong	8,362	8,631	22,236	38.8
Taiwan	8,949	9,128	13,313	68.6
India	3,463	5,303	19,584	27.1
Australasia	335	473	1,408	33.6
N&C America	1,179	1,789	8,676	20.6
USA	649	1,109	5,032	22.0
Caribbean	109	160	8,199	2.0
South America	365	449	5,693	7.9
Oceania	296	345	621	55.6
Not stated	26	34	218	15.6
All areas	41,153	47,545	216,301	22.0

Source: Ministry of Finance and Corporate Relations, BC Stats, 'Migration Highlights' (Victoria: Ministry of Finance and Corporate Relations), March 1998, www.bcstats.gov.bc.ca

Table 8.5 supports these comments as it shows very large numbers of Western Europeans in 1996 and 1991, though the numbers are declining significantly with the passage of time in both relative and absolute terms as aging Western European immigrants die off and as Asian immigration grows.

Educational Gateway Functions

Vancouver is a very attractive educational gateway. The local schools have developed exceptional expertise in educating students with English as a second language (ESL) as a result of the large influx of non-English-speaking immigrants in the past two decades. The region's post-secondary schools are also popular with foreign students: tuition is reasonable, particularly in light of the weak Canadian dollar, and the quality of the establishments is also good. The region possesses two major research universities and half a dozen baccalaureate-degree-granting colleges. The scale and growth of the educational gateway can be gathered from Table 8.7, which shows the numbers of foreign students studying by type of establishment, a number which nearly tripled between 1985 and 1995.

Table 8.7 Number and percentage distribution of international students in British Columbia by host province and level of study, 1985, 1990 and 1995

Year	Elementary/ secondary		College		Under- graduate		Graduate		Total	
	No.	%	No.	%	No.	%	No.	%	No.	%
1995	5,734	21.8	5,452	36.6	1,944	10.7	2,056	15.6	15,186	20.9
1990	5,200	19.8	2,859	16.2	1,613	7.9	1,807	12.2	11,479	14.5
1985	2,534	18.4	563	10.3	1,197	5.8	1,047	11.1	5,368	10.8

Source: Statistics Canada, Cat. No. 81-261, 'International Student Participation in Canadian Education' 1998.

British Columbia also increased sharply its share of Canada's foreign student population. What the data do not reveal is the enormous change in attitude that has taken place during the 1990s in relation to foreign students. Virtually all post-secondary schools are actively seeking international students, both to earn higher foreign student tuition fees and to broaden the educational experience of domestic students by internationalizing the learning environment.

Vancouver's multicultural population, its excellent global access, and its global view have all helped to make Vancouver an attractive locale for international students and this gateway function can be expected to increase significantly in years to come as a result.

Government Gateway Functions

Government is another interesting gateway function that Vancouver performs. From a Canadian perspective, Vancouver is the national gateway to Asia. The federally supported Asia-Pacific Foundation resides here, as do the provincially supported International Commercial Arbitration Centre (ICAC), International Finance Centre (IFC) Vancouver, and the International Maritime Centre (IMC). IFC Vancouver, ICAC and IMC were all created to foster Vancouver's gateway function through federal and provincial legislation. In addition, Vancouver is home to 21 foreign consulates and 11 foreign government trade commissions/organizations. Taken together, this represents a formidable recognition by governments in Canada and abroad of Vancouver's gateway function for governments.

Business, Trade, Finance and Investment Gateway (and Network Hub) Functions

The final gateway function to be considered is Vancouver as an international commercial trade and commercial gateway. There are several dimensions to Vancouver's growing role in international commerce. Looking at financial functions first, there are 23 foreign banks with branches, representative offices or headquarters in Vancouver, including that of the most profitable and largest foreign bank, the Hongkong Bank of Canada. In addition, there are 7 foreign investment dealers and an additional 5 foreign investment advisors with offices or their Canadian headquarters in Vancouver. At the last count there were 19 non-American foreign airline offices active in the city with another 9 US airlines with active offices as well. Finally, there are 16 business organizations which meet monthly with the goal of building ties between Vancouver or Canada and foreign economies. The Hong Kong Canada Business Association is the biggest of these, with almost a thousand members, but all the economies of Asia and Western Europe are active, building on the immigration patterns noted above from Europe pre-1970 and Asia afterwards.

Taking a more statistical view, Table 8.8 provides data on business immigrants coming to Vancouver under the entrepreneurial and investor classes. Three features are notable: first, Asian source countries dominate; second, Taiwan is rapidly overtaking Hong Kong as the principal source country; and third, the sums are non-trivial, totaling some C$2 billion in 1997.

Table 8.8 Total BC business immigrants visaed abroad – entrepreneur and
immigrant investor programs

Country of last permanent residence	1996 No. of cases	1996 Total funds ($'000)	1997 No. of cases	1997 Total funds ($'000)
Hong Kong	762	1,050,875	449	864,098
Taiwan	506	1,072,282	357	633,886
South Korea	79	117,775	60	84,852
China (PRC)	31	33,663	48	80,181
Other	369	569,701	311	403,738
Total	1,747	2,844,296	1,225	2,067,255

Source: Ministry of Finance and Corporate Relations, BC Stats, 'Immigration Highlights' (Victoria: Ministry of Finance and Corporate Relations), April 1998, www.bcstats.gov.bc.ca

Table 8.9 BC origin exports to selected destinations ($ mill.)

Source	1994	1995	1996	1997
United Kingdom	321	386	336	288
Germany	466	694	404	468
PR of China	305	499	514	447
Hong Kong	192	271	258	352
Taiwan	361	482	354	457
Japan	5,658	6,768	6,403	6,005
South Korea	738	982	866	953
India	58	77	50	65
Australia	262	298	243	236
Mexico	77	54	50	63
United States	12,355	13,293	13,883	14,865
Other	2042	3,108	2,380	2,550
Total international exports	22,834	26,911	25,742	26,748

Source: Ministry of Finance and Corporate Relations, BC Stats, 'Exports (BC Origin): 1988–1997' (Victoria: Ministry of Finance and Corporate Relations), June 1998, www.bcstats.gov.vc.ca

Lastly, turning to Table 8.9, we see a reasonably diversified pattern of trade flows, with the US accounting for 56 percent of BC origin exports, Japan and Korea together accounting for another 24 percent and the remaining 30 percent split quite equally between Europe and other parts of Asia. This contrasts markedly with Canada's national trading pattern, where more than 80 percent of Canadian exports go to the US and in Ontario just over 90 percent of its exports are US-bound (mostly auto parts).

DEVELOPMENT AND GATEWAY STRATEGIES

The Federal and Provincial Roles

Vancouver's success in internationalizing its gateway functions was not accidental but rather the result of significant efforts on the part of both the public and private sectors. Perhaps the most important here was the previously noted EXPO '86 event which really opened Vancouver to the world, both in terms of putting Vancouver on people's global maps and in terms of opening local minds to the possibilities that existed in broadening their views, especially across the Pacific.

Following closely was the Asia-Pacific Initiative (API), formed in 1987 as a joint effort between the federal, provincial and private sectors to explore the possibilities for internationalizing Vancouver's economy and world outlook.

The International Commercial Arbitration Centre (ICAC), the International Financial Centre (IFC) Vancouver, the International Maritime Centre (IMC), the devolution of Vancouver International Airport and the Vancouver Port Corporation, and the numerous trade missions to Asia and Europe by provincial trade ministers with the support of the Vancouver Board of Trade all flowed from API recommendations.

API also suggested that greater autonomy for federal agencies such as Canada Customs and the Department of Transportation (which owns major ports and airports), as well as the relocation to Vancouver of all or significant parts of those federal agencies with a large Pacific Rim focus would help (e.g., the Export Development Corporation (EDC), the Canadian International Development Agency (CIDA), and the International Development Research Council (IDRC).

To realize its gateway functions in the future Vancouver will indeed need more decision-making capacity. Moving meaningful federal gateway decision-making capacity to Vancouver is as important now as in 1988–90 when API first broached the issue.

Vancouver's Economic Strategy-Making

Complementing these federal, provincial and private sector efforts were recommendations by the Vancouver Economic Advisory Commission that the City of Vancouver be more active in seeking out global links, particularly in Asia, but also in Europe, building on earlier immigrant ties. The initial strategy sought to build on the region's strengths as a provider of services to the provincial and western Canadian economies, and to promote the city's role as a key link between Canada and the Pacific Rim. Policies were established dealing with Vancouver's position as an international center of finance and business communications, tourism and other service industry exports (Vancouver Economic Advisory Commission, 1983).

In 1988 the original VEAC strategy was extended and revised. First, the overall objective was restated with the objective of developing Vancouver as Canada's 'Pacific Rim Gateway' and as a center for trade, finance, travel, and tourism (VEAC, 1989). Second, it was decided that Vancouver should concentrate on specific policies and plans such as building on links developed in the 1980s with 13 Pacific Rim cities, both under its sister city relations and through other government and commercial contacts.

Regional Economic Strategies

At the same time that the VEAC unveiled its revised strategy, the Greater Vancouver Regional District (GVRD, comprising the City and 16 surrounding municipalities) was developing its own economic vision and action plan for the wider metropolitan area (Stevenson Kellogg Ernst and Whinney, 1988). Since no part of metropolitan Vancouver can function independently, this year 2000 vision complemented the City's Pacific Rim strategy above, while recognizing the residential and manufacturing functions of the outer municipalities. These largely public sector initiatives were strongly supported by leading private sector organizations such as the Vancouver Board of Trade, the Hong Kong Canada Business Association, and half a dozen other very active Asian-oriented business organizations.

Vancouver and the GVRD took steps to implement a number of supporting activities aimed at upgrading the region's community and economic infrastructure – often in conjunction with provincial government funding and program agencies. Thus it was recognized that to succeed, the strategic initiatives mentioned above required efficient transportation and communication services. Consequently, the City worked with the GVRD and provincial agencies to upgrade port, rail and arterial road systems in the region and the Greater Vancouver Transportation Committee called on the province to spend C\$825 million, between 1991 and 1996, on road improvements and bridge widening.

In the intervening eight years, the planned transportation investments were largely put in place: the region's LRT was extended southeast across the Fraser River into the booming city of Surrey; a new commuter rail link is still under development to the exploding northeastern portions of the urban area; new freeways were opened and bus and car pool lanes added. Hundreds of new buses swell the region's transit fleet; and improved river and harbor crossings are in the planning and design stages. Additionally, a new Greater Vancouver Transportation Authority (GVTA) was created in 1998 by the provincial government to take over responsibility for all regional transportation planning and operation in the region, most notably the development of an LRT extension to the booming Northeast Sector centered in Coquitlam.

Planning policy in the GVRD's 'Liveable Region Plan' focused on decentralizing downtown work and cultural opportunities to regional centers (GVRD, 1976 and 1993). The planning strategy explicitly encouraged the development of a multi-nuclear metropolitan structure through establishing Regional Town Centres (RTCs). Four new Regional Town Centres for the metropolitan area were designated in this way: Burnaby-Metrotown and New Westminster in the inner suburbs, and Coquitlam Centre and Whalley-Guildford (City of Surrey) in the outer suburbs.

Office suburbanization is significant, with major gains recorded in Burnaby, North Vancouver City, Richmond, Surrey and Delta, whereas the older suburban centers experienced a relative decline in this period (Map 8.1). Nonetheless, apart from successful development at Burnaby-Metrotown, and the emergence of Surrey's Whalley area as 'Surrey City Centre' with the LRT terminus there, the regional town center plan is not leading to the tightly patterned multi-nuclearization envisioned by the Liveable Region Plan (GVRD, 1989; Hutton, 1998, p. 104–16).

Partly in response to the failure to achieve all of the major initial Liveable Region Goals and partly in response to the dramatic changes in the Vancouver, British Columbia and global economies, the GVRD initiated a review and update of its earlier plan. The 1990 'Creating our Future' plan stressed environmental protection, creation of six RTCs (as opposed to four earlier), with recognition that the Vancouver central business district (CBD) was a unique regional asset (GVRD, 1993). 'Creating the Future' builds directly on the earlier Liveable Region Plan and reinforces many of its goals in the context of the greatly changed 1990s.

It demonstrates that considerable knowledge about growth management and infrastructure investment was gained in the 15 years between the two planning exercises. 'Creating our Future' is expected to lead to a series of communities built around the six RTCs and the CBD in a more flexible and sustainable manner than the more mechanistic 1975 'Liveable Region Plan'. By extension, efforts are under way to put Vancouver and the metropolitan region in a broader provincial and northwest regional context so that planning can be done more effectively.

Other Related Economic Strategy-Making Efforts

Paralleling these governmental efforts, the airport and port have developed significant plans to extend their global reach and enhance the scope and scale of their gateway functions. The VIAA has subsidiaries that manage airports around the world, that design and market airport services globally, and that plan for the future of the VIAA itself. The Port has similarly taken a long-term and broad view of its role in planning for the future and building on its past.

Lastly, even provincial universities are redefining their role in global terms, which strongly complements these other internationalization and planning efforts.

POLITICAL AND OTHER OBSTACLES TO REALIZING STRATEGIES AND GOALS

Vancouver has enjoyed great success in developing a range of gateway functions linking three continents. However, problems face the city and its region at present and in the immediate future, and serve as obstacles to realizing fully its multi-functional gateway potential.

These obstacles are of four sorts: those that are self-generated and basically internal to the region; those deriving from the provincial economy and government; those that are external to the region deriving from being in Canada; and those that are global in origin.

City of Vancouver and Greater Vancouver Regional Obstacles

City of Vancouver obstacles

Vancouver was a pioneer in developing an economic strategy two decades ago. Despite that promising early start, in the past decade the Vancouver Economic Advisory Commission (VEAC) withered and in 1998 was phased out and replaced by a still struggling Vancouver Economic Development Commission (VEDC).

With the demise of the VEAC came the end of the city's Economic Development Office and thereby active development and promotion of economic strategy for Vancouver. As a result, the city lacks any kind of urban economic vision or strategy. The VEDC is underfunded and must itself set its goals and public–private financial arrangements. The absence of a clear economic strategy hinders the city's ability to broaden and deepen its gateway functions and understand better their relationship to the urban economy more generally.

Intraregional obstacles and difficulties

The lack of clear and contemporary economic strategy is not only a weakness of the city of Vancouver, but one affecting the urban region, too. Current regional economic development policy is best characterized as being uncoordinated with much harmful intraregional competition.

Among the specific problems facing the region as a result are the growing inadequacy of the regional transportation system, increasing sprawl and congestion, and lack of any goals to promote an efficient urban form. Additionally, there are awkward regional intergovernmental links. Specifically, the relationship with the province is at best strained and certainly not cooperative.

There are also overlapping regional functions, which make coordination difficult. For example, in addition to the new Greater Vancouver Transportation Authority (GVTA) there is a Greater Vancouver Hospital District (GVHD), a Greater Vancouver Regional Parks District (GVRPD) and a Greater Vancouver Water and Sewer District (GVSWD), which are reasonably independent of each other.

The absence of an overall land use and economic planning group makes it difficult to coordinate these bodies and mold them into a truly effective metropolitan government.

British Columbia Obstacles

British Columbia has long been experiencing wide political swings between free enterprise and pro-labor socialist governments. The political climate has become especially unfriendly of late with the province's weak economy showing further signs of weakening from an ideologically based rent-seeking provincial government which includes support for rent-seeking and rigid labor legislation.

The current government, the New Democratic Party (NDP), is a European-style social democratic government with strong ties to labor. It embraces rent-seeking both by government and labor, shifting labor legislation toward organized labor by making it easier to unionize under the

Labour Code, while raising the costs of using non-union workers through the Employment Standards Act.

The NDP clings to a dated vision of the provincial economy, favoring heavily unionized resource and manufacturing industries over new sectors. Thus the province has spent hundreds of millions of dollars to support inefficient pulp- and sawmills, and great political capital boosting a small and dwindling unionized ocean fishery, while failing to support aquaculture and the province's booming technology sector. It has also acceded to labor demands to apply the industrially-based Employment Standards Act to technology firms in order to limit hours of work and use industrial occupational safety and insurance costs to a sector for which they are dysfunctional.

Regrettably, the private sector is not much further ahead in developing new visions. The resource sector has not shifted from its commodity focus. There has been little understanding that stronger environmental controls are the future for resource extraction, necessitating a shift to higher-value niches because rising costs preclude competing in low-value commodities in the future.

Not surprisingly, the province has a very poor labor–management climate where both sides appear to be stuck in 1930s views of each other. This has discouraged flexible and new approaches from both sides and adversely affected investment and productivity.

Business investment and productivity have badly lagged Canada and the OECD during the 1990s. The provincial capital tax discourages investment, while the pro-labor stance of the government has raised the costs of hiring and retaining labor. The net effect has been falling productivity and rising costs per person employed.

The regulatory environment is in part responsible for low levels of investment and for declining productivity. Provincial economic regulation has grown dramatically, almost doubling since the NDP came to power in late 1991. This has helped raise costs, lower productivity, and weaken the competitiveness of a provincial economy where trade accounts for 40 percent of its GDP.

In addition, provincial fiscal management has been poor, with rising government spending and debt, leading to lower debt ratings from Canadian and US debt agencies. During the NDP tenure, provincial debt has almost doubled while other Canadian provinces and the government of Canada have run budget surpluses, and begun shrinking debt and lowering taxes.

One final and unique source of provincial weakness stems from the current treaty negotiations with Aboriginal groups in British Columbia. Because the province, unlike the rest of Canada, never entered into formal treaties with its Aboriginal peoples, these negotiations are under way now, with the first of dozens of such treaties ready for adoption by the Nish'ga people in northwestern British Columbia and the province of British Columbia. The negotiations have put in limbo the status of many millions of hectares of land, which further discourages investment.

Canadian Obstacles

Obstacles standing in the way of fully realizing its gateway role also arise from merely being in Canada, where the lack of vision and the high degree of centralization by Ontario-based financial institutions hinder the flow of capital and decision-making to Vancouver. There is still a poor understanding of the needs of the Western Canadian economy and the opportunities that exist in Vancouver for positioning Canada more strongly in the global economy. Low Canadian productivity growth and paltry R&D investment further hamper Vancouver's development.

Global Obstacles

Earlier it was noted that the British Columbia and Vancouver economies still rely heavily on commodity exports. As a result, the economy is heavily dependent on global commodity cycles completely outside the influence of the province. This has been exacerbated by the Asian, Russian and more recent Brazilian economic crises, which have depressed demand for commodities and flooded global markets, lowering prices and quantities further. This reinforces the argument made at the outset for the need to move more boldly into new activity and get out from under the present commodity- and resource-dependent forest and mining sectors.

CONCLUSIONS AND A LOOK FORWARD

Vancouver has already made significant progress in developing a diversity of gateway functions as documented above. The dramatic growth of the airport and seaport illustrates some of the major successes of the past decade. Major obstacles must be overcome, though, before Vancouver can realize its full potential as a multi-functional gateway linking North America, Asia and Europe. The current business downturn is notably hindering progress. The severity of the current slump (while the rest of Canada grows nicely) is stimulating a diversity of inquiries, which are searching for new and denser global connections and new economic metaphors, paradigms and strategies.

Given Vancouver's location and Asian–European bridge functions, prospects to expand and deepen its gateway functions appear bright.

Broadening and deepening its gateway functions will likely be a central feature of any future development strategy. Vancouver's income and wealth have been tied to its traditional international trade and transportation roles. These provide a solid base for extending the growing tourism and Asia-Pacific service center roles that are being discussed widely at the present time. The success of current and future regional economic growth and diversification strategies will undoubtedly be closely tied to the gateway functions discussed in this chapter. Their success in turn should bolster these gateway functions.

REFERENCES

Davis, H.C. and M.A. Goldberg (1988), *Determination of the Comparative Advantages of Vancouver as an International City*, Asia Pacific Initiative, Vancouver.

Greater Vancouver Regional District (1976), *The Liveable Region, 1976–1986*, Greater Vancouver Regional District, Vancouver.

Greater Vancouver Regional District, (1989), *The Liveable Region, A Strategy For the 1990's*, Greater Vancouver Regional District, Development Services, Vancouver.

Greater Vancouver Regional District (1993), *Liveable Region Strategy: Proposals (A Strategy for Environmental Protection and Growth Management)*, Greater Vancouver Regional District, Strategic Planning Department, Burnaby.

Hutton, T.A. (1998), *The Transformation of Canada's Pacific Metropolis: A Study of Vancouver*, Montreal, Quebec: Institute for Research in Public Policy.

Hutton, T.A. and H.C. Davis (1985), 'The role of office location in regional town centre planning and metropolitan multinucleation', *Canadian Journal of Regional Science*, **8**, 17–34.

MacLeod, S., D. Edgington and T.G. McGee (1993), 'Vancouver on the edge: Vancouver and the outside world', in T.G. McGee and Y Kato (eds), *Vancouver and Yokohama: Emerging Cities in the Pacific Rim*, Yokohama: Yokohama City University, pp. 25–48.

Morley, A. (1974), *Vancouver: Milltown to Metropolis*, Vancouver: Mitchell Press.

Stevenson Kellogg Ernst and Whinney (1988), *Achieving Greater Vancouver's Potential: An Economic Vision and Action Plan for the Livable Region*, Greater Vancouver Regional District, Vancouver.

Vancouver Economic Advisory Commission (1983), *An Economic Strategy for Vancouver in the 1980s: Proposals for Policies and Implementation*, City of Vancouver, Vancouver, mimeo.

Vancouver Economic Advisory Commission (1989), *A Strategy for Vancouver's Economic Development in the 1990s*, City of Vancouver, Vancouver, mimeo.

PART THREE

Asia-Pacific Gateway Regions

9. Hong Kong as a Regional Strategic Hub for Manufacturing Multinationals[1]

Edmund R. Thompson

INTRODUCTION

The list of superlatives that can be applied to Hong Kong is long and, given the city's population of less than 7 million, impressive. Gross domestic product (GDP) increased over four-fold in the twenty-odd years from 1975 (Hong Kong Government). Per capita GDP is now amongst the highest in the world, at over $25,000 (Asiaweek, 1998). This level of wealth has been achieved by a highly internationally oriented economy, which has ensured that Hong Kong has increasingly acted as a bridge linking the Asia-Pacific and other world economies.

Despite its small size, Hong Kong is ranked the world's eighth largest trading economy. Its trade-to-GDP ratio, at 230 in 1997, is second only to that of Singapore's, which was 260 during the same year (Asian Development Bank, 1998). Hong Kong's trade with the rest of the Asia-Pacific grew to over $250 billion in 1997, far in excess of any other economy in the region, after annualized growth of nearly 20 percent from the early 1980s (Hong Kong Government). In terms of foreign direct investment (FDI), Hong Kong has been amongst the world's top five sources of outward investment every year since 1993 (UNCTAD). Hong Kong is the largest direct investor in Mainland China, accounting for over 50 percent of all foreign investments in the Mainland, whether measured in number of projects or cumulative value (Eng and Lin, 1996).

Hong Kong has also attracted substantial FDI from around the world and has become the Asia-Pacific's major center for foreign MNC regional headquarters (RHQs) and regional offices (ROs).[2] In 1998, over 800 foreign firm RHQs and more than 1,600 ROs were identified by the government of Hong Kong.[3] Just under 10 percent of these offices are accounted for by Mainland China firms using Hong Kong as a window into the rest of the world's economy. A further 25 percent are from other Asia-Pacific economies, predominantly Japan. But the vast majority, 65 percent, are accounted for by United States and European multinational corporations

169

(MNC). Unlike Singapore, Hong Kong has never had any governmental program or overt policy to attract or retain MNC offices (see Chapter 10 by Poon). Hence the MNCs that are in Hong Kong have been attracted by a combination of its geography and business environment. Geographically, Hong Kong is roughly in the middle of the Asia-Pacific. From a business environment perspective, Hong Kong has historically and famously established a reputation for being a highly liberal, transparently regulated, and free-wheeling business environment.[4] That business environment is now overwhelmingly a service-oriented, metropolitan economy (Enright, 1999). Services accounted for over 86 percent of GDP in 1997 (Hong Kong Government, 1998). Manufacturing contributed only around 7 percent of GDP, having shrunk from nearly 25 percent in 1980.[5]

Notwithstanding the service rather than manufacturing orientation of Hong Kong's economy, the city still has a high proportion of foreign manufacturing MNC's, RHQs and ROs. The research on which this chapter is based indicates that around 30 percent of US, Japanese and European MNCs in Hong Kong are manufacturing rather than service firms. A small proportion of these MNCs do sell into the local Hong Kong market, but that market is really too small to justify the presence of an office. An even smaller number manufacture in Hong Kong, but the cost of land and labor make this generally prohibitively expensive. Given this, it is clear that Hong Kong acts predominantly as some form of regional operating hub for the foreign manufacturing MNCs which have a presence in the city. However, precisely what manufacturing MNCs' offices in Hong Kong do, and over what geographical areas, is not known. The research on which this chapter is based was geared to finding out.[6]

WHY ARE MNCS IN THE ASIA-PACIFIC?

Consideration of what MNC RHQs in fact do in Hong Kong needs to begin with the question of why foreign firms are in the Asia-Pacific in the first place.[7] Theories of international firms broadly posit that firms expand across national borders for one or a combination of two reasons (Caves, 1996). First, firms may integrate vertically across national boundaries in order to exploit geographically disparate comparative advantages that cannot effectively be captured through trade (Hennart, 1991). Hence, with vertical internationalization of a firm, the value-adding activities that it internalizes are located where some form of comparative advantage exists. Such advantages may be the result of natural factor endowments, such as raw materials or cheap labor. Or these advantages might be the consequence of specialized local production having given rise to superior goods or services compared to what is available at a similar price elsewhere (Scott, 1998; Enright, 1998). Examples of this might be the precision, small-item engineering and manufacturing capability developed in Switzerland in relation to the concentration of jewelry and watch-making businesses, or the computer software services available in Silicon Valley (Saxenian, 1994). In both these locations nominal labor costs are high, but due to specialization, productivity levels are proportionately higher still.

A second cause of firms internationalizing across borders is horizontal integration to sell into foreign markets (Vernon, 1966). Here firms are not seeking to exploit location-dependent comparative advantages, but rather to exploit competitive advantages specific to their own products in the market place (Hymer, 1976).

Firms internalize production and selling in foreign markets when they cannot effectively exploit and retain their competitive advantages through exporting or licensing (Kindleberger, 1969). This is generally because of unique production and/or managerial processes that can only be performed by the firm, or because competitive advantages rely on factors which are appropriable by competitors if not tightly protected within the firm (Caves, 1971).

Competitor activities have also been shown to stimulate horizontal internationalization among firms in oligopolistic industries, such as those which chiefly characterize advanced industrial economies (Knickerbocker, 1973). In effect, if one domestic competitor moves into a foreign market, its domestic rivals will also enter the overseas markets, fearing that additional sales in new overseas markets will afford the first mover competitive advantage in the home market through economies of scale, increased efficiency of asset utilization and so on. Naturally, many firms internationalize both vertically and horizontally, following a locational structure which combines efforts to exploit both geographical comparative advantages and firm-specific competitive advantages (Dunning, 1977).

To discover to what extent MNCs with RHQs and ROs in Hong Kong are in the Asia-Pacific due respectively to vertical and or horizontal integration, firms were asked how important market- and production-related factors were in determining their presence in the region (See Table 9.1).

Overall, MNCs are primarily in the Asia-Pacific due to horizontal integration. On a scale of 1 to 5, with 1 being very unimportant and 5 being very important, 'market opportunities' obtains a mean of 4.72. 'Competitor activities' comes next with a score of 3.91. Both these variables are indicative of horizontal integration. The two variables relating to vertical integration score somewhat lower overall. 'Low-cost production' obtains a mean of 3.67, and 'raw materials' availability' scores only 3.13, making this variable only slightly above neutral.

Asia-Pacific Gateway Regions

Table 9.1 In deciding to have or maintain a presence in the Asia-Pacific region, how important generally do you think are the following for your parent company?

	All firms n=159	Japanese firms n=50	US firms n=49	European firms n=60
Market opportunities	4.72	4.73	4.71	4.73
Competitor activities	3.91	4.06	3.88	3.82
Low-cost production	3.67	4.38	3.37	3.34
Raw materials availability	3.13	3.76	2.73	2.92

Note: Figures represent mean scores; 1 = very unimportant, 2 = unimportant, 3 = neutral, 4 = important, 5 = very important.

Source: Author's survey.

There can be little question that MNCs from all the rich industrialized nations are first and foremost in the Asia-Pacific to sell. Japanese, US and European MNCs uniformly indicate a mean of just over 4.70 for market opportunities. However, there is some difference between Japanese and 'western' MNCs when it comes to the importance of competitor activities as a reason to be in the region. For Japanese firms, this variable scores a mean of over 4.05, whereas western firms average around 3.85.

However, this is explicable only by comparing the means of variables indicating vertical integration. Japanese firms may be in the Asia-Pacific to sell, but they would seem to be present to manufacture as well. Japanese MNCs score a mean of 4.38 for 'low-cost production', compared to an average of just 3.35 for western firms.

This is reinforced by Japanese MNCs scoring a mean of 3.76 for the variable 'raw materials' availability', which suggests this is also quite an important factor for such firms. This contrasts sharply with western MNCs for which availability of raw materials seems to be unimportant. European MNCs indicate a mean of just 2.92 for this variable, and US firms score an even lower mean of only 2.73.

Hence it would seem that if Japanese firms are slightly more driven by competitor activities to be in the region than western firms, it is not just competition for markets, but competition for lower factor costs that is driving them.

This finding concurs with general assertions that Japanese firms have internationalized partially in response to the rise of labor costs in the domestic economy and also as a way to obtain raw materials unavailable in Japan itself (Thompson and Poon, 1999; Kojima, 1978, 1995; Ozawa, 1979).

WHERE IN THE ASIA-PACIFIC ARE MNCS SELLING AND MAKING PRODUCTS?

If manufacturing MNCs with RHQs and ROs in Hong Kong are in the Asia-Pacific primarily for sales and secondarily for manufacturing reasons, it begs the question of where they sell and make products. Hong Kong, with its small population, both of consumers and, in relative terms, firms, particularly manufacturing firms, could hardly be considered a sufficient market in and of itself to justify any major presence. For some kinds of business service firms, such as accountancy and legal services, Hong Kong arguably represents a significant market. But this cannot be said for manufacturing firms. As a base for production, Hong Kong represents a very high-cost location. Not only is labor very expensive, but land is also. Restrictive government land-use policies and high demand have made Hong Kong property prices some of the highest in the world. Between 1981 and 1990, factory rentals more than doubled, and increased by a further 75 percent in the four years to 1994 (Hong Kong Government).

To find out where manufacturing MNCs with RHQs and ROs in Hong Kong do in fact market and make products, survey respondents were asked in which Asia-Pacific economies their parent companies had significant sales and production activities. In terms of sales activities, overall, a surprising 83 percent of MNCs indicated that they have significant sales activities in Hong Kong (see Table 9.2).

Due to the wording ambiguity of the question, it is not entirely clear that such activities relate to sales to buyers in Hong Kong or to buyers elsewhere which are simply coordinated and closed from Hong Kong. However, undoubtedly the 78 percent of firms overall which indicated sales activities in Japan and Mainland China could reasonably be assumed to be selling directly into those markets. But with the 73 percent of firms recording sales activities in Singapore, as with Hong Kong, it might be concluded that some of these activities are geared to sales outside of that city state, particularly given its smaller population of only 3 million. Taiwan, Malaysia, Thailand and Korea are each indicated to have sales activities by 60–70 percent of MNCs. Just over half of MNCs recorded sales activities in Australia, the Philippines and New Zealand, whereas under 50 percent showed sales activities in India.

Analyzing the findings on sales activities on the basis of MNC origin, generally a smaller percentage of Japanese firms recorded sales activities in most countries than did western firms. This is in keeping with the higher prevalence of vertical integration prompting Japanese firms to internationalize throughout the region. Around 85 percent of both US and European firms reported sales activities in China, whereas only 62 percent of Japanese firms record sales activities there.

Table 9.2 In which of the following Asia-Pacific countries does your parent company currently have significant sales activities?

	All firms n=159 %	Japanese firms n=50 %	US firms n=49 %	European firms n=60 %
Hong Kong	83	72	86	90
Japan	78	86	86	66
China	78	62	84	87
Singapore	73	68	73	77
Taiwan	71	64	69	77
Malaysia	63	56	67	64
Thailand	61	58	59	64
Korea	60	42	73	66
Australia	58	40	73	59
Philippines	55	46	61	56
Indonesia	53	50	53	56
India	47	08	55	56
New Zealand	39	26	47	43

Note: Figures show percentage of firms indicating sales activities in respective locations.

Source: Author's survey.

A significantly higher proportion of western MNCs have sales activities in Korea, Australia, New Zealand and, most particularly, India than Japanese firms. Indeed, whereas over 50 percent of western firms report sales activities in India, only 8 percent of Japanese MNCs do so. Some of the differences might be explained by the closer geographical proximity of Japan to specific markets, such as Korea and China, although this is not likely to explain the lack of sales activities in Australasia and India, which can hardly be regarded as close to Japan.

As might be expected, few firms overall have production activities in Hong Kong (see Table 9.3). Nevertheless, a surprisingly high 20 percent of all MNCs indicated some form of manufacturing presence. Not all firms gave the precise nature of their activities, but a good proportion appeared to be in food and drink sectors. Production in both these sectors is more likely to be carried out in the immediate vicinity of local markets due to the just-in-time inventory practices of retailers and the sometimes perishable nature of products. However, China is by far the location in which most MNCs overall recorded having production activities, some 64 percent of all respondent firms. This was followed by Japan, indicated by half of respondents, then by

Thailand and Malaysia, mentioned respectively by 29 percent and 27 percent of firms.

All other countries were indicated by between 20–25 percent of MNCs, except for New Zealand, in which only 7 percent of respondents recorded having production activities.

Table 9.3 In which of the following Asia-Pacific countries does your parent company currently have significant production

	All firms n=159 %	Japanese firms n=50 %	US firms n=49 %	European firms n=60 %
Hong Kong	20	18	18	25
Japan	50	86	43	26
China	64	66	71	57
Singapore	20	18	24	20
Taiwan	25	32	27	18
Malaysia	27	32	24	26
Thailand	29	44	24	21
Korea	25	22	33	21
Australia	20	8	31	21
Philippines	20	22	16	21
Indonesia	25	30	27	20
India	23	14	29	26
New Zealand	7	0	6	13

Note: Figures show percentage of firms indicating production activities in respective locations.

Source: Author's survey.

The location of production activities differs markedly when looked at by MNC home country. For Japanese firms, for which Japan, naturally enough, is the most commonly recorded location of manufacturing activities, China is the most important foreign production location in the Asia-Pacific, cited by 66 percent. Thailand is also relatively important, indicated by 44 percent of Japanese MNCs.

Next come Taiwan and Malaysia, both mentioned by 32 percent of Japanese firms, and then Indonesia, indicated by some 30 percent. Korea and the Philippines are each cited by 22 percent of Japanese MNCs, with other countries indicated by fewer than 20 percent of respondents as being locations of significant production activities.

For US MNCs, China is the most frequently recorded location of production activities, indicated by 71 percent of US respondents. Japan is the next most important location, with 43 percent of US firms indicating that they have production activities there. With the exceptions of Hong Kong, the Philippines and New Zealand, all other locations are mentioned by between 24–33 percent of US firms. This suggests that US MNCs' production activities are very heavily concentrated in China but otherwise relatively evenly spread throughout the Asia-Pacific, if Japan is excepted.

For European manufacturing MNCs with RHQs and ROs in Hong Kong, China is the most important location for production activities throughout the Asia-Pacific. Indicated by 57 percent of European firm respondents, China has more than double the number of MNCs recording production activities there than any other economy. Such activities are uniformly dispersed amongst other locations at a relatively low level, with only between 13 and 26 percent of firms indicating production activities in all non-China economies.

Combining results for both sales and production activities, it would seem that European firms are the most likely to be in the Asia-Pacific simply to sell and are the most likely to be selling products made in locations outside the Asia-Pacific. Japanese firms are least likely to be in non-Japanese Asia-Pacific countries to sell but are the most likely to have production facilities. MNCs from the US are as likely as those from Europe to have sales activities throughout the Asia-Pacific, but fall somewhere between Japanese and European firms with regard to production activity locations. China is by far the most important manufacturing and sales location for all MNCs.

WHAT IS THE GEOGRAPHICAL AMBIT OF HONG KONG RHQS AND ROS?

Foreign manufacturing MNCs that have some kind of office in Hong Kong may have sales and production activities throughout the Asia-Pacific, but this does not mean that those activities are necessarily controlled or coordinated from Hong Kong. Regional offices can be anticipated to have narrower geographical ambits than RHQs. Local offices should have responsibility solely for Hong Kong based activities (see fnote 2). Consequently, the preponderant geographical purview of foreign MNC Hong Kong offices will depend on the concentration of different types of respective offices located in the city.

The survey found that 52 percent of all firms regard their Hong Kong office as an RHQ, 33 percent regard it as just a regional office, and some 27 percent describe their office there as a local office (see Table 9.4). Over 10 percent of surveyed firms described their offices as having dual functions, usually an RHQ or RO doubling as a local office, too. When looked at by the home country origin of MNCs, it is clear that a lower percentage of Japanese firms in Hong Kong operate RHQs than western firms. Only 38 percent of Japanese MNCs indicated that their Hong Kong office is an RHQ compared with 67 percent of US and 50 percent of European MNCs reporting their offices as being RHQs.

On the other hand, a higher proportion, 36 percent, of Japanese MNCs describe their Hong Kong office as a local office than do US or European firms. Only 27 percent of US firms and just 21 percent of European respondents regard their Hong Kong office as acting as a local office. These findings would anticipate varying ambits of control and coordination for MNCs depending on their home country.

Table 9.4. Does your office in Hong Kong act as a regional headquarters, a regional office, or a local office?

	All firms n=159 %	Japanese firms n=50 %	US firms n=49 %	European firms n=60 %
Regional headquarters	52	38	67	50
Regional office	33	32	31	36
Local office	27	36	27	21

Note: Figures show percentage of firms indicating different types of office. Percentages donot add up to 100 as some offices have dual functions.

Source: Author's survey.

To find out the precise geography of foreign manufacturing MNC offices' sphere of influence, survey respondents were asked over which countries their RHQ or RO had some significant coordination and/or control function (see Table 9.5).

Overall, and putting together results for both RHQs and ROs, it was found that the ambit of such offices does not fully reflect the locations of sales and production activities throughout the Asia-Pacific region. Some 73 percent of Hong Kong offices exercise some coordination and/or control functions over Mainland China, and 54 percent do the same over Taiwan. Between 30 and 38 percent of all MNCs exercise some authority over the Philippines, Korea, Thailand, Singapore and Indonesia. And between 22 and 29 percent have some responsibility for Japan, Malaysia, India and Australia. This would suggest that, apart from Greater China (Hong Kong, Taiwan and

Mainland China), Hong Kong RHQs and ROs generally share some responsibility with other major offices for many parts of the Asia-Pacific.

On the face of it, it could be guessed that Japan is generally controlled directly from the home country head offices or from within Japan itself, while Singapore, Malaysia, Thailand and Indonesia, and, to a lesser extent, the Philippines, and possibly Australia, could be controlled by other Southeast Asian RHQs, based primarily in Singapore (see Chapter 10 by Poon).

When the results are looked at from the perspective of MNC origin, it can be seen that Japanese firms' offices in Hong Kong, as might be expected given their lower proportion of RHQs, have very little responsibility outside Greater China. And even this is misleading as only 20 percent of surveyed Japanese manufacturing firms actually reported having any significant responsibility for Taiwan. It could well be that Hong Kong represents for Japanese firms a center only to cover the local market and China, with Singapore the main RHQ or RO center for covering Southeast Asia, and the Japanese head office controlling Korea and Taiwan, and possibly the Philippines.

Table 9.5 Over which geographical areas does your Hong Kong regional headquarters or office exercise significant coordination and/or control functions?

	All firms n=159 %	Japanese firms n=50 %	US firms n=49 %	European firms n=60 %
China	73	64	73	79
Taiwan	54	20	67	73
Philippines	38	12	53	47
Korea	37	2	51	52
Thailand	34	6	53	40
Singapore	34	8	47	44
Indonesia	30	4	45	39
Japan	29	0	39	37
Malaysia	29	4	47	35
India	23	0	41	23
Australia	22	6	35	24

Note: Figures show percentage of firms in each category indicating a particular country.

Source: Author's survey.

The Hong Kong offices of US MNCs, reflecting their higher prevalence of RHQs, have a considerably wider orbit of control than those of Japanese firms. For US MNCs, Hong Kong is clearly a key center for coordinating and controlling activities in Greater China, with 73 percent reporting control over Mainland China and 67 percent indicating authority over Taiwan. Over 50 percent of US RHQs and ROs also have considerable responsibility for activities in the Philippines, Korea and Thailand. And throughout the rest of the Asia-Pacific, between 35 and 47 percent of US MNC Hong Kong offices exercise significant authority, depending on the particular country. A similar pattern of geographical control and/or coordination is evident for European firms' RHQs and ROs in Hong Kong. The only difference, however, is an apparently slightly lower incidence of authority over Southeast Asia generally, and Australia and India in particular.

Table 9.6 Area of geographical control of regional headquarters and regional offices

	All regional headquarters n=83 %	All regional offices n=36 %
Mainland China	89	87
Hong Kong	88	83
Taiwan	77	49
Philippines	57	30
Sinagapore	55	17
Korea	53	32
Thailand	53	21
Malaysia	48	15
Indonesia	48	17
Japan	47	17
India	36	15
Australia	34	15

Note: Figures show percentage of firms in each category indicating a particular country. Each category comprises only those offices reported as either solely an RHQ or RO.

Source: Author's survey.

Given a distinction between RHQs and ROs, it was decided to divide the overall findings for all firms' ambit of control by each type of office (see Table 9.6). The results show that RHQs in Hong Kong tend to cover the majority of the Asia-Pacific, with the impact of distance evident through a gradually declining percentage of firms being responsible for countries which are geographically further away from Hong Kong. On the other hand, ROs have responsibility for a much more tightly circumscribed geographical region. This region predominantly consists of Greater China, but also, to a much lesser extent, Korea and the Philippines.

WHAT STRATEGIC FUNCTIONS ARE PERFORMED BY HONG KONG RHQS AND ROS?

To find out precisely what MNCs' Hong Kong offices in fact do, they were surveyed on a scale of discrete firm activities (see Table 9.7). Asked to score items for importance using a five-point scale, for all firms, corporate coordination-type activities obtained high means of 3.75 and upwards. Specific variables for 'supporting and coordinating other regional operations' and 'reporting to parent company' all scored means between 4.12 and 4.17.

'Acting as regional liaison center' also obtained a high mean of 3.97, but 'monitoring other regional offices' scored a slightly lower mean of 3.75. Central management-type functions generally obtained lower means overall. 'Regional strategy formulation' scored the highest mean, 3.92, followed by 'competitor intelligence', with a mean of 3.73. Other central management functions, including 'business process development', 'senior personnel' and 'regional information technology management' obtained means of between 3.11 and 3.31, suggesting they are not particularly important RHQ or RO activities. Other central management functions, like 'non raw materials procurement' and 'product design' obtain means of 2.47 and 2.78 respectively, indicating that they are not at all important activities for MNC offices in Hong Kong.

Sales, marketing and customer-service-type activities were generally regarded as highly important RHQ and RO activities. 'Marketing' and 'sales' planning and execution each scored means for importance of over 4.10. 'Customer servicing and support' was also regarded as important, getting an overall mean of nearly 4.00, while 'market research' and 'sales and marketing related procurement' obtained slightly lower means of 3.78 and 3.61, respectively.

All other major firm activity areas, including finance and accounting, distribution, production and research functions, were regarded as relatively less important. Apart from the individual items of 'accounting', 'trade finance', 'order processing' and 'trade documentation', which obtained means for importance of between 3.10 and 3.24, all other items obtained very low means of between 1.90, for 'process technology development', and exactly 3 for 'warehousing', suggesting that all these functions are distinctly unimportant RHQ and RO activities.

Table 9.7 How important is your Hong Kong office as a center for the performance of the following activities and functions?

	All firms, n	Mean	Standard dev.
Corporate coordination			
Coordination of other operations within region	156	4.12	1.15
Supporting regional operations	155	4.17	1.06
Monitoring of other regional operations	154	3.75	1.33
Reporting regional activities to parent company	157	4.13	1.15
Regional liaison center for parent company	153	3.97	1.20
Central management functions			
Competitor intelligence	154	3.73	1.01
Regional strategy formulation	155	3.92	1.11
Product/service development and design	153	2.78	1.28
Business process development	153	3.31	1.21
Senior personnel management	153	3.31	1.29
Regional information technology management	153	3.11	1.23
Non-raw materials procurement	152	2.47	1.34
Finance & accounting			
Trade finance	154	3.10	1.37
Capital-investment finance	153	2.74	1.30
Insurance	152	2.74	1.19
Accounting/auditing	154	3.24	1.27
Sales, marketing & customer service			
Marketing planning and execution	153	4.17	1.00
Sales planning and execution	153	4.14	1.04
Sales- & marketing-related procurement	153	3.61	1.26
Market research	154	3.78	1.07
Customer servicing and support	152	3.99	1.14
Distributional activities			
Warehousing finished goods	154	3.00	1.41
Packaging	153	2.41	1.25
Order processing	153	3.28	1.41
Trade documentation	154	3.31	1.41
Coordinating regional distribution	150	3.27	1.45

(cont.)

Coordinating global distribution	147	2.41	1.34
Land distribution	152	2.43	1.35
Air distribution	152	2.61	1.40
Sea distribution	153	2.79	1.44
Production activities			
Manufacturing	151	2.21	1.46
Assembly/processing	149	2.14	1.41
Quality control	152	2.51	1.56
Testing/certification	150	2.39	1.46
Raw materials sourcing	152	2.41	1.50
Research and development			
New product development	144	2.26	1.45
Process technology development	143	1.90	1.19

Note: Figures represent mean scores, 1 = very unimportant, 2 = unimportant, 3 = neutral, 4 = important, 5 = very important. The n for each variable differs due to some respondents missing out specific items.

Source: Author's survey.

To see if the importance of RHQ and RO functions varies by parent firm nationality, important functions (those recording a mean of 3.5 or above) were compared by MNC home origin (see Table 9.8). For Japanese MNCs, Hong Kong is most important as a location for marketing, sales and customer service functions. Each of these activities obtained a mean greater than 4.00, as does reporting regional activities to parent companies.

However, for Japanese MNCs, Hong Kong is not so important for monitoring other regional operations. This item scores a mean of just 3.34. This contrasts sharply with US multinationals for which Hong Kong appears to be a much more important center for all corporate coordination-type activities than it is for Japanese firms. Indeed, for US MNCs, Hong Kong would seem very important for coordinating, supporting and reporting on regional operations, as each item relating these activities obtains a mean of over 4.40.

Hong Kong is also an important center for US MNCs in developing regional strategy, which records a mean of 4.30. The patterns of importance of Hong Kong as a location for undertaking most activities are broadly similar for US and European MNCs.

However, Hong Kong is a slightly less important center for European MNC strategy formulation and reporting regional activities to parent companies than it is for US MNCs.

Table 9.8 How important is your Hong Kong office as a center for the performance of the following activities and functions?

	Japanese firms n=45–47 Mean	US firms n=46–48 Mean	European firms n=61–62 Mean
Corporate coordination			
Coordination of other operations within region	3.74	4.43	4.16
Supporting regional operations	3.74	4.48	4.26
Monitoring of other regional operations	3.34	4.02	3.85
Reporting regional activities to parent company	4.04	4.43	3.98
Regional liaison center for parent company	3.65	4.13	4.10
Central management functions			
Competitor intelligence	3.57	3.93	3.69
Regional strategy formulation	3.57	4.30	3.89
Sales, marketing & customer service			
Marketing planning and execution	4.17	4.17	4.16
Sales planning and execution	4.13	4.09	4.18
Sales- & marketing-related procurement	3.72	3.33	3.74
Market research	3.85	3.70	3.79
Customer servicing and support	4.13	3.89	3.97

Note: Figures represent mean scores, 1 = very unimportant, 2 = unimportant, 3 = neutral, 4 = important, 5 = very important. The n for each variable differs between to the ranges given due to some respondents missing out specific items.

Source: Author's survey.

Overall, the importance of Hong Kong for performing various activities reflects the differences between what MNCs from different countries in fact do in terms of sales and marketing throughout the Asia-Pacific region, and differences in proportions of RHQs to ROs. Japanese firms are less oriented toward corporate and central management functions than either US or European firms because they tend to base fewer RHQs in Hong Kong.

Likewise, because European firms have a lower proportion of RHQs than US ones, they place slightly less emphasis on corporate and central management than US firms, while they regard Hong Kong as slightly more important for sales and marketing, which are European MNCs' prime activities in the Asia-Pacific.

WHY ARE RHQS AND ROS LOCATED IN HONG KONG?

Because the main functions of RHQs and ROs in Hong Kong are geared towards regional coordination and marketing activities, it might be anticipated that MNCs locate their offices in the city because it is attractive for the performance of those activities. To test if this is the case, survey respondents were asked how attractive Hong Kong is along a range of dimensions necessary for executing coordination and marketing activities on a regional basis (see Table 9.9).

On a five-point scale with 1 being very unattractive and 5 being very attractive, Hong Kong obtained a high mean of 4.69 for the attractiveness of its communications' infrastructure, and 4.49 for the attractiveness of its transportation infrastructure. Excellent communications and transport infrastructures are vital to performing regional coordination activities, and it is unsurprising that Hong Kong should score highly on these dimensions. For European firms, Hong Kong scores particularly highly on these two items, obtaining 4.80 for communications infrastructure and 4.70 for transportation infrastructure.

Table 9.9 How attractive as a regional headquarters or office location is Hong Kong regarding the following factors?

	All firms n=151–157	Japanese firms n=44–47	US firms n=46–47	European firms n=60–62
	Mean	Mean	Mean	Mean
Communication infrastructure	4.69	4.50	4.70	4.80
Centrality to important markets	4.49	4.30	4.48	4.61
Transportation infrastructure	4.49	4.30	4.41	4.70
High-quality local managers	4.22	4.20	4.00	4.43
Supporting and supply industries	3.83	3.50	3.85	4.03

Note: Figures represent mean scores, 1 = very unattractive, 2 = unattractive, 3 = neutral, 4 = attractive, 5 = very attractive. The n for each variable differs between to the ranges given due to some respondents missing out specific items.

Source: Author's survey.

Given that all MNCs are in the Asia-Pacific to sell, it could be expected that their RHQ and RO locations should reflect this, and with Hong Kong they appear to do so. Hong Kong obtained a mean of 4.49 overall for its attractiveness in terms of centrality to important markets. Reflecting Japanese MNCs' greater concern with production for export to elsewhere in the world, they recorded a slightly lower mean of 4.30 for centrality to markets. But for European firms, the MNCs most geared to selling, Hong Kong obtains a substantially higher mean of 4.61 for centrality to important markets.

In order to carry out both coordination and marketing activities on a regional basis, RHQs and ROs need access to appropriate standards and levels of human capital and supporting industries. Overall, Hong Kong obtained a mean of 4.22 for attractiveness in terms of availability of high-quality local managers, and 3.83 for supporting and supply industries. While US firms, recording a mean of 4.00 for the attractiveness of Hong Kong for high-quality human capital, certainly do not view Hong Kong as unattractive on this dimension, their mean is well below that of European MNC respondents, which scored a mean of 4.43, suggesting these latter firms regard Hong Kong as highly attractive for good-quality local managers. As might be expected for Japanese firms, which do more manufacturing around the region, Hong Kong is not as attractive for support and supply industries as it is for European firms. Japanese firms score a mean of 3.50 for this dimension, compared to 4.03 scored by European MNCs which, as predominantly sellers rather than producers in the region, are mostly looking for the types of supporting industry infrastructure that is typical of an overwhelmingly service-oriented economy like Hong Kong's.

CONCLUSION

As a regional strategic hub for foreign manufacturing multinationals, Hong Kong's role reflects to a great extent the objectives such MNCs have for being in the Asia-Pacific region in the first place. While there are many similarities in these strategic objectives, there are substantial differences among MNCs depending on the origin of their parent companies. Japanese, US and European MNCs are all primarily concerned to be in the Asia-Pacific to sell. The huge markets, actual and potential, of the region are what attract MNCs into the Asia-Pacific through a process of horizontal internationalization. So, too, do competitor activities, but to a much lesser extent. For Japanese firms, the Asia-Pacific outside their home country is also a very important region for production. Vertical integration to exploit lower-cost manufacturing locations is almost as powerful a driver of Japanese MNC internationalization within the Asia-Pacific region as is the attraction of the region's markets. However, vertical-integration-driven FDI is significantly less important for both US and European firms. For all firms, sales activities are relatively evenly spread throughout the region, although with a marked focus on Greater China. Production activities are likewise relatively evenly dispersed in the region, although far fewer firms actually manufacture in the Asia-Pacific, and, again, there is a strong focus on Greater China.

These patterns of sales and production are mirrored to some extent in the geographical ambits of RHQs and ROs located in Hong Kong. Many MNC RHQs tend to have spheres of control over much of the Asia-Pacific, but to a lesser degree than the overall extent of sales and production activities might suggest. It would seem that Hong Kong does not act as a strategic RHQ hub for all Asia-Pacific operations, many of which are either run directly from the home countries or from other hub locations, notably Singapore. When it comes to ROs, these have a much more tightly circumscribed geographical responsibility, confined essentially to Greater China.

The strategic functions carried out by MNCs in Hong Kong differ by both what their parent companies' prime objectives are and whether or not their office is an RHQ or RO. RHQs concentrate much more on corporate coordination and control than ROs, which are more highly focused on sales and marketing activities. For performing nearly all other strategic functions outside these parameters, Hong Kong is not an important center. It is probable that these functions are either simply not important at all for MNCs in the Asia-Pacific, or are carried out on a local production or sales location basis.

Why Hong Kong is an important site for regional control and co-ordination clearly has a lot do with geography. Hong Kong is in the right place. However, Hong Kong would seem also to have developed a very highly regarded infrastructure of communications, transportation, personnel and supporting industries. These vital characteristics of Hong Kong as a strategic hub for foreign manufacturing MNCs in the Asia-Pacific have to some degree been developed and refined because of the sheer number of MNCs with a presence in the city. It may even be the case that Hong Kong has developed so strong a competitive advantage as a regional hub for MNCs that it will remain the Asia-Pacific's predominant center for RHQs and ROs, despite increasing competition from existing competitor locations like Singapore and Sydney, and the emergence of other major cities, like Shanghai. Time will tell.

NOTES

1. Data used in this chapter were collected with the help of research funding from the University of Hong Kong Committee on Research and Conference Grants held by the author, grant 337/108/0011, and by the author and M. J Enright, grant 10202111/27959/44000/323/01.
2. The Hong Kong Government has for several years used definitions of regional headquarters and regional offices which were used as the basis for the definitions used in this research. A **regional headquarters (RHQ)** is defined as an organization which has control over the operation of one or more other offices or subsidiaries in other countries or economies in the region and which does not need to make need to make frequent referrals to, or consultations with, the overseas parent headquarters. Note that Hong Kong and Mainland China should be considered as two different economies. A **regional office (RO)** is defined as an office responsible for general business activities in its own and other countries or economies in the region, but which is less autonomous than a **RHQ**. A **local office (LO)** is defined as one responsible for general business activities solely in its particular country or local economy.
3. These figures vastly understate the presence of foreign MNCs in Hong Kong as they represent only those firms that responded positively to particular RHQ- and RO-related items in a questionnaire administered to over 12,000 foreign firms known to be operating in the city.
4. Hong Kong has been rated as one of the top two or three most competitive economies in the world for a number of years. See World Economic Forum (various years) and IMD (various years).
5. Hong Kong still has several thousands of indigenous manufacturing firms. However, many of these have become effectively multinational firms with only service oriented head offices in Hong Kong and manufacturing activities over the border in Mainland China (Thompson, 2000).
6. Questionnaires were administered to 2400 US, European and Japanese MNCs in Hong Kong. A total of 257 usable responses were received. To check for non-response bias and to boost overall number of responses, instruments were administered a second time to all identifiable non-respondents. A further 203 usable responses were received. No non-response bias was found. A total of 161 responding MNCs identified themselves as manufacturers. Of these, 159 identified themselves as either US, Japanese or European MNCs.
7. Literature on RHQs generally, but on those in the Asia-Pacific particularly, is sparse and none of it relates directly to Hong Kong. See Akira and Tachiki 1992; Dunning and Norman, 1987; Hedlund, 1980; Heenan, 1979; Perry, Poon and Yeung, 1998; Roth and Allen, 1992.

REFERENCES

Akira, A. and D. Tachiki (1992), 'Overseas Japanese business operations: the emerging role of regional headquarters', *Pacific Business and Industries*, **1**, 26–39.

Asiaweek (1998), **24** (3), 57.

Asian Development Bank (1998), *Foreign Trade Indicators*, Manila: Asian Development Bank.

Caves, R.E. (1971), 'International corporations: the industrial economics of foreign investment', *Economica*, **38**, 1–27.

Caves, R.E. (1996), *Multinational Enterprise and Economic Analysis*, Cambridge: Cambridge University Press.

Dunning, J.H. (1977), 'Trade, location of economic activity and the MNE: a search for an eclectic approach', in B. Ohlin *et al.* (eds), *The International Allocation of Economic Activity*, London: Holmes and Meier.

Dunning, J. and G. Norman (1987), 'The location choice of offices of international companies', *Environment and Planning A*, **19**, 613–31.

Eng, I. and Y. Lin (1996), 'Seeking competitive advantage in an emergent open economy: Foreign direct investment in Chinese industry', *Environment and Planning A*, **28**, 1113–38.

Enright, M.J. (1998), 'Regional clusters and firm strategy', in A.D. Chandler *et al.* (eds), *The Dynamic Firm: The Role of Technology, Strategy, Organization, and Regions*, New York: Oxford University Press.

Enright, M.J. (1999), 'Globalization, regionalization and the knowledge-based economy in Hong Kong', in J.H. Dunning (ed.), *Regions, Globalization and the Knowledge-based Economy*, Oxford: Oxford University Press.

Hedlund, G. (1980), 'The role of foreign subsidiaries in strategic decision-making in Swedish multinational corporations', *Strategic Management Journal*, 1, pp.23–36.

Heenan, D.A. (1979), 'Regional headquarters decision: a comparative analysis', *Academy of Management Journal*, **22** (2), 410–15.

Hennart, J.F. (1991), 'The transaction cost theory of the multinational enterprise', in C.N. Pitelis and R. Sugden (eds), *The Nature of the Transnational Firm*, London: Routledge.

Hong Kong Government (various years), Census and Statistics Department, 21/F Wanchai Tower, 12 Harbour Road, Wanchai, Hong Kong.

Hymer S.H. (1976), *The International Operations of National Firms: A Study of Direct Foreign Investment*, Cambridge, MA: MIT Press.

IMD (various years), *World Competitiveness Yearbook*, Lausanne: Institute for Management Development.

Kindleberger, C.P. (1969), *American Business Abroad*, New Haven: Yale University Press.

Knickerbocker, F.T. (1973), *Oligopolistic Reaction and Multinational Enterprise*, Boston: Harvard University Press.

Kojima, K. (1978), *Direct Foreign Investment: a Japanese Model of Multinational Business Operations*, London: Croom Helm.

Kojima, K. (1995), 'Dynamics of Japanese direct investment in East Asia', *Hitotsubashi Journal of Economics*, **36**, 93–124.

Ozawa, T. (1979), *Multinationalism, Japanese Style: The Political Economy of Outward Dependency*, Princeton, NJ: Princeton University Press.

Perry, M., J.P.H. Poon and H. Yeung (1998), 'Regional offices in Singapore: spatial and strategic influences in the location of corporate control', *Review of Urban and Regional Development Studies*, **10** (1), 42–59.

Roth, K. and J.M. Allen (1992), 'Implementing global strategy: characteristics of global subsidiary mandates', *Journal of International Business Studies*, **23** (4), 715–35.

Saxenian, A. (1994), *Regional Advantage: Culture and Competition in Silicon Valley and Route 128*, Cambridge, MA: Harvard University Press.

Scott, A. (1998), 'The geographic foundations of industrial performance', in A.D. Chandler et al. (eds), *The Dynamic Firm: The Role of Technology, Strategy, Organization, and Regions*, New York: Oxford University Press.

Thompson, E.R. (2000), 'Business integration across the Hong Kong–Chinese border: Patterns and explanations in the garment industry', in D.E. Andersson and J.P.H. Poon (eds), *Asia-Pacific Transitions*, London: Macmillan.

Thompson, E.R. and J.P.H. Poon (1999), 'Determinants of US, UK and Japanese foreign direct investment in East and Southeast Asia', *Journal of Asian Business.*

UNCTAD (various years), *World Development Report*, Geneva: UNCTAD.

Vernon, R. (1966), 'International investment and international trade in the product cycle', *Quarterly Journal of Economics*, **LXXX**, 190–207.
World Economic Forum (various years), *World Competitiveness Report*, Geneva: World Economic Forum.

10. Reconfiguring Regional Hierarchy through Regional Offices in Singapore

Jessie P.H. Poon

INTRODUCTION

Contemporary multinational systems of production have expanded in the past few decades, popularizing the notion that economic activities are being greatly 'globalized'. Observation that major agents of economic globalism, namely multinational corporations (MNCs), are embarking on a tripolar-supported model of investment and production has led to the notion that commercial networks form the major constituents of the global economy today (UN, 1991; Castells, 1996). Paradoxically, though, as economic activities increasingly assume global dimensions, the need for greater governance coherence and sensitivity to thinner margins of comparative advantage has increased the prominence of regional economic systems in driving worldwide investment, trade and competition (Storper, 1995; Scott, 1996).

The participation of developing countries in global integration has been crucial in accelerating this process. Nowhere is this more clearly seen than in Southeast Asia, which has become a major producer of consumer electronics outside of Europe, North America and Japan (Dicken, 1998), building its comparative advantage on a relatively cheap, disciplined and literate labor force. Southeast Asia is well integrated into changing international product cycles, forming an important base for the exports of MNCs to third countries in Europe or North America. Japan's contribution to this process is also important. Its vision of a potentially self-operating Asian economic system (Fallows, 1994) has seen Japanese MNCs relocating segments of vertically integrated industries to Southeast Asia (Poon and Thompson, 1998). Not surprisingly, Japan has been the largest FDI contributor to Indonesia, the Philippines and Thailand since the 1990s (OECD, 1997).

Southeast Asia, as a region, is highly heterogeneous (Poon, 1997a). Its economic development in the 1960s and 1970s was supported largely by a well-defined regional division of labor that exploited the relatively diverse comparative advantages of Southeast Asian countries. Rather fortuitously, Southeast Asia became incorporated into international subcontracting systems as the process of internationalization intensified during the 1980s with MNCs relocating branches of their assembly-based industries to countries in the region. Japanese firms, in particular, accelerated their investments in Southeast Asia following the 1985 Plaza Accord, setting up both production and sales bases to take advantage of lower-cost Asian suppliers (Tejima, 1996). Singapore, which had neither natural resources nor particularly cheap labor (UN, 1961),[1] quickly moved into a leading nodal position by serving as a port hub for the exports of the region. The country alone accounts for nearly one-half of Southeast Asia's regional trade. Outside of trade, Singapore is also a major financial center both regionally and globally, maximizing its locational advantage in time zones between North America and Asia. Indeed, the country's historical nodal strength has seen heavy intervention by the state that is targeted at constructing a regional hierarchy that favors the country's position geographically through the higher value-added activities of regional offices.

This chapter seeks to document the changing comparative advantage of Singapore via its geographical positioning at the intersection of international capital circuits in Southeast Asia. Such locational advantage is argued to be actively constructed by the state as it seeks to entrench Singapore as the major commercial node and urban center in the region. By aggressively courting regional office establishments, Singapore not only privileges its own position within Southeast Asia's hierarchy of production, but attempts to influence foreign capital behavior, forging an alliance that ensures that the island remains a regional center of sustained accumulation.

MULTINATIONAL CAPITAL IN SINGAPORE

Though it is the second smallest country in Southeast Asia, Singapore has served as an important trading outpost for the region for more than one hundred years. Endowed with a deep natural harbor, it thrived as a regional entrepôt collecting the region's mostly primary exports for re-export to the West, while importing manufactured goods from Europe for redistribution in the region. Singapore's geographical position astride major sea routes between East Asia and Europe has thus been an important advantage to the country.

Following independence from the British, and its break from Malaysia in 1965, the country embarked on an industrialization program that rested on the backbone of foreign manufacturing companies, particularly those that were export-oriented. Foreign direct investment (FDI) has been an important engine in driving the country's high post-war growth rates, reaching nearly S$6 billion in 1996. This makes Singapore one of the top five FDI recipients among developing countries in the period between 1980 and 1990. Singapore's reliance on multinational capital has been so heavy that as late as 1992, wholly and majority-owned foreign companies account for 74.2 percent of the output and 84.1 percent of the direct exports of its manufacturing sector (Huff, 1995).

The island's dependence on foreign capital may be explained by its small domestic market, rendering import-substitution industrialization an untenable strategy, and a weak indigenous manufacturing base. As a result, the government endorsed an elaborate industrial blueprint that was mapped out under the Winsemius Report.[2] The report gave prominence to exports and foreign investments as the major engines of growth for the island. Not surprisingly, exports as a share of GDP have exceeded 100 percent for most years since the 1980s, indicating the country's overwhelming dependence on trade. Similarly, Singapore has been courting FDI since the 1960s, allowing foreign investors to establish wholly owned subsidiaries. Foreign investment in the electronics sector is especially marked, forming some 36 percent of total manufacturing FDI in 1989, and 88 percent of total foreign equity in manufacturing in 1992 (Chia, 1997).

The bias toward the electronics sector is evidenced by the fact that Singapore is among the top ten producers of computer tapes and semi-conductors in the world (Pang, 1995). The Economic Development Board (EDB), a semi-governmental body with full autonomy in its operations, was formed in 1961 to spearhead Singapore's industrial development and has since then been entrusted with the responsibility of turning Singapore into the economic nerve center of Southeast Asia (Haggard, 1990). Furthermore, the island's historical importance as an outlet for the region's trade, and in the 1960s as an offshore assembly base for MNCs, helped to entrench the country firmly in the global–regional production and distribution networks, providing the country with a strong economic advantage over its neighbors.[3]

Within the Asia-Pacific region of the triads (UN, 1991; Lévy, 1995), this advantage has moved Singapore to the apex of a regional hierarchy of production based on the area of Southeast Asia. In particular, Singapore has shifted away from low-skilled assembly-based activities since the early 1980s to a regional control and coordination center for business activities (Perry, 1992). A subregional division of labor is thus apparent, with Singapore specializing more and more in decision-related functions, while its neighbors specialize in low-value-added assembly. In fact, the EDB has been very active in getting global businesses to anchor their global corporate headquarters in Singapore, thus expanding its comparative advantage beyond locational advantages to product design, research and development, manufacturing control and strategic marketing.[4]

While Singapore's geographical location might have been responsible for its historical position as a major trading node for the region, its emergence as a regional business coordination center is a more recent construction. In particular, the state has played a major role in retaining the country's nodal position in the region. Among its initiatives, a subregional arrangement designed to promote economic development in cooperation with the Johor state of Malaysia, and Batam Island of Indonesia, exemplifies such locational maneuvering.

The Singapore–Johor–Batam growth triangle, originally mooted by Singapore's present prime minister, effectively expands the economic space of the country by tapping into its neighbors' abundant supplies of land, gas and labor for industrial development, with Singapore providing management and technical skills. Singapore's role, in effect, is to mediate between MNC activities by providing them with transport and communications infrastructure as well as financial and technical support, while siphoning off lower-end production to Johor and Batam. As one author noted, the impetus for such an initiative stems from Singapore's vulnerability to export markets, especially in electronic goods, which saw a sharp downturn during the 1985–86 recession (Rodan, 1993).

Second, acutely aware of Malaysia's own rapid economic transformation in the 1980s and the industrial progress made by other Southeast Asian countries in terms of catching up, the government introduced a strategy of regionalization in 1993. The motivation behind this is to catapult Singapore to the global echelon of accumulation centers with total business capabilities so that the country not only functions as a major intersecting node for global investment and trade flows, but also as a gateway for MNCs seeking business and market expansion in the region (Economic Development Board, 1995). Singapore's new regional focus is achieved through its government-linked corporations (GLCs) and state-driven entrepreneurship, where the state takes a lead role in providing market and business intelligience to private sector actors interested in regionalizing their activities (Yeung, 1998).

In both instances, the state's alliance with local and foreign capital is clear, with the government fostering implicit goals of exploiting the country's well-established links with MNCs and regional governments. Both initiatives are also designed to move the country into an incontestable commercial confluence, with Singapore acting as the central motor in the region's economic production. In either experience, the attraction of regional offices has become crucial as Singapore's ability to enhance its own position in the regional hierarchy depends on its success in operating as a strategic hub for international business and finance activities.

THE ROLE OF REGIONAL OFFICES

The widespread use of regional offices to coordinate business activities is fairly well established in the literature (Heenan, 1979; Sullivan, 1992; Dunning, 1993). Regional offices have become an increasingly useful mechanism for regional management in an era when globalization effectively operates on a triadized structure based on the United States, the European Union and the Asia-Pacific.

Evidence shows that some four-fifths of total outward foreign direct investment stocks is conducted within the triads (UN, 1991), while world trade flows are organized around a few multinational regions (Poon, 1997b). That interactions within regions have outpaced those with the rest of the world points to a new spatial strategy globally, where production alliances by MNCs combine regional integration with international operations. Castells (1996) notes that this process has increased the spatial concentration of a few nodal centers under a highly hierarchical system, supported by a number of regional centers dispersed throughout the networks of MNCs.

Triadization allows firms to combine ownership advantages with host countries' locational advantages, giving rise to greater possibilities for a more refined division of labor within corporate systems. By 'slicing up the value chain' (Krugman, 1995), firms are able to allocate branches of the industry to sites with favorable factor-cost advantages.

Value-added activities that are more capital- technology- or knowledge-intensive will be allocated to locations with comparative advantages in skilled labor or superior business infrastructures. In other words, global firms now allocate parts of the value chain to locations which best enhance the firm's international competitiveness. The dispersion of horizontal or vertically integrated activities across different countries increases intra-firm investment and trade flows (UN, 1996; Dobson, 1997). Such a new environment brings about the need for greater regional management as relationships between parent firms and subsidiaries or, firms and suppliers/distributors, increase in complexity.

Because of the intermediate position that a regional office occupies between the corporation's head office and foreign affiliates, it is given the following roles:

1. To coordinate and control the activities of subsidiaries in a geographical region
2. To manage different segments of the value-adding chain by directing information upwards and downwards within the corporate hierarchy (Hamel and Prahalad, 1994)

3. To provide services to the parent company and affiliates such as labor, investment and market opportunities
4. To achieve closer integration of home and overseas affiliate operations (Perry et al., 1998).

A number of reasons may be offered as to why regional offices have become a popular corporate entity in the worldwide networks of MNCs.

First, there is the need for a strategic location on the global network of transport and communications so as to keep the key decision-makers in close contact with other spatially dispersed parts of the organization.

Second, the importance of agglomerative forces arising from personal contacts with CEOs or other top company executives are facilitated by close proximity (Dicken, 1998).

Third, the need to respond to changing conditions in local markets makes managing from a distance an increasingly difficult task.

Finally, the emergence of 'heterarchical' MNCs or 'horizontal' structures (Hedlund, 1986, 1993) in decision-making implies that MNCs will likely depend less and less on hierarchical forms of control, and more and more on a matrix of multiple centers of organizing principles.

Under such a structure, the relations between units are multidimensional, the headquarter functions and products geographically dispersed, and no dimension of it is uniformly subordinate. The heterarchical system is insulated from anarchy by normative integration such as a common organizational culture and corporate symbolism. The spatial scatteredness of corporate functions and activities implies that regional headquarters and offices are given more strategic command of resources through the latter's proximity to host regions, as chains of commands within the corporate system become less and less welldefined.

Perry (1992) has identified a typology of regional offices in his work: a *bridgehead* regional office which represents the first stage of a corporation's forays into a region; a *profit collector* which manages the finances and profits of its subsidiaries; a *technical support* center whose primary role is to provide engineering, testing or design skills to its affiliates; and a *regional integrator* which coordinates regional operations, including disseminating the policies and decisions of the corporate headquarters to its subsidiaries.

Whatever the role of regional offices, it seems clear that the parallel trend of globalization and regionalization has increased the strategic importance of managing geographically dispersed operations and markets through a regional framework, making regional nodal positioning an important dimension of corporations' internationalization strategy.

DATA AND SAMPLE

A regional office is defined in this study as an establishment that has control or responsibilities for one or more subsidiary companies outside of Singapore (see also Perry et al., 1998). A survey population of about 250 regional offices was identified, although Singapore's own Economic Development Board estimates that there are about 2,000 regional offices. However, the Board's estimates include representative offices as well as head offices of Singapore companies or MNCs whose only regional organization is in Singapore. Its definition of regional offices was deemed too broad for our purpose.

A postal questionnaire was sent out in 1996, and we received 130 usable responses, which represented 52 percent of the initial population. Results of the survey are presented below.

REGIONAL OFFICES AND REGIONAL HIERARCHY

Table 10.1 Nationality of parent companies

Nationality	Number	(%)
North America	43	33.1
Europe:	62	47.7
Germany	17	13.1
Switzerland	11	7.7
UK	10	7.7
France	7	5.4
Others	17	13.8
Japan	16	12.3
Rest of Asia-Pacific	7	5.4
All other	2	1.5
Total	130	100

Note: Data for Tables 10.1–10.6 are from the author's survey conducted in 1996.

Of the 130 responses received, 33.1 percent were from North America, 47.7 percent from Europe and 12.3 percent from Japan. The remaining 6.9 percent came from other regions such as Australia, New Zealand, South Korea and Saudi Arabia (Table 10.1).

The top three nations from Europe were Germany (n=17), Switzerland (n=11) and the United Kingdom (n=10). Such a strong presence of North

American and European regional offices is consistent with Singapore's trade and investment biases, both of which are highly focused on the two regions.

One-third of the regional offices in the sample are in Singapore primarily to serve the Southeast Asian region, but only 16 percent is found to serve both Southeast Asia and East Asia (Figure 10.1).

Figure 10.1 Area of responsibility

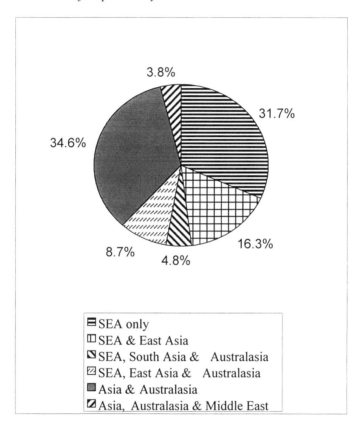

3.8%

31.7%

34.6%

8.7%   4.8%   16.3%

⊟ SEA only
Ⅲ SEA & East Asia
◩ SEA, South Asia & Australasia
☑ SEA, East Asia & Australasia
▩ Asia & Australasia
◪ Asia, Australasia & Middle East

The relatively low share associated with the latter may be explained by the fact that Hong Kong is the other important regional center for foreign MNCs in Asia (see Chapter 9 by Thompson), so that the two areas of Southeast Asia and East Asia are effectively viewed as two separate markets and production units.

Interestingly, the shares of regional offices that are responsible for either Southeast Asia–South Asia–Australasia, or, Southeast Asia–East Asia–

Australasia are rather low at 4.8 percent and 8.7 percent, respectively. But when the geographical area is extended to all of Asia and Australasia, some 36 firms responded positively. Moreover, American and European firms are more likely to cover Asia and Australasia than Japanese firms. It would appear that the bulk of regional offices in Singapore are highly regionalized with primary interests in Southeast Asia only, or, alternatively, that they are extraregional, extending across all of Asia and Australasia.

The above discussion also suggests that Singapore faces its strongest competition from Hong Kong in terms of getting firms to operate out of the country. When asked what other alternative locations the firms had considered before selecting Singapore as their regional base, not unexpectedly, Hong Kong emerged as the most frequent alternative locational competitor, followed by Kuala Lumpur in Malaysia (Table 10.2). No other country came close in terms of being locational substitutes to these two countries.

Table 10.2 Alternative location to Singapore

Country	Number
Hong Kong	49
Malaysia	32
Thailand	8
Japan	7
Australia	6
Philippines	6
Indonesia	3
China	2
Taiwan	2
South Korea	1
Total	116

The most important factors influencing the choice of Singapore are centrality to regional establishments (n=54), telecommunications infrastructure (n=42), access to customers (n=37) and the quality of Singapore's business and financial infrastructure (n=35).

Only 13 firms reported that government incentives had been an important consideration, while a negligible number (n=2) affirmed that favorable costs had influenced their decisions (Table 10.3).

Table 10.3 Key variables in selection of Singapore

Variable	Number
Centrality to regional establishments	54
Telecommunications infrastructure	42
Access to customers	37
Quality of business and financial provision	35
Government incentives	13
Lower operating costs	2

Note: For Tables 10.3–10.5, respondents were asked to select three variables for the relevant question.

Table 10.3 clearly points to two major influences on locational requirements for regional offices: first, the need for regional offices to be strategically positioned geographically in order to monitor the activities of their subsidiaries. This supports the earlier observation that a major function of regional offices is to act as a regional integrator, integrating home and overseas affiliate operations. Such spatial coordination ensures that a degree of flexibility in responding to local markets is possible, placing high emphasis on local–regional markets. Second, it is apparent that unlike other operations, regional offices are drawn to locations with superior telecommunications infrastructure and other business financial services. Both Singapore's port and airport facilities are regarded as among the best in the world. The government is also currently developing a national information infrastructure (NII), with the aim of facilitating the exchange of goods, services, capital and information throughout the island.[5] It has exploited the Internet, setting up a Singapore, Inc. website to market itself, helping foreign firms to establish partnerships with local firms, while aggressively courting businesses through provision of relevant information and data on the country's business climate.[6]

That government incentives play only a marginal role in the choice of regional office location is interesting given the attention that the Singapore government has paid to incentives. For instance, the Economic Development Board introduced tax breaks for regional offices under the Operational Headquarters scheme, and more recently also established the Business Headquarters program in order to attract a wider range of regional offices with the result that eligibility requirements were lowered (Perry, 1995). Similarly, the high costs faced by regional offices in Singapore appear to have been a deterrent, especially with respect to labor costs and office rentals, although regional offices typically rely much more on expatriate labor than most other types of offices. To sum up, Table 10.3 points to locational advantages of centrality, geographical proximity to markets, and business infrastructure rather than costs and host country incentives as the key locational determinants that favor Singapore over other countries in the region.

As noted in previous sections, regional offices serve a rather wide variety of functions. Table 10.4, however, suggests that a key role of regional offices in Singapore pertains to its ability to coordinate spatially dispersed affiliate activities in the Asian region, since a high priority is placed on the geographical centrality and nodal positioning of Singapore in MNCs' regional production and distribution networks.

Table 10.4 Main mechanisms for exercising control over affiliates

Mechanism	Number
Report of local managers	64
Inspection by top management executives	41
Cost control	38
Centralized decision-making	22
Inventory and quality control	15
Production planning	10

When asked about the principal mechanisms by which regional offices in Singapore exercised control over the operations of their subsidiaries, the most important mechanisms turn out to be reporting by local managers (n=64), followed by inspection by top management executives from regional offices (n=41) and the control of costs by regional offices (n=38).

This largely supports the literature's observation that regional management control is facilitated via the geographical positioning of regional offices *vis-à-vis* their proximity to subsidiaries. Other mechanisms of control, albeit far less significant, include the centralization of decision-making (n= 22) as well as inventory control (n=15) and production planning by regional offices (n=10). That Singapore is able to shore up its spatial position within the Southeast Asian regional hierarchy is further confirmed in Table 10.5.

Here, respondents were asked about the special advantages of Singapore as a regional office. An overwhelming number of firms listed its flexibility in local and regional markets and the country's integration within the region as its top advantages. Such advantages point to Singapore's ability to embed itself within the regional framework and strategies of MNCs in order to exploit scale economies and to entrench the country as a value-adding commercial center.

Table 10.5 Special advantages of Singapore as a regional office

Advantages	Number
Flexibility in local and regional markets	87
More integrated with the region	86
Decentralization of decision-making	59
Greater coordination	37
Reduced corporate HQ's administrative burden	34

By offering regional offices greater autonomy, this allows for more decentralization of decision-making, which is typical of the heterarchical model of management. Two other advantages also need to be pointed out: regional offices in Singapore facilitate greater coordination in decision-making within the region (n=37) and help to relieve corporate headquarters of their administrative burden (n=34).

Finally, firms were asked to rate their perceptions of Singapore as a location for their regional offices (Table 10.6).

Table 10.6 Ratings of Singapore as a regional office[*]

Ratings in terms of:	Mean	Std dev.
Political stability	4.58	0.582
Telecommunications infrastructure	4.54	0.600
Quality of business services	4.03	0.666
Centrality to regional establishments	4.03	0.621
Proximity to local establishments	3.99	0.677
Access to customers	3.96	0.780
Government assistance	3.40	0.936
Operating costs	2.32	0.860

* 1= very unsatisfactory, 5= very satisfactory.

Source: Perry et al. (1998).

The ratings were ranked on a scale from 1 to 5, with 1 being very unsatisfactory and 5 being very satisfactory. The most important factors that favor Singapore are: political stability, telecommunications infrastructure, quality of business services, and centrality to regional establishments. All four factors scored means of 4 and above. Political stability also has the highest mean at 4.58 and lowest variability, with a standard deviation at 0.582. In other words, more respondents agreed than disagreed on political stability, followed by telecommunications infrastructure and centrality to regional establishments. Other factors such as proximity to local establishments and access to customers were also ranked highly, but a major negative perception of Singapore relates to its high operating costs, which scored only a mean of 2.3.

Table 10.6 confirms much of the earlier discussion about Singapore's nodal strength within the region. However, that political stability is accorded such a high priority and rating deserves some elaboration here. Heavy intervention by the state in the economic activities of Singapore is widely noted in the literature (Lim, 1983; Huff, 1995). The country's successful export performance since the 1960s has largely relied on institutional reforms that concentrated economic decision-making in the hands of the government. The creation of the Economic Development Board to spearhead Singapore's industrial development is one such example, as are other governmental bodies such as the retirement and savings system under the Central Provident Fund. As noted by Haggard (1990), the government moved in a decidedly interventionist direction through a combination of economic policy and political organization as soon as political power was consolidated. Foreign capital was instrumental to this political strategy because the alternative of fostering indigenous capital, especially among Chinese businesspeople, was untenable since this could potentially complicate political management given the originally relatively strong ties of the Chinese to China.

State intervention has ensured important continuity in economic and social policies, which is highly valued by foreign investors. Krause (1987) has argued that perfect competition in private markets cannot be successful in a case like Singapore because of its small size, thus necessitating a major role for the government in the economic sector in order to correct market failures. By fostering a stable macroeconomic environment, a discouragement of labor organization, and an emphasis on producer over consumer interests, Singapore's political system is seen to be one of the most stable in Southeast Asia. Such a perception is no doubt strengthened by the recent financial crisis. Indonesia approached social anarchy in May of 1998, while Malaysia is witnessing the possibility of social and political changes with the arrest of its liberal former deputy prime minister.

CONCLUSION

While export-based industrialization has been important in integrating Singapore with the global economy, its policy-makers made a decided shift in industrial strategy in the 1980s to capitalize on the more complex and refined patterns of the regional division of labor associated with international capital investments. With Indonesia and Malaysia surging ahead economically in the 1980s, in the hope of leap-frogging into the high-tech era with the aircraft industry in the former, and a multimedia supercorridor in the latter, Singapore instead focused on exploiting its competitive advantage through rational regional integration. Further, the state has attempted to shape international investment behavior in the region by engineering its position within MNC networks. Regional offices provide a means to achieve such spatial privileging as they help transform Singapore into a decision-making center rather than a low-value production-based center. By carving out a particular niche in the ongoing global and regional segmentation of the value chain, Singapore is assured of its nodal lead in Southeast Asia's regional hierarchy.

Our survey results confirm that Singapore continues to remain attractive as a regional office center for foreign MNCs. While it faces competition from Hong Kong and Kuala Lumpur, recent political dynamics associated with the handover of Hong Kong to China and Malaysia's ambivalence towards foreign capital with the imposition of capital controls clearly enhance Singapore's locational advantage. That it is rated highly for its regional centrality, telecommunications and business–financial infrastructure further suggests that it will be some time before its lead in the regional hierarchy changes. Despite the 1997 monetary crisis in Southeast Asia, US oil company Caltex has announced plans to move its entire global corporate headquarters to Singapore from Irving, Texas. Further, the state has been aggressively courting MNCs to base the design of products for the world in Singapore. All this will likely move Singapore up the global value chain.

On the other hand, MNCs clearly make political stability a condition for locating their regional offices in Singapore. Despite the internal stability of the country, Singapore is highly dependent on its neighbors for economic sustainability, ranging from water supply to outward investments, trade and labor.[7] Recent dissent in ASEAN over the political fallout between Malaysia's current prime minister and its former deputy prime minister[8] suggests that Singapore's own position within the region is vulnerable as negative sentiments against the domination of Chinese capitalism rise. Singapore's ability to continue to operate as a gateway in the region, therefore, is likely to depend on treading a careful line between the sensitivities of its neighbors and the demands of international capital.

NOTES

1. The 1961 UN report suggests that wage costs in Singapore were historically 20–30 percent too high for international markets.
2. United Nations Industrial Survey Mission (1961).

3. Compared to its neighbors, Singapore does not have the problem of a large agrarian sector as well as territorial fragmentation and control. That Chinese constitute some 70 percent of the population also means that the country faces less of the racial competition between the Chinese and indigenous population that characterizes its neighbors in the region. Its transition to national sovereignty was marked by a relatively non-acrimonious relationship with Britain, having suffered no xenophobic hangover from colonialism (Lee, cited in Huff, 1995, p. 1431), thereby making the country far more receptive to foreign capital than many other countries in the region.
4. See http://www.sedb.com.sg.
5. Singapore's NII plan aims to establish an electronic network throughout the island that will help transform Singapore into an intelligent island following the year 2000. Smart cards will be used in place of monetary transactions while portable cellular data screens will be introduced to facilitate the flow of traffic throughout the island. All houses, schools, businesses and government agencies are expected to be connected through an electronic grid so as to plug the country into the global information network (Harvard Business School, 1996).
6. See www.singapore-inc.com.
7. It is estimated that there are at least 200,000 guest workers in Singapore (Huff, 1995).
8. Both ex-President Habibie of Indonesia and President Estrada of the Philippines have expressed dismay at the arrest of ex-deputy prime minister Anwar Ibrahim, departing from ASEAN's previous commitment to consensual consultation and non-interference in domestic politics (*Asiaweek*, 7 August 1998). Singapore also had a series of fallouts with Malaysia in 1997 with the latter expressing anger over Lee Kuan Yew's perceived negative remarks about Johor, and subsequently, Senior Prime Minister Lee's interpretation of the Malaysian–Singapore split in the early 1960s in his recent book *The Singapore Story.*

REFERENCES

Castells, M. (1996), *The Rise of the Network Society*, Cambridge, MA: Blackwell.

Chia, S.Y. (1997), 'Singapore: advanced production base and smart hub of the electronics industry', in W. Dobson and S.Y. Chia (eds), *Multinationals and East Asian Integration*, Singapore: Institute of Southeast Asian Studies, pp. 31–62.

Dicken, P. (1998), *Global Shift: Transforming the World Economy*, London: Paul Chapman.

Dobson, W. (1997), 'East Asian integration: synergies between firm strategies and government policies', in W. Dobson and S.Y. Chia (eds), *Multinationals and East Asian Integration*, Singapore: Institute of Southeast Asian Studies, pp. 3–30.

Dunning, J.H. (1993), *Multinational Enterprises and the Global Economy*, Reading, MA: Addison Wesley.

Economic Development Board (1995), *Yearbook*, Singapore: EDB.

Fallows, J. (1994), *Looking at the Sun*, New York: Pantheon.

Haggard, S. (1990), *Pathways from the Periphery: The Politics of Growth in the Newly Industrializing Countries*, Ithaca: Cornell University Press.

Hamel, G. and C.K. Prahalad (1994), *Competing for the Future: Breakthrough Strategies for Seizing Control of Your Industry and Creating the Markets of Tomorrow*, Boston, MA: Harvard University Press.

Harvard Business School (1996), *Singapore Unlimited: Building the National Information Infrastructure*, Boston, MA: Harvard Business School Publishing.

Hedlund, G. (1986), 'The hypermodern MNC – a heterarchy?', *Human Resource Management*, 25, 9–35.

Hedlund, G. (1993), 'Assumptions of hierarchy and heterarchy, with applications to the management of the multinational corporation', in S. Ghoshal and D.E. Westney (eds), *Organization Theory and the Multinational Corporation*, New York: St Martin's Press, pp. 211–36.

Heenan, D.A. (1979), 'The Regional Headquarters Decision: A Comparative Analysis', *Academy of Management Journal*, **22**, 410–25.

Huff, W.G. (1995), 'The developmental state, government and Singapore's economic development since 1960', *World Development*, **23**, 1421–38.

Krause, L.B. (1987), 'The government as an entrepreneur', in L.B. Krause, A.T. Koh and Lee T.Y. (eds), *The Singapore Economy Reconsidered*, Singapore: Institute of Southeast Asian Studies, pp. 107–27.

Krugman, P. (1995), 'Growing world trade: causes and consequences', *Brookings Papers on Economic Activity*, I; pp. 327–76.

Lévy, B. (1995), 'Globalization and Regionalization: toward the shaping of a tripolar world economy', *The International Executive*, **37**, 349–71.

Lim, L. (1983), 'Singapore's success: the myth of the free market economy', *Asian Survey*, **23**, 752–64.

OECD (1997*), International Direct Investment Statistics Yearbook*, Paris: OECD.

Pang, E.F. (1995), 'Staying Global and Going Regional: Inward and Outward Direct Investments', in *The New Wave of Foreign Direct Investment in Asia*, Singapore: Institute of Southeast Asian Studies and Nomura Research Institute.

Perry, M. (1992), 'Promoting corporate control in Singapore', *Regional Studies*, **26**, 289–94.

Perry, M. (1995), 'New corporate structures, regional offices and Singapore's new economic directions', *Singapore Journal of Tropical Geography*, **16**, 181–96.

Perry, M., J.P.H. Poon and H. Yeung (1998), 'Regional offices in Singapore: spatial and strategic influences in the location of corporate control', *Review of Urban and Regional Development Studies*, **10**, 42-59.

Poon, J.P.H. (1997a), 'Inter-country trade patterns in Europe and the Asia-Pacific: regional structure and extra-regional trends', *Geografiska Annaler*, **79**(b), 41–53.

Poon, J.P.H. (1997b), 'The cosmopolitanization of trade regions: global trends and implications 1965–1990', *Economic Geography*, **73**, 390–404.

Poon, J.P.H. and E.R. Thompson (1998), 'Foreign direct investment and economic growth: evidence from Asia and Latin America', *Journal of Economic Development*, **23**.

Rodan, G. (1993), 'Reconstructing Divisions of Labor: Singapore's New Regional Emphasis', in R. Higgott, R. Leaver and J. Ravenhill (eds*)*, *Pacific Economic Relations in the 1990s: Cooperation or Conflict?*, St Leonards, Australia: Allen and Unwin, pp. 223–49.

Scott, A. (1996), 'Regional motors of the global economy', *Futures*, **28**, 391–411.

Storper, M. (1995), 'The resurgence of regional economies, ten years later', *European Urban and Regional Studies*, **2**, 191–221.

Sullivan, D. (1992), 'Organization in American MNCs: The perspective of the European regional headquarters', *Management International Review*, **32**, 237–50.

Tejima, S. (1996), 'Foreign direct investment by Japanese firms in the Asia-Pacific region', in D.K. Das (ed.), *Emerging Growth Pole: The Asia-Pacific Economy*, New York: Prentice-Hall, pp. 122–56.

United Nations Industrial Survey Mission (1961), *A Proposed Industrialization Scheme for Singapore*, UN Commission for Technical Assistance, Department of Economics and Social Affairs.

United Nations (1991), *World Investment Report: The Triad in Foreign Direct Investment*, New York: UN.

United Nations (1996), *World Investment Report 1996: Investment, Trade and International Policy Arrangements*, New York: UN.

Yeung, H. (1998), 'The political economy of multinational corporations: a study of the regionalization of Singaporean firms', *Political Geography*, **17**, 389–416.

11. Gateway Sydney – from the Tyranny of Distance to Strategic Hub

Wolfgang Kasper

OF PLACE AND TIME

Sydney began as a gateway to nowhere. In 1788, a British fleet arrived to establish a convict colony, and soon an impressive colonial city was laid out at the edge of an unknown, remote and hostile-looking Southland. In the intervening 210 years, the Sydney region – spanning some 200 km along the coastal fringe from Port Kembla in the south to the city of Newcastle in the north, and some 50 km inland to the Blue Mountains – has developed into the premier metropolis in that third of the earth's surface that lies between the equator, Africa's east coast and South America's west coast.

This statement is not all that impressive, since Sydney lies in the middle of the empty third of the world. Only 5 percent of humankind live here. This is one way of drawing attention to the central theme about Sydney, namely that it has developed under the 'tyranny of distance'.[1]

In its first century, the Sydney region's population rose from a few bands of Aborigines and a few shiploads of administrators, military and convicts to about half a million inhabitants. And a little more than another century later, as of 1998, the wider Sydney region is home to close to 5 million people, nearly a quarter of all Australians. The more narrowly defined Sydney Metropolitan Area had about 4 million inhabitants.

The Sydney region is the central place in the southwest Pacific, ranking ahead of the dynamic Brisbane region (700 km to the north), Melbourne (700 km to the southwest), and Auckland (some 2200 km to the east in New Zealand). Sydney is the leading gateway to Australia and the southwest Pacific region and has become one of the central nodes in the global market-place for ideas, products and services. Although it does not count among the world's top centers, such as New York, London or Tokyo, it ranks without doubt among the second tier of world cities as a global hub in financial, research, transport, trade and artists' networks. Its distinguishing feature is that it lies further away from the other major central places than any other.

The distance to the nearest comparable world city, Singapore, is further than New York to Paris.

Nowadays, the Sydney region is one of the metropolitan places on the globe where innovative ideas, products, services and methods of organization are tried out and from where they are marketed globally. In Sydney's case, innovation is often based on a youthful Australian can-do spirit and inspired by a unique European–Asian cultural mix coupled with Anglo-Saxon institutions and traditions.

In many ways, contemporary Sydney, as it now competes globally, finds itself in a challenging open economy position similar to the city states of ancient Greece, when each polis was an independent, open testing unit for ideas, but the poleis operated within a shared system of competition and exchange. In short, interjurisdictional rivalry has often been crucial to amazing outbursts of commercial, technical and cultural creativity.[2] Likewise, rivalry had earlier promoted creativity among the Sumerian and Phoenician trading centers, and rivalry among the cities of Renaissance Italy and the early modern Netherlands also served to pave the way for innovation and subsequent economic growth.

The historically minded reader may conceive of the Sydney region as a distant colony of the old world which flourishes from interaction with its more immediate surroundings, in the mold of Greek Marsilia (Marseilles) in Antiquity. The prosperity of such 'outlier centers' depends on continuing trade and factor flows, a degree of independence coupled with shared concepts and institutions, such as the commercial, legal and financial culture of the core economies (OECD and East Asia) in the global system of the present day. As we shall see, this constellation of circumstances has been developing in Sydney.

OF CENTER AND PERIPHERY

The peculiarities of the Sydney region, its past and present problems, and its potential for future prosperity can best be analyzed within a Thünen-type framework of center and periphery.[3] The economic, geographic and historic context against which to interpret Sydney's evolution may be sketched for the purposes of our analysis as follows.

The economic development of most nations and regions is nowadays shaped by the observation that capital, high technical and organizational skills, knowledge and entrepreneurship (as well as organized bundles of these production factors, called 'firms') are increasingly mobile, whereas labor, land and government administration are the major immobile production factors. This means that the owners or controllers of immobile labor, land and administrations can attract mobile resources to compete in global markets only if they bear the costs of transport and communications to the central marketplaces of the world. Those who operate near the periphery and who are immobile thus have to accept lower incomes, lest the mobile factors desert them.

The long-term trend in transport and communications costs has been downward, so that the 'periphery handicap' of places like Sydney has been reduced over time (Tables 11.1a and 11.1b). Owners of land, workers and government authorities on the periphery of trading networks therefore derive a direct gain from technical, organizational and infrastructural developments which reduce these costs. While the fall in shipping and air travel costs has been considerable over the past two generations, the costs of telecommunications have plummeted over recent decades. These trends can be expected to continue.

Table 11.1a The secular decline in transport and communications costs percentage changes p.a., in constant 1990 US$

	1930–50 %	1950–95 %
Average cost of freight and port handling (per ton) in international trade	– 2.8	– 0.5
Average air revenue per passenger mile	– 4.0	– 2.6
Cost of London–New York phone call (3 min.)	– 7.3	– 7.5

Source: G. Hufbauer (1991), 'World Economic Integration, The Long View', *International Economic Insights* (May/June), p. 26; updated by own estimates.

Table 11.1b The recent plummeting of the costs of transmitting information

	Index of US$ cost of transmitting 1 million bits of information over 1 km, 1975 = 100	Bandwidth (mill. bits/sec) in optical fibre transmission
1975	100.0	45
1985	9.8	400
1995	0.1	10,000
2000(projected)	0.06	40,000

Source: J. Bond (1997), 'The Drivers of the Information Revolution – Cost, Computing, and Convergence', in World Bank, *The Information Revolution and the Future of Telecommunications* (Washington: World Bank).

What matters to the profitability of the owners of the mobile factors, who make the locational decisions, is not the factor price, but factor unit cost, i.e., the price of using a production factor relative to the efficiency of its use (e.g., the wage relative to labor productivity). Productivity increases thus make a location more attractive to mobile factors. They facilitate the 'immigration' of capital and enterprise, and this may well trigger further productivity increases, producing a 'virtuous circle' of growth. By contrast, obstacles to productivity growth tend to induce outflows of capital, know-how and enterprise and lead to the decline of regional economies.

Given that there is some friction in factor mobility in the form of risks and transaction costs, those in control of immobile factors in a peripheral location are well advised to offer even lower unit costs than are merited by mere transport-cost differentials. As original peripheral centers such as Singapore have demonstrated, this sacrifice to attract sufficient mobile resources to promote its growth is only temporary. Once a good reputation and a critical mass of activities are established, the 'periphery sacrifice' can be ended and local incomes can rise without causing a setback to the growth process.

In this context, one must not look merely at production cost. One also has to take into account what is typically the other half of all costs of producing and distributing the national product, namely transaction costs. These are the costs of finding and testing knowledge about economic opportunities, as well as of concluding, monitoring and enforcing contractual commitments. Transaction costs are determined to a large extent by institutions, the rules that pattern human conduct and inflict penalties for their violations (Kasper and Streit, 1998, chs. 5 and 6). They are, so to speak, the software that facilitates the effective use of a community's hardware, its capital, labor and infrastructures. The quality of institutions and their impact on transaction-cost levels varies greatly among jurisdictions.

Not only do the government-made institutions, such as legislation and regulations, differ, but above all the internal institutions, which evolve within society and which are largely self-enforcing (such as ethical norms, customs and work practices) vary greatly. The external and internal institutions of a community or region determine the effectiveness with which scarce resources can be combined. Therefore, institutions have to be seen as a production factor whose presence and effectiveness influence the productivities of all other factors. Good government is an important component part of that institutional capital (Kasper and Streit, 1998).

The quality of institutional capital has particular impacts on two increasingly important classes of economic activity: (i) innovation and (ii) services which are at the core of any enduring gateway region to the global economy.

(i) Entrepreneurs who want to innovate are heavily exposed to institutional conditions because the transaction costs in new ventures are much higher than in routine production and because the transaction costs of finding and testing new knowledge can be more easily predicted if uncertainties about the behavior of others are constrained by reliable institutions.

(ii) Services are nowadays often tailor-made for the individual client. Their efficient production depends on the level of trust, which the prevailing rules of conduct establish. Thus bankers, accountants, traders and the providers of headquarter services have to rely to an unusual degree on trust based on the credible enforcement of rules.

At the same time, the communications revolution is now permitting long-distance trade in more and more services, so that institutions are becoming increasingly important to the overall cost competitiveness of service industries in a specific location.[4] The world cities, which are predominantly centers of innovation and service provision, can therefore nowadays only flourish in a climate of expedient and low-cost institutions. The basic economic gameplan of the Sydney region differed in important respects from, say, your average European gateway region in that its location on the global periphery imposed a 'tyranny of distance', i.e., high transport and communication costs in communicating and trading with other gateway cities. The other dominant theme for most of Sydney's history was that labor, too, had to be treated as an internationally mobile factor. Workers had to be attracted by high wages to overcome the high transport and transaction costs of intercontinental migration and to compete for new settlers with the better-established United States.

Because Sydney was the archetypical immigrant-attracting gateway to a young nation, public attitudes and policy settings had to differ fundamentally from those centers that grew in or near labor-surplus regions: when both capital and labor are to be attracted, profits and wages have to be relatively high, making growth harder. The more recent decline in transport costs and the sea change from labor shortages to surpluses have fundamentally altered the driving forces behind Sydney's continuing ascendancy, coincidentally at a time when economic dynamism shifted into the Asia-Pacific neighborhood. These changes have inflicted adjustment costs and have led to disorientation and confusion in the perceptions of policy-makers and the public.

A 'MIRACLE ECONOMY' OF THE 19TH CENTURY

It took some 25 years after the landing of the first British fleet untill some enterprising young men managed to find an opening through the Blue

Mountains barrier into the vast, open spaces of inland Australia. In the course of the nineteenth century, the colony of New South Wales (about 800,000 square km, roughly the size of France and the UK combined) developed rapidly. Exports were channeled through Sydney, making it the focal node of a radial system of roads and railway lines and of shipping networks up and down the coast and to the Pacific islands. The economy of the colony grew fast as exportable, land-intensive goods suitable for long-distance transport – primarily wool and wheat – were found and developed.

From a low base in 1790, the economy of New South Wales grew at a break-neck rate of 9.8 percent p.a. for the 60 years to 1850 (Butlin, in Vamplew, 1988, p. 128). By the middle of the nineteenth century, Sydney and its New South Wales hinterland accounted for nearly half the product of the entire continent, although six separate colonies had been set up around the coast and on Tasmania. Sydney's record economic growth was due to a number of factors:

(a) The Sydney region attracted many talented, enterprising people and considerable amounts of British capital. While a first generation of entrepreneurs came to Sydney to make a fortune before retiring to Britain, many soon stayed and became Australians in outlook and spirit, reinvesting their profits in new Australian ventures (Shann, 1930; Blainey, 1994).

(b) Land and natural resources were abundant in Sydney's hinterland. During the nineteenth century, they could be exploited by new technologies and new forms of economic organization and delivered to the markets of industrializing Britain and Europe.

(c) From the outset, labor was the bottleneck to economic growth. Labor scarcity, together with economic opportunities, drove up wages, but also living standards. This created strong incentives to go about one's business in labor-saving ways, shaping attitudes and favoring technical and organizational pragmatism still visible some 150 years later. Not perfection, but a certain can-do improvisation became the hallmark of work and life in Sydney.

(d) The growing shipping trade eased Sydney's isolation. Innovations and deregulation reduced transport costs from and to 'the Motherland'. Australian ports also gained from the competition of fast and big Yankee clippers, and liberal reforms (such as the repeal of the Navigation Acts) removed barriers to trade. The need to apply for licenses from the East India Company if one wanted to trade with Sydney fell prey to the liberalization of the early Victorian era (Blainey, 1966, ch. 3). This reduced the transport cost burden which had to be borne by those living in the arguably most peripheral city of the world economy. The flip-side was of course that relatively high transport costs encouraged local improvisation and inventiveness.

(e) Immigrants brought with them the internal institutions of early nineteenth century British capitalism which facilitated commerce and development.[5] They also imported the time-tested British rule of law, rule systems that made for small and expedient government, and trustworthy basic organizations of government. Different from colonies with large indigenous populations, New South Wales inherited a rule system that was spontaneously adhered to by almost all.

This made for low costs of transacting business. The imported institutional capital therefore facilitated the influx of capital and people and their ready and productive absorption into the local economy. However, when the imported institutions did not address their purposes and circumstances, Sydneysiders were quick to reform the rules, soon through a rough-and-ready local democracy.

During the second half of the nineteenth century, Sydney's population and production continued to grow at a fast pace. But what had been the premier colony in Australasia was now overshadowed by the even more dynamic expansion of Melbourne and the colony of Victoria, after substantial gold deposits had been discovered there in the 1850s. 'Marvelous Melbourne' – a much more affluent place than contemporary New York, let alone the overcrowded cities of Europe – overtook Sydney in size and dynamism. From the mid-1850s to 1890, the lead in the rivalry between Sydney and Melbourne was taken by the Victorians. The more larrikin, more individualistic character of Sydney came to be overshadowed by the more orderly, sober ways subscribed to by the Melbourne establishment.

Since the early days, Sydneysiders have probably always been biased in the direction of individual initiative, irreverence, short-termism, spontaneous ordering and the enjoyment of life, whereas Melbournians tended to have more of a preference for collective action and top-down ordering and governance. These differences in the *genius loci* still linger. They may well constitute a competitive advantage for Sydney in the fast-changing circumstances of the twenty-first century as spontaneous responses may again have an advantage over coordinated, orderly reaction.

The boost from the gold boom was soon enhanced by steam-powered transport and shipping. This made it easier to open up a vast continent the size of Europe. Australia was developed by surprisingly few people: only some 3 million lived in the entire continent in 1890 (Vamplew, 1988, p. 34). Rapid economic growth in Sydney and elsewhere in the Australian colonies came to an abrupt end in the 'Land Crash of 1888', a financial and economic crisis similar to the East Asian crash of 1997–99. The crisis had been brought on by the careless and poorly audited accumulation of domestic and external debts and speculative real-estate developments with little regard to rates of return. Yet the responses to the crisis of 1888 differed greatly between Sydney and Melbourne:

The colony of Victoria opted for tariff protection, relying on a wave of populist local patriotism, whereas the free-trading party of New South Wales Premier George H. Reid enacted a series of financial, agrarian and fiscal reforms 'which set free ... the resources of the land and the energies of its people ... Reid removed protective duties. New South Wales made a recovery in bold contrast with the long stagnation that followed ... in Victoria and South Australia' (Shann, 1930, pp. 336–41). Sydney soon overtook Melbourne again in population and economic prowess. It has not looked back since.

FEDERATION AND THE 'AUSTRALIAN SETTLEMENT'

Sydney's resurgence from the setback of the 1890s was to have an unexpected long-term side-effect. The next generation of Sydneysiders were drawn to commerce and industry where they propelled the 'Federation boom' after the Australian colonies had united in 1901. By contrast, the Melbourne establishment channeled much more of its talent into government, imprinting a fairly *dirigiste* approach on the constitutional make-up of the new Commonwealth of Australia for most of the twentieth century.

The new nation had its government and high court in Melbourne until a new national capital was built decades later. The political élites that shaped the life of the new nation relied on the country's extraordinarily high per capita incomes (at the time considerably ahead of the United Kingdom and the United States) to construct a socially reformist electoral democracy which was inspired by the collectivist, Fabian fashions of late nineteenth century Europe. An 'Australian Settlement' was soon put in place by federal politicians and judges. This was a social compact that aimed to provide security for all, promising a paternalistic, egalitarian welfare state and a central wage-fixing system to distribute Australia's bounty to all. This compact had to be protected from outside interference. It therefore rested on immigration control (the 'White Australia Policy'), industrial protectionism, and British military protection (Kelly, 1992, pp. 1–12).

The emphasis on the top-down provision of security and inward-looking policies in the new Federation led to a pronounced and lasting slowdown in long-term economic growth nationwide. During the first half of the twentieth century, Australian real per capita incomes grew by only 0.6 percent p.a. (Kasper et al., 1980, pp. 27–31), and Australians, who had been some 20 percent better off than west Europeans in 1950 are now 10–20 percent less affluent. Inward-looking policies and redistributional interventionism are diagnosed as the main causes of the slowdown in the growth trend, but of course two world wars, the Great Depression, strong and often obdurate unions, and the 'tyranny of distance' also took their toll.

Despite slow economic progress nationwide, Sydney's growth continued. It was fed by the secular drift to the urban and coastal areas and by the influx of international migrants. Many of the new migrants stayed within 50 miles of where they had stepped off the boat, adding to congestion costs and urban sprawl. The interventions on which the 'Australian Settlement' rested were intended to redistribute the bounty of the land from mining and agriculture to urban voters and the emerging, protected manufacturing industries. In the first half of the twentieth century, the Sydney region attracted many 'tariff factories'. Trade protection of manufacturing was a means of keeping Australia attractive both to internationally mobile capital and labor. Tariffs were handed out, often 'on demand', in order to raise prices and industry profits. Central wage-fixing was then used to redistribute industry profits to the workers, spreading middle-class living standards and amenities to all, but also raising costs in primary and tertiary activities. The centralization – and de-marketization – of wage-fixing politicized labor markets and gave rise to strong unions who enjoyed numerous political privileges.

For Australia's affluent workers, the wage was no longer something that one earned by being productive, but rather a benefit handed down after much political posturing by interest-group representatives before quasi-judicial tribunals. This bred attitudes inimical to productivity growth in industry and made the entire industrial culture, indeed the entire suburban culture, look toward government for material security and advancement. The proliferating interventionism weakened the spontaneous forces that might have overcome the effects of the Great Depression. Redistribution and egalitarianism made entrepreneurship unrewarding, instead breading contented mediocrity and boredom in economic life. But at least for Sydneysiders there was always the consolation of competition in sport and life on the beach as safety valves for spontaneous energies.

The culture of protectionism not only raised production costs, but gradually also transaction-cost levels. In open economies, the discipline of interjurisdictional competition tends to induce communities and governments to reform and streamline their internal and external institutions as a means of developing competitive transaction cost levels. People cooperate to control the costs of doing business simply because they sit in the same boat and have to face a common adversary, foreign competition.

By contrast, closed, protected economies can be run by the costly visible hand of political case-by-case intervention. Over time, this makes for high transaction costs – an unintended side-effect of an inward-looking interventionism of the sort that Australia practiced from the beginning of the twentieth century. This handicapped the competitiveness of centers such as Sydney. As a result, headquarters and the production of intermediary services, such as in trade and international finance, could not be easily attracted to Sydney. In this situation, the Second World War came as a shock. When Japanese pocket submarines did some minor damage in Sydney Harbour, the idyll of a distant, comfortable 'Britannia Downunder' suddenly looked threatened. After the war, when all of Australia still had only 7 million inhabitants, the national government endorsed the slogan 'populate or perish' and launched one of the most remarkable migration campaigns in human history. During the ensuing three decades, Australia's comparatively high natural population growth was doubled by immigration; the country's population rose by about one million every four years. Sydney received a fair share of that growth, leading to urban sprawl. By the 1980s, massive immigration had transformed Australia, now with a greater share of overseas-born residents than any other country except Israel.

Sydney became Australia's major gateway for immigrants, who filled up new, protected industrial workplaces and suburbs. An increasingly cosmopolitan mix of immigrants, initially from Europe, but since the 1970s increasingly also from Asia and the Middle East, added to Sydney's growth. Successive immigration waves turned what had been a British colonial city into an ethnic melting pot with an arguably wider selection of foods, lifestyles, and cultural manifestations than any city of that size in the world. The mixing of cultures went along with surprisingly little friction. This was facilitated by the British-inherited rule of law, an open, egalitarian democracy, and access to subsidized education, health and other social services – features of Australian life that many new migrants embraced enthusiastically.

Integration in the 1950s and 1960s was also helped by the fact that government was not very intrusive in daily life, that the incumbent population was easy-going and tolerant and that most immigrants were eager young workers with welcome skills. Many a small immigrant business probably thrived because the newly arrived entrepreneurs could not read the fine print of existing regulations, and many an immigrant began to feel Australian because there was much leeway to live one's private life as one pleased.

More recently, some social tensions have surfaced in those Sydney suburbs where certain immigrant groups concentrated and after politicians had engaged in organizing the 'ethnic vote' and subsidizing those 'ethnic industries' which thrive on organizing a degree of separateness and the durable cohesion of immigrant groups. Nonetheless, compared to other newly multi-ethnic centers, Sydney has to be considered a success of multicultural peace and harmony.

THE CREATIVE DESTRUCTION OF THE 'AUSTRALIAN SETTLEMENT'

By the 1970s, it was evident that the 'Australian Settlement' had led to a benign, tolerant, but mediocre society, poor economic growth, high costs and a pervasive industrial malaise. It was no longer tenable. Sydney had become a gateway not only to long-distance flights to London and Los Angeles, but increasingly also to Tokyo, Jakarta, Singapore and Hong Kong. Exports of raw materials – in the case of the Sydney region, mainly local coal, as well as foodstuffs and fibers from the hinterland – flowed increasingly to the new expanding economies of East Asia. Japan became Australia's main trading partner in the 1960s, and in the 1980s the 'tigers' and China added new export demand. They also were the source of much inflation-controlling competition in consumer goods markets. By contrast, Britain and Europe receded into the background, not only in trade, but also as a cultural and political reference point. Australians, who had fought during two world wars in Europe and around the Suez Canal, will never do so again. Australian interests now lie in the Pacific.

Sydney probably began to look across the Pacific and to East Asia earlier than the other centers of Australia. At the same time, Sydney became a magnet for Asia's newly well-to-do tourists and for Asian students, artists and businessmen who wanted to experience first hand how things were done by the only major European culture in their neighborhood. Some stayed and added to Sydney's cultural and economic tapestry and the cross-fertilization between Western and Asian ideas and concepts.

The chain reaction of cultural interaction in Sydney continues unabated. It has become a draw card for overseas businesses with an interest in Asia. In Sydney, you can easily hire people who know Asia's cultures, institutions and languages and who retain ties to East Asian networks. Here, you can set up shop if you have business in Asian time zones, but harbor reservations whether you can cope in one of the crowded and costly new centers of Asia. Being near and involved in Asia, yet at some distance, safe and full of familiar amenities, has become one of Sydney's major draw cards. It explains why so much intermediation between new and old industrial countries now takes place in Sydney.

During the 1980s, some politicians even tried to cast Australia as an integral part of a successful Asia, much to the disbelief and bewilderment of many Asians. As of the late 1990s, it seems widely accepted that Australia is a distinct country of British heritage, but with a destiny of its own and that it need not force its way into foreign regional clubs to survive and prosper.As the external protections of the 'Australian Settlement' fell prey to creative destruction and as advances in transport and communications (such as the jetliner, the container, satellites, fax, e-mail) reduced Sydney's traditional transport cost disadvantage, the economic–geographic context in which Sydney operates shifted dramatically. The center of gravity in the global economy has been shifting to the Pacific, faster than most Sydneysiders realize. This trend will continue. Whereas most of the world's megalopolises were clustered around the North Atlantic and most sea-borne trade had crossed between Europe and North America 50 years ago, the bulk of the biggest cities has been moving to the Pacific Rim and South Asia (Table 11.2).

Table 11.2 Shifts in economic geography. Megalopolises1950 and 2015.

Megalopolises 1950		Megalopolises 2015 (forecast)	
Rank order 1950	Inhabitants (mill.)	Rank order 2015 (forecast)	Inhabitants (mill.)
1. New York	12.3	Tokyo	28.7
2. London	8.7	Bonbay	27.4
3. Tokyo	6.9	Lagos	24.4
4. Paris	5.4	Shanghai	23.4
5. Moscow	5.4	Jakarta	21.2
6. Shanghai	5.3	Sao Paolo	20.8
7. Essen	5.3	Karachi	20.6
8. Buenos Aires	5.0	Beijing	19.4
9. Chicago	4.9	Dhaka	19.0
10. Calcutta	4.4	Mexico City	18.8
11. Osaka	4.1	New York	17.6
12. Los Angeles	4.0	Calcutta	17.6
13. Beijing	3.9	Delhi	17.6
14. Milan	3.6	Tianjin	17.0
15. Berlin	3.3	Manila	14.7

Source: UN, Urbanisation Prospects.

Already for some time more trade has been flowing across the (north) Pacific than the Atlantic. This shift of economic and industrial weight into the Sydney time zone will continue, in effect restoring original historic patterns. East Asia had long been ahead of the Far West of the Eurasian continent in science, technology, administration and economic achievement. It was only the European ascendancy from the sixteenth century onwards and China's secular decline in the nineteenth and early twentieth centuries that had turned the tables (Jones et al., 1994; Linder, 1986). Consequently, the

Sydney region was born as an outpost of a distant Europe that saw itself – with some justification for a time – as the center of the world economy.

Sydney's traditional mind-set was thus that of a distant outpost on the periphery. This conception has now been largely shed. The world has become truly polycentric and the biggest weight of economic and industrial mass has shifted back to the Pacific. The partial liberalization of Asian economies enhanced Sydney's geo-economic position. In addition, the creation of a free-trade area between Australia and fast-liberalizing New Zealand offered further opportunities for Sydney to become the prominent gateway in the southwest Pacific.

These shifts and the evident economic failures of Australian protectionism drove home a reluctant recognition that tariff protection and capital controls had to go, even if 'tariff factories' had to be closed. It was slowly realized during the 1970s that Australia had to find new niches in open global trade and financial networks, and that tariffs and other border controls constituted artificial transport costs which worked only to the detriment of local wages, land rents and tax revenues. Booming resource demand in East Asia and the rise of Sydney's service sector helped to attenuate the pains of the liberalization process that gathered steam during the 1980s.

It took political leaders and the public a long time to realize that the other legacies of the 'Australian Settlement' – regulated labor markets, high transaction costs, and an interventionist, though benevolent, state – would also have to be jettisoned if Australian locations were to be competitive in the global age. As of the late 1990s, Australia has one of the most open economies, with low tariff rates and a very liberal regime governing trade in banking, insurance and securities services, far more liberal than the Asian economies except Hong Kong and Singapore (Productivity Commission, 1998). Some interest groups and populist politicians are admittedly still fighting rear-guard actions against the opening of the economy and the deregulation of internal markets. However, most citizens now realize that – among the old industrial countries – Australia is in a front-line position *vis-à-vis* the emerging Asian industrial societies and can compete only on the basis of open, expedient and business-supporting institutions.

The Sydney region adjusted to the changing economic circumstances much more easily than the other industrial centers of Australia. Indeed, as a gateway city with an educated workforce, it benefited from the new circumstances disproportionately. First, there had been less reliance all along on protected industries in Sydney, but the steel centers to the north and south of Sydney (Newcastle and Wollongong) are suffering continuing adjustment pains. Relatively fewer industrial capacities than in Melbourne or Adelaide had to 'die' after the climate change of the 1980s and numerous new jobs were 'born' in the lightly regulated, competitive service industries. Sydney's tariff factories, such as car assembly plants, therefore closed amid much less agony than in the 'rust-belt states' to the south.

Liberalization turned the 1980s and 1990s on balance into a time of economic and cultural revival for Sydney. In the years from 1991 to 1997, the volume of jobs in the Sydney region was growing by 10 percent p.a., roughly as fast as during the concurrent revival of London, but less than in the boom cities of East Asia (Committee for Sydney, 1998, p. 17). As the shackles of inward-looking policies and collective action were eased, Sydney could draw on its traditional assets of individualism, irreverence, a can-do spirit, good weather and an attractive lifestyle to become one of the archetypical service centers within international webs. New assets, such as a cosmopolitan population mix, high education levels, and privatized, competitive service infrastructures added to Sydney's competitive strengths.

The change in activity mix from heavily unionized, regulated manufacturing to non-unionized, lightly regulated services de-activated many of the growth handicaps that had hampered traditional industries. At the same time, institutional reforms helped to lower some transaction costs, although much remains to be done, especially in labor markets, taxation and governance.

THE NEW BALLGAME

At the start of the new millennium, the fundamental economic conditions in which the Sydney region develops differ fundamentally from those that have shaped most of its history.

(a) What was an inward-looking transshipment place and an export port for bulk materials became an outward-looking center with a primary commitment to service activities. Of course, all major cities in history have moved from production to trade and on to finance and services. But the shift happened much more quickly in Sydney because of the conjunction of economic liberalization, the rise of East Asia and the changes in the technology, organization and marketing of communications.

(b) Globalization and the Asian ascendancy reduced the transport-cost handicap of what had long been an 'outlier center' by more than in those world cities that are fairly close to others. This accelerated the change.

(c) Fortuitously, the shift in Sydney's product mix from manufacturing and bulk-handling to high-level services was a shift from areas of collectively boosted transaction costs – manifested by discriminatory tariffs, industry regulation and a confrontational, privileged industrial-relations system – to activities where Australia's older political, legal and cultural traditions allow competitive transaction costs. Many of the new service industries can rely on fairly expedient institutions, in particular relative to most centers in East Asia which are now suffering from an 'institutional deficit' and relatively high transaction costs (Kasper, 1999).

At a time of labor surpluses, immigration is no longer a priority. Australians can import labor indirectly in the form of labor-intensive goods from Asia. Consequently, the challenge now is to make Sydney attractive to mobile capital and enterprise by, among other things, undoing artificial labor privileges and fostering a culture of productivity growth. Deeply entrenched attitudes and institutions need to be changed so that Sydney's workers act on the maxim that their jobs compete with jobs in Singapore, Taipei or San Diego. This culture change is under way, but far from complete.

Another necessary culture change stems from the realization that the role of government has irreversibly changed from being a ruler with hierarchical power over a closed economy to acting as a support organization for internationally competing niche exporters of goods and services. Governing service industries requires a different approach from the traditional forms of ruling over agriculture, mining and manufacturing. Mistakes of governance now have much more immediate feedback because capital and enterprises simply vote with their feet against artificially high transaction-cost levels. The faster feedback enhances the evolutionary quality of the system, but imposes unfamiliar strictures on the political agents.

These culture changes have to be made in a world in which the number of globally competing jobs has been rising dramatically. Whereas modern industry was, by and large, the possession of the Western countries at the middle of the twentieth century, huge new workforces of increasingly well-educated and well-led industrial workers elsewhere have now joined in global competition. They are prepared to work for less and are raising their productivity so that the competition among world-market-oriented jobs has intensified. Some workers in established high-income centers such as Sydney now find it hard to cope, because incomplete reforms inflict costs which make it harder to face the new competitors.

As a consequence, the Sydney region now has pockets of high unemployment and low incomes. These problems are not readily visible from the booming city center and the high rises that have transformed the skyline. Yet the fight is tough for people of poor education, immigrants with poor English-language and work skills and mental attitudes that stand in the way of pragmatic adjustment. This is of course a universal problem. In Sydney at least there has been much growth and there are more opportunities to escape poverty than in many older centers overseas that face the same challenges of globalization.

A SNAPSHOT OF SYDNEY AT THE TURN OF THE CENTURY

A recent private report on the future of Sydney found that the region performed reasonably well against comparable benchmark cities on a range of quantitative measures. It also shared problems with other world cities, such as urban sprawl, environmental and traffic problems, congestion, social and safety concerns, and concerns about sustaining prosperity (Table 11.3).

Table 11.3 Sydney by comparison with other benchmark cities

	Sydney Metro-politan	Van-couver Region	N Y City	London (Greater)	Frankfurt (Rhine Main)	Singa-pore
Population (mill.)	4	1.8	8.6	7	4.7	3
Av.annual temp.(°C)	17.6	9.9	14.2	11.2	9.9	26.7
Airport–city (km)	8	20	20-25	42	9	20
Nonstop flights (no. of cities)	41	55	130	116	77	25
Air passenger (mill., 1996)	20.2	14.0	81.0	84.6	38.0	23.1
Air freight ('000tons, 1996)	413	191	2,423	1,412	1,328	1,190
Workforce (mill.)	1.85	0.85	3.34	3.61	2.2	1.75
HQ of Fortune-500 companies	3	0	25	24	7	0
Stock exchange capital (US$ mill. end-97)	294,240	19,048	8,988,133	2,058,78	825,133	106,216

Source: Committee for Sydney (1998)

Nonetheless, the report concluded that 'in world city terms, Sydney is an attractive, vibrant city with a unique quality of life and environment; and our reputation as a business center is improving' (Committee for Sydney, 1998). Symptomatically for Sydney, this stock-take was the initiative of concerned citizens and businesses that lamented the centrifugal and fragmented political approach to the future of the region. There is no single local government covering the region, not even the Sydney Metropolitan Area.

Sydney's function as a node in worldwide networks can be illustrated further by statistics on shipping and air traffic, there being no statistics for its place in Cyberspace traffic (other than the comparatively high Internet connection rates of Australians).

Figure 11.1 shows where Sydney's sea-borne trade routes go with regard to high-value imports and exports (Australia's trade in bulk resources is handled mainly from ports further north). As of the late 1990s, East Asia was the dominant source and destination of trade out of Sydney's ports. Together with Southeast Asia, it received more than half of all containers loaded in Sydney and was the source of nearly half of all inbound container traffic. It is also interesting to note how little is being shipped these days to the traditionally dominant markets on both sides of the north Atlantic, although sizeable import volumes of sophisticated equipment still come from these old industrial countries.

Figure 11.1 Sydney ports: exports and imports of full containers, 1995–96

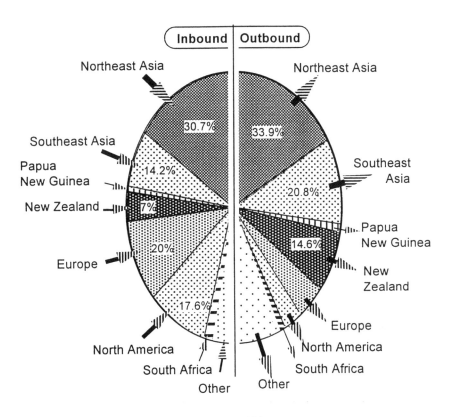

Source: Sydney Ports Corporation, *Annual Report*, 1996.

Figure 11.2 reports on the passenger traffic through Sydney's airport.
With 277,650 aircraft movements it is one of the major hubs of the global air
traffic system, though Sydney falls far short of centers like New York or
London (compare Table 11.3). The number of passengers that pass through
Sydney's airport was split roughly one-third to two-thirds between
international and domestic passengers. About half of all direct international
arrivals came from East Asia in 1997, reflecting the rapid growth in tourism
exchanges with that region prior to the Asian crisis, as well as by growing
business links. Sizable New Zealand and North American shares indicate
another priority in Sydney's mutual exchanges these days.

Figure 11.2 Sydney Airport: air passengers by major destinations/sources,
*   1997*

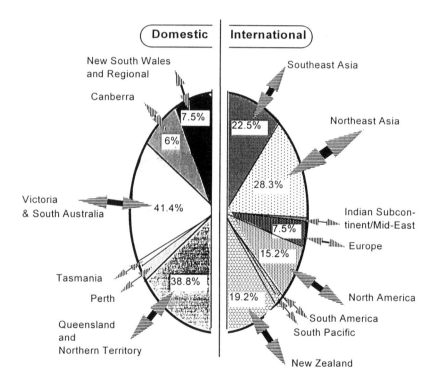

Source: Sydney Commonwealth Department of Transport and Regional Development.

The domestic passenger numbers indicate that Sydney is the hub of Australia's domestic air network, with Melbourne and Adelaide to the southwest and Queensland to the north dominating the traffic. This of course reflects the distribution of Australia's population, apart from indicating that the Queensland coast some 1,000 or 2,000 kilometers to the north has become a playground for Sydneysiders on short-stay holidays.

PROSPECTS: COMPETITIVE STRENGTHS AND WEAKNESSES

Future trends will be influenced by Sydney's traditional competitive attributes, emerging global competitive advantages, and the handling of competitive weaknesses, some of which are the result of the region's very economic success.

A major gateway city has to reinvent itself continually to remain a leader and to provide an attractive environment for innovators and trend-setters elsewhere. And it has to cope with the agglomeration costs that are the byproducts of its growth. This requires, as we said, transaction-cost saving institutions (low taxes and expedient regulations), thriving clusters of growth activities, the creation of new skills, and the elimination of obstacles to enterprise. Tendencies towards a hollowing-out of city centers and unstructured urban sprawl need to be counteracted, for example, by efficient traffic infrastructures, the provision of cultural goods, and the cultivation of an attractive living environment in the city. In an era of intensifying locational competition and a growing 'placelessness' in globalized markets, it no doubt also helps to develop a distinctive character and feeling of place.

Of the conditions necessary for continuing vigor, Sydney has quite a few. Among the attractions, one would first have to rate the good weather, the beaches and other natural assets, a vibrant urban and outdoor lifestyle, and good educational, cultural and other service facilities. The city's reputation as a place to do business and to invest has been improving, mainly as a consequence of nationwide liberalization and institutional reforms. Australia's international competitiveness now shows a growing list of assets, among them a good infrastructure, technology-friendly conditions and stable, reasonably favorable institutions and financial market conditions, although Australia tends to miss out on being among the top dozen most competitive locations (see, for example, World Economic Forum, 1999).

One factor that helps Sydney's strength in the communications age is the possession of English, which gives people confidence to communicate. This ties in with the cultural openness of an immigrant society, where different cultural approaches are readily accepted and responded to and where there is a preparedness to experiment with different concepts. In such a setting, professionals from around the world can quickly become productive. This is reflected in the steep increase in the number of business visas for internationally mobile expatriate experts. To many foreign observers, the easy-going Australian approach to alien concepts may seem over-confident if not naive, but it is a great asset in the discovery procedures of the global communications age.

Another factor that contributes to the Sydney region's competitive strength is a comparatively low level of executive living costs. They are about a quarter below New York's, and more below those in Tokyo and Hong Kong (*The Economist*, 23 January 1999, p. 108). In addition, communication costs have been falling, thanks to privatization and competition, energy costs are low and Sydney land, office and housing costs are very competitive in comparison with most other major cities.

Space availability and local pro-development policies have allowed the Sydney region to expand and have kept congestion – though on the increase – at internationally competitive levels. Although Australian governments do not normally offer systematic tax holidays and other selective government-made inducements to foreign investors, foreign-owned enterprises join a community where they are treated as equals and do not have to hand over brown paper bags to be allowed to do business. The overcrowded new centers of Asia, which are plagued by lags in infrastructure development, fuzzy institutions and sometimes high costs, are therefore increasingly losing out to Sydney when multinationals choose to establish a branch in the Asia-Pacific region.

Pragmatic attitudes, reasonably high levels of education, the relative youthfulness and the cultural diversity of the Australian population have fostered a much greater receptiveness to cost-saving computer and communication devices than in most other countries. As of 1998, a third of adult Australians use the Internet (*The Australian*, 26 November 1998). The long Australian tradition of having to cope with distance and labor scarcity has no doubt alerted people to the benefits of technology and now enables them to exploit the space-bridging skills one has to acquire in a vast country. For the same reasons, one Sydney-based transport company, TNT, has gained market share in private parcel services around the world. Sydney-based developers, construction and mining companies have gained much experience with working in the rough outback conditions and greenfield sites of Australia. This has given them competitive skills in similar ventures to develop Asian projects. Australian staff of Asian descent often add extra competitive strength in competing for Asian construction and development projects.

As the East Asian crisis of the late 1990s unfolds and reveals deep-seated institutional deficiencies in East Asia, Australia's relative strengths are becoming more pronounced (Kasper, 1999). But, at the same time, some of the dynamics of the west Pacific is likely to be lost in the immediate future, a circumstance that will detract to some degree from Australia's competitive position. In any event, Australia's international competitiveness profile also shows distinct and durable competitive weaknesses, most notably in the quality of government and above all in the governance of labor markets – both long-term legacies of the 'Australian Settlement'. Many aspects of the labor-market policy – strike rates, autonomy to hire and fire, industrial relations interference and minimum wages – as well as the tax system, with its heavy reliance on direct taxes, have long been diagnosed as in urgent need of reform (World Economic Forum, 1999; Kasper, 1999). The political resistance of interest groups, as well as a lack of political leadership and vision, has impeded faster progress.

As we saw, the challenge in the 1980s was to compete internationally for more of those mobile factors that everyone is now trying to attract or retain, namely capital, technology and high skills. The shift from being an attractor of labor and capital to being an attractor of capital and knowledge made it necessary to adjust factor-price proportions and to inculcate a culture of raising labor productivity. The full, pervasive political–organizational consequences, namely to abandon central wage-fixing and untargeted welfare hand-outs, have not yet been fully drawn, although the experience with openness has done much to promote tendencies in this direction over the past decade.

Table 11.4 highlights those factors that influence a business's long-term profitability in Australia which are most frequently mentioned when one consults with business enterprises about locational comparisons and which underpin systematic, comparative competitiveness ratings, such as those by the World Economic Forum (1999). These national conditions of course affect the Sydney region's competitiveness, too.

One possible weakness in Sydney's perceived position seems to be a divergence between the self-critical assessments of those who live there and more favorable perceptions of those who visit or are potential investors. Admittedly, residents acknowledge the lifestyle values and the cultural diversity, but tend to have negative perceptions of aspects such as high taxation, political fragmentation, rising crime rates, growing pollution and traffic congestion (Committee for Sydney, 1998, p. 30). These perceptions derive partly from comparisons with the past and partly point to growing agglomeration costs. But self-criticism may also be useful in mobilizing corrective collective action, even if it cannot be justified by comparisons with other gateway cities (compare Table 11.3 above).

Table 11.4 Australia-wide competitive strengths and weaknesses

Competitive strengts	Competitive weaknesses
Low and falling communications costs	Economy still not completely open
The world language, English	Trade policy inconsistent
Information readily available	Exchange rate volatile (a result of
Known British codes of conduct and law	dependence on volatile raw-material exports)
Low corruption	Tax system heavily reliant on income
Leisure, climate, natural environment make for pleasant lifestyle	and corporate taxes
	Low savings
Same time zone as East Asia, yet great differences in factor prices that can be exploited	Financial risk ratings on the low side
	Geographic isolation
	Engineering capabilities limited
Pragmatic culture, ethnic variety	Management often inward-looking,
Sophisticated, high-income markets	limited entrepreneurial orientation
Low land and office costs, low living costs	High product-liability costs
	Residual class antagonism at
Labor-unit costs moderate by OECD standards	workplaces, concentrated in key sectors such as ports
High acceptance of computing and the Internet	Featherbedding of labor, restrictive work practices; workplace regulations
	Government based on the notion of ruling, rather than being a support organization for internationally competing business
	Contradictory, confusing enviomental policies and landrights

Source: Own assessment based on World Economic Forum (1999).

The challenge remains to address the region's competitive weaknesses and reinforce its strengths. In Sydney, there is a professed intent to strengthen the economic base by attracting a greater share of the Asia-Pacific region's inward investment into key sectors. Some of them already have great strength and depth, namely in construction and property development, the food and hospitality industries, financial and other business services, health services and education (Committee for Sydney, 1998, p. 34). Another competitive cluster is an emerging media and entertainment complex that has seen inward investments such as the new Fox Studio for film and television. Some promoters want to target certain activities for promotion, the picking of winners of course always presupposes knowledge about the future which central authorities rarely have.

In the past, Sydney has managed without much of the formal planning paraphernalia of other big centers. The alternative strategy to unwieldy planning for economic expansion, namely concentrating on getting obstacles out of the road and enhancing business's spontaneous capability to innovate and expand, may well be more appropriate at a time of complex and dynamic evolution. When circumstances are changing as much as they have in Sydney over the past decade, the role of collective action may well be to keep tax and compliance costs low, and to ensure that low-cost infrastructures are accessible to all comers.

This does not mean that governments must produce and own these public-domain infrastructures, as several private and fee-paying traffic facilities in Sydney (inner-city monorail, motorways, a road tunnel under the harbor) and the increasingly privatized and competitive telecommunications and power infrastructures demonstrate. Technical and organizational innovations are reducing the transaction costs of monitoring the use of such public domain infrastructures and user-fee collection. For example, transponders are now making private city roads economically feasible. Sydney has moved further along the way to private infrastructure provision than, say, European gateway cities where there seems to be a more deeply entrenched commitment to socialized property.

EMERGING TRENDS

A visible reminder of Sydney's growing presence in national and global service networks is the changing skyline. The inner city has been transformed by numerous gleaming high-rises that dwarf the historic remnants, and substantial new high-rise business centers have sprouted north of the Harbour, in Parramatta to the west and elsewhere, as space becomes more expensive and commuting to the city is more of a burden. Different from other metropolises, Sydney has the space to seed major new centers at a few kilometers distance from the city and to grow at less cost than some older, densely packed cities.

The Asian crisis has strengthened Sydney's comparative advantage. Sophisticated services have often proved much harder to establish in Asia because of trust-destroying political interference and political risks and because of the discovery that many Asian institutions were not 'load-bearing' in a crisis (Kasper, 1999). At a time when many services have become transportable thanks to the new telecommunication technology, Sydney is well positioned to exploit that competitive advantage. Thus the international section of Singapore's *Straits Times* is edited in Sydney and transmitted by Internet to the printer in Singapore. Moreover, huge construction projects in Laos or Vietnam can be managed on an hourly basis out of headquarters in the Sydney region, and the control by the Hong Kong triads over the settling of bets on horse-racing can be avoided by letting housewives on the Australian coast acquit the bets and remit pay-out slips electronically to Hong Kong.

This new Cyberspace business, combined with internationally competitive telephone costs since deregulation, accounts for Australia's large excess of outgoing over incoming international telephone calls (if measured on a percapita basis; source: TeleGeography, as reported in *The Economist*, 23 January 1999, p. 116). An additional important Asian linkage is that Australian universities have become big exporters of higher education to Asia. They are now beginning to enroll Asia-based students in their distance-education courses and give them continual feedback over the Internet and video links. Sydney-based medical specialists are furthermore involved in diagnosing diseases and surgical problems of patients tens of thousands of kilometers away.

The new distance trade in services is not a one-way street. Less skilled and less transaction-cost-dependent services can be imported. Thus daily entries in business journals and stock-keeping accounts can be prepared by cheaper office workers in Manila and remitted back overnight to Sydney. Being in roughly the same time zone, and having big differences in factor prices to Asia, has given Sydney a lead in this new trade, much of which is so new that it is not even known to statisticians. The spatial specialization from which the Sydney region has been benefiting has attracted many headquarter services in finance, logistics, publishing, transport, construction, industrial management and real-estate development to Sydney and made Sydney headquarters the center of webs which allow the farming out of lower-skilled work to cheaper providers elsewhere. This sort of specialization is an important source of sustained growth in mature city economies.

The new Cyberspace activities also open frontiers that permit private actors to evade government controls as well as the standardization by centrally supervised collective action. This is of course the open frontier where the well-defined nation state of the steam and automobile age is losing its traditional grip. As in pre-modern states, the openness of Cyberspace again allows individuals to operate in control-free spheres. To date, government policies have not been playing a major role in the e-commerce revolution, although politicians have tried to stay ahead of the moving flock, claiming leadership and worrying about how to extract taxation. Yet the new developments are too diffuse and dynamic for bureaucrats, politicians and slow-moving collective action to take a decisive lead.

What constraining influence has been exercised and what rules have been set up to facilitate the new activities have originated in professional bodies and associations involved in the new global business in services, for example self-regulating accountants, real-estate bodies, arbitration services or the Sydney Stock Exchange. They are now cultivating institutions that enhance international trust in them, but they do so in polycentric competitive markets and not as regional monopoly providers of rules and enforcement (Bell, 1998). Thus Sydney's financial intermediaries have used the – initially unsettling – financial deregulation of the early 1980s as an impetus to develop their own more expedient rules and procedures. They have installed monitoring and enforcement procedures which establish trust while using computer technology to do away with paper documentation. The computer-based land-title registries and the CHESS system of paperless stock exchange transactions are examples of a trend where Australian operators tend to be ahead of the overseas competition.

Population growth in the Sydney area over the past decade has led to the emergence of a local green and anti-immigration movement. Although the urban sprawl is open to the ocean in the east and is broken up by large areas of green space and protected natural bush land which few other cities of Sydney's size can match, many of Sydney's incumbent residents lend support to political movements to stop further expansion. This can be seen as an attempt to preserve good access to free goods. In many respects, Sydney's environmental movements reflect those in other affluent parts of the world, but in Sydney this is coupled with demands to stop international immigration, one of the traditional driving forces of the Sydney region's development.

One telling sign of changing public attitudes (and of government ineptitude in handling a difficult problem) has been the growing civic resistance to Sydney's big international airport, which lies close to the city center. Traffic through the airport, Australia's premier landfall, is hampered by high landing fees, night curfews and cumbersome landing procedures to reduce noise pollution. The airport, once built on the southern outskirts of Sydney at Botany Bay, is now surrounded by urban sprawl, and citizens who chose to move there now agitate against aircraft noise, turning this into a major political issue. A much talked-about second major Sydney-region airport has not progressed beyond the discussion stage.

The ports of the Sydney region have been molded by the legacy of featherbedding, scarce labor, the British heritage of militant waterside unions and the granting of near-monopoly status to few stevedoring companies. Poor port-handling productivity adds to transport-cost disadvantages. Many traditional local industries are hampered by Sydney's intractable, high-cost port culture. However, the troubled Sydney ports are now facing growing competition from other ports, in particular to the north along the Queensland coast, which are a steaming day closer to East Asia and North America. Noisy political and organizational reform attempts have been only a partial success. They can be expected to succeed when interport competition intensifies.

Major infrastructural developments – such as airports, subways and motorways – may in the past have been hampered by Sydney's individualism, the fragmentation of local government and happy-go-lucky attitudes. Problems that can be sorted out by decentralized, private action tend to be solved more expediently in Sydney than those dependent on strategic public action. But technological changes and an attitude shift in favor of privatization are now under way, allowing private enterprise to tackle infrastructural bottlenecks. Traditional growth handicaps may therefore be eased by the new gameplan that allows for more private, for-profit action.

CONCLUSION

Can one convey the essence of a complex, changing metropolitan economy such as Sydney's and its relations to the world on a few pages? Possibly not when so many major changes coincide, as has been the case in long-inward-looking Sydney. If one steps back from the detail, one cannot help but be astounded by the spontaneous energy with which the Sydney region has been exploiting the new opportunities. The 2000 Olympics have injected more of a centrally driven initiative, and that may not be a disadvantage given the tradition of decentralized muddling on.

What stands out is the multifaceted diversity of Sydney life. If one were to impress on a stranger what is special about this city, one would mention the beaches, but above all the great economic and cultural diversity. In Sydney, you can worship in neo-Gothic cathedrals, a huge mosque, a Baha'i temple and Buddhist monasteries; you can eat the food of virtually any province on earth and listen to most dialects known to humanity.

The English, Irish and Scottish inheritance is dominant, but the Sydney mix is transforming into something new, yet unknowable. Sydney citizens interact and adjust, as they chat in Mediterranean-style fruit markets, Vietnamese baguette bakeries, cappuccino cafés, on the beaches, in work-places and when they applaud a passing Bavarian or Brazilian band. The major image a cosmopolitan visitor takes away is of tolerance, a youthful can-do mentality, openness, and good-natured, though at times sardonic, cheer.

NOTES

1. This alludes to the book by Australian historian GeoffreyBlainey which is rightly celebrated for having made distance (and labour-scarcity) the dominant theme of Australia's short history since White settlement (Blainey, 1966).
2. For compelling, detailed historic evidence on the connections between interjurisdictional rivalry, innovation and economic progress, see Bernholz et al. (1998), as well as the work by Douglass North and Eric Jones cited in that book.
3. For a modern sketch of a Thünen-type framework of a spatial economic order, see Giersch (1993); also Thünen (1826/1966); and Kasper (1993 What is said below of Sydney can be applied to Australia and, for that matter, of the other late-developed, peripheral 'Antarctic rim countries' – New Zealand, Chile, Argentina and, to some extent, South Africa.
4. It used to be said that service providers have to locate where the demand is. But low communications costs now make it possible to buy insurance, banking or advisory services overseas, turning services into tradable goods. With the gradual adoption of the General Agreement on Trade in Services (GATS) that was ratified in the Uruguay Round of the world trade negotiations, many artificial barriers to distance-trade in services will be eliminated, and international competition in services will become even more intense.
5. Sydney's inspiration by the ideas and concepts of the early nineteenth century is still made visible by its Georgian buildings. By contrast, the oldest built monuments of somewhat younger cities in the region, such as Melbourne and Auckland, date from the mid- to late nineteenth century, a more collectivist, more statist era (Park, 1973; Morris, 1992).

REFERENCES

Bell, T.W. (1998), 'Polycentric law in a new century', *CATO Policy Report* (November–December), pp. 1–11.

Bernholz, P., M.E. Streit and R. Vaubel (eds) (1998), *Political Competition, Innovation and Growth, A Historical Analysis*, Berlin and New York: Springer.

Blainey, G. (1966), *The Tyranny of Distance*, Melbourne: Macmillan/St. Martin's Press.

Blainey, G. (1994), *A Shorter History of Australia*, Melbourne: W. Heinemann Australia.

Committee for Sydney (1998), *Sydney 2020, The City We Want*, Sydney: The Committee for Sydney.

Giersch, H. (1993), 'Labor, wages and productivity', in H. Giersch, *Openness for Prosperity: Essays in World Economics*, Cambridge, MA: MIT Press, pp. 119–36.

Jones, E., L. Frost and C. White (1994), *Coming Full Circle: An Economic History of the Pacific Rim*, Oxford and New York: Oxford University Press/Westview Press.

Kasper, W. et al. (1980), *Australia at the Crossroads, Our Choices to the Year 2000*, Sydney and New York: Harcourt Brace Jovanovich.

Kasper, W. (1993), 'Spatial economics', in. D.R. Henderson (ed.), *The Fortune Encyclopedia of Economics*, New York: Warner Books, pp. 82–6.

Kasper, W. (1999), 'Rapid development in East Asia: institutional evolution and backlogs', in R. Thillainathan (ed.), *Malaysian Journal of Economic Research*, 1998 vol., (Special Issue on Financial Markets and the Future of the Asian Miracle).

Kasper, W. and M.E. Streit (1998), *Institutional Economics: Social Order and Public Policy*, Cheltenham, UK: Edward Elgar.

Kelly, P. (1992), *The End of Certainty*, Sydney: Allen & Unwin.

Linder, S.B. (1986), *The Pacific Century: Economic and Political Consequences of Asian-Pacific Dynamism*, Stanford: Stanford University Press.

Morris, J. (1992), *Sydney*, Ringwood, Vic.: Penguin.

Park, R. (1973), *Companion Guide to Sydney*, Sydney and London: Collins.

Productivity Commission [Australian Government] (1998), *Australia's Restrictions on Trade in Financial Services*, Canberra and Melbourne: Productivity Commission, Staff Research Paper series.

Shann, E. (1930), *An Economic History of Australia*, Cambridge: Cambridge University Press.

Thünen, J.H.v. (1826), *Der Isolerte Staat in Beziehung auf Landwirtschaft und Nationalökonomie* (Hamburg), English translation (1966), *Von Thünen's Isolated State*, Oxford: Pergamon Press.

Vamplew, W. (ed.) (1988), *Australians, Historical Statistics*, Sydney: Fairfax, Syme & Weldon.

World Bank (1998), *Knowledge for Development, World Development Report 1998/99*, Washington: The World Bank.

World Economic Forum (1999), *The Global Competitiveness Report 1999*, Geneva: WEF.

12. Exploiting Gateway Externalities: the Future of Kansai

Kiyoshi Kobayashi and Mikio Takebayashi

INTRODUCTION

Seemingly insignificant events in history may create a formation of a world urban system different from the one that exists today. Especially, locational patterns of interaction-intensive activities such as services, finance and knowledge production follow paths that depend upon history. Agglomeration economies introduce an indeterminacy; when agents want to congregate in the same location as others, one or a few locations may end up with the entire industry. If we bypass this indeterminacy by arguing that historical accidents determine the dominant locations, we must then define historical accident and how they act to select the winning locations.

Osaka, including Kobe/Kyoto (referred to as Kansai), is a peculiar example of how a city rises and falls by historical accident. Japan's early gravitation of population to Kansai was mainly due to its geographical advantage for administrative affairs. Shotoku Taishi (578–622), regent to the Empress Suiko, founded the nation's first Buddhist temple, Shitennoji, near Osaka's present downtown. Because of its location and proximity to the major ports of the time, Osaka flourished as a port city for centuries. However, Osaka (and Kansai) was devastated in the fourteenth century by repeated civil wars, and did not recover until the early 1660s.

Toyotomi Hideyoshi, the shogun who unified seventeenth century Japan, put his government headquarters in Osaka. As the seat of central power, Osaka attracted merchants and craftsmen from all over Japan. Rivers and canals crisscrossed Osaka during the feudal era. Local shipping firms organized river trade with Edo (Tokyo), and Osaka became the center of commodity distribution for the nation. Starting in the eighteenth century, Osaka began to flourish as an economic and financial center and played a leading role in the development of fine arts and culture. The most monumental event in Osaka of the time was to innovate a market for agricultural produce futures. It was the first such market in the world. Tokyo, with an estimated one million inhabitants, was the largest city in the world, and Osaka was probably third in the world urban hierarchy after London. Since then, Osaka has continued to generate a wide variety of businesses, the majority of which were wholesalers.

People in Osaka reestablished their city as Japan's center of international trade after the Meiji Restoration in 1868. By the 1880s, Osaka's textile industry was leading Japan's industrial revolution. Osaka was the gateway for virtually all of Japan's trade, and during the Meiji era it served as the launching pad for Japan's modernization. However, Osaka lost its industrial standing during the 1930s, when military expenditures came to dominate the economy. The tight business connection with the central government drew companies to Tokyo. This sort of gravitation has persisted to the present day. Osaka's economy, however, boomed after the Second World War, with capital-intensive heavy manufacturing in coastal industrial complexes. Since the 1970s, the city has emphasized the development of knowledge-intensive production in the interior as well as in the coastal zones. Now, 17 million people reside within a 60-kilometer radius. The size of Kansai's economy is considerable, comparable in size to the Australian or Canadian economies.

Thus Osaka has faced many crises in its long history, population decline being the most recent one. Although Osaka City had a record population of 3.25 million in 1940, in 1990 the resident population had diminished to 2.6 million, in part because of rapid growth in the nearby suburbs. Osaka has witnessed remarkable changes in its economic, social and geographical conditions. Comprehensive strategies blending urban and industrial policies have been employed to create new futuristic urban cores within the Osaka Metropolitan Area. However, Osaka's relative magnitude in terms of administrative and management functions compared with that of Tokyo has been steadily declining over the last three decades.

The spatial economics literature tends to see the spatial ordering of cities as economic responses to geographical endowments, transport possibilities and firms' needs. The locational pattern is an equilibrium outcome of individual agents' decisions. From this point of view, development history is not an issue, since the equilibrium outcome is unique. The urban system is deterministic and predictable. Recently, however, urban development has been viewed as being path-dependent – much like an organic process – with new agents very much influenced by inherited locational patterns already in place. Geographical differences and transport possibilities are important but the main driving forces have been agglomeration economies – the benefits of being close to other agents. Latecomers may be attracted to places by the presence of earlier economic actors, rather than by geography.

What the economic history of Osaka, and its repeated repositioning in the national urban system, tells us is that the agglomeration of interaction-intensive activities is a positive feedback process, which is by nature cumulative and self-reinforcing. This is because the emergence of a particular site as a major agglomeration does not solely depend upon the intrinsic nature of this site. In other words, historical events such as political initiatives have appeared to be essential in the selection of a particular equilibrium. It is furthermore well known that minor changes in the socioeconomic environment occurring at some critical periods may well result in very different geographical configurations (Batten et al., 1989; Kobayashi, et al., 1991; Krugman, 1991; Arthur, 1994; Fujita and Krugman, 1995; Matsuyama, 1995).

This chapter attempts to provide a sound empirical example of the historical accident from an agglomeration viewpoint by revealing Osaka's development story. The following section reviews the source of increasing returns in spatial agglomerations. Then the geographical landscape of knowledge networks is discussed. Specific attention is paid to the evolutionary locations of industrial research laboratories. The chapter then highlights transport networks and sets out the dynamic features of network structural change. This is followed by a consideration of the monocentric nature of the financial network. We conclude by discussing the relevant policy strategies for the future of Osaka/Kansai.

A GATEWAY PARADIGM

A gateway city paradigm posits a distinct role for certain cities in the global system. Gateway cities develop hierarchical relationships with other cities that rise and fall over time according to controllable factors and accidental social, political and economic fluctuations in the system. As commanding nodes in the global network, gateway cities are defined by dense patterns of interaction between capital, information, ideas and knowledge. The rapidly expanding logistical systems, such as knowledge, transport and financial networks, facilitate this interaction. In turn, the globalization of finance, production, service, culture, information and knowledge has given impetus to extraordinary advances in logistical systems.

The role of logistical systems in the evolving world city system is both crucial and fundamental. The mobile features of administrative, information and knowledge activities argue for geographic dispersion in a variety of places. Advances in transport and communication technology have removed many of the spatial and temporal barriers, encouraging decentralization of certain types of information-based activities. By contrast, a gateway city paradigm suggests that a gateway city can be characterized by a combination of highly complementary economic activities, which, when taken together, make a coherent whole of what we call gateway externalities. Being a gateway to the global network, a gateway city can be assumed to be endowed with flexibility, reliability and diversity for the movement of people, goods, information and knowledge, and can attain a high degree of coordination among these diverse activities; each gateway city may possess a limited amount of knowledge and information concerning these activities.

The economic history of a city is a process of structural change; productivity growth is achieved through an evolution of a highly complex system of activities. 'Activities' refers to the production of various types of goods, services, ideas and knowledge that have potential economic value. Cities grow and the quality of life improves because we continuously develop and add new activities to the list of those that we are already engaged in. Development may thus be regarded as a continuously evolving process of adding new sets of activities, while dropping others (Matsuyama, 1995). To achieve well-coordinated economic development, activities must be guided somehow into making complementary production, consumption, investment and saving decisions. The activity of one agent creates a substantial positive externality for a number of other agents. More commonly we can observe that the performance of many agents depends highly upon the performance of a number of others.

This sort of complementarity, stemming from the mutual interdependencies among many agents, is best exemplified by a basic feature of communications (Kobayashi and Fukuyama, 1998). In communications, the decisions made by an agent cannot be independent of the decisions and/or intentions of other agents. One's decision on one's communication is more or less affected by the decisions of others. For instance, in various aspects of daily life, one organizes meetings. The objective of business trips, such as those for negotiations, as well as personal trips with friends and loved ones, is the meeting itself. Many institutional conditions that rule daily behavior, such as school, hospital, work or shopping trips, derive from the need for meetings. The essence of a meeting is the discovery of the existence of interaction partners.

In face-to-face interactions, two kinds of externalities are important. The first is a 'thick-market externality', and the second is a congestion externality. The 'thick-market externality' arises from matching technology. When some people increase their search for interaction partners, this reduces the 'thinness' of the partners and induces a further round of increased communication as long as congestion does not matter. If people expect a lot of aggregate demand for communication, then they expect communication costs to be relatively low. This will encourage high communication levels, which in equilibrium will result in high aggregate demand, thereby fulfilling the original expectation. By the same token, the expectation of low communication levels can also be self-fulfilling, because the associated prospect of thin markets and high communication costs will discourage activity. The reason is that there is a strategic complementarity arising from non-price interaction – specifically the thick-market externality.

The problem is not merely coordinating day-to-day communications among a fixed set of agents. The major part of this problem is to discover new agents to communicate with, which brings about a better outcome for the economy as a whole. This problem would be relatively simple if all agents had access to perfect knowledge about potential interaction partners. We should steadily progress to improve the quality of communication by routinely experimenting with meeting new interaction partners, and by determining whether or not a long-term relationship is desirable. The problem arises, however, because of the inherent complementarity of activities.

The prevalence of coordination failures in communications suggests the importance of coordination experiments through private and public initiatives. The government in each region or even national economy should pursue studies about its role in coordination. The experiments may include improvement of matching technology, encouragement of communications, or arrangement of new types of infrastructure. In other words, a city should be a gateway to new experiments. The gateway city is a city that is endowed with a well-coordinated combination of highly complementary economic activities, thanks to being a gateway to the global network and to experimental efforts.

The economic activities are guided by various gateway functions to make a coherent whole of more than a simple sum of outcomes of the respective activities. In what follows, by highlighting some important functions of gateway cities, nodality in knowledge, transport and finance networks, we examine the past development and the current state of Osaka in the world gateway city network.

KNOWLEDGE NETWORKS

Knowledge Production and Externalities

Path dependency is omnipresent for evolutionary locations of knowledge-intensive agents such as headquarters of business firms, financial agents, consulting firms and research laboratories. An increasing number of knowledge-intensive agents want to agglomerate because of the various factors that allow for a larger diversity and a higher specialization in knowledge production, and the wider array of knowledge available for consumption. Setting up new research centers such as Tsukuba gives rise to new incentives for researchers to migrate there because they can expect better matching for research requirements. This in turn makes the place more attractive to knowledge-intensive agents who may expect to find the types of agents and services they need, as well as new outlets for their products. Hence both types of agents benefit from being together. This idea was already discussed by Marshall (1920).

In general, the Marshallian externalities arise because of (1) internal economies, (2) the formation of a highly specialized labor force based upon the accumulation of human capital, (3) the availability of specialized input services, and (4) the existence of modern infrastructures. The propensity to interact with others is a fundamental human attitude, and distance is an impediment to interaction, thus making cities the ideal setting for the development of social contracts.

Economic life is creative in the same way as art and science. As pointed out by Romer (1986) and Lucas (1988), personal communications within groups of individuals sharing common interests can be vital inputs to creativity. In this respect, it is well known that face-to-face communications are most effective. Given that different people have different skills, the size of such groups also gives rise to significant scale effects.

There is a circular causation for the agglomeration of knowledge-intensive agents and knowledge workers through forward linkages (an increased concentration of knowledge-intensive agents enhances researchers' amenity) and backward linkages (a greater number of researchers attracts more knowledge-intensive agents) (Fujita and Thisse, 1996). Through these linkage effects, scale economies at the individual agent level are transformed into increasing returns at the level of the city as a whole. The spatial ordering is not unique when these types of scale economies are functioning in locational fields.

Early firms locate by historical accident in one or two locations; other firms are attracted by their presence. A different set of early events could have steered the locational pattern to a different outcome, so that settlement history becomes crucial. Because of the existence of multiple equilibria, minor changes in the values of the critical parameters may generate dramatic changes in the equilibrium spatial configuration. This suggests that historical matters explain actual industrial patterns, and that circular causation generates a snowball effect that leads knowledge-intensive agents to be locked within the same region for long time periods (Arthur, 1994). This is especially apparent in the evolutionary location of industrial research laboratories.

The Tsukuba Phenomenon

Among other things, we focus on the location of industrial research laboratories of industries with high R&D investment, such as electrical and electronic engineering, general machinery, and the chemical, medical, and automobile industries. Among these industries, 142 industrial research laboratories were chosen from the *Directory of National Experimental and Research Organizations* published by the Science and Technology Agency.

The locational pattern of the laboratories shows that there is a strong tendency to locate in large cities, especially in the Tokyo Metropolitan Area. The total number of newly established research laboratories peaked during the 1961–70 period. In the sample, 27 laboratories are located in head offices (19.0 percent) 63 in manufacturing plants (44.4 percent), and 52 are stand-alone ones.

Related to the fact that head office functions concentrate in the large cities, the research laboratories located within the head office congregate around the Tokyo Metropolitan Area. While many research laboratories of the located-with-factory type are found in the Tokyo and Kansai Metropolitan Areas, the number of research laboratories located in these areas has nevertheless been declining. Recently, there is a strong tendency for the located-with-factory types to decentralize to other areas. In contrast, the concentration of stand-alone laboratories in Tsukuba is prominent. However, before 1980 there was a concentration of stand-alone laboratories in Yokohama and Tokyo. There were no laboratory locations in Tsukuba, but after 1985, the number of laboratories there has dramatically increased. At the same time, new locations in Tokyo and Yokohama have decreased.

The concentration in Tsukuba after 1985 is most clear for the chemical industry. The laboratories are clustered in the spatially delimited region within the Tsukuba Research and Academic City. Undoubtedly, the emergence of new research agglomerations has affected the new locations of industrial research laboratories. These dynamics reflect the so-called 'Tsukuba Phenomenon'.

'The Tsukuba Phenomenon' is a striking example of a dominant location for industrial research laboratories of the stand-alone type. Tsukuba is a science city, which is a new settlement planned and built by the central government, and which aims at generating scientific excellence and synergetic research activities by concentrating a critical mass of research organizations and scientists within a high-quality urban space. However, the initial progress of Tsukuba was slower than expected. Particularly slow, at the first stage around the 1970s, was the response of the private sector. But a major change occurred after 1985, when the mass in Tsukuba became large enough to outperform the existing agglomerations in Tokyo. After 1985, the location of private research laboratories to Tsukuba became important.

Shaping a New Scientific City in Kansai

As we have observed, the location of knowledge-intensive agents such as research laboratories is path-dependent since latecomers' choice of locations is very much influenced by inherited locational patterns already in place. Scale effects refer to critical thresholds that need to be reached for the provision of particular ideas, knowledge and services. Once scale effects start to function, the agglomeration of knowledge-intensive activities has the nature of a cumulative self-reinforcing process. In other words, historical events such as political initiatives appear to be essential in the selection of a particular equilibrium.

Kansai Science City is a huge development that began to take shape in the 1980s. It includes five cities and three towns in three prefectures – Kyoto, Osaka and Nara – and covers an area of some 15,000 hectares and has an eventual projected population, in the year 2000, of 380,000. The location is approximately 30 kilometers south of Japan's ancient capital of Kyoto, 10 kilometers north of an even older capital, Nara, and 30 kilometers northeast of Osaka. Departing from previous conventional models – including Tsukuba and most other technopolis developments – Kansai Science City abandoned the single-point concentrated approach in favor of a linked, multi-nuclear development, in which the 12 areas will be integrated via traffic and information networks into an organic whole. Unlike any previous Japanese model, Kansai was built from the start upon public–private partnerships in order to avoid becoming a monotonous and inflexible agglomeration. Kansai Science City is expected to be a vital experiment in forming a complex knowledge agglomeration of diversified activities related to industrial research, academic research, culture and the fine arts, so as to serve as a dynamic gateway to the world knowledge network.

THE TRANSPORT NETWORKS

The Air Transport Network

Gateway cities are connected by hierarchies of transport networks and services that provide both horizontal linkages (connectivity among cities of equal status) and vertical linkages (connectivity between cities of equal and lesser status) on a number of different scales. They are connected not only to other gateway cities, but also to a variety of centers of regional economies.

These connections are facilitated at the global and regional levels primarily by air transport, telecommunications circuits, and non-voice data transfer systems. The airline network offers the best illustration of communication patterns in the world city system.

The airline network can be characterized by the discrete features of its structure. Through facilitating point-to-point interactions between spatially dispersed locations, air transportation networks have been integrated as global logistical networks. The air transport network in the Pacific Rim also has this discrete structure with a hub-and-spoke character.

Figure 12.1 compares the number of international air passengers in 1995 across the world's major airports. The largest airport in the world is London/Heathrow, followed by Frankfurt. In the Pacific Rim, both Hong Kong and Singapore are dominant, followed by Narita, Los Angeles, Bangkok, Seoul, Taipei and Kansai. Figures 12.2 and 12.3 describe the major intercontinental non-stop flight routes involving the Asian countries in December 1993 and December 1998.

Figure 12.1 International air passengers for major airports (1995)

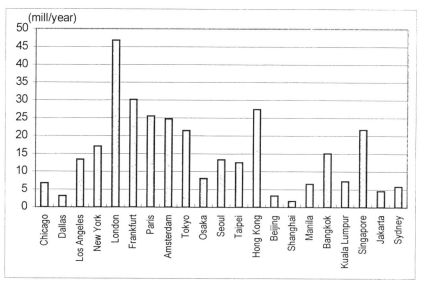

Non-stop scheduled flights to major gateway cities symbolize both the globalization of society and trade and the emergence of an information-based economy. A map of international non-stop air connections clearly illustrates the major global linkages between New York, London, and Tokyo, and the role these cities play as dominant global hubs in 1993 (see Figure 12.2).

Although intercontinental flights are quite limited compared to the volume of intraregional and domestic flights, London, New York and Tokyo dominate the international airline network. Notice, however, that Tokyo/Narita ranks only seventh in the total number of international air passengers. Tokyo/Narita is not the most important center of Asian regional air traffic, but Tokyo is the dominant city for intercontinental flights in that region in the world city hierarchy. This highlights the dominance of the Japanese economy in the Asian region, as well as its importance in the global system. However, in 1998, as shown in Figure 12.3, an apparent structural change in the world air corridor can be observed: The New York–Hong Kong–London axis has become a new parallel world corridor. The London/Frankfurt–Bangkok/-Singapore axis is also showing signs of becoming a world corridor.

Figure 12.2 Intercontinental major non-stop passenger flights (over 20 flights per week in 1993)

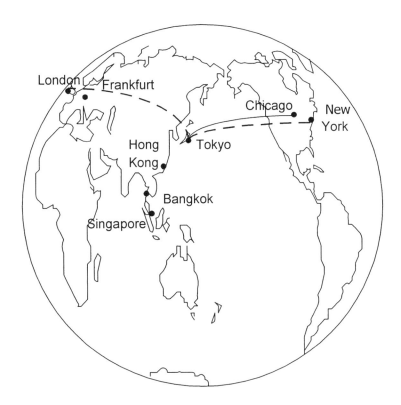

Figures 12.4 and 12.5 illustrate the Pacific Rim sub-network in 1993 and December 1998 respectively, which is focused on Tokyo, Hong Kong and Singapore, with extensions to Oceania, South Asia and West Asia. In the five years between 1993 and 1998, the complexity of the airline network increased substantially. At both points in time, there can be found strong connections between Japan and Pacific Asian countries. In 1993, Tokyo played a dominant role as the principal gateway to Pacific countries, resulting from its strong local markets within Japan and from its being a fuel stop on transpacific flights. After the Kansai airport opened in 1994, Kansai became a regional hub connecting Osaka to Asian countries in 1998. Thus, the regional air sub-network with Japan as a departure and arrival point has become characterized by its two-hub structure with Narita and Kansai. It should also be noted that there is an important regional corridor between Hong Kong and Taipei; Hong Kong plays an important pivotal role stemming from its connections with China, and Bangkok's prominence arose from its function as a fueling base on the one-stop Australia–Europe flights. Singapore offers 831 non-stop flights each week serving 39 cities, thereby operating twice as many flights as Narita.

Figure 12.3 Intercontinental major non-stop passenger flights (over 20 flights per week in 1998)

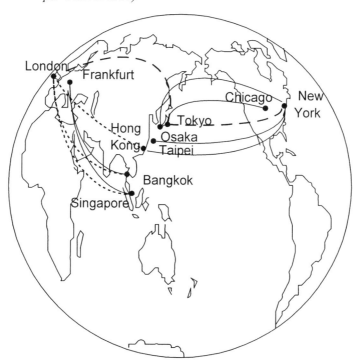

Figure 12.4 Major non-stop passenger flights in the Pacific Rim (over 20 flights per week in 1993)

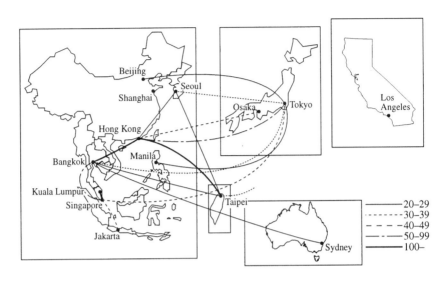

Figure 12.5 Major non-stop passenger flights in the Pacific Rim (over 20 flights per week in 1998)

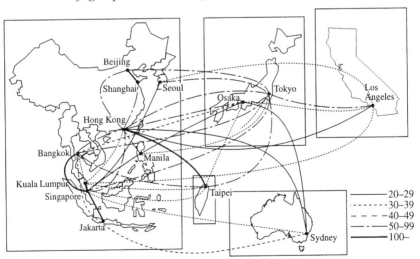

To summarize, the analysis of the air transport network has revealed the existence of a few dominant hubs dispersed around the world. Traffic at the global level seems to be quite limited and concentrated in a few dominant world cities. The greatest number of flights is of the medium- or short-haul type, which highlights the importance of regional and domestic connectivity. The connectivity among gateway cities is extremely dynamic: a city's position in the global network rises and falls depending on myriad factors, including market conditions, government initiatives, infrastructure arrangements, the influence of economic integration, historical inertia, local circumstances and the changing perceptions of a place.

The Sea Transport Network

A prominent feature of the sea transport network in the Asian Pacific Rim is the emergence of regional hub ports. An examination of the dynamic change of container port patterns in the Asian Pacific Rim during 1990–97 shows the concentration of cargo at a limited number of hub ports. As shown in Figure 12.6, Kaohsiung, Pusan, Keelung, Yokohama and Kobe were pivotal load centers of the regional sea network. Japanese ports, especially Kobe port, have benefited from being the closest to North America, and were also the hubs for the Asian Pacific Rim for several decades after the Second World War.

However, with the growth of East and Southeast Asian economies and large investments in port infrastructure outside Japan, the major transshipment function of ports has shifted to Hong Kong, Kaohsiung, Pusan and Singapore.

Another important feature that can be observed in Figure 12.6 is the decline of the magnitude of Kobe's port during the period. This was a consequence of the Kobe earthquake. That earthquake hit Kobe on 17 January 1995. Port facilities together with road, railways and other lifelines collapsed. About 32 percent of greater Kobe was partially destroyed, and more than 50 percent of its central areas was obliterated. After the earthquake, international shipping firms shifted their transshipment base from Kobe to Pusan, Keelung or Kaohsiung, and some domestic firms built new bases at Osaka's port. By 1999, though, Kobe's port had completely recovered its original capability.

However, the economic weight of Kobe's port in the sea transport network has not recovered its original magnitude (see Figure 12.7). The relocated shipping firms have already made major investments at the new sites and will probably never come back to Kobe.

Figure 12.6 Container ports in the Pacific Rim (in 1995)
(Unit: million TEU/ year)

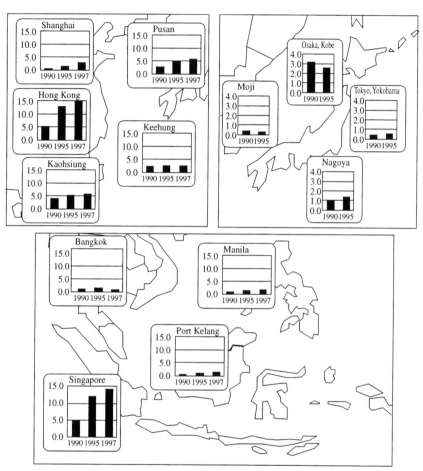

Osaka as a Gateway City

A regional perspective on gateway city linkages is particularly important as gateway cities are becoming increasingly distinct from their host countries. Patterns of transport growth in the Pacific Rim raise some important questions concerning the possible development impetus of Osaka at the national level. Two possible scenarios are suggested by these network patterns: (i) a development that focuses on Tokyo (centralized), or (ii) a development that disperses the benefits of gateway externalities among Tokyo, Osaka and other cities (decentralized).

Figure 12.7 Comparison of handled cargo volume at the Port of Kobe, 1993–97

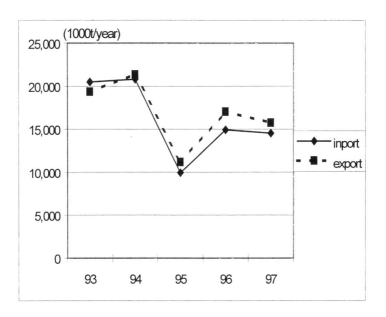

The Japanese scenario assumes the latter case with a development pattern composed of growth axes and chains of urban centers. The major one is the linear chain of urban development extending through Nagoya into Tokyo along the old Shinkansen line. In order to resolve the capacity shortage of the Shinkansen, and to reinforce interactions between Tokyo and Osaka, the maglev (magnetic levitation) linear motor system, guaranteeing 500 km/hr in speed is regarded as a promising countermeasure. Osaka also has a new 24-hour international airport on reclaimed land in Osaka Bay that is attracting traffic away from the heavily congested and inconvenient Tokyo Narita airport. Eleven regional and 13 international cities now have non-stop flights to Osaka, compared with only a handful of cities ten years ago. Both air and surface transport are thus playing a crucial role in helping spread the development impetus of both Tokyo and Osaka along the urban corridor linking the two centers. Such a pattern offers the possibility of diffusing the development impetus of world cities both vertically and horizontally throughout a region.

FINANCIAL NETWORKS

After the Stock Exchange Ordinance was enacted in 1878, stock exchanges were established in both Tokyo and Osaka. Since then, Tokyo and Osaka have been major domestic centers for the financial market. World financial and corporate capital centers have also emerged in Tokyo and Osaka. In particular, headquarters and control functions have been centralizing further into becoming an elite group of command centers in Tokyo. Symptomatic of the move toward a monocentric structure, Tokyo's leadership was confirmed by the further globalization of the Japanese economy. It was highlighted by Japan's capital surplus and by Tokyo becoming, with London and New York, one of the pivotal international financial centers.

Japan's financial market has lately become internationalized, creating a new market environment. Thanks to the improvement of the disclosure system for foreign companies in 1984 and a revision of the listing standards for privatized companies in 1985, the number of foreign firms listed on the Foreign Section of the Tokyo Stock Exchange has continued to increase, amounting to 127 companies in 1991. However, the trading volume of foreign stocks listed on the Foreign Section dropped sharply on account of the sluggishness of the domestic stock market as a whole since 1992. Some of the foreign firms began to pull out of the Tokyo market because of decreases in the number of Japanese stockholders and trading volume, and by the end of October 1996, their number dropped to 67. Aiming to meet the financing needs of rapidly growing regions, including Asian countries, and diversifying investor preferences, the Tokyo Stock Exchange has, since January 1995, relaxed the business scale requirements of foreign firms seeking to list their stocks on the Exchange and has simplified disclosure documents to help them absorb the cost of maintaining the listing of their stocks.

In the meantime, in December 1991 the Osaka Securities Exchange started trading country funds (closed-end investment trust funds of the company type) based in foreign countries that invest their funds in equities of specified countries or regions, and the number of such funds listed on the exchange increased to 12 at the end of 1996 (all of these funds are listed on the New York Stock Exchange). In October 1996, the Osaka Securities Exchange opened a foreign section aiming to encourage foreign firms in Asian and Pacific Rim countries (which have relatively close business relations with firms based in Kansai) to list their stocks on the Osaka Securities Exchange. Japanese stock exchanges took various measures in February 1996 – the relaxation of short-selling regulations and the introduction of stock certificate lending systems to facilitate stock trading through market making – to increase the liquidity of foreign stocks (Japan Security Institute, 1999).

Looking at the share of the trading volume of each exchange, we find that in 1996, the Tokyo Stock Exchange accounted for 79.19 percent; the Osaka Security Exchange, 16.44 percent; the Nagoya Stock Exchange, 3.24 percent; and five other stock exchanges, 1.13 percent, clearly demonstrating the leading position of Tokyo as the central market (see Figure 12.8).

Figure 12.8 Percentage of volume of transactions on all stock exchanges, 1996

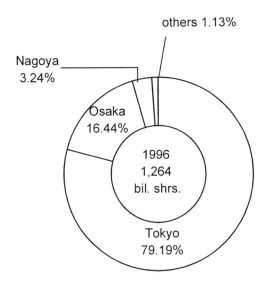

The concentration of stock trading in Tokyo has intensified markedly in recent years owing, besides economic factors, to the rapid development of telecommunications and information systems, which have increased the trend toward centralization. The recent story in the financial market illustrates the fact that once the agglomeration of interaction-intensive agents is formed, it becomes very difficult to change the existing spatial structure by any policy means because of the lock-in effects associated with existing agglomeration.

CONCLUSIONS

This chapter has attempted to provide an empirical example of the dynamic change of a gateway city by explaining Osaka's experience. The dynamics of a gateway city as it rises or falls in the global network are difficult to predict. The major challenge when developing a theory of gateway cities is to explain divergent performances across gateway cities. Here arises a major question that awaits careful scrutiny: why have certain gateway cities been more successful than others in developing a complex economic system?

In recent years, this question has been partially answered by a large number of studies applying the so-called 'New Growth Theory'. One school of thought approaches economic development as a coordination problem. Applying this view to a theory of gateway cities, the diverse performances of gateway cities could be postulated by the selection of equilibrium states. Due to the fundamental complexity of coordination problems, there are equilibrating mechanisms by which the state of a city evolves into one of a large number of inefficient equilibria. What differentiates a gateway city with a certain performance from other ones is simply a matter of degree. A historical accident, including coordinating efforts by private and public agents, determines the selection of the equilibrium states.

As Hicks once pointed out, the great mercantile expansion in the Mediterranean was associated with a system of city-states and their political autonomy (Hicks, 1969). Many historians who ask why Western Europe became the first region in the world to industrialize attribute the rise of the West to its political fragmentation. The success of capitalism depends not so much on a particular set of institutions as on its ability to maintain an environment that encourages open experimentation, by preserving the freedom to form new institutions and letting existing institutions be constantly replaced by those that are more successful (Matsuyama, 1995). Coordination is an inherently difficult matter to control. Cities have never evolved in a manner that precisely follows predetermined blueprints formulated by governments. The only way to sustain a continuous transition from lower states of the equilibria to higher ones is thus to keep searching for a better system.

This observation suggests a policy that may direct the future development of Osaka. It is essential for the future of Osaka to maintain the freedom to pursue and experiment with new ways of coordinating economic activities.

A small change initiated by a small group of agents may start a long chain reaction, in which the change in one strategy is continuously supported by changes in complementary strategies. The role of the government may be to foster private sector coordination rather than to substitute for it. The government's role would then be to facilitate the development of the private sector by providing public goods with diffused externalities such as the transportation infrastructure. People in Osaka have been making huge investments inside Kansai by private initiatives. The arrangement of a global infrastructure driven by private initiatives, most typically exemplified by

Kansai airport and Kansai Scientific City, to connect local knowledge and production systems more firmly with the rest of Japan, Asia, and the rest of world could be further promoted by fully exploiting the gateway externalities in the Osaka/Kansai Region.

REFERENCES

Arthur, W.B. (1994), *Increasing Returns and Path Dependence in the Economy*, Ann Arbor: The University of Michigan Press.

Batten, D.F., K. Kobayashi and A.E. Andersson (1989), 'Knowledge, nodes, and networks: an analytical perspective', in A.E. Andersson et al. (eds), *Knowledge and Industrial Organization*, Heidelberg and Berlin: Springer-Verlag.

Fujita, M. and P. Krugman (1995), 'When is the economy monocentric? von Thünen and Chamberlin Unified', *Regional Science and Urban Economics*, 25, 505–28.

Fujita, M. and J.-F. Thisse (1996), 'Economic agglomeration', Discussion paper No. 430, Kyoto Institute of Economic Research, Kyoto University.

Hicks, J. (1969), *A Theory of Economic Theory*, Oxford: Oxford University Press.

Kobayashi, K., D.F. Batten and A.E. Andersson (1991), 'The sequential location of knowledge-oriented firms over time and space', *Papers in Regional Science*, 70, 381–97.

Kobayashi, K. and K. Fukuyama (1998), 'Human contacts in knowledge society: an analytical perspective', in M.J. Beckmann, B. Johansson, F. Snickars and R. Thord (eds), *Knowledge and Networks in a Dynamic Economy*, Heidelberg: Springer-Verlag.

Krugman, P. (1991), 'History versus expectations', *Quarterly Journal of Economics*, **106**, 651–67.

Lucas, R.E. (1988), 'On the mechanics of economic development', *Journal of Monetary Economics*, **22**, 3–22.

Marshall, A. (1920), *Principles of Economics*, 8th edition, London: Macmillan.

Matsuyama, K. (1995), 'Complementarities and cumulative process in models of monopolistic competition', *Journal of Economic Literature*, **33**, 701–29.

Romer, P.M. (1986), 'Increasing Returns and Long-Run Growth', *Journal of Political Economy*, **94**, 1002–37.

13. Shanghai: a Gateway to China's Economic Modernization

Wei-Bin Zhang

INTRODUCTION

Great cities rise and fall. A place may grow into a great city because of its military or political importance or because of economic factors such as geographical accessibility, an entrepreneurial culture or natural resource endowments. A great city may lose its prominence because it no longer possesses comparative advantages over other regions. However, internal mechanisms for growth and external factors for change interact in such a complex fashion that it is difficult to provide any general analytical conclusions about the dynamic process of urban development.

Shanghai presents an interesting case for examining the dynamics of cities. Shanghai, with a population of 13 million in 1994, is the largest city in China. It is situated at the midpoint of China's east coast. Walsh (1992) describes Shanghai as follows: 'The name summons up a world of compradors and foreign concessions, gunboat diplomacy and opium, afternoon tea at the Cathay Hotel and death by starvation in the streets outside Western cantonments. It recalls a landscape of gangsters, sweatshops, strikes and revolution, fierce intellectuals and vengeful Red Guards.' Over the past hundred years it has played a leading role in China's modern development. From being an insignificant town before the Opium War, it had grown into an international metropolis by the end of the Second World War. It experienced chaos as well as cultural enrichment and economic development before the Communists came to power.

Shanghai was not only the center of prewar capitalism, but also the cradle of Chinese communism. After the Chinese Communist Party was founded in Shanghai in 1921, the Party used the city as a base to organize students and workers. The city therefore became the hub of communist-led movements in the 1920s and underground communist activities in the 1930s and 1940s. During the period of isolation from 1949 to 1979, Shanghai became less important internationally but still upheld its prestige as China's cultural and

254

economic center. After the economic reforms were introduced in 1978, Shanghai's relative economic position in China has declined, even though its economic performance has improved greatly.

SHANGHAI BEFORE THE OPIUM WAR

The first significant human settlement on the site of Shanghai occurred in the Tang dynasty. During the Tang and Five Dynasties periods, the population of the area grew and became increasingly prosperous. During the Song dynasty, Shanghai developed into a local center for trade. At that time, commerce began to replace agriculture as the dominant sector of the economy. Shanghai people by then primarily made a living from handling and transporting goods. Shanghai continued to prosper during the Yuan dynasty. By the end of the Yuan dynasty the dominant sectors of Shanghai's economy were textiles and trade. It is held that spinning and weaving techniques were introduced at the end of that dynasty. In the Ming era, Shanghai became a major center of cotton production that served the entire empire.

With the introduction of a more efficient technology in the thirteenth century, cotton gradually became the leading cash crop of the coastal Jiangnan region including Shanghai (Johnson, 1993). Shanghai and neighboring Songjiang counties became centers of cotton cultivation, processing, spinning and weaving. The sandy alluvial soil of Shanghai was marginally suited for rice cultivation. It was ideal for cotton. The humid climate provided suitable conditions for spinning long-fiber cotton yarn with a high tensile strength. The soil and climatic conditions implied that it would not be economically efficient for Shanghai to cultivate both rice and cotton. It would be more efficient if Shanghai imported rice and other commodities and exported cotton and cotton-related products. A large percentage of arable land in Shanghai county was therefore taken over by cotton plantations.

The specialization in cotton production implied that interregional trade had to play a significant role in Shanghai's economy. There was also another important factor that connected Shanghai with other regions. Cotton cultivation exhausted the soil easily and required additional nutrients for sustained yields. The main source of fertilizer was soybean cake, which led Shanghai to import beans, bean products, and fermented soycake fertilizer from the north in exchange for cotton yarn and cloth. In conjunction with the increasing interregional trade, the number of market towns in Shanghai county increased from the fifteenth to nineteenth centuries. Many people came to earn their living as brokers and transport merchants. Internal services such as banking and construction also grew in association with the expansion of commerce and population growth. Johnson (1993, p. 180) wrote: 'between

1685 and 1840 Shanghai grew from a typical county seat and local marketing center to a major coastal port city. In the mid-eighteenth century the city's population was around 120,000. One hundred years later, in the mid-nineteenth century, European visitors estimated the population at around 230,000. Shanghai was clearly a city of substance and importance by anyone's measure.'

SHANGHAI AFTER THE OPIUM WAR

In the eighteenth century Chinese contact with the West was limited to trade through the port of Guangzhou. The British motive for a relationship with China had been primarily economic. A Chinese product, tea, was in great demand in Britain. Tea imports reached 15 million pounds sterling in 1785 and double that amount in the decade preceding the Opium War. Tea was considered a necessity of British life. The popularity of this staple was such that the British Parliament passed an act requiring the East India Company to keep a year's stock in supply at all times. Not only the East India Company was dependent on the income from the tea trade. The British government received about one-tenth of its entire revenue from a tax on Chinese tea. Britain's problem was that there was no market for British woolens in China and the trade in manufactured goods was insufficient to pay for the tea. At the beginning of the nineteenth century, the import of tea and the poor market for British goods in China resulted in an unfavorable balance of trade for London. But Britain soon discovered that it could make a huge profit by exporting opium to China, which was produced in the British possessions of Bengal and Madras. By the 1820s, the expansion of the Chinese market for opium reversed the balance of trade. By 1828, opium was responsible for 90 percent of the value of all foreign goods imported into China. But in 1839 the imperial court decided to prohibit opium. In March 1839, an imperial commissioner, Lin Zexu, arrived at Guangzhou. He demanded that the foreigners hand over all the opium, worth over two million pounds, which they had stored in Guangzhou. The British merchants saw this demand as being unjust and refused to hand over the newly illegal drug. Lin then put them under house arrest. Eventually the merchants gave in and Lin then destroyed the opium. The British insisted on their right to sell opium in China in the name of free trade. They used the disagreement over opium as an excuse for declaring war on China. The conflict led to the Opium War (1839–42), in which China was defeated. The defeat led to the first of many unequal treaties forced on China.

In Nanking, on 29 August 1842, the treaty that brought the war to a close was signed. The Treaty of Nanking (together with the supplementary Treaty of the Bogue, October 1843) set the pattern for treaties China later signed with other foreign powers. It established the basic pattern for China's relations with the West for the next century. The Treaty of Nanking stipulated that China cede Hong Kong to the British. In addition, five Chinese ports (including Shanghai) were to be opened to foreign trade. China was forced to abolish the restrictions on trade within the treaty ports. In addition to Britain, the United States, France, Germany, Italy, Russia and Austria demanded special concessions inside China and privileges for their traders and missionaries. Westerners were placed under the legal jurisdiction of their own consuls and determined Chinese import duties. China could thus no longer interfere with the opium traffic. But the Westerners wanted more privileges whereas Chinese officials and local groups made efforts to resist Western demands. War broke out again in the mid-1850s and China was badly defeated once more. An Anglo-French expeditionary force took Beijing in 1860. The imperial summer palace was burned and a new set of treaties was forced upon China. Missionaries received the right to live and proselytize anywhere in the country. China's rivers were opened to foreign ships and gunboats. In some cities, Westerners gradually opened 'concession' areas, which were under complete foreign control, and Chinese officials were excluded from authority. Opium was legalized, leading to its production in China.

According to the Treaty of Nanking of 1842, the British secured rights to station a consul in the British Settlement in Shanghai. The American Settlement was established in 1863. The International Settlement resulted from the amalgamation of the British and the American Settlements in 1863. Until 1943, three separate municipalities, the International Settlement, the French Concession, and the Chinese County of Shanghai, existed in Shanghai side by side. Each of them had its own government and laws. Foreign powers obtained special rights of extraterritoriality for tariff collection and for navigating the East China Sea, the Yellow Sea, and along the Yangtze River. The first party of English traders was soon joined by an increasing number of Western traders and missionaries, of whom many were French or American. After the turn of the century, Japanese, White Russians, Indians, Vietnamese and other foreigners came to Shanghai. By 1875 there were 2,297 residents and about the same number of military and naval personnel in the International Settlement. By the end of the century, this number reached a few thousand more. However, by 1930 there were almost 100,000 foreigners in Shanghai's settlements (Wei, 1987). It is estimated that in its heyday Shanghai's foreign community comprised almost 60 nationalities, even though the size of this community never seemed to have exceeded a total of 150,000 people. Foreigners were known as Shanghailanders, and the Chinese, classified into West-influenced Chinese and native Chinese, were called Shanghainese. They worked together for their mutual benefit, but there was very little social intercourse between the Chinese and foreign residents. No single group dominated Shanghai's city culture. No wonder that in the 1930s and the 1940s it was described as a metropolis 'as crowded as Calcutta, as decadent as Berlin, as snooty as Paris, as jazzy as New York'.

The development of Shanghai thus became an international undertaking. In 1851 the establishment of a shipyard by the British marked the beginning of modern industrial development in Shanghai. During the treaty port years, the most important light industries in Shanghai were textiles, including cotton spinning and weaving, silk reeling, wool spinning and weaving, as well as dyeing and printing designs onto finished materials, and garment knitting and manufacturing. By 1895, the Chinese introduced foreign coloring and design for the manufacture of cloth. It is estimated that in the 1930s there were 75,242 workers in 567 textile factories in the International Settlement and 73,445 in 690 factories in the Chinese Municipality (Wei, 1987). Between 50 and 60 percent of the city's labor force was employed in textile production and 40 to 60 percent of the value of the industrial output was produced by this sector.

The Treaty of Shimonoseki in 1895 opened the way for Japan to develop mining and manufacturing activities in China. Other nations soon demanded and garnered similar privileges from the Qing government. The resulting treaty allowed Japanese and Westerners alike to make direct capital investments on Chinese soil. As a result, Western investments in Shanghai increased dramatically. In 1899, the area of the International Settlement expanded to nearly ten times its 1854 size, and the French Concession grew by an even larger factor. Railways, telegraph lines, and other means of communication and transportation were constructed. New foreign ventures attracted increased investment and know-how to Shanghai. In addition, many Chinese entrepreneurs and peasant laborers went to Shanghai. These Chinese, together with foreigners, mainly lived and worked in the foreign settlements. It is estimated that out of more than 620,000 Chinese living in the International Settlement in 1915, more than 75 percent had originally come from other regions to Shanghai (Wei, 1987).

The development of railways and steamships made the transportation of raw materials and finished products faster and cheaper. After it was opened as a treaty port, Shanghai gradually become the largest commercial center in China. Its functions became increasingly diversified and Shanghai's industrial development accelerated. Consequently, it became a trade, financial, entrepôt trade and transportation center during the 1920s and the 1930s. According to customs records, Shanghai's total exports reached US$993 and US$963 million in 1920 and 1926 respectively (Tian, 1996). Shanghai firms purchased different products all over China and then exported them. Between 1926 and 1930, Shanghai's share of the value of the total export of goods from China was 68 percent on average. In 1933, the foreign trade of Shanghai accounted for 1 percent of the world total (Fung et al., 1992).

Western knowledge was also brought in through Shanghai. Some young Chinese received Western education at institutions established in Shanghai by foreign missionaries. Some went to study abroad. These Western-educated Chinese played an increasingly important role in the development of Shanghai into a modern economic center of China. While they tended to keep Chinese mores and manners, they did business in new ways and were philosophically influenced by the doctrine of *laissez-faire*. These Chinese further helped Shanghai develop a taste for keeping abreast of new ways in economic and social life. Due to the existence of the foreign concessions, Shanghai also provided a social environment relatively free from the Chinese government. Artists, musicians, scholars and thinkers made their homes in Shanghai. Before the Communists took over China, Shanghai was China's indisputable cultural center.

Shanghai's population increased tenfold between 1842 and 1945. The increase mainly resulted from Chinese in-migration. Chinese entrepreneurs and laborers came to Shanghai to seek investment and employment opportunities. The number of people in the International Settlement doubled between 1895 and 1910 and doubled again between 1910 and 1930, while the number of people in the French Concession almost tripled between 1895 and 1915 and more than tripled between 1915 and 1930. In less than a century, Shanghai developed into the leading metropolis of Asia. In 1936, it was the seventh largest city in the world, with a population of 3.81 million (Yeung, 1996).

SHANGHAI DURING THE PERIOD 1953-78

After the Second World War, the foreign concessions were closed and Shanghai fell under Chinese administration. When the Communist forces took over, private enterprises had transferred their movable assets out of China and moved their centers of operation to Hong Kong. Shanghai was soon transformed from being a financial and commercial center into a leading industrial city. In the 1930s and 1940s, Shanghai had been an important financial and trading center on the western Pacific coast. After the Communist takeover, Shanghai's overseas connections were severed and most foreigners left the city. Murphey (1988) describes the development of Shanghai prior to the economic reforms and open policy initiated in 1978 as follows:

> During the first three decades of Communist rule, Shanghai was periodically viewed officially as more problem than promise, an unwelcome leftover from a humiliating and resented semicolonial past. There was official talk in the early 1950s of dismantling Shanghai and distributing its factories and experts over the previously neglected rest of the country. Shanghai was never dismantled completely, but skilled workers, technicians, machine goods and tools, and some whole factories were

reallocated from the city to aid in developing new inland industrial centers, and Shanghai's own growth was sharply restricted.

In the early 1950s, the central government wanted to reduce the inequalities between the coastal and interior regions. In order to achieve a balanced growth of cities, the government favored small and medium-sized cities, especially those in the inland provinces. The central government designed a policy of restricting Shanghai's growth and its economic connection with the outside world. On the other hand, the government treated the city as a source of funds and human capital. In order to guarantee the growth of the interior regions, Shanghai was assigned to play the role of the most important contributor of fiscal revenue, foreign exchange, scientific and technological know-how, and human capital. Partly because of this assignment, Shanghai did not lose its leading role in China's economy in the pre-1978 command economy. The central government transformed Shanghai into the industrial center of the country. Heavy industries were concentrated in Shanghai. Shanghai continued to maintain its supremacy as China's largest metropolis and key economic center during the period.

During the First Five-Year Plan (1953–57) the industrial structure experienced dramatic changes. The central government favored the development of heavy industries. In 1952, about 80 percent of the gross value of Shanghai's industrial output was produced by light industries. The major products were textiles, flour, cigarettes, leather and rubber goods, matches and soap. Heavy industries such as machinery, metallurgy and the chemical, electricity and shipbuilding industries were then still at an early stage of development. Later, the gross value output of heavy industries soon caught up with that of light industries. In 1988, the output proportions of light industry and heavy industry were 55:45.

In comparison with most regions in China, Shanghai enjoyed some superior endowments, which included an experienced labor force, superior managerial and technical skills, and an established industrial foundation, relatively high productivity and strong historical ties with the rest of the world. Shanghai maintained high productivity levels during the period between the early 1950s and the later 1970s because of its traditions of skill, efficiency and innovation. Its older firms were actually more innovative and responsive than better-equipped newcomers. Shanghai's industries had China's highest technological efficiency throughout the period of central planning. In the 1980s, Shanghai led the nation in the value of industrial output per factory worker, per capita national income, and energy utilization ratio. In 1978, it accounted for one-seventh of the industrial output, one-sixth of the revenue and one-third of the exports of the entire country. In the 1953–78 period, the annual growth rate of Shanghai's national income amounted to almost 9 percent.

After the establishment of the People's Republic of China (PRC), there was no freedom of migration even within China. Migration was subject to strict controls after the imposition of the household registration system in the late 1950s. During the early 1950s, Shanghai was allowed by the central government to adopt several measures to control in-migration. In order to solve urban social and economic problems, the government implemented several large-scale migration programs that reduced the size of the urban population. The net rate of population increase was the lowest among all large cities in China. During the period 1968–77, Shanghai experienced a net loss of about one million people due to China's migration policy

SHANGHAI AFTER THE ECONOMIC REFORMS

The late 1980s witnessed a major transformation of China's economy (Zhang, 1998, 1999). This transformation of the national economy was mainly expressed as structural changes in the regional economies. Over the past two decades, the complex process of economic reform has profoundly changed the economic geography of China. After 1979, the government moved the country toward a market economy and introduced an open-door policy toward trade, financial flows and foreign investments. It emphasized the coastal region for economic as well as political reasons. In this way, the speed of 'opening the doors' of the various regions was controlled by the central government. The reform policy allowed uneven income distribution among regions and included an 'experimental strategy' of forcing rapid growth to occur in particular areas. It was argued that if a specific region succeeded in promoting economic growth, other regions could emulate the successful region. This argument about regional economic evolution, even though it proved to be successful in some cases, perhaps stemmed from the leaders' limited understanding of regional economics and the enforced homogeneous regional development in the preceding three decades.

The government's open-door policy initially did not include all regions. The first focus was on the Special Economic Zones on China's south coast in the early 1980s. These areas were supposed to grow rapidly and play a leading role in expanding foreign trade, transmitting knowledge and directing national economic growth. Due to this policy and differences in geographical and cultural factors, economic development in China has been spatially unbalanced. The coastal regions have experienced a disproportionate share of the economic growth. One might reasonably expect that Shanghai should first benefit from the open policy because of its location, industrial foundations and human resources. But it is perhaps rational for Chinese politicians in power to emphasize stability when social stability and economic efficiency conflict, at least in the short term, since stability tends to secure politicians' current power. Although Shanghai's industries had proved to be among the most efficient in the nation, the central government did not grant Special-Economic-Zone-like autonomy to Shanghai in matters affecting external economic relations. Instead, the government carried out the initial experiments in economic reforms and preferential policies in Guangdong in southern China. Guangdong's contribution to China's treasury was only about 5 percent of that of Shanghai in 1982. A failure in Guangdong would not matter so much for the central government. To reform Shanghai was not an easy matter because the city was politically and economically far more complex than Guangdong. A rapid reform in Shanghai might easily have led to instabilities in the national system. Partially due to its comparative advantages, Shanghai did not obtain favorable treatment from the government in the initial stage of the economic reforms. Shanghai actually experienced relative stagnation in comparison with other coastal cities. In terms of export volume, utilization of foreign capital, and overall economic growth, Shanghai did not play a catalytic role in China's industrialization after the reforms were instituted.

True, in 1984, together with some other coastal cities, Shanghai was designated an open-port city. This policy was designed to help Shanghai to attract capital investment and to transfer technology rapidly from developed economies. It was argued that if the economic development of Shanghai succeeded, the economic reforms would diffuse through the entire Yangtze Delta and eventually spread to the lower and middle Yangtze Basin. Shanghai was considered as a catalyst for urban and regional development in Central and East China. Since Shanghai opened to foreign investment in 1984, economic cooperation with foreign countries has indeed been rapidly strengthened. Advanced technology and different types of industrial goods and services have been introduced. Export-oriented industries have benefited from foreign technology transfer and the number of joint ventures between Shanghai's enterprises and foreign firms have increased. Still, during the 1979–90 period, Shanghai was not supposed to play a leading role in the economic reform program. Over those 12 years its manufacturing sector lost its dominant position in the domestic market. Annual economic growth averaged 7.5 percent which was below the national average. In 1978, China's top five contributors to its national income were Shanghai, Jiangsu, Liaoning, Sichuan and Shandong; but in 1990 they were Shandong, Jiangsu, Guangdong, Sichuan and Liaoning. Shanghai had fallen from number one in 1978 to number ten in 1990. Shanghai's share of China's national income also fell from about 8 percent in 1978 to 4 percent in 1990.

Since the end of the 1980s, Shanghai has been involved in a continuing struggle to regain its position as the economic center of China. During the early years of the economic reforms, when Guangdong and Fujian developed rapidly,

Shanghai experienced rather modest growth. The rise of the southern regions and the decline of Shanghai's relative economic position were noticed by Shanghai's government as well as the central government. But Shanghai lacked space for expansion. The city center at Puxi was very dense. It would be difficult and expensive to further develop in this area. It seems that Pudong was only one possible direction for the further development and urban growth of Shanghai. The official announcement by Premier Li Peng on 18 April 1990 about the development of Pudong encouraged some observers to believe that Shanghai would develop into a world city again.

Pudong is located opposite the Shanghai city center at Puxi on the eastern side of the Huangpu River. It is immediately opposite the Bund, the central business district of Shanghai. Pudong occupies some 350 square kilometers. When it was announced to be an open area for development, there were already some industrial activities in the area. It had a built-up area of 38 square kilometers and a population of 1.33 million. On becoming a special development area, ten preferential policies were introduced in Pudong. These policies related to, for example, the income tax on foreign investors, custom duties and the tax on equipment. Pudong was planned to become a well-integrated district with an advanced communication network, a complete infrastructure and convenient communication and information systems. The development was supposed to help Shanghai to become one of the major economic and trading centers on the western Pacific Rim in the next century.

During the 1980s, Shanghai was able to attract a total of US$3.3 billion in foreign investment. After Pudong was established as an open area, the amount of foreign investment in 1992 alone was equivalent to that of the entire preceding decade. It attracted direct investment of US$2.3 billion and 3.2 billion in 1993 and 1994, respectively. After Pudong was declared an open area, large-scale investments in infrastructure were made in Shanghai. The Nanpu Bridge and the Yangpu Bridge were completed, respectively, in 1991 and 1993. The 16-km Line One of the subway system linking north and south Puxi was opened in 1994. An inner ring road linking Pudong with Puxi was opened to traffic in 1994.

In contrast to the 1980s, Shanghai has lately become the focus of economic development in China. At the 14th Party Congress held in October 1992, the central government announced that Shanghai should develop as a 'dragon head' with 'economic, financial and trading center' functions to lead the Yangtze River Basin and China at large into the twenty-first century. Due to its strategic location, its abundance of skilled manpower and national policies highly favorable to Shanghai, it was expected that Shanghai would soon recover its pre-war dominance as the center of China's economy. Shanghai has consequently experienced significant economic structural changes in the 1990s. The tertiary sector has developed especially rapidly. In 1994, the value of the tertiary sector accounted for 39.6 percent of Shanghai's GRP. Industrial development has concentrated on steel, automobiles, petrochemicals, energy, telecommunications and computer products. The industrial sector accounted for more than 56 percent of Shanghai's GRP in 1993.

Irrespective of its recent growth, however, Shanghai's share of China's industrial output declined from 12.1 percent in 1978 to 5.5 percent in 1994. Guangdong surpassed its industrial output in 1988. The opening of Pudong did not help Shanghai to regain its leading role in industrialization. In 1994, Guangdong's industrial output was nearly 1.7 times that of Shanghai (Sung, 1996). This is similar for other sectors. In 1994, Guangdong's service output was 1.8 times that of Shanghai.

THE FUTURE OF SHANGHAI

As noted in the introduction, great cities both rise and fall because of factors such as geographical location, institutional quality, technological progress and the distribution of wealth and consumption. A great city neither arises by accident nor does it fall by whim. Modern non-linear economics shows that capital, knowledge, population and institutions interact over time and space in such a complicated path-dependent manner that it is almost impossible to forecast the future of a complicated urban system in the long term. In the global economy, no single economy is able to dominate the world for very long. This is similarly true within a large national economy. As technology and economic geography change, centers relocate. China seems to be moving toward a modern economy with multiple centers. This multi-nuclear development pattern is different from the traditional pattern with one or a few centers. Main economic forces for this multi-nuclear pattern are technological change, structural changes in the regional division of labor associated with technological changes, the spread of education, and improvements to the communication and transportation infrastructures.

As China carries out economic reforms on a national scale, market forces and production relationships are experiencing great changes. These changes will bring about a redistribution of comparative advantages among regions. Shanghai is thus faced with increasing competition on a national scale. Cities and regions compete not only in merchandise and services trade, but also, more fundamentally, in imitation, innovation and other intangible assets, such as management skills and entrepreneurship. As market mechanisms further penetrate China's economy, regions improve their communication and transportation infrastructures as well as their education and knowledge levels, resulting in improved overall efficiency. Different from the semi-colonial period when the conditions for industrialization were limited to a few treaty ports, many regions in contemporary China are trying to bring about the conditions for industrialization. It would therefore be unreasonable to predict that Shanghai would play an economic role as important as it did in the past within China.

Shanghai is no longer China's economic, trade and transport center. For example, Guangdong has overtaken Shanghai in terms of output, foreign investment and exports. Moreover, Shanghai's transportation system is inefficient and many provinces along the Yangtze have better linkages to other cities than Shanghai. For instance, most of Sichuan's foreign trade goes through Hong Kong rather than Shanghai. This means that Shanghai no longer enjoys the advantages in transport, communication and coordination within the country and with other countries that played such a significant role in facilitating the process of Shanghai's industrialization in the past. Shanghai's relative shares in the total value of exports and in cargo handled at ports have both declined. Conversely, Guangzhou and Hong Kong handle a growing proportion of China's trade. Since the Shanghai port cannot handle fourth- and fifth-generation container ships and 10,000-ton vessels, there is little hope that it will become a hub port in the global container network.

In Shanghai, factories are mainly located in the central city. Although this may imply agglomeration economies, the negative impact of industrial concentration may become dominant, especially when other cities gain better access to capital and knowledge. The problems partly derive from inadequate accumulated investments in urban renovation and infrastructure. In the 1949–83 period, less than 4 percent of Shanghai's total expenditures was spent on urban maintenance. Since the launch of the Pudong project, Shanghai has been expected to accelerate its economic development. But since the state is heavily involved, the project may fail to induce sufficient levels of competition and risk-taking behavior. The heavy involvement of the state, for instance, led to very costly mistakes in infrastructure construction. As pointed out by Sung (1996), the central government chose to build the Nanpu Bridge instead of constructing a less costly and more efficient tunnel simply because a bridge is a highly visible monument. Moreover, Shanghai remains poor in environmental quality not only in absolute terms but also in comparison with other Chinese cities. The Huangpu River is often called 'a chemical cocktail' made up of raw sewage, toxic urban waste, and huge amounts of industrial discharges.

Shanghai's economic system also suffers from serious administrative and fiscal problems. Its economic structure was formed during the three decades of socialist industrialism. Industrial enterprises were unusually large and the number of workers employed in the state sector was higher in Shanghai than in other cities. It will not be easy to revitalize the large enterprises and adapt them to the market economy. In 1974, the share of people employed in individual-owned and private-owned businesses of total employment amounted to only 2.8

percent in Shanghai, but 3.3 percent in Tianjin and 9.8 percent in Guangzhou. In 1994, the state sector still accounted for over 72 percent of total urban employment in Shanghai. The amounts of subsidies that are used to support ailing state-owned enterprises have increased substantially over the years. These state-owned enterprises have diverted resources from more efficient uses to an especially great extent in Shanghai.

Shanghai is well endowed with education. Its technological capacity is second only to Beijing in terms of the number of institutes of higher learning and scientific research as well as in the number of technical personnel, engineers and scientists engaged in research and development. In 1990, Shanghai had 638 tertiary graduates per 10,000 population, much higher than Guangdong's ratio of 133. This does not however automatically translate into higher productivity. It is said that in the 1980s Shanghai's managers often waited for policy guidance before taking any action. Shanghai's educated bureaucrats tended to adopt a strategy of strict adherence to central directives. In addition, Shanghai is now facing a brain-drain problem. According to the 1990 Population Census, there are almost 70,000 persons from Shanghai residing abroad. These emigrants tend to have higher educational backgrounds than the general population in Shanghai.

One of Shanghai's ambitions is to become a financial center. It will be quite difficult for Shanghai to realize its potential as the financial center of China if the financial and banking system is not reformed. It is often speculated that Shanghai will overtake and replace Hong Kong. In comparison to Shanghai as one of the major cities of underdeveloped China, Hong Kong is a global financial and industrial center. On the one hand, Hong Kong has the advantages of modern infrastructures, worldwide trading connections and a sound legal system. Shanghai, on the other hand, has the advantages of its geographical location, a huge hinterland and a strong science and technology base (Wong, 1996). Since Shanghai lacks a functioning legal system, it will be difficult for the city to become an international financial center in the near future unless China rapidly reforms its institutions.

Modern technology makes it difficult to predict future urbanization processes. Traditional increasing-returns-to-scale economies through urbanization may disappear because of new technology and the possibility of huge capital investments in one region in a short time. The impact of changes in the mechanisms of industrial location may have profound implications for urban growth. Shanghai is a skill-intensive city by domestic standards, but it is not skill-intensive in a global sense. It is labor-intensive within the international division of labor. The comparative advantage resulting from its labor-intensive character may be lost to other regions in China. Labor costs are still lower in Shanghai than in some cities in southern China, not to mention Hong Kong, Taiwan or Singapore. But in comparison to most regions in China, Shanghai's wage level is not low at all. It is therefore expected that labor-intensive production will gradually relocate to other regions. Because domestic and international transportation costs are coming down, other regions with cheap labor and low land rents can increasingly produce labor-intensive goods more efficiently as long as the technology and capital are available. The improvements to the transportation and communication systems in China have greatly increased customers' and producers' global awareness. This has allowed for the spatial dispersion of related activities: no longer do manufacturing and services always occur in the same region. The decentralization of production has been facilitated by increased economic freedom at the international, national, and regional levels. Thus it seems that Shanghai has to develop into a knowledge- or skill-intensive city if it wants to attain global gateway status. But highly specialized skills are information-intensive, complex, largely tacit and difficult to imitate. They may be embodied in individuals, organizational routines or production processes. It is difficult to tell whether or not Shanghai will become a less labor-intensive economy in the near future. Moreover, in order to become a modern city, it seems necessary to become a center of innovation and agglomeration. Entrepreneurship, imitative learning and the love of money are not alone sufficient for a city to become innovative.

It is not easy to predict the dynamics of a city, especially into the future. Since China is at a historical turning point and Shanghai is one of the key cities in China, one should be cautious in speculating on its future. Although Shanghai faces many difficulties, it still has some favorable traits. It has a hard-working labor force and a cultural tradition of capitalism. Despite three decades of socialist egalitarianism, the work ethic is still very strong as a normative value among Shanghai residents. Diligence and personal progress are highly appreciated in the cultural environment. Its entrepreneurial spirit fosters a readiness for innovation. The local culture emphasizes educational aspirations and moneymaking as well. This predilection for education, diligence and money may yet play a future role in helping Shanghai attain a position as a commercial center in China and, perhaps, in the world.

REFERENCES

Fung, K.I., Z.M. Yan and Y.M. Ning (1992), 'Shanghai: China's world city', in Y.M. Yeung and X.W. Hu (eds), *China's Coastal Cities — Catalysts for Modernization*, Honolulu: University of Hawaii Press.

Johnson, L.C. (ed.) (1993), *Cities of Jiangnan in Late Imperial China*, Albany: State University of New York Press.

Murphey, R. (1988), 'Shanghai', in M. Doggan and J.D. Kasarda (eds), *The Metropolis Era: Mega-cities*, vol. 2, Newbury Park: Sage Publications.

Sung, Y.W. (1996), 'Dragon head' of China's economy?', in Y.M. Yeung and Y.W. Sung (eds), *Shanghai – Transformation and Modernization under China's Open Policy*, Hong Kong: The Chinese University Press.

Tian, G. (1996), *Shanghai's Role in the Economic Development of China*, London: Praeger.

Walsh, J. (1992), 'Shanghai', *Time*, 5 October.

Wei, B.P.T. (1987), *Shanghai – Crucible of Modern China*, Oxford: Oxford University Press.

Wong, S.L. (1996), 'The entrepreneurial spirit – Shanghai and Hong Kong compared', in Y.M. Yeung and Y.W. Sung (eds), *Shanghai – Transformation and Modernization under China's Open Policy*, Hong Kong: The Chinese University Press.

Yeung, Y.M. (1996), 'Introduction', in Y.M. Yeung and Y.W. Seung (eds), *Shanghai – Transformation and Modernization under China's Open Policy*, Hong Kong: The Chinese University Press.

Zhang, W.B. (1998), *Japan versus China in the Industrial Race*, London: Macmillan.

Zhang, W.B. (1999), *Confucianism and Modernization*, London: Macmillan.

14. Institutions and Networks: the Case of Taiwan's Export-Oriented Production Zones

David E. Andersson

BACKGROUND

For at least 30 years, there have been three major export-oriented production zones on the west coast of Taiwan, to use Sassen's terminology and a functional regional approach (Sassen, 1994). While a wide range of goods has been exported from Taiwan since the onset of industrialization, the role of the economy as a whole in the global division of labor has been unambiguous. The Taiwanese in all three regions (Taipei, Kaohsiung and Taichung) have specialized in being producers of increasingly advanced manufactured goods for the world market. The seaports of Kaohsiung and Keelung as well as the international airport near Taipei have for this reason become much more important as transport nodes in the global network for trade in manufactured goods than in any of the service networks.

On the surface, the role of Taiwan as a whole in the world economy may seem similar to South Korea or – taking a time lag into account – Japan. But this is only true of the overall specialization in manufacturing. Compared with South Korean or Japanese firms, Taiwanese firms tend to be smaller and more integrated in international production networks. The relative internationalization of Taiwanese businesses is also evident in the extensive linkages to overseas firms, ranging from American high-tech companies to Southeast Asian subcontractors. Overall, the stable comparative advantage of Taiwan seems to be small-scale manufacturing that involves spatially dispersed networks of firms.

The purpose of this chapter is both to analyze the general competitiveness of the Taiwanese economy, as well as to speculate on what the ongoing institutional and spatial restructuring may imply for Taiwan's future positioning in various global networks. Institutionally, Taiwan is evolving toward a variant of Western-style liberal democracy with some unusual features. Taiwan's spatial restructuring refers to various infrastructure projects that may cause a new configuration of regions.

A presumption of the arguments presented here is that entrepreneurs (in business as well as in idea creation) are the driving forces in the network economy and further that the networks are becoming increasingly globalized. Whether a region becomes a node or gateway in one or more networks depends on whether the region provides a hospitable environment for domestic or external individuals and firms. I argue that the odds for a region becoming a gateway are influenced by three factors: institutional quality, accessibility and productivity. Productivity is in this context closely related to spatial agglomerations of knowledge.

REGIONS AND INSTITUTIONS

The institutions of a region include the internal institutions of the community, such as ethical norms and customs, and the external institutions embodied in the constitution, the legal system or legislation. For the individual entrepreneur, the institutional setting primarily influences the transaction costs he or she faces, including both the expected transaction cost and the level of uncertainty associated with it. Uncertainty differences can arise because of heterogeneity in the internal institutions across individuals, or because of uncertain outcomes associated with law enforcement or new legislation.

Any evaluation of the institutional quality of a region necessarily involves normative criteria. My approach is normative individualism with a subjectivist foundation (see Buchanan, 1991). An implication of this approach is that the removal of coercive obstacles to gains from trade represents a quality improvement, as evidenced by individuals' voluntary exchanges. Other improvements include transaction-cost reductions and the right of individuals to choose the institutional structure under which they live. The subjectivist approach thus enables us to assess the quality of the external institutions of a region. On the other hand, no such (interpersonal) assessments can be made regarding the quality of the internal institutions, since these represent the internalization of values to which individuals voluntarily adhere.

A rejection of the possibility to evaluate the quality of the internal institutions does not, however, make them unimportant. Indeed, internal institutions are often much more important than external institutions in explaining a region's role in the global division of labor. Conversely, the quality of the external institutions is to a large extent determined by how well they complement the internal institutions (e.g., a society that mostly relies on informal sanctions needs fewer formal laws).

TAIWAN'S INTERNAL INSTITUTIONS

With a population that is predominantly ethnic Chinese, the internal institutions of Taiwanese society closely resemble those of other Chinese societies in East and Southeast Asia. Important institutional traits include a general acceptance of private property, the importance of kinship and *guanxi* relationships and the principle of equal inheritance (Hamilton, 1996). The informal sanction that is of overriding importance is loss of face. Loss of face can refer both to a loss of moral authority and to insufficient accomplishments (Redding and Ng, 1982). Taken together, these institutional traits have far-reaching implications for the economic structure.

The importance of kinship relationships affects both the objectives of individuals and interpersonal trust. According to Redding (1990), individuals are expected to look to the best interests of the (extended) family, even at the expense of others. Loss of face is also considered especially severe if it occurs within the family. Complementary but somewhat weaker than kinship relationships are so-called *guanxi* relationships. These relationships arise from a personal establishment of mutual dependence and investments in face, and tend mostly to occur between people with similar socioeconomic backgrounds. Chinese society is therefore both familistic and personalistic.

Interpersonal trust is crucial for the functioning of the internal institutions of a culture (Dasgupta, 1988). A high-trust society can rely to a much greater extent on internal institutions, which is a considerable advantage since internal institutions tend to be more flexible, less expensive to enforce and have greater evolutionary capacity than external institutions (Kasper, 1998). Whether Chinese society is a high-trust society is, however, not generally agreed upon. Redding (1990) argued that it is essentially a high-trust society, whereas Fukuyama (1995) singled out Taiwan as one of his low-trust case studies. Perhaps Chinese societies are best characterized as having differentiated trust, with high-trust extended families and – to a lesser extent – *guanxi* networks operating in a low-trust environment.

The identification of individual interests with family interests and the high level of trust within families have induced an economic system that mainly relies on family enterprises (Fei, 1992). Moreover, the state has historically not played a major role in the institutionalization of Chinese capitalism. Relational networks have instead been responsible for promoting the market order (Hamilton, 1985). The leading role of relational networks in institutional development and a cultural tradition of emphasizing family rather than national interests have meant that the internal institutions of Chinese capitalism are not associated with any particular political space (Hamilton, 1996). Instead, these institutions evolve with the relational networks, sometimes encompassing firms in several nation states.

Another characteristic feature of Chinese capitalism is the prevalence of small and medium-sized enterprises (SMEs). The preponderance of SMEs has several causes. First, the tradition of equal inheritance among sons means that large firms are likely to be broken up after the death of the firm's founder. Second, the lack of trust in people outside one's relational network makes it more difficult to bring in professional managers and also implies a general distrust of employees from outside the family. According to a survey of overseas Chinese executives by Redding (1990), employees are not only distrusted, but there is a cultural abhorrence of being an employee. A reflection of this is that Taiwan and Hong Kong have the world's highest labor turnover rates. Redding's survey also showed that satisfaction from owning a firm is a core personal value, which may explain the extremely high levels of entrepreneurship in both Taiwan and Hong Kong. In contrast to many Westerners and Japanese, the Chinese seem to have a predisposition to supply their own employment.

Overall, the internal institutions in Taiwan are conducive to a highly decentralized and flexible form of competitive capitalism with few large firms. Because of a tradition of informal institutional evolution unconstrained by political space, Taiwanese businesses can be expected to continue to increase their role in cross-border investment, production and distribution networks.

TAIWAN'S EXTERNAL INSTITUTIONS

The quality of the external institutions of a region depend both on 'meta-institutions', such as the constitution and the legal system, as well as on the legislation and laws that derive from decisions taken at lower institutional levels. At the meta-institutional level, desirable traits include the rule of law, the principle of universality and constitutional constraints on legislative power, because these traits tend to reduce the coercion, friction and uncertainty that individuals face (Epstein, 1995). The external meta-institutions determine the feasibility and likelihood of specific laws and regulations.

Several historical circumstances explain why the West rather than the East developed relatively efficient external institutions. Chief among them are the universalistic and individualistic world view of the Christian religion (Gregg, 1999) and interjurisdictional competition, arising both from the separation of church and state and the political decentralization in pre-industrial Europe (Jones, 1981).

By contrast, the Chinese empire lacked the philosophical prerequisites for the rule of law or a constrained state. According to Lin Yu-sheng: 'In traditional China, there was no conception of the separation of the sacred from the profane, the spiritual from the secular. Political legitimacy rested on the Mandate of Heaven, which defined politics in terms of morality' (Lin cited in Huntington, 1991). Moreover, political centralization was typical of traditional China, even though most of its technological development took place when power was temporarily fragmented (Needham, 1954) or when foreign institutions were imposed on China (i.e., in the treaty ports). The indigenous external institutions of China, however, were based on unconstrained political power and the rule of men. While the internal institutions of China evolved to support a market order, China's external institutions made the full realization of that order impossible.

The external institutions adopted by the Kuomingtang regime in Taiwan after 1949 have been crucial for Taiwan's rapid economic development. Lacking an indigenous Chinese foundation for the rule of law, Taiwan's government inherited a Japanese legal system, which was introduced under Japanese colonial rule. This legal system was in its turn adopted from continental European civil law, which is one of two manifestations of a legal system based on equality under the rule of law (the other being Anglo-Saxon common law). While the authoritarian Chiang Kai-Shek regime did not introduce any internal checks and balances into the political system, there were substantial external constraints on its power. These included the carrot of US support, the stick of the Chinese military threat and the discipline of having to perform well in export markets.

US aid and military support for Taiwan was conditional on the creation of a private enterprise system and a semblance of democracy (Jacoby, 1966). The American education that a growing number of Taiwanese received was also instrumental in promoting the internalization of liberal and democratic values, at least in the long run. The mainland Chinese threat, meanwhile, induced the regime to emphasize economic growth in order to ensure lasting security (Kasper, 1998). The smallness of the economy and the lack of natural resources, finally, ensured that Taiwan faced the pressures of inter-jurisdictional competition, especially from other emerging trading economies.

Taiwan's current institutional challenges are particularly interesting, because Taiwan represents the only predominantly Chinese society that is also a liberal democracy (Engberg, 1999), categorizes Hong Kong as a 'liberal autocracy' and Singapore as an 'illiberal democracy'.) While Taiwan is a nation under the rule of law, the legal system still has several shortcomings. A general shortcoming of continental civil law is that it has less evolutionary capacity than common law (Hayek, 1973). Surveys on institutional competitiveness also tend to rank common-law jurisdictions as offering the most competitive 'institutional package's (World Economic Forum, 1998). A specific consequence of Taiwan's authoritarian past is that the principles of due process and the presumption of innocence are less entrenched in Taiwan than in Western Europe.

While liberal democracy is likely to endure in Taiwan, its constitutional aspects have yet to take root. Horse-trading between the two major political parties has, over the past few years, led to constitutional changes such as a more powerful presidency, the abolition of the provincial government, and the mid-term time extension of the current national assembly (the constitution-making assembly).

Turning to the individual laws and regulations that have been enacted within the meta-institutional framework, we can observe certain distinctive tendencies. Internally, the Taiwanese economy has been burdened with relatively little rent-seeking legislation. Under martial law, most rent-seeking was confined to politically well-connected parts of the mainlander minority. Low taxes, few urban land-use regulations and a flexible labor market have instead been hallmarks of the domestic economy (Andersson, 1999). Externally, however, there have been substantial restrictions against the free flow of goods, services and, especially, capital and labor.

At present, we are witnessing two conflicting trends. Due to World Trade Organization (WTO) and US pressure, international trade and financial flows are being gradually deregulated. This can only improve Taiwan's institutional quality and transaction-cost level. Domestically, meanwhile, democracy has empowered the non-mainlander majority to engage in rent-seeking for the first time. While the public sector is still relatively small by OECD standards, it has increased from less than 20 percent of GDP ten years ago to between 25 and 30 percent in the late 1990s. Unlike Western Europe or North America, however, most political redistribution benefits local *guanxi* networks rather than organized industry and labor.

TAIWAN'S ACCESSIBILITY

Like other parts of Asia, Taiwan's accessibility to world markets has improved markedly over the past 30 years. Because of technological improvements in aviation and, particularly, telecommunications, space-bridging costs are a small fraction of what they were a generation ago. Almost equally important for Taiwan has been the concurrent rapid development of other Asia-Pacific economies, so that the geographical accessibility to product markets has improved.

In a spatial analysis of air passenger flows in the Asia-Pacific, Kobayashi (1993) found that there are two major air corridors in the region; a Southeast Asian corridor stretching from Jakarta to Taipei and a Northeast Asian one from Tokyo to Hong Kong. Interestingly, Taiwan and Hong Kong are the only two economies that link up to both corridors. Moreover, the Hong Kong–Taipei route is one of the top three international routes in the world in terms of total passenger load (the other two being New York–London and London–Paris). On the other hand, Taipei does not – unlike Bangkok, Hong Kong, Singapore and Tokyo – have a high percentage of international transit passengers.

Taiwan also plays an important role in the sea transport network. Kaohsiung has the world's third largest container port, behind Hong Kong and Singapore. In fact, Kaohsiung's trade-adjusted accessibility would be the best in Asia, were it not for the ban on direct transport links with China. While sea transport has been in decline in Europe and America, this is not the case in Asia since road transport is not a feasible option for connecting the Asia-Pacific's most advanced economies (Japan, the NICs and Australia) with one another.

As noted in the introduction, the densely populated west coast of Taiwan consists of three contiguous functional regions, rather than an urban corridor, which Batten (1995) claimed would be the final stage in the evolution of a link in a network. The main reason for the economic separation of the three regions is the persistently high transport costs.

In their chapter on the Milan–Venice corridor (Chapter 17), Magrini and Martellato claim that the space between Milan and Venice should be considered a network city, rather than a link between two urban nodes. A notable similarity between that corridor and the space between Taipei and Kaohsiung is the distance (280 and 300 kilometers, respectively), the high proportion of networking SMEs (especially in the small towns), and a high population density on a relatively flat surface. Congestion problems, however, are much more severe in the Taiwanese case. The average travel time by car between Milan and Venice amounts to little more than three hours, ranging from two-and-a-half to four hours. The corresponding figure for Taipei to Kaohsiung is about six hours, ranging from four to as much as 12 hours on some Sundays and holidays. In addition, the rail link from Taipei to Kaohsiung is not particularly fast either, with the fastest trains taking more than four hours. For that reason, the mean commuting time per unit of distance is probably at least double the Western European figure, especially if feeder road congestion is accounted for.

While western Taiwan at present does not constitute an integrated economic region, a future reconfiguration is still possible. A high-speed rail link, modeled on the Paris to Lyon TGV, is currently under construction. When completed, it will cut the travel time between Taipei and Kaohsiung from over four to one-and-a-half hours. In effect, central Taipei and Kaohsiung can then both be reached from downtown Taichung in about 45 minutes, a manageable commuting time distance. In addition, a second, parallel, freeway is now under construction, which could possibly reduce road congestion levels, depending on the future rate of automobile use.

While by no means a foregone conclusion, an integrated west coast metropolitan area would imply the largest conurbation in Asia south of Japan. It would be three times as populous as the Hong Kong SAR and have a regional GDP comparable to Hong Kong and Singapore combined.

AGGLOMERATIONS OF KNOWLEDGE

The search cost for finding knowledge (a transaction cost) depends on the geographical location. Although people can search for knowledge in distant geographical locations as well as in the home region, the transportation costs that must be incurred may be prohibitive. This is especially true of businesses that are in engaged in the production of knowledge, which normally implies regular face-to-face interactions with (potential) knowledge suppliers. The high price of land in the downtown areas of large cities is a reflection of this knowledge accessibility advantage. Especially for high-technology manufacturing and knowledge services, there are strong agglomeration economies associated with being located in centers with a high level of related or complementary knowledge production, due to lower search costs for finding new knowledge. For less knowledge-intensive producers, there are still agglomeration economies associated with being in proximity to competing producers and subcontractors. If a producer of air conditioners introduces a technological improvement, other producers that are clustered in the same location can learn about it faster than elsewhere. Also, firms will not be disadvantaged *vis-à-vis* competitors when total transportation costs change due to unforeseen changes to their interactions with subcontractors or customers.

That agglomeration economies exist in Taiwan is in itself of little interest. Rather, the question is what kinds of knowledge agglomerations exist in Taiwan, and whether any particular agglomeration makes a Taiwanese region an important node in some global network.

Taiwan's share of total employment in manufacturing amounted to 38.2 percent[1] in 1997. By developed-country standards, this is a very high share.

In Western Europe, the only regions with higher shares are Lombardy (42.4 percent) and Baden-Wurtemberg (42.3 percent). An exception to the manufacturing profile is Taipei proper, where services account for 77.1 percent of employment. In the Taipei region as a whole, however, manufacturing makes up 39.1 percent of employment. Taipei is not, however, a major location for the regional headquarters of MNCs, not even for manufacturing ones (see Chapter 9 by Thompson). Rather, it serves as a transaction services center for Taiwanese exporters, as is epitomized by the gigantic World Trade Center.

Most manufacturing in Taiwan can be described as 'medium-tech' – relatively high-value-added products but with little original research and development. An exception is the R&D-intensive Hsinchu Science-based Industrial Park, where more than 80 percent of the workforce is engaged in the production of integrated circuits, computers and computer peripherals (Kung, 1994).

Observations on education and research activity levels reinforce the impression of Taiwan as a medium-tech manufacturing center, assuming that such manufacturing benefits from agglomerations of a high general level of knowledge rather than a high concentration of original research. Consequently, 20.2 percent of the adult population had at least two years of post-secondary education in 1997, reaching 36.6 percent in Taipei City. On the other hand, the number of published scientific papers in the natural sciences, medicine or engineering is not sufficient to make any Taiwanese region a major world research center. More scientific papers originate in medium-sized European regions, such as Sheffield–Leeds, Mannheim–Heidelberg or Barcelona than in any of the Taiwanese regions (see Chapter 2 by Wichmann Matthiessen et al.). Likewise, in 1990, per capita scientific output as measured in published papers per 1 million inhabitants amounted to 392, not far from the world average of 395. While high compared with India (55) or China (19), it is low by developed-country standards (e.g., Britain: 3,099, Japan: 1,150, Spain: 774) (Wichmann Matthiessen and Andersson, 1993).

CONCLUSION

In the global infrastructure networks, Taiwan has an important nodal function in the sea transport network, with Kaohsiung being the world's third largest container port. Together with Hong Kong, Taipei is a node in both the Southeast Asian and Northeast Asian air transport corridors, although it is primarily an origin and destination airport rather than a transit hub. These transport networks support Taiwan's role as a major exporter of 'medium-tech' goods as well as more R&D-intensive computer hardware. The three main Taiwanese regions are therefore major nodes in the global trading network. While the Taipei region has the greatest production of scientific papers south of Osaka, it is at most a second-level node in the global science network. Science is still heavily concentrated in North America and Northwestern Europe.

We can expect to see the above nodal functions to be reinforced in the future, assuming further trade liberalization and rising educational levels. What may change is that high-tech manufacturers may become increasingly important outside of Hsinchu, especially with the establishment of a second science park in southern Taiwan. In fact, Hsinchu has already achieved the function of being Asia's gateway to Silicon Valley, since many Taiwanese and some American IT firms operate in both locations. Taipei, Taichung or Kaohsiung are unlikely to become important nodes in the general science network, although the Taiwanese educational preference for engineering and computer science may engender nodal functions in particular sub-networks. The possible integration of the three west coast regions into a corridor city could increase Taiwan's role in international knowledge networks, owing to agglomeration economy thresholds. But it will probably also require the internationalization of Taiwanese universities and the deregulation of faculty salaries (all professors in Taiwan earn the same salary, regardless of university or discipline). Another knowledge network where Taiwan may play an increasing role is information, owing to its good communication infrastructure and press freedoms (which face an uncertain future in Hong Kong).

Unless conditions change drastically in Hong Kong, it is unlikely that even the emergence of a west coast corridor city will allow Taiwan to rival Hong Kong as a financial center or a regional operations center for MNCs. This would require an unlikely combination of reforms. First, it would require a substantial liberalization of factor flows, including white-collar labor. Second, it would require direct transport links with China. Moreover, the rule of law would have to be strengthened and modernized and, finally, the use of English would have to become widespread.

NOTE

1. Unless indicated otherwise, the statistical sources are the Urban and Housing Development Department (1998) and *Eurostat* (1997).

REFERENCES

Andersson, D.E. (1999), 'Land-use controls and economic freedom: the diverging histories of Singapore and Taipei', in D.E. Andersson and J.P.H. Poon (eds), *Asia-Pacific Transitions*, London: Macmillan.

Batten, D.F. (1995), 'Network cities: creative urban agglomerations for the 21st century', *Urban Studies*, 32, 313–27.

Buchanan, J.M. (1991), 'The foundations for normative individualism' in J.M. Buchanan, *The Economics and the Ethics of Constitutional Order*, Ann Arbor: The University of Michigan Press.

Dasgupta, P. (1988), 'Trust as a Commodity', in D. Gambetta (ed.), *Trust: Making and Breaking Cooperative Relations*, Oxford: Blackwell.

Engberg, J. (1999), 'Illiberal democracy in Southeast Asia', in D.E. Andersson and J.P.H. Poon (eds), *Asia-Pacific Transitions*, London: Macmillan.

Epstein, R. (1995), *Simple Rules for a Complex World*, Cambridge, MA: Harvard University Press.

Eurostat (1997), *Regions – Statistical Yearbook 1997*, Luxembourg: Office for Official Publications of the European Communities.

Fei, X.T. (1992), *From the Soil: The Foundations of Chinese Society*, Berkeley, CA: University of California Press.

Fukuyama, F. (1995), *Trust: The Social Virtues and the Creation of Prosperity*, New York: The Free Press.

Gregg, S. (1999), 'Religion and liberty: Western experiences, Asian possibilities', paper presented at the Special Regional Meeting of the Mont Pelerin Society, Bali.

Hamilton, G.G. (1985), 'Why no capitalism in China?', in A.E. Buss (ed.), *Max Weber in Asian Studies*, Leiden: E.J. Brill.

Hamilton, G.G. (1996), 'Overseas Chinese capitalism', in W.M. Tu (ed.), *Confucian Traditions in East Asian Modernity*, Cambridge, MA: Harvard University Press.

Hayek, F.A. (1973), *Rules and Order*, vol. 1 of *Law, Legislation and Liberty*, Chicago: University of Chicago Press.

Huntington, S. (1991), 'Religion and the third wave', *National Interest*, Summer, pp. 29–42.

Jacoby, N.H. (1966), *U.S. Aid to Taiwan: A Study of Foreign Aid, Self-Help, and Development*, New York: Frederick A. Praeger.

Jones, E.L. (1981), *The European Miracle: Environments, Economies and Geopolitics in the History of Europe and Asia*, Cambridge: Cambridge University Press.

Kasper, W. (1998), 'Regional competition by institutional innovation', paper presented at the 11th European Advanced Studies Institute in Regional Science, Munich, Germany.

Kobayashi, K. (1993), 'The emerging new arena of transportation and communication in Japan', in R. Thord (ed.), *The Future of Transportation and Communication*, Berlin: Springer-Verlag.

Kung, S.F. (1994), 'From Science Park to Science City: The case of Hsinchu Science-Based Industrial Park development in Taiwan, R.O.C.', paper prepared for the conference 'Cities, Enterprises and Society at the Eve of the XXIst Century', Lille.

Needham, J. (1954), *Science and Civilization in China*, Cambridge: University Press.

Redding, S.G. and M. Ng (1982), 'The role of "face" in the organizational perceptions of Chinese managers', *Organization Studies*, 3, 201–19.

Redding, S.G. (1990), *The Spirit of Chinese Capitalism*, New York: de Gruyter.

Sassen, S. (1994), *Cities in a Global Economy*, Thousand Oaks: Pine Forge Press.
Urban and Housing Development Department (1998), *Urban and Regional Development Statistics 1998*, Taipei: UHDD.
Wichmann Matthiessen, C. and A.E. Andersson (1993), *Oresundsregionen – Kreativitet, Integration, Vaekst*, Copenhagen: Munksgaard/Rosinante.
World Economic Forum (1998), *Global Competitiveness Report*, Geneva: WEF.

PART FOUR

European Gateway Regions

15. Frankfurt and the Rhine Main Region – the Transport and Finance Gateway of Germany

Knut Koschatzky

INTRODUCTION

The Rhine Main region hosts a population of nearly 4.8 million people, i.e., 5.8 percent of all Germans live in this region (Table 15.1).

Table 15.1 Basic indicators

Indicator	Frankfurt city (1)	Rhine Main region (2)	Germany (3)	(2)/(3) in %
Size (km²)	248	11,061	356,959	3.1
Population[a]	643,500	4,769,000	81,817,000	5.8
Employees[b]	452,000	1,772,000	28,060,000	6.3
Share of services[c] (%)	83	69	67	
Purchasing power index	131.3	119.5	100.0	+19.5
Gross value added/ Employee 1992 (DM)[d]	129,509	54,617	36,388	+50.0
R&D intensity 1995[e] (%)	10.3	–	3.4	–

Notes:
a   Frankfurt city 1997, others 1995
b   Employees subject to social security contributions
c   Frankfurt city: in GDP, Rhine Main and Germany: in Gross Value Added
d   Frankfurt 1995
e   Share of R&D employment in total employment

Source: IHK Frankfurt 1999; Umlandverband Frankfurt Region Rhein Main 1998

The region, as defined by regional authorities such as the Umlandverband Frankfurt Region Rhein Main and the regional chambers of commerce and industry, includes parts of the federal state of Rhineland-Palatinate to the west (the city and district of Mainz), the greater Frankfurt area up to the southern border of the federal state of Hesse (including the cities of Darmstadt and Offenbach), as well as the westernmost part of Bavaria (Aschaffenburg and Miltenberg; cf. Figure 15.1). This regional definition is based on functional criteria, reflecting economic networking and commuting behavior (Koschatzky et al., 1993 p. 4).

Figure 15.1 The Rhine Main region

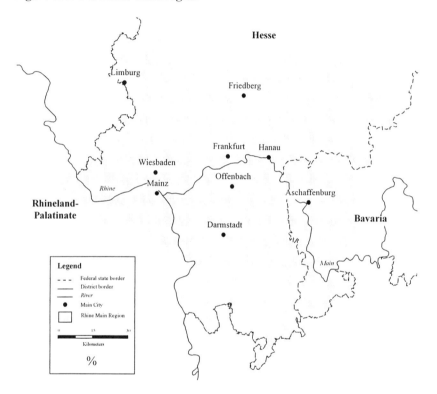

Within the region, the roots for economic specialization between the constituent cities are historical. According to legend, the emperor Charlemagne succeeded in fleeing from the wild Saxons at a ford across the river Main. In gratitude for his survival, he founded 'Franconofurd' (Umlandverband Frankfurt, 1990). In the following centuries, the free royal city of Frankfurt became the place where the German king was elected. Between 1562 and 1792, all 'Rulers of the Holy Roman Empire' were crowned in the imperial cathedral and in 1848 the first German national assembly convened in the Paulskirche.

Frankfurt was not only politically important for centuries, but its advantageous location at the crossroads of north–south and east–west trade routes has attracted traders since its early years, although a regime of free trade was not introduced until 1864 (Bördlein and Schickhoff, 1998). Industrialization first took place in neighboring cities like Offenbach (mechanical engineering), Aschaffenburg (wood and paper production), Hanau (metal processing), Darmstadt (pharmaceuticals), Wiesbaden (administrative headquarters, now the capital of the federal state of Hesse), Mainz (harbor services) and Rüsselsheim (car production) as well as in small villages just outside the borders of Frankfurt (e.g. Höchst) (for more details see VDI, 1995).

Up to the early 1940s, the Rhine Main region developed into one of Germany's major economic agglomerations, although its industrial base was weaker than in the Ruhr area, in Saxony and in Berlin. Moreover, its role as a financial center was eclipsed by Berlin (Freund, 1991). A revival of Frankfurt's economic and political impact can be attributed to the need for economic and financial regulation in postwar Germany. Frankfurt and the Rhine Main region became the headquarters of the American military (Rhine Main Air Base) and the political center of the three western occupation zones. In 1947, the bizonal (later trizonal) economic council was founded and in 1948 the bank of the German states, predecessor of the Deutsche Bundesbank, was established.

After the Second World War, Frankfurt was a candidate to become the capital of the Federal Republic of Germany, but was outvoted in favor of Bonn by the German parliament. Anticipating the possible state capital function of Frankfurt, several organizations such as economic councils and labor unions moved their headquarters to the city and remained there, even after it became clear that Bonn was to become the provisional capital of Germany. In the years after 1945 the region also benefited from the relocation of several industrial and service enterprises formerly located in Berlin or East Germany (Bördlein and Schickhoff, 1998):

- Deutsche Bank, Dresdner Bank and Commerzbank moved their headquarters to Frankfurt;
- several insurance companies located either in Frankfurt or in Wiesbaden;
- industrial and retailing enterprises (e.g. Woolworth) selected Frankfurt as their German operations base;
- the fur industry moved from Leipzig to Frankfurt;
- several fairs and exhibitions were hosted by Frankfurt (motor vehicles), Offenbach (leather products) or Wiesbaden (sports articles).

Besides economic aspects, Frankfurt and the Rhine Main region also provide a vast variety of cultural activities. In Frankfurt alone, 33 theatres, 37 museums, 109 art galleries and 56 cinemas supply cultural services to the regional population as well as to approximately 2 million visitors per year, of which more than 50 percent originate from foreign countries.

FRANKFURT – CRITERIA FOR A GLOBAL CITY

Frankfurt claims to be an international finance, communications and transport center and a gateway to Europe. 'Mainhattan' and 'Bankfurt' are terms often used to describe its international orientation (Heller and Martin, 1990). In order to analyze whether the city and the region fulfill the criteria of being a gateway to Europe and the world, a brief look at the theoretical literature on global nodes and cities seems necessary. The recent debate on globalization and internationalization is characterized by the dichotomy between regional aspects on the one hand and global thinking and acting on the other. Porter, in his book on the competitive advantages of nations (Porter, 1990), and also in later contributions (Porter, 1996), stresses the importance of a national or regional home base for globally operating enterprises. This home base not only serves as a cultural backbone offering social identity, but also as a test market for international market penetration. While Porter focuses on firm strategies, other approaches like those dealing with industrial districts, flexible specialization and innovative environments emphasize the importance of localized Marshallian factor externalities for economic development. These are interpreted as localization economies resulting from close linkages between flexible and specialized SMEs of the same industry contributing to the production of a specific product group (Braczyk et al., 1995). Firms in an industrial district are interlinked in a specific market (e.g., textiles, clothing, watch-making) in which cost and quality competition forces them to innovate and interact closely. In an innovative milieu, defined as a 'complex network of mainly informal social relationships on a limited geographical area, ... which enhance the local innovative capability through synergetics and collective learning processes' (Camagni, 1991), the low territorial mobility of productive factors contributes to the emergence of a regional environment which supports innovation and competitive production (Camagni, 1994; see also Bramanti and Ratti, 1997). Therefore Storper analyzes territorial development in a global economy under the heading of 'the regional world' (Storper, 1997).

In virtually all contributions dealing with industrial districts, innovative environments and competitive post-Fordist flexible production modes, the importance of networking, interacting and learning between the different actors in a nation, region or production chain is stressed (Florida, 1995; Morgan, 1997). The region as a nexus of learning processes (Cooke and Morgan, 1998) serves as the basis for the establishment of intraregional and interregional network relations. Especially learning by interacting (Lundvall, 1988), which describes learning and knowledge exchange processes linked to the interaction between users and producers, can contribute to the accumulation of knowledge originally not available in a firm or region. Interaction can take place via personal contacts, be they formal or informal, via the integration of a customer–supplier production or service chain. The interactions are often supported or made possible by physical telecommunication and information technology networks (see the different contributions in Batten et al., 1995). Although business and science networks are of great importance for regional development (Chisholm, 1997; OECD, 1996; Staber et al., 1996), physical networks such as water, energy, transportation and telecommunication networks and their intelligent use also contribute to regional income and wealth. A region equipped with numerous regional, national and international businesses, social and physical networks, by which the economic actors can communicate, exchange knowledge and learn, has an advantage over those regions in which the amount, international integration, quality and creative use of networks is lower. Especially the connection to and interaction with other globally oriented knowledge centers stimulate and foster information exchange, knowledge accumulation and learning processes. Regions that possess these gateway functions become attractive locations for knowledge and skill-intensive firms and organizations, searching globally for suitable sites. Andersson (1995) termed these suitable locations C-regions 'which provide education *of cognitive* skills, *creative* organizations (i.e., R&D activities, scientific institutions, libraries, etc.) and *cultural* facilities. Such regions, almost invariably, provide modern communications and are fast growing areas of economic activity' (ibid., pp. 30–31). In other terms, these are neo-Marshallian nodes in global networks which act, like a collective brain, as international centers of excellence (Amin and Thrift, 1994). Three types of location seem to fulfill the criteria of such global nodes: export-oriented production zones, offshore-banking centers and global cities (Jacobs, 1969; Sassen, 1994). According to Sassen (1996), global cities are characterized by:

- a broad supply of knowledge-intensive and high-order services,
- access to fast global communications,
- the presence of headquarters of globally acting enterprises,
- being centers of global finance and service markets fulfilling important economic and political steering functions.

This characterization leaves it open if only a few cities such as London, New York or Tokyo meet these criteria, or if a specialization in specific functions qualifies more cities as global nodes in specific markets. Nevertheless, for assessing the global and gateway function of Frankfurt and the Rhine Main region, it is important to emphasize that all of the above discussed approaches highlight the global integration of the respective cities or regions and their international economic impacts. Based on this criterion it will be shown that Frankfurt is at least in certain aspects a gateway to Europe and a globally operating European city.

GATEWAY FUNCTIONS OF THE REGION

Transport and Communications

The area around Frankfurt is characterized by its function as an infrastructural crossroads of Germany and Europe. In the region, the two international freeways (autobahns) of the A5 – linking northern Germany and the Scandinavian countries to France, Switzerland and Italy – and the A3 – linking the Netherlands and the Ruhr area with Bavaria, the Alps, Austria and neighboring countries – fulfill a key function in Central European motor vehicle transportation. The 'Frankfurter Kreuz', where these two freeways intersect, is Europe's busiest freeway cloverleaf (Airport Frankfurt, 1998b). In 1996, a five-year redevelopment program was launched in order to increase the transportation capacity of this network intersection, including rail tunnels for the new ICE track (high-speed rail transportation) between Frankfurt and Cologne.

Access to fast passenger and cargo transportation by rail is another important gateway function of the region. Frankfurt's railway station is one of the busiest stations in Europe and an important junction for domestic and continental rail transportation. Fifteen international railway lines meet at Frankfurt's main station, which is served by more than 1,600 trains and where more than 250,000 travelers arrive, depart or connect each day, including 160,000 commuters (Umlandverband Frankfurt, 1990).

The ICE track now under construction to Cologne will not only reduce the travel time to that city to about 1 hour and shorten travel times to Brussels and Paris (via the high-speed THALYS train) as well, but also further improve the railway hub function of the region. Already, Hamburg can be reached in 3 hours and 40 minutes, Zürich in less than 4 hours and Munich in less than 3 hours. Regarding short-distance transport, the Rhine Main region also occupies a leading position in Germany. The Rhine Main Transport Authority (RMV), which operates a dense network of short-distance transit services (railways, subways, buses) is Germany's largest coordinated regional transit system (Region Frankfurt Rhein Main, 1999).

Table 15.2 Flight and freight activity at European airports, 1998

Airport	Passengers (in mill.)*		Flights		Air freight (100,000 t)*	
	Total	Rank	Total	Rank	Total	Rank
Frankfurt	42,143,000	2	407,859	3	1,333,481	1
London Heathrow	60,336,560	1	441,162	1	1,209,187	2
London Gatwick	29,034,312	5	241,991	7	275,082	6
Paris– Charles de Gaulle	38,465,440	3	421,461	2	940,274	4
Paris–Orly	24,930,956	6	242,020	6	202,283	7
Amsterdam	33,952,148	4	376,810	4	1,171,256	3
Zürich	18,902,826	7	251,424	5	329,842	5

Note:
* without transit.

Source: Flughafen Frankfurt Main AG (1999).

From an international viewpoint, the region's gateway function in the international air transportation network is of even greater importance. With respect to the number of passengers, Frankfurt's airport is the second busiest in Europe and the eighth busiest in the world (Airport Frankfurt, 1998b). According to Table 15.2, only London Heathrow records more passengers than Frankfurt, while Paris-Charles de Gaulle follows in third place. Regarding the number of flights, Heathrow and Charles de Gaulle occupy the first two positions, leaving Frankfurt in third place. On the other hand, its 1.33 million tons of air cargo makes Frankfurt Europe's largest and the world's seventh largest cargo airport. Within Germany, Frankfurt is the most important airport with respect to the number of flights, the volume of freight, and the number of passengers much ahead of Munich and Düsseldorf. A third of all arriving and departing passengers enter Germany via Frankfurt and two-thirds of all air cargo handled in Germany is shipped via Frankfurt.

BANKING AND FINANCE

Frankfurt was an important European financial center as early as the sixteenth century (it has had a stock exchange since 1585 and private banks since 1674). Trade and banking are also the foundations of Frankfurt's postwar economy. Table 15.3 shows the number of banks located in the city from 1953 to 1996.

Table 15.3 Number of banks in Frankfurt, 1953–96

	1953	1970	1982	1994	1996	Share 1996 (%)
Headquarters of German banks	69	73	74	67	68	17.3
Branches of German banks	11	35	56	75	76	19.4
Foreign banks	–	8	39	108	95	24.2
Branch establishments of foreign banks	3	13	46	52	48	12.3
Representative offices of foreign banks	–	14	90	118	105	26.8
Not classified	2	14	2	–	–	
Total	85	157	307	420	392	100.0

Source: Bördlein and Schickhoff (1998); IHK Frankfurt (1999).

In 1953, only eight years after the end of the Second World War, 80 headquarters and branches of German banks indicate the city's prewar function as one of the major German financial centers. Nevertheless, only three branch establishments of foreign banks demonstrate that Frankfurt was not regarded as an important international financial center in those days. During the following years, especially in the 1970s and 1980s, many new foreign banks, their branch establishments, or representative offices located in Frankfurt's CBD. As a consequence, rentals for office space and property prices increased drastically and displaced less profitable uses of land to other parts of the city. Today, about 90 percent of all primary locations of banks can be found within one square kilometer in the city of Frankfurt. This concentration is characteristic for all major financial centers in the world (Bördlein and Schickhoff, 1998; Heller and Martin, 1990).

Between 1994 and 1996, the number of banks decreased by 7 percent to a total of 392 in 1996, of which a third are German and two-thirds are foreign banks. Major reasons for this decrease are mergers and the increased use of international computer networks for financial transactions (IHK Frankfurt, 1999). The development of Frankfurt as a financial center was supported by the decision not to relocate the Bank of the German Federal States, which was founded in 1948 and which is the predecessor of the German central bank (since 1957 German Federal Reserve), to the capital of that time, Bonn. Frankfurt's stock exchange, the most important in Germany, further fostered the concentration of financial activities in Frankfurt. In 1994, a further stimulus was expected by the decision to let Frankfurt be the location for the European Currency Institute and the European Central Bank, which took over the steering and control functions from all national central banks belonging to the European Monetary Union. The Frankfurt Stock Exchange (Frankfurter Wertpapierbörse, FWB) is the largest among Germany's stock exchanges with 78 percent of the total turnover, 79.5 percent of exchanged shares and 76.9 percent of bonds traded at German stock exchanges (Deutsche Börse, 1999). Depending on the indicator used for measuring the economic impact, the Frankfurt Stock Exchange is the world's fourth largest stock exchange in the turnover of shares (see Table 15.4) and the sixth largest in terms of market capitalization.

Table 15.4 Listed companies and turnover of shares on international stock exchanges 1998

Country	Exchange	Listed Companies			Shares (in mill. DM)		
		Domestic	Foreign	Total	Domestic	Foreign	Total
USA	NYSE	2,722	392	3,114	11,299,782	943,146	12,242,928
UK	London	2,399	521	2,920	3,682,943	6,376,317	10,059,260
USA	NASDAQ	4,572	438	5,010	n.a.	n.a.	9,233,197
Germany[a]		741	2,784	3,525	4,892,548	345,140	5,237,688
Japan	Tokyo	1,838	52	1,890	1,412,656	1,276	1,413,932
Switzerland[b]		232	193	425	1,136,728	58,370	1,195,098
Spain	Madrid	481	5	486	1,112,182	2,243	1,114,425
France	Paris	784	178	962	998,480	21,302	1,019,782
Italy	Milan	239	4	243	858,354	999	851,353
Netherlands	Amsterdam	214	145	359	701,680	3,347	705,027

Notes:
a Frankfurt and regional stock exchanges (share of Frankfurt: approx. 78 % of German total).
b Zürich and regional stock exchanges.

Source: Deutsche Börse, (1999).

INNOVATION, HIGH-TECH PRODUCTION AND RESEARCH

To obtain information about the structure of high-tech and innovative industries in the Frankfurt region, a study was carried out in 1993 on the high-tech potential of the region (Koschatzky, 1997). Following an evaluation of the product and service features of appoximately 20,000 enterprises, a total of 2,300 high-tech firms were identified as knowledge-intensive firms characterized by an R&D intensity (R&D expenditures related to turnover) of above 3.5 percent. Although employment figures were not available for all firms, it can be assumed that the share of high-tech firms in total employment in the region at the time was between 10 and 15 percent, or around 250,000 employees.

Rhine Main ranks third compared with other German industrial regions, preceded only by the agglomerations of Stuttgart and Munich. The majority of the high-tech enterprises are small and medium-sized firms (around 95 percent), with a high degree of regional attachment.

The technological emphasis in the Rhine Main region was found to be information and communication technology. A total of 1,054 firms, corresponding to 39.5 percent of all high-tech activities in the region, are active in this field. This includes eight main offices among the world's 40 largest software firms.

FURTHER DEVELOPMENT PROSPECTS

The polycentric economic, research and innovation activities make the region an attractive location and support its national and international gateway functions. From nearly every place within the region, sufficient communication and transportation networks ensure good national and international accessibility. Serving as a transport and financial junction in Germany and Europe, and offering additional locational advantages such as a well-developed R&D infrastructure, it seems justified to classify Frankfurt and the Rhine Main region, centrally located within the major Europan development axis, the 'blue banana', as one of the leading European gateway regions (Wolf, 1995). Nevertheless, even Frankfurt has to keep pace with the ongoing changes in international transport management and financial markets. The fact that land in a densely populated urban area is scarce will limit the airport's growth, at least in the medium term. Capacity increases will in the future only be possible through logistical improvements, not by building a new runway. Whether the airport will be able to maintain the growth rates of the past in the coming years will not only depend on how its management succeeds in handling a steadily increasing number of passengers and aircraft, but also on whether a regional consensus is reached between business groups and residents favoring the *status quo*.

Although it was hoped that the choice of Frankfurt as the location of the European Currency Institute would further stimulate and improve its function as a financial center in Europe, developments in recent years indicate that this hope will not be fully realized. As pointed out, the number of banks decreased between 1994 and 1996. Some banks moved their investment activities from Frankfurt to London to be closer to the global financial networks (Bördlein and Schickhoff, 1998). On the other hand, the introduction of the Euro in most European countries in the year 2002, excluding Britain among a few other countries, will strengthen Frankfurt's centrality in continental Europe and further link the city to the top global financial networks.

Because of its federal and decentralized structure, wisely installed after the Second World War, Germany did not give birth again to a major metropolis with an economic and political impact reaching beyond the German borders. In Germany, it is not one but at least a handful of agglomerations which each fulfill specific functions and contribute to the overall competitiveness of Germany. At least with respect to Germany's economic performance during the last 50 years, this decentralized spatial structure seems to have paid off. In this division of labor between the trading house (Hamburg), Germany's silicon valley (Munich), the innovative summit (Stuttgart), and the capital (Berlin), Frankfurt serves as Germany's transport and financial hub. In this respect, the city cannot compete with other global agglomerations that combine all these different functions in one place. However, in international transportation and finance, Frankfurt is among the top European and global cities. And although it will face some challenges in the coming years, the city has the potential and prospects to remain there.

REFERENCES

Airport Frankfurt (1998a), *All Routes Lead to Frankfurt Airport: Europe's Intermodal Traffic-Port*, Backgrounder BG 4/98, Frankfurt: Flughafen AG.

Airport Frankfurt (1998b), 'Frankfurt Airport records nearly six percent growth in passenger traffic for the first nine months of 1998', *ANR 19/98*, Frankfurt: Flughafen AG.

Airport Frankfurt (1999), *Company Information – Facts and Figures*, Frankfurt: Flughafen AG.

Amin, A. and N. Thrift (1994), 'Neo-Marshallian nodes in global networks', in W. Krumbein (ed.), *Ökonomische und politische Netzwerke in der Region. Beiträge aus der internationalen Debatte*, Muenster: Lit-Verlag, pp. 115–39.

Andersson, Å.E. (1995), 'Creation, innovation and diffusion of knowledge: general and specific economic impacts', in C.S. Bertuglia, M.M. Fischer and G. Preto (eds), *Technological Change, Economic Development and Space*, Berlin: Springer, pp. 13–33.

Batten, D.F., J. Casti and R. Thord (eds) (1995), *Networks in Action – Communication, Economics and Human Knowledge*, Berlin: Springer-Verlag.

Bördlein, R. and I. Schickhoff (1998), 'Der Rhein-Main Raum', in E. Kulke (ed.), *Wirtschaftsgeographie Deutschlands*, Gotha: Klett-Perthes, pp. 466–95.

Braczyk, H.-J., G. Schienstock and B. Steffensen (1995), 'The region of Baden-Wuerttemberg: a post-Fordist success story?', in E.J. Dittrich, G. Schmidt and R. Whitley (eds), *Industrial Transformation in Europe – Process and Contexts*, London: SAGE Publications, pp. 203–33.

Bramanti, A. and R. Ratti (1997), 'The multi-faced dimensions of local development', in R. Ratti, A. Bramanti and R. Gordon (eds), *The Dynamics of Innovative Regions: The GREMI Approach*, Aldershot: Ashgate, pp. 3–44.

Camagni, R. (1991), 'Introduction: from the local "milieu" to innovation through cooperation networks', in R. Camagni (ed.), *Innovation Networks: Spatial Perspectives*, London and New York: Belhaven Press, pp. 1–9.

Camagni, R. (1994), 'Space-time in the concept of "milieu innovateur"', in U. Blien, H. Herrmann and M. Koller (eds), *Regionalentwicklung und regionale Arbeitsmarktpolitik*, Nürnberg: Institut für Arbeitsmarkt- und Berufsforschung, pp. 74–89.

Chisholm, R.F. (1997), 'Building a network organization to foster economic development', *International Journal of Public Administration*, 20, 451–77.

Cooke, P. and K. Morgan (1998), *The Associational Economy: Firms, Regions, and Innovation*, Oxford: Oxford University Press.

Deutsche Börse (1999), *Frankfurter Wertpapierbörse (FWB). Description, structure and history*, Frankfurt: www.exchange.de/fwb/fwb.html.

Europäische Kommission (1999), *Sechster Periodischer Bericht über die Regionen*, Brusssels: European Commission.

Flughafen Frankfurt Main AG (1999), *Geschäftsbericht 1998*, Frankfurt: FAG.

Florida, R. (1995), 'Towards the learning region', *Futures*, 27, 527–36.

Freund, B. (1991), 'Das Rhein-Main-Gebiet. Ein grenzüberschreitender Wirtschaftsraum', *Geographische Rundschau*, 43, 272–82.

Heller, J. and W. Martin (1990), 'Mainhattan. Das Finanzzentrum Frankfurt/M', *Praxis Geographie*, 9, 16–19.

IHK Frankfurt (1999) (Chamber of Commerce and Industry Frankfurt am Main), *Economic Data*, Frankfurt: www.ihk.de/frankfurt-main/.

Jacobs, J. (1969), *The Economy of Cities*, New York: Random House.

Kauffmann, J. (1995), 'Ohne Airport kein Cash-Flow. Was die Nachbarn vom Fliegen haben', in J. Heppner (ed.), *Airport City. Flughafen Frankfurt – eine Stadt für sich*, Frankfurt: Societätsverlag, pp. 28–31.

Koschatzky, K. (1997), 'Regional high-tech potentials in Germany. The Rhine-Main agglomeration', *Zeitschrift für Wirtschaftsgeographie*, pp. 41, 17–30.

Koschatzky, K., S. Breiner, R. Bördlein and R. Sternberg (1993), *Technologieprofil der Region Rhein Main*, Frankfurt: Umlandverband Frankfurt.

Lundvall, B.-A. (1988), 'Innovation as an interactive process: From user–producer interaction to the national system of innovation', in G. Dosi, C. Freeman, R. Nelson, G. Silverberg and L. Soete (eds), *Technical Change and Economic Theory*, London: Pinter, pp. 349–69.

Morgan, K. (1997), 'The learning region: institutions, innovation and regional renewal', *Regional Studies*, 31, 491–503.

OECD (Organization for Economic Cooperation and Development) (1996): *Networks of Enterprises and Local Development: Competing and Co-operating in Local Productive Systems*, Paris: OECD.

Porter, M. (1990), *The Competitive Advantage of Nations*, London: Macmillan.

Porter, M. (1996), 'Competitive advantage, agglomeration economies, and regional policy', *International Regional Science Review*, 19, 85–94.

Region Frankfurt Rhein Main (1999), *Region Frankfurt/Rhein Main online*, Frankfurt: www.region-frankfurt-rheinmain.de.

Sassen, S. (1994), *Cities in a Global Economy*, Thousand Oaks: Pine Forge Press.

Sassen, S. (1996), *Metropolen des Weltmarktes: Die neue Rolle der Global Cities*, Frankfurt: Campus Verlag.

Staber, U.H., N.V. Schaefer and B. Sharma (eds) (1996), *Business Networks: Prospects for Regional Development*, Berlin: Walter de Gruyter.

Statistisches Bundesamt (1997), *Statistisches Jahrbuch 1997 für die Bundesrepublik Deutschland*, Stuttgart.

Storper, M. (1997), *The Regional World: Territorial Development in a Global Economy*, New York: The Guilford Press.

Umlandverband Frankfurt (1990), *Leben voller Kontraste*, Frankfurt: Verlag Waldemar Kramer.

Umlandverband Frankfurt Region RheinMain (1998), *Statistik Trends. Region Frankfurt RheinMain*, Frankfurt: Umlandverband.

VDI (Verein Deutscher Ingenieure) (1995), *Technischer Fortschritt und wirtschaftliche Entwicklung. Beiträge zur Geschichte des Industriestandorts Frankfurt-Darmstadt*, Frankfurt: Societätsverlag.

Wolf, K. (1995), 'Frankfurt am Main und das Rhein-Main-Gebiet im Europa der Regionen', in G. Meyer (ed.), *Das Rhein-Main-Gebiet – Aktuelle Strukturen und Entwicklungsproblem*, Mainz: Selbstverlag des Geographischen Instituts der Universität Mainz, pp. 9–27.

16. The Role of the Randstad Region in the European Urban System

Folke Snickars

EMERGENCE OF A EUROPEAN URBAN POLICY ARENA

The aim of the current paper is to discuss the future prospects of the European urban system with an emphasis on the Randstad region, which includes Amsterdam, Rotterdam, the Hague and Utrecht. The Randstad region as a gateway to the Benelux countries is a long-standing core of the European urban system.

Public decision-making has always encompassed the provision of common goods. The nature of the common or public goods, however, has changed over time. The geographical scope of the commons has also increased. We are now entering the era of identifying and defining the global commons. The local village, which had to sustain its local assets, is being replaced by the global village. What were Europe's original villages later developed into towns, cities and metropolitan conurbations. The challenges of joint public decision-making remain, but now also at the supranational level. What regional roles are emerging in the European urban system?

In the farming villages of medieval Europe rules developed, which prescribed how activities that could not be handled by individual households were to be performed for the benefit of the community. These rules were inherited as a sort of genetic code from one generation to the next. Agricultural society could only be sustained by managing the cultivation of the land. The diversity of European culture has its roots in these adaptations to nature. Over the centuries there emerged a variety of strategies to manage the local commons. In the towns and cities of Europe rules emerged which prescribed how the inhabitants were to interact to sustain the value of the commons. These rules were inherited as codes of honor in artisan guilds.

Acquired skills made the towns and cities prosper. The city wall protected and contained. The contents of the commons changed. But the need for public decision-making did not. Another layer of cultural diversity was added to the European cultural fabric.

The farmer never left his land. He could not, for he was continuously battling with nature. This added to the local character of European culture. The market, and the marketplace, was invented as a common good. Once a year, goods were traded and cultural assets exchanged at a central marketplace. The city dweller was more mobile, since trade required mobility. The wealth of cities was spurred by the growth in trade, and later production of artisan goods emerged in the city. While innovations were promoted through the guild system, apprentices wandered to the central cities in the contemporary European network to acquire new ideas and skills. This was the beginning of the innovative city. It was also the emergence of the network society (Andersson and Strömquist, 1990). Specialization created common interests strong enough to forge links between distant locations, which made written communication of fundamental importance. Messages were separated from messengers and trade commenced to globalize with the discovery of the New World.

The industrial revolution was a European innovation. Energy could be channeled to make machines out-compete human skills. This was the irreversible development step. The innovations in the financial institutions also irreversibly provided the option to exploit the future. However, wealth was also created outside of the cities, since natural resource assets determined where industrial production could be established, which later led to the emergence of the factory town. A common problem was the establishment and management of the local society, as a new political class of organized labor arose. Democracy ultimately emerged as a successful innovation that addressed this problem. Public decision-making also became concerned with networks along with territories, and the authority to control the networks was given to the nation state.

Transport and communications slowly changed the relationships between cities and regions, while education changed the relationship between social classes. Telecommunications made the networks wider and stronger and mobility continued to rise. Firms again moved closer to markets as at the time when cities were established, but wealth was increasingly accumulated in global networks.

The common good came to be managed by the welfare state within nation-state borders and power was again shifted from territories to networks. Institutions tended to become obsolete once again as the contents of the common good changed, which was in part due to the opportunities that were created by the emergence of the international economy. However, threats to the global environment were emerging.

The obvious answer to the question posed is that any global commons are also local, since global problems have local origins. This observation may be more important today than ever before. The problem is that the link between cause and effect tends to become less distinct. Therefore, effective policies will need to be implemented at the appropriate sectoral and geographical level. Where is that level going to be in the future? What areas of competence should be delimited and defined for public decision-making? It seems obvious that considerations of this problem need to embrace the daily life of the citizens in their roles as producers and consumers. This places the emphasis at the regional level.

OF CORE AND PERIPHERY

The urban system of Europe has a distinct core and periphery structure. The nation states embed regions and influence their development via the political and administrative structure. Most capital regions have a peculiar role in their nation with a concentration of activities associated with the political and administrative functions. As the economy becomes more international, the primary city of a country will be playing a more important role to link the country to the outside world. This function can be called a gateway.

Table 16.1 gives a summary of the economic specialization of five Western European countries in the middle of the 1990s. Norway and Sweden represent the northern welfare states. Germany and the Netherlands are among the founding members of the European Union and core economic regions. The UK is peripheral to continental Europe, while serving important global gateway functions to and for the Commonwealth countries.

The most conspicuous trait of the Dutch economy is that international trade amounts to four-fifths of GNP, a share which is not matched by any other European country. The Dutch use air transport to a great extent and Randstad's airport, Schiphol, is one of Europe's largest. The dense urban network makes train travel more competitive for the mobile Dutch population than air travel.

It should be noted that the Dutch economy is not specialized in shipping to the extent of, for example, the Nordic economies, where Norway is the prime actor. By comparison, Sweden uses more rail transportation for commodity shipments, which is of course a reflection of the dependence on basic industries. Otherwise, the Swedes stand out as the ones making most use of postal and telephone communication, a fact that is explained by the dispersed structure of the territory.

Dutch society has a tradition of consensus-seeking, political life thus being relatively calm. It is also internationally oriented and its population has a high average level of education. The Netherlands has traditionally been a promoter of welfare-state ideals. It is also, however, a small open economy which at the same time is a culturally open society.

Table 16.1 Some economic indicators for five European countries, 1995.

Economic indicators 1995	Sweden	Norway	Nether-lands	Germany	UK
(Imports+Exports)/GNP (%)	60	54	84	41	47
Shipping/GNP (tonnage/million US$)	58	310	15	8	18
Air travel/GNP (passenger km/1,000 US$)	39	51	122	26	132
Motor vehicles (per 1,000 population)	447	473	402	523	406
Train travel (passenger km/1,000 US$)	25	12	35	27	26
Newspapers (copies/1,000 persons)	460	468	329	344	313

The Netherlands is the most densely populated country in Europe and has a central position in continental Europe as a gateway for the continent and embodies a long tradition in transport and trade. It has thus had a node and trade function in the European economy for many centuries. Moreover, the country was a very active global power in the colonial period. The specialization in trade was thus established long ago. The merchant functions of the Dutch cities with Amsterdam as the prime example have historical roots in the medieval period.

The Randstad region is one of the leading European conurbations. It is comparable in its economic character to its neighboring competitor: the Ruhr area. However, whereas the Ruhr area specializes in industrial production and economies of scale, the Randstad is a trading region employing economies of scope. The two regions have a similar spatial structure with towns and cities linked by efficient road and rail systems that are separated by green areas. In the Randstad there are four dominant cities, Amsterdam, Utrecht, Rotterdam and The Hague. In the Ruhr area there are a number of industrial cities with Dortmund, Bochum, Essen and Düsseldorf being some of the leading ones.

The Netherlands has a three-tier political system with small municipalities, relatively strong provinces and a dominant national government level. Taxation is performed at the national level. Table 16.2 shows the administrative structure with the 12 provinces as the base. They are grouped in four larger regions following the European level NUTS definitions.

Table 16.2 The administrative structure of the Netherlands and the economic strength of the regions in 1995.

Province	Popula-tion (1,000s)	Munici-palities	Municipal size (1,000s)	Relative income/capita
Groningen	557	25	22.2	106.2
Friesland	599	31	19.4	79.1
Drenthe	437	34	13.0	81.0
Noord-Nederland	**1,593**	**90**	**17.8**	**89.1**
Overijssel	1,010	45	22.8	91.1
Flevoland	194	6	37.0	70.6
Gelderland	1,783	86	21.1	90.3
Ooost-Nederland	**2,987**	**137**	**22.4**	**89.3**
Utrecht	965	38	27.0	97.8
Noord-Holland	2,353	70	34.2	106.4
Zuid-Holland	3,208	95	34.2	109.5
Zeeland	356	30	11.9	118.6
West-Nederland	**6,882**	**233**	**30.2**	**107.3**
Noord-Brabant	2,156	120	18.4	102.7
Limburg	1,096	56	19.8	94.1
Zuid-Nederland	**3,252**	**176**	**18.9**	**99.8**
The Netherlands	14,714	636	23.6	100

The Dutch population is close to 15 million and the somewhat less than 640 municipalities thus have on average 24,000 inhabitants each. The Randstad basically corresponds to the West-Nederland region. It is richer than the others and the populations of its municipalities are larger than in the rest of the country. Amsterdam forms the core of the Noord-Nederland province. A main discussion point in the Netherlands is how to increase the political responsibilities at the province and city levels. The argument is that in a situation when competition increases between metropolitan regions in Europe, the Dutch economy will benefit from increasing the freedom of action at the regional level, including having access to more direct economic resources within the public sector (see also Kreukels and Salet, 1992).

The Netherlands has experimented with complementing regional policy in the classical equity mode, which emphasizes peripheral regions, with policy in the growth mode, focusing on the suburban parts of the metropolitan regions, particularly in the Randstad.

The gateway functions of modern cities and regions are to a large extent connected to infrastructure systems. In the Netherlands the political hold over infrastructure provision is tighter than in many countries with more ministries involved in the preparation of investment decisions (see also Hall et al., 1994). At the same time the power of the national level to make decisions is substantial. There is a special planning process for large-scale infrastructure investments where stakeholders are brought into the process at an early stage. The same public agency has the responsibility for the provision of all transportation infrastructures.

THE EMERGENCE OF A EUROPEAN URBAN SYSTEM

The urban systems of Europe are not yet – economically, socially or politically - fully connected to one another. A hierarchy of central places for each part of the continent has been formed by economic specialization and political and administrative actions over long time-periods. The multifaceted European urban system is one of the main inheritances from the pre-industrial and industrial periods. The transport and communication infrastructures were mainly built to fulfill national needs. One of the main initiatives in the earlier phases of the European integration project has been to extend the networks in a coordinated fashion over the whole of the European territory. The Netherlands, with its very close connection to the German city system and to the rest of Benelux and to Britain, will have had an influence on its urban system hierarchy from these network vicinities.

Figure 16.2 includes a summary description of the rank-size hierarchies for seven urban subsystems in Europe. The information in the figure covers the bulk of the functional urban regions of Western Europe and involves a data base of some 280 city regions (see Snickars, 1992). The data set has been developed by using information from statistical sources to delineate functional urban areas in the earlier EU countries and then combining it with information that has earlier existed in separate data bases for the Nordic area on so-called labor market regions. In the data set presented in Figure 16.2, the cities of Austria, Finland, Norway, Sweden and Switzerland have been added to the earlier EU data set. The result makes it possible to compare the structure of the urban systems of Europe, either by country or sub-region, or for the whole of the Western European territory.

In Figure 16.1, the urban systems of the Alpine countries have been counted as a part of the German system. Benelux consists of the Netherlands, Belgium and Luxemburg. The Nordic area contains Denmark, Finland, Norway and Sweden. The Iberian peninsula has been counted as one urban system.

Figure 16.1 The urban systems of selected regions of Europe at the beginning of the 1990s

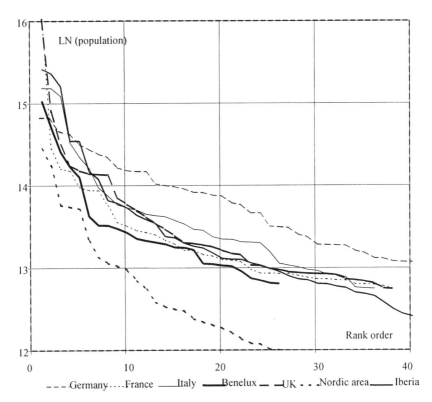

The urban systems of the macro regions of Western Europe cannot be regarded as independent of one another. There is a general tendency for the larger functional regions to be more populous than the rank-size rule would forecast (see Table 16.2). The exception is the German urban system, which follows Zipf's law surprisingly well. The main deviation is France, where the Paris agglomeration is much larger than central place theory would suggest. This corroborates the influence of the spatial centralization policy that has been promoted in France over a long time-period. The European urban systems furthermore seem to become forged together from top to bottom. For several of the subsystems the largest regions are bigger than would be reasonable if they each had their home country as the hinterland. The Benelux urban system is no exception to this rule.

The urban system of the Nordic area differs from the others not so much in the structure of the larger metropolitan regions but rather in the smaller settlements. In a European perspective, the Nordic urban systems lack medium-sized labor-market regions similar to the ones that are found in continental Europe. The graphical representation also shows that the character of the Nordic urban system is indeed different from the rest of Western Europe. The Nordic achievement in this perspective is to have been able to make the sparsely populated periphery competitive in a way that has not materialized in the other countries. In this sense the capital regions of each of the Nordic countries serve as a dominant gateway for their countries. A clear reflection of this is the hub functions that have been introduced for the domestic airline systems in Finland, Norway and Sweden. The difference between the north and the south is not the larger settlements. It is rather the domestic urban systems.

One question to be addressed is whether there has already emerged an integrated European urban system where functional urban regions in one country may contain regions in other countries as members of their hinterlands. We know that the emergence of the multi-layered transport and communications networks will promote this process but in a way which is not as easy to foresee as if only one means of transport had existed. The guess is that the urban rank-size hierarchy will not have been established yet. Figure 16.2 shows clearly that the slope of the curve differs between segments, implying that several processes are at work concurrently.

Figure 16.2 The urban system of Western Europe as represented by the rank-size rule

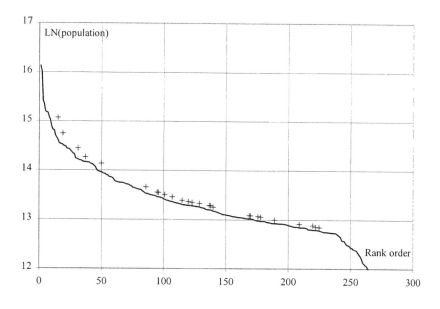

The logical development would be that the European integration processes should be most felt in the medium-sized cities. Some of them will move up the hierarchy as a consequence of the free movement of capital, labor and people and the removal of public sector barriers. Some of them will move down and continue to be embedded in the domestic hierarchies, as they have been historically.

The essence of the discussion about the increased competition between urban regions in Europe lies with these medium-sized regions with between 500,000 and 1.5 million people. Some of them will attain new gateway functions associated with important infrastructure or market and trade functions. The specialization in the production chain is not likely to be as influential for determining the role of the urban system in the future, as was the case in the industrial period.

Our observation is that there are three concurrent urban systems in Europe at the moment. One is reflected in the right part of Figure 16.2 and shows the superimposition of national systems of functional urban regions. The middle portion exhibits the regions with an emerging pan-European reach. In the leftmost part of the curve we find those regions of Europe which have become integral parts of the global urban system. The likely development scenario for the European functional urban regions is that the rank-size rule becomes more prominent, leading to an almost linear curvature. This development will have important and differential consequences for different parts of the continent. The development will most likely be strongly influenced by the situation that will emerge in the central and eastern parts of Europe.

With the emergence of a post-industrial society it is thus safe to say that Europe by now will have moved into a new global regime. This regime bears the typical characteristics of a multi-layered network society where node and network operators develop their schemes of maintaining supremacy over economic and social functions across networks and within nodes. The political function is historically connected to the node function and the territory. It will presumably remain with this connection. The operation range of the network operators may vary from the local to the global. It is actually not globalization which is the most important aspect of the emerging society. It is the increasing speed, and the enhanced reliability, of fast connections over long distances. The consequences of this development are many and far-reaching.

Some of the most important ones relate to the emergence of a global urban system. Urban areas traditionally used to be conceived of as a hierarchy of members of a national settlement system. Now the most logical way of looking at them is as members of a network-based global system of central places.

Table 16.3 Development of the passenger numbers at some European airports during the later part of the 1980s and a forecast of the future ranking in 2010

Rank 1990	Airport region	Passengers 1990 (million)	Yearly % change 1985–90	Average rank 2010
1	London	63.9	6.6	1.7
2	Paris	46.8	7.7	2.6
3	Frankfurt	28.7	8.0	3.1
4	Rome	17.9	6.0	5.9
5	Amsterdam	16.2	7.3	5.1
6	Madrid	15.9	8.3	6.6
7	Stockholm	14.8	10.3	7.3
8	Zürich	12.3	6.2	8.8
9	Copenhagen	11.8	4.6	8.9
10	Düsseldorf	11.6	7.9	9.8
11	Milan	11.6	7.9	10.0
12	Palma	11.6	5.1	11.0
13	Munich	11.3	7.8	10.3
14	Manchester	10.1	10.9	10.7
15	Barcelona	9.0	10.9	10.7
16	Helsinki	8.0	11.3	10.9
17	Hamburg	6.7	7.4	10.8
18	Oslo	6.4	2.2	11.0
19	Vienna	5.5	8.9	10.9
20	Geneva	5.5	4.0	11.0

Some infrastructure systems are more important in determining the long-term characteristics of this emerging urban system than others. In transportation, the obvious candidate is the combined airline and airport system. A continuous transformation will be taking place in this system over the coming years. It is connected with the development of the most important network infrastructure systems of all: the regional, national and international telecommunications systems. It is important to understand that changes are occurring at all three geographical levels of these systems concurrently. The interconnectedness of them makes it necessary not to separate the perspectives but to keep them together to understand how they work. This is the essence of the network aspect of the so-called global village concept.

Table 16.3 gives a picture of the position of different airport regions in Western Europe in the first part of the 1990s. The information in the two left-hand columns was given to a set of transport experts in Sweden as a part of a scenario study (see also Snickars 1990, 1992, 1995, 1999; Grübler and Nakicenovic 1993; Nijkamp et al., 1995; and Spiekermann and Wegener 1994). The experts were asked to provide a rank ordering of the likely situation in 2010 in view of the anticipated European air transport market development. They also were asked to give a statement of the level of certainty that they associated with their judgement. The result was that the London region was expected to retain its supremacy as an air transport node. The positions of Paris and Frankfurt as airport regions were assessed to be closer than today. Amsterdam was expected to overtake Rome. The situation among the medium-sized airports was basically that the German airport regions were often ranked somewhat higher than during the 1990s. The assessment of uncertainty in the ranking showed that the top ranking of the London, Paris and Frankfurt airports was not questioned whereas the ranking for Amsterdam, Rome and Stockholm was much less unanimous.

This analysis can be complemented with studies on the effect of airline deregulation on the network structure in Europe and on the likely candidate for a primary Western European hub (Berechman and de Wit, 1996). The main question in their study was which major Western European airport is most likely to attract most service following the deregulation of the European airline system, thus becoming the European gateway hub. Competition between deregulated airlines will lead to the promotion of a primary airport which will serve the role of the primary city in the urban hierarchy.

The main result is that deregulation will generate more intensive use of hub-and-spoke networks for airlines in order to reap maximum profits from their operations. Five airports were selected as candidates to be primary hubs: Heathrow, Charles de Gaulle, Frankfurt, Schiphol and Brussels, and simulation exercises were performed where a number of airlines chose profit-maximizing hub locations. The principal result was that Heathrow will increase its leading position while Brussels will emerge more strongly. The tendency for other regions like Frankfurt will be a decline in their importance. The central role of air transport and airports for the future mobility of Europe implies that this result can provide a reflection of the future development of the urban system itself.

Even though the transport systems will continue to have a strong role in Europe, the most important nodal infrastructures in the future will relate to education, research and innovation. They can develop in a private setting like many of the classical infrastructure systems of the industrial revolution such as the telephone, the car or even the train. There is also room for collective action at the regional, national and international level to construct knowledge-creating institutions that adhere to the network rather than the node paradigm. Novel mechanisms are likely to cause structural changes in the global, national and regional economies. It seems essential to understand what role technical change – primarily in the information technology and telecommunication industries – plays in this context. The task for the regional policy-makers is to compose a policy mix consisting of economic incentives and environmental restrictions to safeguard the environment without sacrificing, but rather boosting, economic efficiency.

EUROPEAN SPATIAL POLICY ISSUES

It is a trait of the development of Europe during the recent phases of the EU integration process that different constellations of regional actors have emerged at the European level. These actors have shared interests either in the promotion of resources that they house or in the sharing of experiences in coping with problems of economic and social transformations. Some of the coalitions have emerged as a part of the pressure group and lobbying system that exists around the EU headquarters. Other constellations have been formed on a basis of bilateral interests as in the case of border regions. Yet others have been initiated by Europe-wide organizations of industries, government agencies, and non-profit organizations.

In a way one can say that these new developments are a reflection of the potential value added by joint action at the European level. They are a reflection of the expectation that jointly created value can bring more net benefit to the individual members than staying outside. These non-tangible networks may be seen as forerunners of more tangible and mutually beneficial structures. In a sense they correspond to the strategic alliances which seem to be emerging in institutional arrangements in the corporate sector and which are often summarized by the term value-added networks. According to this philosophy, the long-term challenge at the corporate level lies in the identification of such value-added networks which can be exploited through a mix of financial strategies, acquisitions and mergers, and market actions. These informal and self-organized institutions, so-called soft institutions, focusing on their contribution to the establishment of spatial policy and planning at the comprehensive European level, are interesting to compare across nations and regions. The industrial and political actors in the Netherlands have cleverly used these new structures. In fact, the suspicion exists that they have indeed invented them for their own benefit.

A proposal has been forwarded by the EU of a polycentric urban system in Europe as an ideal model to strive for through policy action at the national and international level. These considerations have been put forward in policy documents within the work on the so-called European Spatial Development Perspective (ESDP), see also European Commission (1999). If we regard the EU area in an economic policy perspective, the area has economic growth problems if compared to other global regions such as North America or the Pacific Rim. Economic analyses have shown that mobility across state borders in the US is high since people migrate to growth areas. Europe does not exhibit the same pattern because of barriers such as language and culture, but also because of historically established urban hierarchies. One question is whether a mobility policy for economic growth would be at all possible in the EU. It is an important policy issue to find alternatives to the US mobility model which will promote a balanced development across the European territory.

The EU faces important decisions for the twenty-first century such as reducing the support to agriculture and shifting it towards urban areas for social cohesion reasons. This support could be an important factor for keeping people in areas that are or threaten to become stagnation areas. A Europe-wide urban policy can play a role here. ESDP promotes the view of cities as engines for economic development. The challenge is to design territorial policies outside of the agricultural area favoring a balanced spatial development. The promotion of urban networks is at the heart of these policy ideas, alleviating the pressure on urban areas while at the same time allocating resources to urban economic activities.

There is a need to perform empirical studies on the location decisions among major European industries when those are faced with the increased movement of production factors. Studies could also be done for service industries, i.e., for industries that were formerly local, regional or national in extent. Examples can be taken from the consultancy sector, the culture industry and the transport industry. The example of the transport industry is particularly important in view of the environmental impacts throughout the European territory of the increase in interregional trade. The integration of Europe coupled with a deregulation of the airline industry, and the establishment of a private airport industry, will fundamentally change the competitive situation among European regions. The credibility of spatial planning action crucially depends on the credibility of analyses of the impacts of such secular trends.

The changes fundamentally interact also with the development of the urban system. In the long run it is likely that the manufacturing industries of Europe will look for both economies of scale and scope, and locations which reduce their need for transport input in a situation when governments point to the need to economize on transport. This may give rise to substantial location changes not only because of the relocation of existing capacity but also because of emergent differences in profitability. The other important factor for the European urban system is the impacts of deregulation and rapid technical development in the service industries. These processes may have substantial impacts on labor demand, but also on location developments.

The long-term question is what location patterns will emerge at the European level for those sectors which have been nationally protected. A particularly important example is provided by the higher education industry, both because of its market potential and because of its stated importance as an engine for regional development. Another important example is the financial sector which exhibits a dual development pattern for the moment, becoming local to approach customers with more complex service offers, and becoming international to secure risk capital and fund large-scale investment projects.

These developments will provide both opportunities and threats for core regions of Europe such as the Randstad. For the Randstad, the long-term challenge is to retain the competitive edge in the emerging knowledge economy. The Randstad region houses some of the leading European R&D environments with a strong association to the classical trading functions.

One of the strategic choices for the actors in both regions is to position themselves in the appropriate global networks. The actors in the Randstad are doing this by further strengthening the transport and communications infrastructure for both persons and goods. The region is a designated gateway for Europe in the global economy. However, the threat is that globalization will promote the development in even larger conurbations than the Randstad, which is already extremely densely populated and struggles with increasing environmental problems. On the other hand, it will be important for the macro-regional stability in the European urban system at large that there are stable nodes of development in gateway locations. The Randstad will surely play such a stabilizing role for northwestern Europe with positive impacts as far away as the Stockholm region.

REFERENCES

Andersson, Å.E. and U. Strömquist (1990), *The Future of the C-society*, Stockholm: Prisma.

Berechman, J. and J. de Wit (1996), An analysis of the effects of European aviation deregulation on an airline's network structure and choice of a primary west European hub airport, *Journal of Tranport Economics and Policy*, 30 (3), 251–74.

European Commission (1999), *European Spatial Development Perspective. A strategy for balanced and sustainable development in Europe, European Issues in the Debate*, Office for Official Publications of the European Communities, Luxembourg.

Grübler, A. and N. Nakicenovic (1993), 'Economic Map of Europe: Transport, Communication and Infrastructure Networks in a Wider Europe', Working Paper, IIASA, Laxenburg.

Hall, P., R. Prud'homme and F. Snickars (1994), *The Impacts of the Dennis Agreement: Regional Development*, Department of Infrastructure and Planning, Royal Institute of Technology, Stockholm.

Kreukels, A. and W. Salet (eds) (1992), *Debating Institutions in Cities*, Proceedings of the Anglo-Dutch conference on urban regeneration, Netherlands Scientific Council for Government Policy, The Hague.

Nijkamp, P., S. Rienstra and J. Vleugel (1995), *Long-run Scenarios for Surface Transport*, Department of Regional Economics, Free University, Amsterdam.

Snickars, F. (1990), 'Transport, communications and long-term environmental sustainability: a futures study of the Swedish transport and communications sector', Working Paper, Department of Infrastructure and Planning, Royal Institute of Technology, Stockholm.

Snickars, F. (1992), *Two Scenarios of Transport and the Environment in Sweden 2010*, Swedish Board for Housing and Physical Planning, Karlskrona.

Snickars, F. (1995), *Mobility Sustained*, Department of Applied Geography and Planning, University of Utrecht, Utrecht.

Snickars, F. (1999), 'The sustainable network society – a scenario study of transport and communications', in J. Brotchie et al., *East-west Perspectives on 21st Century Urban Development*, Aldershot, UK: Ashgate.

Spiekermann, K. and M. Wegener (1994), *New Space-time Maps of Europe*, Working Paper 132, Institute for Spatial Planning, University of Dortmund.

17. The Network Profile of the Milan–Venice Corridor

Stefano Magrini and Dino Martellato

INTRODUCTION

Assuming that the Milan–Venice corridor is a spatial system, how could it be characterized? We see a corridor, a network city, probably a creative one, many networks of firms, some network infrastructures. Also, the concept of nodal region appears to us almost indispensable. We are not alone in this. Johansson, for instance, observed some time ago that 'the criterion for identifying a region should be based on the nature and intensity of the interaction between its nodes' as a spatial system is nothing more than 'a set of layers of networks'.[1]

Four distinct aspects appear to us particularly relevant. First of all, we consider the qualitative change undergone by the Milan–Venice corridor. Milan and Venice were once two distinct gateways. But the subsequent territorial evolution represents a textbook example of how some small settlements evolved into medium-scale nodes with their own systems of subnodes and networks and eventually forming a corridor with a network of cities.

Secondly, we focus on the numerous networks of small and medium-sized firms that makes the Milan–Venice corridor of today look like an archipelago of labor and, above all, competence pools. In this context, we draw particular attention to the concept of Marshallian industrial districts.

The subsequent section is devoted to the network infrastructure of the Milan–Venice corridor. The water, rail, road and air networks in the corridor all seem undersized. Arguably, there should be a greater role for transport policy and public–private partnerships, but the area encompasses many administrative bodies and there are obvious difficulties in coordination as well as administrative rivalries. We limit our discussion to the traffic flows on the 'E' arteries and note significant differences in the rate of growth of flows. The final section focuses on the relation between creativity and regional development, which Andersson has brought to our attention at least from 1980.[2] Information, knowledge, competence and creativity are very elusive concepts, hard to quantify, but crucial in understanding the development performance of any network region. The analysis we offer is tentative, but suggests that the stronger the connectivity of the network of cities, the higher the average growth performance of its cities.

THE EVOLUTION OF THE MILAN–VENICE CORRIDOR

It is well known that the physical survival of Venice requires some form of regulation of the tidal flow in its lagoon. Whether this regulation will take the form of mobile gates at the entrance of the lagoon is not yet completely clear. However, it is fairly obvious that, if the gloomy scenario assuming a marked climate change and a rise in sea levels proves to be true, Venice will be disproportionately affected and its competitive position completely eroded. This event will probably bring to an end the era of Venice as a seaport. Although the Venetian economy is no longer based on its port since tourism has become the dominant activity, the port still provides an important way of diversifying the economy of the city.

The scenario described above will bring the decline of Venice to its conclusion – a decline which started a long time ago. As far as the position of Venice in the European economy is concerned, and particularly its position within the southern hinterland of the Alps, the turning point can be traced back to the sisteenth century.[3] When the old mercantile power of Venice – a global gateway in those days – started to decline because of the commercial and financial crisis in the first half of that century, the Venetian government realized that the cities in its hinterland (mainly Verona and Padua) were starting to gravitate towards Milan. While the hinterland gained from the newly established trade links, the Venetian government tried to force Venice to remain the hub of its historical hinterland. In some sense the government tried to reproduce artificially what had earlier been spontaneous, i.e., the transit of commodities though its port hub. However, Venice was not able to prevent the inevitable: the progressive diversion from the lagoon to the hinterland of an increasing part of the value created by production and commercial distribution.

New road connections created a spontaneously evolving regional market that triggered further expansions of the road system, rather than an expanding port. It is probably fair to say that in the second half of the sixteenth century, Venice did not completely understand that it had reached a juncture in its development. Venice was facing a strategic choice: only by changing its direction could it have continued its expansion.[4] However, not fully aware of the situation, the Venetian government was unable to change its policy in any significant way and, remaining entirely focused on the maritime gateway, was gradually being overtaken by the economically growing cities along the corridor.

Many seaports have continued to prosper even after the initial advantage of accessibility to the sea has been eroded. This has not been the case of Venice as the area between Venice and Milan has been able to grow faster than Venice without any special infrastructure endowment and without ever constituting a conventional metropolitan area.

To better explain the economic evolution of the area between Milan and Venice, we need to clarify briefly a few concepts and consider a simple theoretical framework. A gateway and a corridor cannot be mechanically paralleled to such concepts as nodes and links, respectively. However, a gateway or hub can be understood as a node in a cross-border network and, in view of this, a hierarchically important spot in economic space. In this respect, it is useful to refer to Perroux's definition of economic space: 'as a field of forces, economic space consists of centers (or poles or foci) from which centrifugal forces emanate and to which centripetal forces are attracted' (Perroux, 1950). A corridor, on the other hand, is the area surrounding the link or edge connecting two different nodes; the area which, having been able to grow comparatively faster than the nodes or gateways, has then become a field of forces able to compete with those present in the nodes. A corridor is hence more than a link and could be conceived as the final stage in the evolution of a link. Indeed it is, in its own right, an economic region with its own characteristics and profile, which do not necessarily fit those of the gateways. It is an area that experiences a structural change from a node-link structure to a corridor structure by virtue of a growth process in the area surrounding the link. This growth process has the defining characteristic of consistently higher growth in the corridor than in the original gateways.

A related concept is that of network or corridor cities, which has been suggested by Batten (1995). Indeed, growing attention has recently been paid to the emergence of urban systems based on the idea of nodality in a network of linked settlements (see, for instance, Hohenberg and Lees, 1985). This model of spatial distribution of economic activity is usually interpreted as an alternative to the traditional central place model derived from Christaller (1933, 1966) and Lösch (1954). In the latter model, each central place supplies the hinterland around it with different services; by ranking these services in order of importance it is then possible to derive a hierarchy of centers. This theory, therefore, derives a spatial ordering of urban centers over the national economy from definite relationships between the size and function of central places and inter-urban distances. On the other hand, the network approach emphasizes the functional interdependence between its individual components or nodes. Central to this approach are the concepts of complementarity and cooperation among nodes. As Batten puts it, a network city forms when 'two or more previously independent cities, potentially complementary in function, strive to cooperate and achieve significant scope economies aided by fast and reliable corridors of transport and communication infrastructure' (Batten, 1995). The classical example of such a city is Randstad Holland.

The evolution of the area between Milan and Venice can probably be better understood by resorting to this theoretical framework. As pointed out at the outset of the present paper, Milan and Venice once represented the gateways of the Italian West–East link. They were both examples of central place cities, concentrating functions and services of higher order and serving their respective hinterlands.

As explained above, however, at the turn of the sixteenth century Venice had started to lose its supremacy over its hinterland and, consequently, to relinquish its role as a central place city. A group of centers in the Veneto region (primarily Padua and Verona, only later followed by Vicenza and Treviso), traditionally under Venice's sphere of influence, started to increase their own economic importance and independence as evidenced by the expansion of trade flows to destinations other than Venice. Although an important share of the flows originating from these emerging centers were directed towards Milan, flows between the subnodes in the Veneto region grew in importance over time.

The area between Milan and Venice has thus slowly (in the eighteenth century Venice was still among the ten largest cities of Europe) evolved into a complex corridor. To the west, Milan has retained many of the features of a central place city, preserving its role of international gateway for selected commercial, financial and transport services as well as for some selected manufacturing activities, while at the same time enlarging its sphere of economic influence.

To the east, Venice has instead progressively lost its supremacy over its surrounding hinterland. In this area, the central place hierarchy has been substituted by a more complex spatial organization in which relational linkages among centers tend to be horizontal rather than hierarchical. In other words, what we find to the east is a network city – the Veneto Network City – i.e., a composite city-region which encompasses Venice, Padua, Vicenza, Treviso and Verona, and where close links have been forged in terms of complementarity.

Finally, a group of Lombard cities around the West–East link have emerged from their role of mere parts of a transport link, forming a distinct economic region although, in many respects, functionally linked to Milan.

NETWORK OF FIRMS

An obvious feature of northern and central Italian regions is both the relatively large number of small and medium-sized firms and the presence of numerous spatially networked agglomerations of small firms and dependent subcontractors. Particularly well known are the industrial clusters that were studied as early as the 1970s (Becattini, 1975, 1979). There are various types of networks as there are various types of relationship between firms. Broadly speaking, there are: (1) branched or networked firms, (2) agreements that individual firms make with each other in order to cooperate on specific projects, and (3) real networks of firms. If we limit ourselves to the last class, i.e., to networks, and adopt a conceptual point of view, a further subtle, but rather interesting, distinction can be made (Brusco, 1986, 1991) between a Marshallian industrial district proper (MID) and a subcontractor network or a district-like cluster. The idea put forward by Becattini was that some particular territorial clusters cannot be handled properly with the conventional concept of industry. The alternative concept, i.e., the industrial district, is larger than the simple firm or company (in an industrial district there can be thousands of small firms) and different from an industry. The MID combines the smallness of its firms with productive efficiency through strategic interaction and flexible specialization of the district itself. In an industrial district, the small firm is part of a larger network in which cooperation and competition coexist. What matters for the broader national and international market in which the network's product is sold is more the characteristics of the network than those of a specific firm. The way in which the competitive and cooperative features blend to form the local business climate of a specific area makes it difficult to distinguish real Marshallian industrial districts from other systems or district-like clusters, such as subcontractor networks and plain agglomerations.

In the subcontractor network there are few, and sometimes only one, medium or large firms – the leader firms – and many (small) subcontractors. The leader firm acts as a true monopsonistic customer as it limits itself to outsourcing and squeezing the profits of smaller firms. But this is puzzling because it has been noticed that: 'at the origin of an industrial district there are one or more large firms which – sometimes a long time ago – have worked in the field where small firms and artisan firms are now operating' (Brusco, 1986). In a real MID there is competition between subcontractors as well as between subcontracting firms, but cooperation prevails over sheer competition. In the subcontractor network, competition between subcontractors and monopsony prevail. From a certain point of view – that of availability of capital – a subcontractor cluster represents an early stage in the evolutionary process which gives rise to a Marshallian district.

The network of small firms in an MID as well as the dependent sub-contractors located in a restricted area specialize in some specific final consumer good, usually a durable one, and often also in the machine tools needed to produce the final good. Usually each firm and each subcontractor[5] specializes in one phase of the production process. Firms are small, but the intensive division of labor allows them to avoid the inefficiencies of small scale. This is because there are economies of scale external to the firm but internal to the network. The industrial district reduces the transaction costs of the market relationship and the inefficiencies of large firms and corporations as they introduce some form of contractual relationship into a vertically integrated network of firms, where strategic interaction tends to increase reputation and cooperation effects. An important effect of the type of organization described above is that on transport demand. As production is distributed over a number of plants the derived transport demand is quite high. The delivery of intermediate goods and services require that commodities and people move from plant to plant, which has a strong impact on transport demand.

All of this is well known, but a crucial point is raised by Brusco (1986) on the role of capital accumulation in Marshallian industrial districts. What is relevant to understanding MIDs is that the evolution process they represent is more the result of an accumulation and diffusion of competence than an increase in savings and physical capital.[6] The capital invested in these areas does not represent the usual alternative to consumption, but rather an alternative to leisure, as it is nothing more than the transformation of leisure into work, work into income and income into physical and knowledge capital. When knowledge capital is sufficient, spatially diffused and properly differentiated, division of work and cooperation – which are obvious features of Marshallian industrial districts – are facilitated and the subcontracting network or the aggregation of artisans has come to the final phase of evolution into an industrial district.[7]

The Emilia Romagna, Veneto, Lombardy and Piemonte regions are famous for the large number of industrial districts they contain. The manufacturing clusters of specialized producers of cars (Modena and Turin), textiles (Biella, Como, Prato, Schio), food (Parma, Cremona, Udine), tiles (Sassuolo), machine tools (Busto Arsizio), jewelry (Valenza Po, Vicenza), glasses (Padua, Belluno), artistic glass (Murano), sports shoes (Treviso), shoes (Riva del Brenta), furniture (Udine, Verona, Vicenza) are well known, but the districts or district-like clusters are many more than those just listed. From a practical point of view, it is sometimes difficult to identify such complex small systems of firms and in making a clear distinction between real Marshallian industrial districts and mere subcontractor networks or district-like clusters. The existence of different definitions of such networks proves this point. For the definition of industrial districts it is customary nowadays to use official criteria, at least since 1991, when a national law was passed in order to promote innovation in small-scale industrial firms. The national and regional regulations[8] basically refer to such indicators as industrial location quotients and entrepreneurship density, where a small firm is defined as having no more than 200 employees.[9] According to the official Italian definition there are 19 such districts in the Veneto region (Regione Veneto, 1997). But the official definition of industrial districts is by no means the only one. A national financial daily paper[10] recently conducted a survey of Italian industrial districts. Lombardy and Veneto together have 23 industrial districts, but if one adds the regions adjoining them[11] one has a total of 25, which is more than two-thirds of the total number of Italian industrial districts.

The most popular definition of industrial districts, however, is that based on commuting data and industrial location quotients, i.e., census data (Sforzi, 1991, 1997). The identification procedure indicates that out of a total of 784 Italian local labor markets in 1991,[12] 199 can be conceived of as districtareas. This is a rather large number when compared to the previous total (see Table 17.1). This difference reveals how difficult it can be to detect the industrial district, not to mention its geographical delimitation. Also an economic characterization is difficult because quite often two or more distinct districts – i.e. the products of two typical and different districts – partially overlap.

Table 17.1 Regional location of Italian industrial districts

Regions	Sforzi (1991)		Il Sole-24 Ore (1991/2)	
	No.	%.	No.	%.
Piemonte	50	6.4	7	11
Valle d'Aosta	4	0.5	0	0
Liguria	16	2.0	3	5
Lombardia	70	8.9	15	23
Trentino A.A.	35	4.5	2	3
Veneto	48	6.1	8	12
Friuli V.G.	12	1.5	3	5
Emilia Romagna	48	6.1	7	11
Marche	42	5.4	5	8
Toscana	51	6.5	4	6
Sub-total	376	48.0	54	83
Other regions	408	52.0	11	17
Italy	784	100.0	65	100

It has been noted (Baffigi et al. 1999) that the largest city located in an industrial district is Padua (215,000 inhabitants in 1991), and that only nine industrial district municipalities have as many as 100,000 inhabitants. The average population is just above 5,500, less than the average of non-district areas, which is a confirmation that networks of small and medium-sized firms tend to locate in networks of small cities and not in gateways.

TRAFFIC FLOWS IN THE WEST–EAST CORRIDOR

Almost all the Italian motorways and a few of the national roads are part of the 'E' network. The 'E' network has undergone a process of upgrading, which has been a factor of economic growth. The Italian motorway network increased by roughly 65 percent between 1979 and 1995 while state roads grew only by 6 percent and provincial roads by 26 percent. As far as the northern part of Italy is concerned, there are three different 'E' arteries which can be considered the backbone of the West–East corridor: the basic one is the motorway connecting Turin to Milan, Verona and Venice; the other is the motorway connecting Switzerland to Milan, Bologna and Florence. But also the other orthogonal motorway connecting Austria to Rimini through Verona and Modena can be considered an integral part of the same network. As a result, the connection between the so-called 'Third Italy', i.e. the seven regions of northeast and central Italy, and the earlier industrialized area of the northwest is basically covered by the network.

The relation between the provision of transport infrastructure and economic development has long been considered both strong and obvious. According to Andersson and Strömquist (1989), all major economic transitions in Europe were accompanied by major changes in transport and communications infrastructure. The improvement of transport infrastructure is also necessary to eliminate bottlenecks and foster further economic expansion. However, it is widely recognized that the increase in road capacity cannot always cater for the forecast increase in traffic. From this point of view, the improvement of transport infrastructure is more a necessary than a sufficient factor of growth. The economic mechanism by which the improved transport network is capable of influencing the development process is rather complex, but the interaction between transport costs and economies of scale would seem the most obvious. The idea is that the reduction in shipping and transit costs – as well as the abolition of trade barriers – allows a wider market area to be served and thus allows the exploitation of economies of scale in production and distribution. The creation of a larger and better networked economic space, however, is deemed to be able to yield more specialization and spatial concentration than a dispersion of economic activities. Krugman and Venables, at least since 1990, have been writing extensively on how the enlargement of a market area adds scale effects, which bring about a centripetal force favoring a more pronounced core–periphery pattern of production. In the new geography, even without the assumption of any significant comparative advantages, increasing returns to scale turn out to be sufficient to explain the uneven spatial distribution of economic activities. Sufficiently large economies of scale may encourage concentration of production in high-cost locations with sufficiently good market access, rather than in low-cost locations. This means that transport improvements which reduce transport costs in combination with economies of scale may increase peripherality, i.e., shape and reshape the existing economic space, thus making the history of places important.

This is the basic tenet of the new theory of international trade and geography. However, it can be argued, and also statistically observed, that congestion effects produced by a transport demand constantly growing faster than network capacity could counteract the centripetal force, adversely affecting the congested regions forming the core, thus producing a centrifugal force bringing an advantage to peripheral and less congested regions. Complete specialization then becomes less likely than generally believed, even though a dampened core–periphery pattern does not immediately imply lower transport demand in certain corridors and nodes.

It is generally believed that the creation of the Single European Market and transport network improvements will combine to produce an improved allocation of resources and thus a new powerful push to investment and economic growth, which should be accompanied by a general upgrading of the infrastructure.

Road freight (goods vehicle kms) is a transport component which is rather elastic with respect to GDP and is probably more elastic than car transport. Some recent OECD estimates, however, show that in Europe the rate of growth of road freight is 3.7 percent and is equal to that of car use. As the rate of growth of European GDP is about 2.8 percent, the above estimates imply an elasticity equal to $0.037/0.028=1.3$. This means a more than proportional increase in road freight and car use with respect to the increase in GDP or that the elasticity of transport demand with respect to economic activity is higher than 1. One explanation of the continued growth of freight transport in excess of the growth of economic activity is the additional transport demand produced by changes in logistics and recycling.

The inability not only to satisfy the additional transport demand, but also to halt the switch from rail to road is particularly evident in the Eastern European countries. There are indications that the creation of the European Internal Market and the opening up of Eastern European markets will be able to yield an increase in income, trade and transport, which puts the 'E' network under continuous strain and will continue to do so in the early part of the next century.

One could argue that the role of transport infrastructure could be very different depending on the stage of growth. In the early stages, infrastructure investment reduces barriers and acts as an integrating factor. Later it can both trigger the take-off of certain areas and act as a reinforcing factor of core–peripherality. When transport costs are low even a slight difference in accessibility can set off a relocation process which by its very nature yields a core–periphery pattern.

One particular location becomes a core and when the location concerned is equipped with an airport or a seaport the so-called hub effect (Fujita and Mori, 1996) – i.e., the existence of positive feedback between economies of scale and accessibility – comes into play. It is interesting to note that, especially in relation to many ports where the hub effect is particularly evident, the initial advantage of cheap sea access had ceased to play an important role long before these seaports became urban cores.

In conclusion, although transport infrastructure may be critical as the triggering mechanism in the early stages of growth, in the late stages infrastructure investment is necessary only to keep congestion costs at a low level and, consequently, weaken the mechanism that induces core–peripherality.

In the 1980s, the United Nations Economic Commission for Europe adopted a resolution inviting the governments of the 30 member countries to take a road traffic census with 1995 as the reference year. The census data give some clues about the growth of traffic flows on the 'E' arteries with reference to 1995. Figures 17.1, 17.2 and 17.3 show the level of the flow and its percentage change from 1990 to 1995 at different locations on the three 'E' arteries in northern Italy.

While the flow level gives an idea of the activity taking place both in the surrounding area and in the transit function of an artery, the percentage change gives a clear indication of the speed with which the activity level and the transit level increased in the period.

The first observation that can be made is that although the relative increase in 1990–95 of the road traffic at the various locations is rather uneven, it does have a pattern. It tends to be lower where the 1995 flow level is higher and vice versa, but with some exceptions we will comment on below. First, we observe that the existence of an inverse relation between the flow and the relative rate of change could be an indication that artery capacity is close to saturation at some locations.

Figure 17.1 Major traffic flow on the 'E' roads (1995): Torino-Trieste

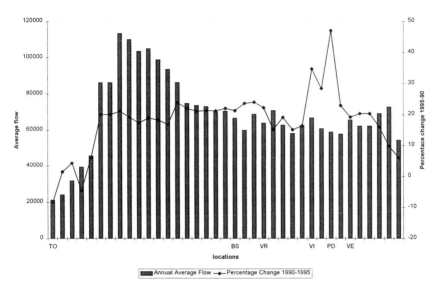

Figure 17.2 Motor traffic flow on 'E' roads (1995): Brennero–Rimini

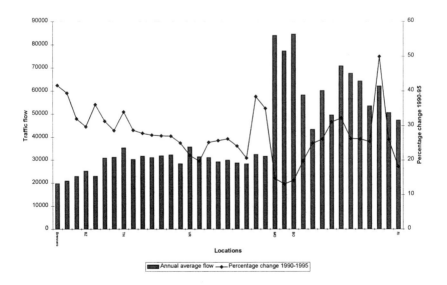

At full capacity, the flow is at its maximum and it is common knowledge that as the concentration of vehicles on a road increases, vehicle velocity decreases. This means that as vehicle concentration increases, the flow increases, but at a decreasing pace, as speed decreases. Thus the observed inverse relation between the flow and the percentage rate of increase seems to indicate that the average flow is reaching full capacity. The closer the average flow is to capacity, the higher the probability of congestion with a resulting lower speed.

As regards the exceptions to the inverse relation between the flow and its percentage increase – typically at the locations around Padua and between Bologna and Rimini, where the flow increased sharply – we can assume that this is an indication of a particularly high local transport demand. We are of course aware that the traffic increase, in general, is the result of many factors, but common factors, such as mode switching and car or truck ownership, can hardly explain the wide local differences in the increase in the rate of demand observed at the locations reported in the figures. These differences could only be explained by the increase in derived demand in the area concerned, which is the outcome of the rate of increase in local economic activity *per se* and of the changes in logistics within the networks of firms located in the surrounding area.

Figure 17.3 Motor traffic flow on 'E' roads (1995): Como-Firenze

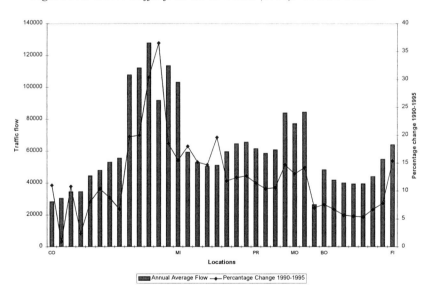

INNOVATIVE CAPACITY AND INCOME GROWTH

The Veneto Network City has recently received attention from scholars for its dynamism and economic growth performance. Indeed, the explanation of regional and national differences in growth and per capita income levels has generally been subject to a revival of interests in recent years, both in its theoretical and empirical aspects, which has focused on the relation between economic growth and technological progress. Within the traditional neoclassical model, technological change is interpreted as a purely exogenous phenomenon and thus no economic explanation of its evolution is provided. By contrast, the 'evolutionary approach' has developed a framework in which technological change is explained by the action of economic agents. Much of the theoretical work within the evolutionary tradition has relied primarily on appreciative theory, that is on less abstract, more descriptive, modeling. This work has then been a source of inspiration for recent work on 'endogenous growth' within the formal modeling tradition of mainstream economics, which has tried to codify some of the fundamental elements of the evolutionary view. As a result, although differing profoundly in many ways, both frameworks interpret technological progress as either the byproduct of other economic activities or the intentional result of research efforts carried out by profit-seeking agents. They therefore consider human capital and innovation as fundamental elements in the explanation of the process of economic growth.

From an empirical point of view, studies on European urban regions suggest that regions specializing in research-intensive activities and good communications and transport infrastructures are expanding their employment and income base more quickly than cities relatively specialized in manufacturing activities (Cheshire and Carbonaro, 1995 and 1996; Magrini, 1998 and 2000, among others). In what follows we shall briefly try to assess whether the Veneto Network City can be though of as a creative network city, that is as a city placing 'higher priority on knowledge-based activities like research, education and the creative arts' (Batten, 1995). After an evaluation of the recent per capita GDP growth performance of the region, we analyze its innovative capacity and its endowment of education infrastructure.

However, before presenting the data, it is necessary to consider the very important issue of the statistical units used in the analysis. It is well known that national territories may be subdivided into regions according to different criteria which, in general, range between two extremes: normative criteria and functional criteria. One example of the definition of regional units according to normative criteria is represented by the administrative regions for which data are normally published and which, hitherto, have constituted the set of regions analyzed in most studies. The use of administrative regions, however, will very often distort the results. The boundaries of administrative regions are the result of political and historical factors, which bear no relationship to the socioeconomic factors that form the basis of a functional region. By contrast, because of the very nature of regional economic disparities, any empirical study on the subject should take space into consideration and opt for a definition of region which is economically as self-contained as possible and is defined by the spatial sphere of socioeconomic influence of foci of economic activity. Moreover, an important and practical reason for using functional regions rather than administrative ones is simply that the economic indicator which is of interest – per capita GDP – is a product of two components, total regional GDP and population, which are measured with respect to different organizational methods. GDP is measured at workplaces while population is counted on residential basis. Thus if population centralizes or decentralizes with respect to the location of employment, entirely spurious 'growth' will result. As is shown in Cheshire (1997) it can be as much as 39 percent of actual growth once changes in commuting have been allowed for. In addition, this source of statistical distortion of measured growth rates will tend to be systematically concentrated in the richest regions given the existence of net inward commuting. In the context of an 'underbounded' region, such as Milan, not only does positive net inward commuting bias measured GDP upwards but changes in net commuting over time are far more likely to distort measured growth rates. Since the functional links between spatial units are limited by space, functional regions take explicit account of the distance factor and appear thus as the best alternative. The data analyzed here, therefore, refer to the Functional Urban Regions (FURs) proposed by Hall and Hay (1980) for 1971, and which were adopted by Cheshire and Hay (1989) in their analysis of urban problems in Europe between 1951 and 1981.[13]

We can now turn our attention to the available data on per capita GDP to evaluate the economic performance of the region. Table 17.2 shows the growth rates of per capita GDP over the period 1979–96:[14] Padua and Treviso are the two fastest-growing FURs in Italy over the period 1979–96, while Vicenza is the fifth fastest. Venice and Verona are respectively the sixth and twelfth fastest-growing cities with growth rates well above the Italian average of 0.063.

The relative performance of the Veneto Network Region compared to the area dominated by Milan can be evaluated from Figure 17.4. The former region shows a high and homogeneous growth rate with a relative peak centered on the FUR of Padua.

Table 17.2 Fastest- and slowest-growing FURs in Italy (1979–96)

Rank	FUR	Growth rate	Rank	FUR	Growth rate
1	Padua	0.077	32	Lecce	0.055
2	Treviso	0.076	33	Caserta	0.053
3	Bologna	0.076	34	Foggia	0.052
4	Pescara	0.075	35	Catania	0.050
5	Vicenza	0.075	36	Siracusa	0.042

On the other hand, Milan dominates its hinterland in terms of per capita GDP growth, with a rate substantially higher than those of the surrounding FURs. It is also worth noting that while the growth rate of Milan is similar to those of the centers belonging to the Veneto Network City, all the other FURs within its sphere of influence show a growth rate smaller than the average Italian rate.

Figure 17.4 Growth rate of per capita GDP (1979–96) in the East–West link

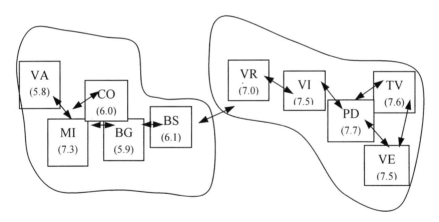

Note:
BG=Bergamo; BS=Brescia; CO=Como; MI=Milano; PD=Padova; TV=Treviso; VA=Varese; VE=Venice; VI=Vicenza; VR=Verona.

It is now possible to examine the possible determinants of the region's dynamism. To evaluate the creativity of a region we make use of data on patents awarded by the US Patents and Trademark Office and classified by location of assignee. In particular, we use the growth rate in the number of patents awarded over the period 1978–94 as a rough measure of innovative capacity.[15] The ten highest rates among the Italian FURs are reported in Table 17.3.[16]

Table 17.3 Innovative capacity in Italy: highest growth rates of patents (1978–94)

Rank	FUR	Growth rate	Rank	FUR	Growth rate
1	Parma	0.14	6	Florence	0.09
2	Padua	0.14	7	Modena	0.08
3	Vicenza	0.12	8	Como	0.08
4	Treviso	0.11	9	Rome	0.07
5	Bologna	0.10	10	Verona	0.07

Notes: Data for a particular year are calculated as the 3-year average centered on that year.

Source: US Patent and Trademark Office and authors' own calculations.

With the only exception of Venice (growth rate of 0.04), whose patenting activity has certainly been affected by the decline of petrochemical activity concentrated in its industrial area, it is worth noting that all the other FURs belonging to the Veneto Network City appear in the table. Moreover, the growth rates for these FURs appears to be substantially homogeneous, as emphasized also in Figure 17.5 where the growth rates for the centers in the Veneto Network City can be compared to those for the area dominated by Milan.

From this figure, on the other hand, the high degree of heterogeneity characterizing the measure of innovative capacity of the latter area is evident, with rates ranging between a large, negative value (–8.4) in Varese and a rather large positive one (9.6) in Bergamo, with Milan lying in the middle, achieving a rate marginally above zero (1.4).

A comparison between Figures 17.4 and 17.5 thus suggests a close correspondence between the innovative capacity and economic performance of the two areas. The FURs belonging to the Veneto Network City all have similarly high growth rates of both per capita GDP and patents, while the area dominated by the central place city of Milan is characterized by a greater variety in performance around a generally lower order of magnitude. It is also interesting to notice that Milan seems to be able to exploit its role of central place by taking advantage of scope economies which may be derived from knowledge exchanges with creative centers within its hinterland.

Figure 17.5 Innovative capacity in the Italian East–West link (1978–94)

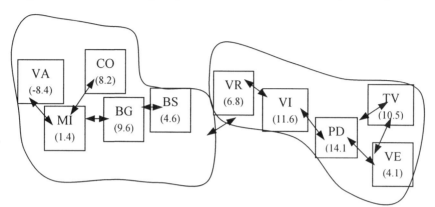

Note:
BG=Bergamo; BS=Brescia; CO=Como; MI=Milan; PD=Padua; TV=Treviso; VA=Varese; VE=Venice; VI=Vicenza; VR=Verona.

The final piece of information we consider concerns the education infrastructure. Indeed, the education system and, in particular, universities and other higher education institutions, play a fundamental function in the development of an environment conducive to innovation through the provision of human capital. Universities also play an essential local role as they are themselves producers of new knowledge that can positively influence the research effort of private corporations as found by Jaffe (1989), Acs et al. (1992 and 1994), Suarez-Villa and Hasnath (1993), and Feldman (1994).

Table 17.4 describes the ten most important Italian FURs in terms of number of students in universities and higher education institutions per thousand population in the 1980–81 and 1997–98 academic years. Padua is one of the three FURs with the highest relative number of students in both years and Venice enters the table in 1997–98, which illustrates the important role played by this type of infrastructure within the Veneto Network City.

Figure 17.6 describes university and higher education infrastructure along the Italian East–West links at the beginning of the 1980s. Quite interestingly, the distribution of this type of infrastructure follows closely the distribution of per capita GDP growth in Figure 17.1. Padua emerges again as the absolute peak along the East–West Link, while Milan, consistent with its role of being a central place city, dominates its hinterland.

Table 17.4 Students in Italian universities and higher education institutions

Rank	FUR	1980–81	Rank	FUR	1997–98
1	Bologna	67	1	Bologna	115
2	Padua	65	2	Perugia	92
3	Perugia	63	3	Padua	79
4	Florence	47	4	Parma	75
5	Parma	47	5	Florence	67
6	Rome	39	6	Trento	57
7	Genoa	36	7	Genoa	53
8	Catania	29	8	Milan	51
9	Milan	28	9	Rome	50
10	Cagliari	27	10	Venice	50

Source: *The World of Learning*, Europa Publications Ltd and authors' own calculations.

Note: Data are expressed in per thousand population terms.

Figure 17.6 University infrastructure along the East–West link (1980–81)

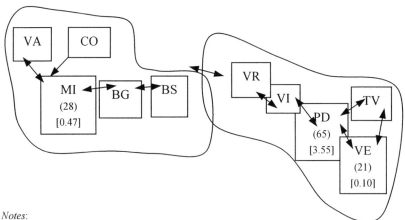

Notes:
Figures for university and higher education institutions students (per 1,000 population) are within parentheses; figures for university and higher education institutions academic staff (per 1,000 population) are within brackets.
BG=Bergamo; BS=Brescia; CO=Como; MI=Milan; PD=Padua; TV=Treviso; VA=Varese; VE=Venice; VI=Vicenza; VR=Verona.

Source: *The World of Learning*, Europa Publications Ltd and authors' own calculations.

To sum up, we have found evidence suggesting that the group of FURs belonging to the Veneto region have been particularly dynamic during the 1980s and mid-1990s, achieving the highest growth rates of per capita GDP in Italy. Moreover, the growth rates for these FURs have been remarkably homogeneous, supporting the view that they actually form a single creative network city in which fast corridors of transport and communications infrastructures allows these nodes to take advantage of dynamic synergies of interactive growth via reciprocity, knowledge exchange and creativity. Moreover, both the actual size and spatial distribution along the East–West link of the chosen indicators of innovative capacity and university infrastructure provide some support to the idea of a creative network city consisting of the FURs of Venice, Padua, Treviso, Vicenza and Verona.

NOTES

1. Johansson (1989).
2. In the paper presented at the Eighth Pacific Conference in Tokyo, 1983 (1985, p. 5), for instance, Andersson argued that Milan would be of potential interest for closer scrutiny as a possible creative region.
3. Braudel (1979) calls it a city-world.
4. From a certain viewpoint a saddle is a top; from a different viewpoint a saddle is a bottom.
5. Or a small number of firms and subcontractors.
6. With a regression analysis of fixed investment rate in a sample of 4,000 companies (1985–1994), Baffigi et al. (1999) found that investments made by firms operating in MIDs is more closely correlated to their cash-flow than those of non-MID firms, but also that this is not generally true. The financial constraint seems to be stronger for MID firms in sectors such as machinery and furniture and, in addition, in Lombardy and Veneto, particularly.
7. The already cited work of Baffigi et al. (1999) reports various forms of 'mutual banking' in Italian MIDs.
8. The regional laws follow the national law which dates back to 1991.
9. 250 employees according to EC regulations, but Italian small firms are traditionally those with less than 20 employees.
10. *Il Sole-24 ore*, 16 April 1992 and Becattini (1998), p. 61.
11. Piemonte, Liguria, Emilia Romagna, Trentino and Friuli.
12. In 1981 there were 955, a reduction which shows that over the ten years the average distance traveled by commuters has increased and local labor systems have grown in size.
13. A full discussion on the importance of the definition of regions for empirical analyses and a detailed description of the FURs can be found in Cheshire et. al. (1996).
14. GDP data are expressed in purchasing power parities in US\$. The growth rate is calculated as $Log(GDP_{96}/GDP_{79})/17$.
15. The rate is calculated in the same way as the one for per capita GDP.
16. Among the FURs with the highest growth rate of per capita GDP, Pescara had no patents awarded at the beginning of the period under analysis. However, its number of patents grew at a rate slightly smaller than that for Padua over the period 1987–94.

REFERENCES

Acs, Z.J., D.B. Audretsch and M.P. Feldman (1992), 'Real effects of academic research: comment', *American Economic Review*, **82**, 363–67.

Acs, Z.J., D.B. Audretsch and M.P. Feldman (1994), 'R&D spillovers and recipient firm size', *Review of Economics and Statistics*, **100**, 336–40.

Andersson, Å.E. (1985), 'Creativity and Regional Development', *Papers of the Regional Science Association*, **56**, 5–20.

Andersson, Å.E. and U. Strömquist (1989), 'The emerging C-society', in D.F. Batten and R. Thord (eds), *Transportation for the Future*, Berlin: Springer-Verlag.

Baffigi, A., M. Pagnini and F. Quintiliani (1999), 'Industrial districts and local banks: do the twins ever meet?', *Temi di Discussone del Servizio Studi della Banca d'Italia*, **347**, March.

Batten, D. (1995), 'Network cities: creative urban agglomerations for the 21st century', *Urban Studies*, **32**, 313–27.

Becattini, G. (ed.) (1975), *Lo sviluppo economico della Toscana (IRPET)*, Firenze.

Becattini, G. (1979), 'Dal settore industriale al distretto industriale: alcune considerazioni sull'unità di indagine dell'economia industriale', *Rivista di Economia e Politica Industriale*, **1**, 7–21.

Braudel, F. (1979), *Civilisation matérielle, économie et capitalisme (XVe–XVIIIe siècle), Les temps du monde*, Paris: Librairie Armand Colin.

Brusco, S. (1986), 'Small firms and industrial districts: the experience of Italy', *Economia Internazionale*, **39**, 85–103.

Brusco, S. (1991), 'La genesi dell'Idea di Distretto Industriale', in F. Pyke, G. Becattini and W. Sengenberger (eds), *Distretti Industriali e Cooperazione fra Imprese in Italia, Studi e Informazioni*, Supplemento 1, Quaderno **34**, 25–34.

Cheshire, P.C. (1997), 'Economic indicators for European cities and regions: why boundaries matter', paper presented to the EUROSTAT Conference on the Quality of Life in the Cities and Regions of the European Union, Barcelona, 14–16 April 1997.

Cheshire, P.C. and D.G. Hay (1989), *Urban Problems in Western Europe: An Economic Analysis*, London: Unwin Hyman.

Cheshire, P.C. and G. Carbonaro (1995), 'Convergence–divergence in regional growth rates: an empty black box?' in H.W. Armstrong and R.W. Vickerman (eds), *Convergence and Divergence Among European Regions*, London: Pion.

Cheshire, P.C. and G. Carbonaro (1996), 'Urban economic growth in Europe: testing theory and policy prescriptions', *Urban Studies*, **33** 1111–28.

Cheshire, P.C., A. Furtado and S. Magrini (1996), 'Quantitative comparisons of European cities and regions', in L. Hantrais and S. Mangen (eds), *Cross-National Research Methods in the Social Sciences*, London: Pinter.

Cristaller, W. (1933, 1966), *The Central Places of Southern Germany*, Englewood Cliffs, NJ: Prentice-Hall.

Feldman, M. (1994), *The Geography of Innovation*, Boston: Kluwer Academic Publishers.

Fujita, M. and T. Mori (1996), 'The role of ports in the making of major cities: self-agglomeration and hub effect', *Journal of Development Economics*, **49**, 93–120.

Hall, P. and D.G. Hay (1980), *Growth Centres in the European Urban System*, London: Heinemann.

Hohenberg, P.M. and Lees, L.M. (1985), *The Making of Urban Europe: 1000–1950*, Cambridge, MA: Harvard University Press.

Jaffe, A.B. (1989), 'Real effects of academic research', *American Economic Review*, **79**, 957–70.

Johansson, B. (1989), 'Economic development and networks for spatial interaction', CERUM, Centre for Regional Science Research, Umeå, CWP, 28.

Lösch, A. (1954), *The Economics of Location*, New Haven: Yale University Press.

Magrini, S. (1998), 'Modelling Regional Economic Growth: The Role of Human Capital and Innovation', unpublished Ph.D. thesis, London: London School of Economics.

Magrini, S. (2000), 'The Impact of Research Activities on the European Urban System', in D.F. Batten, C.S. Bertuglia, D. Martellato and S. Occelli (eds), *Innovation and Urban Development*, Kluwer, MA.

Perroux, F. (1950), 'Economic space: theory and applications', *The Quarterly Journal of Economics*, **64**, 89–104.

Regione Veneto (1997), *Studio per l'individuazione di distretti industriali nel Veneto*, Venezia.

Sforzi, F. (1991), 'I Distretti Marshalliani nell'Economia Italiana' in F. Pyke, G. Becattini and W. Sengenberger (eds), *Distretti Industriali e Cooperazione fra Imprese in Italia, Studi e Informazioni*, Supplemento 1, Quaderno **34**, 91–117.

Sforzi, F. (1997), *I Sistemi Locali del lavoro 1991*, Roma: Istat.

Suarez-Villa, L. and S.A. Hasnath (1993), 'The effect of infrastructure on invention: innovative capacity and the dynamics of public construction investment', *Technological Forecasting and Social Change*, **44**, 333–58.

18. Barcelona – the Logistical Center of Southern Europe

Javier Revilla Diez

INTRODUCTION

Barcelona is trying to become the logistical center of Southern Europe. Spurred on by the successful modernization of the city within the framework of the Summer Olympic Games in 1992, the city administration is making efforts to play a very active role in a second transformation of Barcelona. In its Development Plan 2000, Barcelona's planning authority is paying special attention to the promotion of activities and infrastructures connected with mobility, logistics, and the distribution of commercial facilities and people. The concrete goals are to (Barcelona Regional, 1999):

1. design and realize integrated training activities to give substance to the objective of becoming a city important as a distribution center for Southern Europe.
2. persist in and extend improvements to the transport infrastructure (e.g., to compile an integrated logistics plan for merchandise), to consolidate the port Logistics Activities Zone (Zona Actividades Logisticas – ZAL), to develop the modular service area of the airport, and to give support to the high-speed railway line Montpellier – Barcelona – Madrid.

In order to succeed in doing this, Barcelona is depending on increased regional cooperation within the so-called C-6 network. In addition to Barcelona, this network includes the cities of Toulouse, Montpellier, Zaragoza, Valencia and Palma de Mallorca (Asociación Plan Estratégico Barcelona 2000). This network aims:

- to complete the major road axes structuring the region (the transversal axis, the Pyrenean axis, the axis of the Llobregat and the Ebro–Toulouse axis),
- to reinforce the railway network by introducing high-speed trains,
- to develop a joint airport strategy and coordinated management of the ports

with the objective of creating a strong economic growth pole in the north-west Mediterranean. Barcelona sees itself as the driving force within this city network.

This paper tries to determine whether or not Barcelona has the potential to achieve this ambitious goal. The discussion focuses on Barcelona's intention to become the most important logistical center of Southern Europe. Which criteria does Barcelona have to fulfill in order to develop into a gateway for the western Mediterranean? If one looks at Rotterdam, New York or Singapore it is not difficult to identify important influencing factors. They can be divided into economic and infrastructural factors.

- Infrastructure requirements:
    - the availability of large and developed areas
    - an excellent transportation infrastructure, combining different means of transportation (airport, port, railways, highways)
- Economic requirements:
    - rapid business services growth, especially in transport and communications
    - a large manufacturing base or access to a large hinterland
    - a large number of multinational companies (MNCs) (including regional headquarters).

INFRASTRUCTURE REQUIREMENTS

One precondition for becoming a logistical center is an excellent infrastructure. Besides the size and quality of the facilities, much depends on the interlinkages between different means of transportation. Intermodal freight transport becomes increasingly important if a larger hinterland is to be reached. In this respect, well-developed links, e.g. railways or motorways, are crucial. Along with cargo handling, the storage and manufacturing of goods in a logistical area are of particular importance. The special strength of Barcelona's location near the Llobregat Delta is the geographical proximity of logistical networks to industrial and commercial agglomerations (see Figure 18.1). The seaport, with its logistics area (ZAL), the Poligono Industrial de la Zona Franca, one of the largest enclosed industrial areas in Spain, the free-trade zone (Zona Franca Comercial), the Mercabarna central market and the airport are situated immediately next to each other (see Table 18.1).

Further industrial and commercial areas, such as Famadas de Cornella, Prat de Llobregat, between Sant Boi and Gava, are situated within a radius of between 5 and 10 kilometers (Robusté and Clabera, 1997).

Figure 18.1 The logistical center in the Llobregat Delta of Barcelona

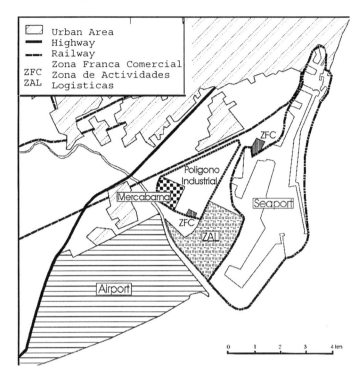

Source: Robusté and Clabera (1997).

Table 18.1 Areas and size of the logistics center at the Llobregat Delta

Areas	Size in ha
Seaport and Logistics Area	
Seaport	527
Logistics Area	68
Airport and Cargo Area	
Airport	950
Cargo Area	75
Industrial Area de la Zona Franca	600
Zona Franca Comercial	10
Mercabarna	90
Total	2,320

Source: Molbay (1995).

THE SEAPORT

The increase in international trade has led to greater demand for maritime transportation. On the one hand, the movement of freight between the continents has increased rapidly, and on the other hand the goods structure has shifted from the transport of individually packaged goods to bulk goods. The technological changes occurring parallel to this, which were marked particularly by the increase in the size of ships and the growing importance of container transport, have increased the competition between the ports.

After the introduction of large specialized ships, the seaports required the construction of suitable terminals with efficient loading and unloading facilities, appropriate storage capacities and good links for further transportation into the hinterland (Nuhn, 1994; Hoyle and Pinder, 1992).

Table 18.2 Container tonnage of European seaports ('000 tons)

Port	1991	1992	1993	1994	1995	1996	% change 1996/91
Atlantic ports							
Rotterdam	31,747	35,114	35,711	38,981	38,870	41,018	29.2
Antwerp	18,934	19,657	20,330	24,336	25,795	29,460	55.6
Hamburg	17,853	18,725	21,225	23,507	24,543	25,931	45.2
Le Havre	8,769	6,863	8,399	8,262	9,066	9,518	8.5
London	–	3,493	3,423	3,877	3,231	4,109	–
Amsterdam	813	899	1,062	1,059	1,111	1,721	111.7
Mediterranean ports							
Marseilles	4,898	3,919	4,573	4,530	5,251	5,769	17.8
Genoa	3,275	3,210	3,173	4,244	5,371	7,333	123.9
Barcelona	5,001	5,702	5,143	6,097	7,443	7,628	52.5
Venice	717	803	877	883	928	1,169	63.0
Trieste	1,137	1,168	1,270	1,188	1,155	1,326	16.6
Tarragona	234	307	367	391	404	283	20.9
Algeciras	6,588	6,869	8,100	9,403	11,893	13,777	109.1

Source: Institute of Shipping Economics and Logistics (1997).

Based on container tonnage, Barcelona, with its total container volume of 7.6 million tons (1996), is the most important container port in the Mediterranean region, closely followed by Genoa (7.3 million tons) and Marseilles (5.7) (Table 18.2).

The Mediterranean ports have not succeeded in taking full advantage of their favorable location regarding trade with Africa and the Near and Far East. The only exceptions are crude oil and refinery products, which are sent northward via pipelines from Trieste, Marseilles and Genoa.

Since multinational businesses are increasingly transferring their stocks to several regional centers in order to achieve greater flexibility, this provides the ports in the northwest Mediterranean region with growth opportunities. Ports that have a favorable location, quick and reliable transshipment facilities and complementary transport systems in the sense of multimodal freight transport, have good preconditions for passing on additional flows of goods from the Far East. When compared with its direct competitors, Barcelona has drawbacks as far as the linking of different transport systems is concerned. The port's link with the railway network is particularly weak.

The possibilities for expansion have also been exhausted. The completed extension of Moll Sud to 66 hectares and the raising of the container transshipment capacity to 800,000 TEU (Twenty Feet Equivalent Units) are already completely insufficient today, and additional reserves of land are not available.

THE AIRPORT

The number of passengers at Barcelona Airport has risen sharply in the past few years. In 1993, 9.3 million passengers passed through the airport, while in 1997 the figure was already 15 million. Thus the airport is comparable in size with the airports at Copenhagen, Stockholm, Munich and Düsseldorf, while the intercontinental hubs London (85 million passengers), Paris (60 million), Frankfurt (40.2 million) and Amsterdam (32 million) have two to three times the number of passengers (Table 18.3).

The development of freight traffic has, however, been sluggish. While the largest European airports (London, Paris, Frankfurt) had increases of 40 percent or more between 1993 and 1997, the rise in Barcelona was only a moderate 18 percent. Although the gap between Barcelona and the largest European airports has been reduced as regards passenger numbers, Barcelona has fallen behind as far as freight is concerned.

In 1997, London and Frankfurt each handled 1.5 million tons, Paris 1.3 million tons, and Rome and Zürich 0.3 million tons each. The corresponding figure for Barcelona was only 0.08 million tons.

18.3 Passenger and freight figures for European airports

	Passengers			Air freight		
	in millions		% change	in million tons		% change
Airport	1993	1997	1997/93	1993	1997	1997/93
London	64.6	85.0	31.6	1002	1547	54.4
Paris	51.5	60.3	17.1	887	1309	47.6
Frankfurt	31.7	40.2	26.8	1080	1514	40.2
Amsterdam	19.9	31.5	58.3	–	1207	–
Madrid	17.3	23.6	36.4	189	282	49.2
Rome	–	25.0	–	243	288	18.5
Milan	14.1	14.2	0.7	153	123	-19.6
Zürich	12.5	18.2	45.6	271	355	31.0
Copenhagen	12.4	16.8	35.5	–	387	–
Stockholm	11.9	15.1	26.9	–	146	–
Munich	10.9	17.9	64.2	–	123	–
Düsseldorf	10.1	15.3	51.5	–	71	–
Barcelona	9.6	15.0	56.3	72	85	18.1
Hamburg		8.6	–	–	53	–
Marseilles		5.4	–	38	58	52.6
Genoa		6.1	–	–	–	–

Source: Airports Council International (1999).

When compared to its main competitors – Marseilles and Genoa – Barcelona is clearly ahead with regard to passenger and freight handling. However, in order to develop into a central hub for Southern Europe (Cambra Oficial de Comerc, 1996c), Barcelona Airport should handle 30 million passengers and 0.5 million tons of air freight.

A particular weakness is the small number of intercontinental connections, which may prove very detrimental to the future development of the airport (Table 18.5). The transit figures, an indicator for the hub function of an airport, amount to only about 3 percent of the overall passenger figures. The structure of the destinations shows that the majority of the passengers, approximately 63 percent, travel on to other Spanish airports. A further 19 percent of the passengers fly to European hubs, such as London, Paris and Frankfurt, while only 3 percent of the passengers take intercontinental flights (Robusté and Clabera, 1997).

High growth rates, with regard to both passenger and freight figures, can only be achieved through direct intercontinental flights. In this context the question must be asked whether or not Barcelona can succeed, like Copenhagen for the Scandinavian region, in becoming a gateway for the western Mediterranean. This will depend decisively upon whether or not Barcelona can establish itself as the central hub for the airports of Zaragoza, Valencia, the Balearics, Toulouse, Lyon, Marseilles and Nice. With a population of more than 20 million inhabitants, a total number of passengers amounting to 50 million, and an overall air freight turnover of approximately 0.3 million tons per year, the cities mentioned have a notable development potential (Robusté and Clabera, 1997).

So far, air connections between these cities, and especially those between Barcelona and the southern French cities, have played only a subordinate role. As a rule these airports act as feeders for the airports in Madrid, Rome, Milan, Zürich, Paris, Frankfurt and London.

The insufficient airport infrastructure also represents a further bottleneck. A passenger turnover of 20 million, which is predicted for 2003, implies that the handling capacity of the airport will be exhausted. Freight handling must also be urgently modernized and extended. Without a separate freight terminal the transshipment figure of 0.5 million tons per year cannot be achieved.

THE ROAD AND RAIL NETWORKS

The Road Network

During the past 20 years a strong process of suburbanization, which was brought about by industrial settlement patterns and also by the development of new housing areas, has increased the intensity of the interlinkage between Barcelona and its hinterland. The metropolitan conurbation now has a radius of up to 30 kilometers from downtown Barcelona. The increase in traffic intensity caused by the larger flows of commuters into and out of the center has led to a congested road network. On the main roads out of the city and the ring roads, the traffic frequently comes to a standstill several times as day. On the A-18 to Sabadell and Terrassa, industrial towns within the commuter belt of Barcelona (a 30-kilometer distance from the center), as well as on several ring roads, more than 100,000 vehicles are counted each day. Although new toll roads have been constructed to relieve the situation, these roads are hardly used by commuters. Only 10,000 vehicles per day use the new roads (Cambra Oficial de Comerc, 1996b). Additionally, numerous construction measures, e.g. the Baix Llobregat motorway and the Sitges–Vendrell motorway, which will bring a lasting improvement to the road system, are additionally hindering the traffic flow at present (Nel·Lo, 1997).

THE RAIL NETWORK

Over the past few years the demands made on the rail network have increased drastically. In addition to the local public transport system, long-distance passenger traffic is also growing in importance regarding high-speed trains and freight traffic. Since each of these types of transportation creates special demands on the infrastructure, separate rail tracks have been laid out over the course of time. While a sufficient local public transport system has been achieved, new routes must be built for long-distance passenger traffic and freight traffic.

The different gauge on the Iberian Peninsula presents a special problem, since it is broader than the European standard gauge (1,668 mm and 1,425 mm, respectively). Although the high-speed route Sevilla–Madrid–Barcelona–Montpellier, which has already been built, does conform to the European norm, the freight traffic routes, which are important precisely with regard to the future development toward becoming the logistical center of Southern Europe, have the Iberian gauge. Even though technological progress has been made with the freight cars, which can, for example, adapt their gauge to the European width, or with the speed of loading the containers between different cars, delays in onward transportation into the core areas of Europe nevertheless occur at the Spanish-French border (Cambra Oficial de Comerc, 1996c).

In addition to the gauge problem, the links with the logistical center are also unsatisfactory. The result is that rail freight is almost insignificant: only 7 percent of the total transport of goods is done by rail. The situation for the transport of containers is only slightly better: 18 percent of the containers landed at the port are transported onward by freight trains (Ayuntament de Barcelona, 1999).

THE DELTA DE LLOBREGAT DEVELOPMENT PLAN – THE DELTA PROJECT

The discussion of the infrastructure pointed to several features that could harm Barcelona's development toward becoming the logistical center of Southern Europe. The seaport and the airport, as well as the facilities in the ZAL, must be modernized and expanded, and the links with the interregional road and rail network must be improved. In order to redress this situation, the Barcelona city administration, the Catalan government and the Spanish central government have agreed upon the Delta de Llobregat Development Plan. The goal is, on the one hand, to extend the existing infrastructure facilities and, on the other hand, to push forward the development of an intermodal logistical center that facilitates the interlinking of different transportation systems. The development plan, which covers the years 1993 to 2007, provides for investments to the tune of PTS1.8 billion. Roughly 70 percent of these investments are being borne by the Spanish central government. The measures concentrate on the extension of the seaport and the airport, the development of the ZAL and of the road and rail networks. The individual measures are (Barcelona Regional, 1999):

- Seaport: the enlargement of the port areas in order to extend the terminal and free zone activities from the current 436 to 773 hectares. The extension is to be achieved by altering the course of the Llobregat River and by constructing new dikes.
- ZAL: as a result of the alteration to the course of the river the ZAL is also to be enlarged from the current 68 to approximately 200 hectares.
- Airport: the extension to the airport provides for the enlargement of the existing terminals, the construction of a new terminal, the conversion of the old airport building into a cargo terminal, and the construction of a third runway. By 2015 the airport capacity is to be raised to 30 million passengers and 0.5 million tons of air freight.
- Road and rail networks: the expansion includes investments in the road and rail networks in order to improve the inner and outer accessibility. The airport is to be linked to the high-speed track, the seaport to new freight traffic tracks with the European standard gauge, and the whole area is to be linked to the newly built highway of the Baix Llobregat.

ECONOMIC REQUIREMENTS

Besides the infrastructure which, as a precondition for international competitiveness, must in any case satisfy the highest demands, economic preconditions are very decisive. In the final analysis it is the entrepreneurial decisions and activities on which the development of Barcelona into the logistical center of southern Europe depends. For their part, entrepreneurial decisions are determined by the economic potential of Barcelona and its hinterland, which thus represents a decisive influencing factor in the city's becoming Southern Europe's gateway.

Since 1986, the year when Spain became of member of the EC, the development of the economy in Catalonia, with Barcelona as the economic center, has been particularly successful. It is precisely the Catalonian businesses that have succeeded in adapting to the new and extremely dynamic framework conditions that were characterized by increasing competition. The situation before 1986 was completely different. The firms, which were mostly small ones, had for decades been directed toward the provision of local, regional and, at most, national markets, and until a few years ago they were protected from foreign competition by high duties and restrictive laws concerning direct foreign investment (Tamames and Rueda, 1997).

Today, Catalonia is the leading industrial region in Spain. In 1995 a large part of the Spanish industrial production (25 percent of Spanish industrial production and 23 percent of Spanish industrial employees), exports (27 percent of Spanish exports), gross domestic product (20 percent of the Spanish GDP) was generated in Catalonia (Instituto Nacional de Estadística, 1995). The current economic structure is marked by the great significance of the manufacturing sector (1996:31 percent of the Catalan GDP) (Generalitat de Catalunya, 1998).

As far as the number of employees is concerned, in 1995 the metalworking industry (including car manufacturing, with 146,000 employees), the textile industry (91,800 employees), the food industry (72,900 employees), the chemical industry (58,200 employees), and the paper industry (47,500 employees) are the most important sectors (Generalitat de Catalunya, 1998). The metalworking, textile and chemical industries are strongly export-oriented sectors. Between 1986 and 1996 the number of people employed in industry was reduced by almost 100,000 employees (– 43 percent).

In contrast, the growth in the service sector was especially pronounced, since over the same period it increased its number of employees by roughly 150,000 (+48 percent) (Table 18.4). While commerce and the hospitality sector attained strong growth, the transport and communications sector developed considerably more slowly, with a growth of only 11 percent. Between 1986 and 1993 the number of employees in the transport and communications sector, an indicator of the importance of logistical activities, even dropped from 41,657 to 32,937.

Apart from the global economic slowdown at the beginning of the 1990s, however, a clear structural change took place in the transport sector. Due to the transition from the personnel-intensive traditional mixed general cargo loading and unloading installations to a semi-automated container-loading system, a not inconsiderable number of port workers lost their jobs. Only with the reorientation of the port in the direction of a distribution center could the number of employees be distinctly increased after the middle of the 1990s (Port Authority of Barcelona, (1996), Bascombe, 1997).

Table 18.4 Sectoral changes in the City of Barcelona

| Branches | No. of employees | | | | % change |
	1986	1991	1993	1996	1996/86
Industry	218,319	140,009	158,915	124,889	–42.8
Construction	35,757	23,580	40,246	30,035	–16.0
Services	340,089	356,843	445,080	502,037	47.6
Trade, hotels, restaurants, repair	95,491	107,630	130,151	141,054	47.7
Transport, communication	41,657	40,705	32,937	46,345	11.3
Finance, producer services	76,772	76,992	99,534	135,781	76.9
Other services	126,169	131,516	182,458	178,857	41.8

Source: Ajuntament de Barcelona (1999).

The presence of multinational corporations (MNCs) is absolutely essential for the development of a logistics platform. The interlinking relationships between large businesses, suppliers, customers and/or markets and headquarters increasingly develop at the international level. In simple terms, the greater the number of MNCs, the greater the use of the transport facilities, no matter whether for people or goods. Since Spain joined the EC, Catalonia has succeeded to a special degree in attracting foreign direct investments (Table 18.5). Roughly 50 percent of all the foreign investment projects in Spain until 1994 were located in Catalonia, and especially in and around Barcelona (Generalitat de Catalunya, 1998). The automobile industry and its associated suppliers, the production of motorcycles, the production of consumer electronics, paper and chemical products are important investment fields. The following are among the well-known investors: VW, Nissan, Sony, Benckiser, Honda and Hewlett Packard, which, in addition to production plants, has also established its regional headquarters in Catalonia. The internationalization of Catalan businesses in the form of direct investments abroad has not progressed very far yet. The ratio between foreign and Catalan direct investments still reveals imbalances. The proportion of Catalan direct investments abroad compared with foreign direct investments in Catalonia only amounted to about 13 percent in 1996.

Table 18.5 Direct foreign investments in and from Catalonia (in million PTS)

	1988	1990	1992	1994	1996
Direct foreign investments in Catalonia	201,298	547,857	553,248	570,027	499,773
EU	112,899	374,356	364,900	409,541	266,4933
USA	4,376	12,990	25,231	35,321	24,086
Japan	7,110	10,697	2,765	3,449	3,249
Reinvestments and other countries	76,913	149,814	160,352	121,716	205,945
Catalan direct investments abroad	49,719	85,121	64,752	59,328	69,297

Source: Fontrodona and Hernandez (1998).

PROSPECTS FOR THE FUTURE

The question of whether Barcelona can develop into the most important logistical center in Southern Europe cannot be answered conclusively at this point. Due to the situation of its infrastructure, Barcelona has good starting conditions. Current bottlenecks, e.g. in the area of cargo handling at the airport or the seaport and the insufficient links to the interregional rail and road networks, will disappear during the next few years in the course of the delta project.

A new infrastructure is being created in the delta region of the Llobregat River, and this will link different transport systems in a comprehensive way. Intermodal container traffic, which, in the future, will permanently alter the traditional foreland and hinterland relations of ports, has outstanding preconditions for expansion.

The future development is decisively dependent on the extension of the current hinterland of Barcelona. It is true that, during the past few years, the amount of goods passing through the port or the airport has risen substantially, but the port and airport are still much smaller than the primary logistical centers in Northwestern Europe. It is questionable whether the businesses in and around Barcelona can make full use of the capacities that will be installed during the next few years. A larger hinterland has to be opened, stretching to the south of France. The initiative of the C-6 city network, which so far is a loose association between Barcelona, Valencia, Zaragoza, the Balearics and the southern French cities of Toulouse and Montpellier, is a step in the right direction. This is also the case with the strategic alliance with the ports of Marseilles and Genoa, which the Port Authority of Barcelona entered into in July 1997. The intention is to lobby the EU jointly and to work together on data exchange, promotional campaigns, commercial studies and initiatives on the environment, security and training. Barcelona's planned link with the French high-speed network, the construction of a freight route with the standard European gauge from Barcelona to France, will lead to a better link between Catalonia and southern France. Whether more intensive interlinking within this macro-region can be initiated and whether Barcelona can establish itself as the central gateway depend on cross-border action by representatives from politics, trade and industry.

REFERENCES

Airports Council International (1999): at http\\www.airports.org.
Asociación Plan Estratégico Barcelona 2000 (1999), 'Pla estrategic economic i social Barcelona 2000, Barcelona.
Ayuntament de Barcelona (1999), *Anuari Estadístic, 1998*.
Barcelona Regional (1999): Projects at http:\\www.bcn.es/BR
Bascombe, A. (1997), 'A question of strategy', *Containerisation International*, September.
Cambra Oficial de Comerc, Indústria i Navegacío (1996a), 'Barcelona, plataforma logistica del Sud d'Europa', *Bulletí d'estadística i conyuntura*, December.
Cambra Oficial de Comerc, Indústria i Navegacío (1996b), *Les infraestructures metropolitanes de l'àrea de Barcelona*, Barcelona.
Cambra Oficial de Comerc, Indústria i Navegacío (1996c), *Memòria econòmica de Catalunya 1995*, Barcelona.
Fontrodona, J. and J. Hernandez (1998), 'Les multinationals industrials catalanes', *Papers d'economia industrial*, Barcelona: Generalitat de Catalunya.
Generalitat de Catalunya (1998), *Anuari Estadístic de Catalunya 1998*, Barcelona.
Hoyle, B. and D. Pinder (1992), *European Port Cities in Transition*, London: Belhaven Press.
Institute of Shipping Economics and Logistics (1997), *Shipping Statistics Yearbook 1997*, Bremen.
Instituto Nacional de Estadística (1995), *Anuario Estadístico de España 1995*, Madrid.
Molbay, S.A. (1995), *Diagnóstico del potencial de la comunidad logística. Método general y aplicación al caso del Delta de Llobregat*.
Nel·Lo, O. (1997), 'Las grandes cuidades españolas: dinámicas urbanas e incidencia de las políticas estatales', *Papers Regió Metropolitana de Barcelona,* 27, July, 9–70.
Nuhn, H. (1994), 'Strukturwandlungen im Seeverkehr und ihre Auswirkungen auf die Europäischen Häfen', *Geographische Rundschau*, H. 5, 282–9.
Port Authority of Barcelona (1996), *Memòries del Port de Barcelona*, Barcelona.
Robusté, F. and J. Clabera (1997), *Impacto economico del aeropuerto de Barcelona*, Madrid: Civitas Aena.
Tamames, R. and A. Rueda (1997), *Estructura Económica de España*, Madrid: Alianza Editorial.

19. The Stockholm Region in the Global Economy

Åke E. Andersson and Börje Johansson

COMPARATIVE ADVANTAGES AND GATEWAY PROPERTIES

Comparative advantages were with a few exceptions mostly derived from resource-based models as late as in the early 1980s. This is a heritage of the economic modeling of international and interregional trade as formulated by Bertil Ohlin (1933). Recent decades have seen an almost revolutionary change within interregional and international economics. In this new approach the advantages of regional specialization of production and trade is assumed to be caused by the advantages of a large market potential in combination with various forms of increasing returns to scale. These models may be referred to as 'scale-based' (Henderson, 1974; Krugman, 1979).

According to this new scale-based theory and the associated models of location and trade, imperfect competition and increasing returns are pervasive features of contemporary industrial and post-industrial economies. With increasing returns as the basic explanation, trade develops because there exist advantages of specialization among both regional and national economies that are very similar to each other in terms of factor supply. If specialization and trade are driven by economies of scale in combination with pre-located durable resources, the gains from trade arise because production costs fall as the scale of output increases – at least as long as the participating regions continue to develop the necessary supply of knowledge and other infrastructural resources. This phenomenon is especially important for novel products and production activities and provides a particular locational advantage in knowledge-intensive metropolitan regions.

In accordance with this theory we suggest that the locational advantages and the gateway properties of the Stockholm region (as well as many other metropolitan areas) ought to be analyzed in a two-pronged framework as illustrated by Figure 19.1.

Figure 19.1 Two basic concepts of a new theory of location and trade

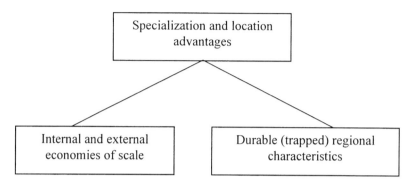

What are the most important durable characteristics of a metropolitan region such as Stockholm? A high density of demand on a matching infrastructure for interaction provides the region with a large *internal market* in which to operate economic activities at low transaction costs. The other closely related aspect is international interaction, especially the conditions for international air transport.

These two factors are reflected in the internal and external market potential of the region in terms of output and input transactions. In this context we can define and identify the gateway properties of the metropolitan region as a *saddle point* into which resources flow from a wide economic environment and from which the same (sometimes improved) resources are reallocated to other urban nodes that have established interaction links with the gateway region.

Hence gateway activities represent a particular and important form of specialization for any gateway region. By means of a large and dense internal market potential a gateway region can attract flows from the rest of the world. Thus an extended external market potential is a prerequisite for the redistributive flows. In order to examine the role of these factors in the Stockholm region, the internal market potential is illustrated in the following section.

THE INTERNAL MARKET POTENTIAL OF THE STOCKHOLM REGION

The economic density of the Stockholm region and the market potential associated with economic density can be measured in terms of the number of inhabitants, the number of firms and the gross regional product. These density measures are reported in Table 19.1.

Table 19 The relative density of the Stockholm region, 1995/96

	Density relative to the average density in Sweden
Inhabitants per square kilometer	15
Firms per square kilometer	18
Gross regional product	19

Source: Johansson et al. (1998).

The Stockholm region is obviously of much greater economic density than the rest of Sweden, at around twenty times the average value of Swedish regions.

The internal market potential of the Stockholm region can also be related to the market potential of other metropolitan regions in Europe. Table 19.2 illustrates the market potential as measured by the gross regional product of the largest functional regions in Europe.

Table 19.2 Functional regions in Europe with a larger per capita GRP than Stockholm, 1995

Region	GRP, billion ECU	GRP/capita , ECU*
Ile de France	310	28,500
Oberbayern	260	27,500
Mittelfranken	260	21,600
Stuttgart	220	23,800
Karlsruhe	220	22,000
Lombardy	210	23,000
Greater London	170	24,100
Darmstadt	160	30,000
Antwerp	120	24,100
Emilia Romagna	90	22,800
Vienna	70	28,500
Stockholm	60	21,300
Hamburg	60	23,600
Bremen	20	26,500

* GRP/capita is measured in terms of purchasing power parity.

Source: Johansson et al. (1998).

Stockholm currently belongs to the major metropolitan regions of Europe, although its size in terms of total GRP is about one quarter of the six largest regions.

The other important factor determining the development potential of the metropolitan region within this theoretical framework is the availability of durable regional characteristics of importance in the contemporary global economy. Table 19.3 illustrates the density of input resources and durable capacities, especially in terms of knowledge resources.

Table 19.3 Density of input resources and durable capacities in the Stockholm region, 1995/96

Input resources	Density relative to the rest of Sweden
Property value	19
Total labor supply	18
Labor with some tertiary education	18
Labor with bachelor's degree	20
Labor with graduate degree	32

Source: Johanssonet al. (1998).

As can be seen from this table, Stockholm has much greater access to labor with post-graduate education than would be expected from the density as measured by total labor supply. The importance of knowledge resources within a European context is discussed further in a later section of this chapter.

ECONOMIC DENSITY AND DIVERSITY

What types of advantages are brought about by economic density, and is density by itself enough to create advantages? Obviously, a dense urban region provides better opportunities than a less dense region in terms of person-to-person contacts. Hence activities which require face-to-face interaction would have superior locational conditions in a dense region, and also, if demand is growing, superior conditions for generating growth. However, suppose that density continues to attract contact-intensive activities and products. If this is the case, density will generate increasing densities, which sooner or later causes congestion phenomena, and thus increased transaction costs. Since metropolitan regions obviously *can* continue to grow over decades, one may ask if there are any facilitating remedies to this conflict. The answer lies in infrastructure investments. Improvements of the built environment and especially of the transport system may have the capacity to match the increasing density in such a way that a high density continues to provide advantages in a sustainable way. One counteracting and regulated force will always remain in the form of the increasing cost of space, which will continue to grow in a metropolitan area as long as the density and the infrastructure grow in balanced and parallel trajectories.

The Stockholm region provides illustrations of both strong and weak infrastructural development. In a Swedish, Scandinavian and Nordic context, it provides a relatively rich supply of R&D-related labor as well as of established organizations and industries that are R&D-intensive. A negative development factor is the supply of floor space for office, production and distribution activities within the region. In a continuous and rapid development of a metropolitan region it is vital that the region can facilitate the relocation of firms to premises with alternative attributes and versatility regarding space. Rigidities in this adjustment process may hamper the expansion of firms and give incentives for mobility out of the region.

Over the last three decades the annual rate of increase in floor space has continued to decline in the city of Stockholm, which is the core of the functional region (Strömquist, 1999). This has led to increasing rents, especially during the second half of the 1990s. Already in the mid- 1990s only a few metropolitan regions in Europe had as high floor-space costs as the city of Stockholm. This was true both for the CBD and other Stockholm locations. This provides a partial explanation for some of the relocation of headquarters away from Stockholm towards the Netherlands and England. The rigidities in the supply of space in Stockholm have probably reinforced the advantages of being located close to transport nodes such as Schiphol of the Randstad region in the Netherlands and the two major international airports of the London region.

An infrastructural advantage of the Stockholm region has been the capacity of its intra-urban passenger transport system. And still this system offers better conditions than in most other European metropolitan regions. But the long-term position of the Stockholm metropolitan region has not improved for a long time.

Quantitative measures of the density and scale of the market and the capacity of the infrastructure and the supply of highly skilled labor is of importance to the efficiency and growth potential of a metropolitan region. However, for a gateway region not only size and density but also *variety of economic activities* constitutes an even more important factor of development and attraction of flows from other economies. The combination of economic density and a large variety of economic activities stimulates interaction with other regions. In Sweden and possibly also in Northern Europe, there is no other region that has the variety of economic activities found in the Stockholm region. This can be illustrated by a sector classification that distinguishes between almost 750 different product categories.

Sweden has been subdivided into 110 functional regions (LA regions, i.e., labor-commuting market regions). For each such region, the number of private sectors (product categories) have been counted, excluding the smallest firms (with less than five active persons).

Table 19.4 Size of functional regions (LA regions) and scope of economic activitie,s 1997

LA region	Population size (Thousands)	Number of sectors *Scope*	Number of sectors with high knowledge intensity *Knowledge scope*
Stockholm	1,810	592	165
Göteborg, Malmö	881–651	546–545	149
7 largest medium-sized	292–169	440–357	112–85
15 other medium-sized	160–97	370–279	93–65
Smaller regions	90–51	262–210	72–46
Small regions	ca. 10	ca. 100	ca. 20

Source: Johansson et al. (1998).

The fact that small regions have such a limited scope of their economies is caused by the internal market potential being too small to cover the fixed and variable costs of production. This is especially pronounced for products that have recently been introduced, for example new financial instruments, media products and IT products. In the introductory phase intraregional interaction is a vital part of the growing demand, which means that both internal and external economies influence the growth process.

METROPOLITAN EXTERNALITIES

Economic Clusters

External economies of scale and other forms of positive externalities are referred to under many different headings in the economic literature, such as localization, agglomeration and urbanization economies. In more recent times the catchword 'regional cluster' has also become popular. Three major factors explain the existence of these phenomena:

- Diffusion of information and knowledge
- Neighborhood firms
- Specialized labor markets.

When firms with similar output mixes, customer markets and input requirements locate in the same place they have a tendency to attract each other as a consequence of positive externalities that each of them can benefit from. Interdependently, they form an environment for one another. In other words, they become a local public good. These firms may be referred to as a 'cluster core'. In principle this requires that for these firms external economies are stronger than internal scale economies. Moreover, when such firms locate jointly they can attract specialized labor through migration, education and the development of a 'tradition' in a regional learning process. In a similar way firms with output similarities have a tendency to attract specialized input suppliers which flock around the core cluster in order to exploit their own internal scale economies. Due to the attraction of a specialized labor supply and of specialized input suppliers, this gives rise to a location advantage in a cumulative process. This process is reinforced when customers of the core cluster also locate in the same region. The neighborhood firms consist of specialized input suppliers and customers. Together with the core firms they can form a regional cluster.

In a cluster of this type one can observe a process of information spillover both between the core firms and the neighborhood firms. Outside the market, these firms spread information and knowledge to each other about (i) production techniques, (ii) product attributes, (iii) input suppliers, and (iv) customers and the development of markets. Since information is diffused without any charges, the spillover has the form of a public good.

Which are the clusters of the economy in the Stockholm region? Before answering this question we may observe that in order to classify a certain economic sector as a member of a cluster we should require that the sector has a visible positive effect of its location. The requirement applied here is that the sector should be disproportionately large, i.e., have a large location quotient and hence be specialized.

Among the almost 600 sectors that we can find in the Stockholm region in 1997, as many as 170 have a high degree of specialization, employing 300,000 persons (38 percent of total employment). Of these, 230,000 were employed in sectors characterized by cluster economies, often in combination with internal scale economies. Another 70,000 persons were active in sectors for which internal scale economies was the dominating property.

The different clusters can be organized as macro-clusters, which in turn can be subdivided into specific clusters as follows:

- Media, marketing and advertisement – of which media-related activities are the largest cluster
- Financial activities
- Information, communication and office equipment – with IT consultants as the largest subsector
- Travel, transport and business services – where management consultants and public transportation represent the largest sub-sectors
- Medical and hygiene services, with pharmaceutical products being the largest subsector.

Table 19.5 Illustration of Stockholm's media cluster, 1996

Sector	Number of jobs	Sector	Number of jobs
Radio and TV transmitter equipment	11,460	News & photo distributors	790
Radio and TV companies	4,990	Supply of recorded music	620
Book publishing	2,870	Wholesale of recorded music	570
Theatre and concert firms	3,040	Other designers	440
Magazine & journal publishing	2,880	Other publishers	380
Film & video production	1,640	Cable TV companies	330
Production of radio and TV receivers	1,280	Distribution of film & video	290
Radio & TV, wholesale	860	Reproduction of film & video	70
Newspaper printing	830	Reproduction of recorded music	30
Other printing	820		
Graphical design	800	SUM	34,900

Source: Johansson et al. (1998).

The media cluster may be used to illustrate the spectrum of subsectors that form a cluster. Table 19.5 describes its composition. The striking picture that emerges is one of a very rich diversification, including both production and services, as well as the export and import of both products and ideas. A large share of the persons working in this cluster are potential movers between firms and different segments of the cluster. And this happens all the time.

The media cluster is typical in its correspondence to the schematic description given in the text.

Figure 19.2 emphasizes the systemic and synergistic conditions. Competitors, suppliers, customers and durable factors in the economic milieu are equally important.

Figure 19.2 Synergy interdependencies in a regional cluster

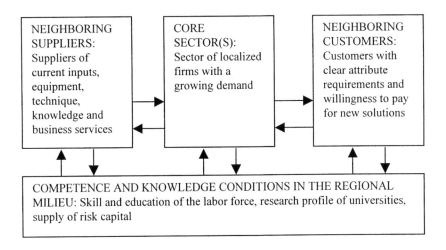

Export Intensity

As already stressed, the density of demand in a large urban region provides opportunities for diversified production, export and import activities. In a smaller region, the specialization has to be more narrow and concentrate on products which have a comparatively low distance sensitivity in existing export networks. As a consequence, one should expect a much larger number of sectors involved in export activities in the Stockholm region than elsewhere in Sweden.

In 1997 one could identify 295 such sectors, each including firms with regular export operations. Taking this as a reference and forming an index of the export diversity in Swedish functional regions, we obtain the following very skewed distribution:

- Export diversity in the Stockholm region   100
- Export diversity in the Göteborg and Malmö regions   64
- Export diversity in the Helsingborg region   43
- Export diversity in other medium-sized regions   20

A large home market with a diversified supply (in a functional region) also seems to provide similar opportunities to develop a diversified export pattern.

Sweden's Gateway for Import Flows

Eli Heckscher's classical statement about import flows being more diversified and embodying more novelties than export flows is indeed supported by the fact that the number of economic sectors with regular import activities is 40 percent larger than the number of sectors with export activities. The skewness of the regional distribution import activities is illustrated by Figure 19.3.

Figure 19.3 Regional distribution of import activities in Sweden

Number of importing sectors

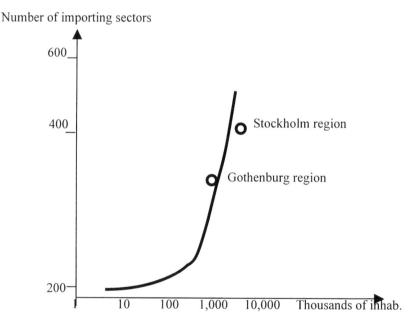

Import activities influence the change processes in the regional economy by bringing news and novelties from the world economy, and these provide incentives for entrepreneurs to develop both their own substitutes and complementary goods and services. The import flows reveal the demand and even the nature of the demand to local innovators. Moreover, product attributes and the composition of customers can be observed. The most important aspect is perhaps that regional firms in a large gateway economy can scan and assess novelties.

Import activities are primarily found in the following four groups: (i) trade technology, (ii) media-related firms, (iii) advanced business services and (iv) goods and services related to information and communication, including information technology. Table 19.6 enumerates sectors in which the number of importing firms is especially large.

Table 19.6 Sectors with a large number of importing firms in 1996

Sector	Number of firms	Stockholm's share of Swedish importers (%)
Wholesale of office equipment	220	64
Wholesale of telecommunications equipment and electronic components	168	66
Wholesale of medical equipment and pharmaceuticals	137	57
Wholesale of metering and precision instruments	97	62
Agency trade with non-computer machinery and industrial equipment	93	59
Computer consultants	39	68
Wholesale of perfumes and cosmetics	30	52
Wholesale of fuels	28	56
Agency trade with special assortments	26	59
Book publishing	21	64
Wholesale of music recording and video cassettes	20	69

Source: Johansson et al. (1998).

ENDOGENOUS KNOWLEDGE AND TECHNOLOGY IN REGIONAL GROWTH

Static economies of scale, due to the indivisibility of resources, and dynamic economies of scale, which are caused by 'learning by doing', are both important for the formation as well as the growth of metropolitan areas. In addition, these internal economies are reinforced by external economies of scale. These factors have together accounted for urban growth for more than a century of industrialization.

However, internal and external economies of scale have become much more important in the post-industrial reorientation of economies. Beginning in the 1960s, research and development have become strategic corporate investments.

New products, processes and designs have become subject to conscious profitability evaluations along the lines of what was earlier reserved for investments in machinery, buildings and other physical assets. This non-Schumpeterian view of investments into new technologies and products has deepened the meaning of economic dynamics. Increasing the investments into existing machinery can increase growth rates, especially if there are substantial internal economies of scale. Investing into new machinery adapted to the production of newly invented products may, however, generate internal and external economies of scale that did not exist before the innovation. The greater the research and development investments are, the more dominant these second-order dynamical effects will become.

The increasing tendency to endogenize technological development implies an increasing importance of metropolitan areas with good internal and external accessibility to markets. It is also evident that regions with a well-developed infrastructure of scientific research and education will have a long-term advantage in the transition from an industrial economy to an economy characterized by endogenous technological growth. The following sections of this chapter are devoted to a discussion of the scientific infrastructure of the Stockholm region in a comparative perspective.

THE STOCKHOLM REGION AS A GATEWAY OF GLOBAL SCIENTIFIC INTERACTION

Extensive continental and global interactions among scientific and industrial researchers have existed for a long time. Especially in the postwar period, large groups of scientists have regularly come together in international conferences, seminars and workshops. The face-to-face contacts of these gatherings have often led to the formation of international scientific research projects, resulting in jointly published papers in internationally distributed scientific journals.

During the last three decades of this century, international scientific collaboration leading to the publication of scientific papers in refereed journals has been growing at two-digit annual growth rates. The scholars of the Stockholm region are no exceptions to this global trend. The two campuses of the Karolinska Institute and the medical faculty of Uppsala University have been especially important in the development of the Stockholm region into a global gateway for scientific collaboration.

The metropolitan region of Stockholm (including Uppsala) is part of a growing interactivity within the scientific world. Table 19.7 gives the pattern of the scientific cooperation between Sweden as a whole, the metropolitan region of Stockholm and different scientifically prominent European countries in the second half of the 1980s.

Table 19.7 Scientific cooperation between Sweden, the metropolitan region of Stockholm and different European countries in the second half of the 1980s

Cooperation with	Stockholm	Sweden
UK	17	18
Germany	14	15
Denmark	10	13
France	11	10
Norway	9	10
Finland	10	9
Italy	9	7
Switzerland	8	7
The Netherlands	5	5
Belgium	4	3
Austria	2	2
Spain	1	1
Total	100	100

Source: Olle Persson, Inforsk, Umeå, On line search in the Science Citation Index.

As can be seen from this table, the pattern of interaction in the production of scientific papers is very similar for Sweden as a whole and the Stockholm metropolitan region. This is of course not surprising, as the Stockholm metropolitan region accounts for more than 50 percent of Sweden's scientific activity. Some small differences can however be noted.

The Stockholm metropolitan region shows a less concentrated pattern of interaction. The Nordic profile is not as pronounced. Especially the interaction with Denmark is much weaker than for the country as a whole, which is primarily explained by the rather intensive interactivity taking place between Lund and Copenhagen, which will probably intensify even more after the completion of the bridge between Malmö and Copenhagen.

The pattern of global scientific cooperation can be represented by a gravity equation in which the driving forces are the total scientific activity of the cooperating regions, while the intensity of cooperation is dampened by the time distance by air transport between the regions, and linguistic and cultural differences.

According to this (estimated) equation, the largest volume of scientific interactions will be found between two large regions in terms of total scientific activity and which are close to each other in terms of transport distance, language and culture. This explains the high degree of interaction between the Stockholm region and the metropolitan regions of the other Nordic countries, as well as the large interaction flows between the Stockholm region and medium-sized and large scientific regions in Britain, the United States and Canada. Scientifically, the Stockholm region is now integrated into an Anglo-American cluster of regions with strong links to other parts of the Nordic region but also to Germany, France, Italy and Switzerland.

STOCKHOLM AS A KNOWLEDGE GATEWAY

Currently and even more in the future, patterns of location and trade, the productivity of regions and their employment structure will increasingly be determined by a combination of specialized accumulation of knowledge by research and development and the dynamics of internal and external economies of scale.

Scientific strategies initiated long ago will generate comparative advantages that are successively reinforced by specialization in techniques initially derived from the strategically developed scientific platform. This is clearly the case of the Stockholm region.

As early as in the 1940s, the Swedish government initiated a health improvement strategy, intimately related to a science policy oriented towards the life sciences in general and biomedicine, clinical medicine and pharmacology in particular. A similar trend was followed in a number of Northern European countries. By the end of the 1970s the scientific profile of Sweden had become highly specialized, as illustrated by Table 19.8.

Table 19.8 Relative scientific specialization measured by a bibliometric publication index (OECD = 100)

Field Country	Bio-medi-cine	Clin. medi-cine	Bio-logy	Physics	Tech-nolo-gy	Chem-istry	Geo-science	Mathe-matics
Sweden	129	125	110	71	67	64	62	45
Denmark	116	133	97	91	45	45	78	74
UK	106	118	95	83	79	79	95	70
Norway	105	110	141	56	50	50	194	72
Finland	98	123	107	86	47	47	73	81
Holland	107	106	105	91	86	86	98	90
Germany	7	86	90	145	116	116	97	117
France	104	99	92	120	104	104	113	133
Switzerland	108	99	97	144	97	97	85	59
Italy	93	105	81	125	109	109	102	131
Austria	74	121	75	108	89	89	87	143
Japan	110	73	95	132	152	152	49	68
Australia	89	100	131	63	72	72	175	113
Canada	97	85	124	77	81	81	156	132
New Zealand	66	104	160	47	69	69	177	97
Iceland	114	131	99	50	24	24	328	78

Source: Inforsk, Umeå, 1990.

The benchmark for this specialization table is the vector of relative proportions allocated to the different fields for the OECD region as a whole. Relative scientific specialization is calculated as relative deviations from the OECD vector. The material is subdivided into three distinguishable clusters of countries according to their pattern of scientific specialization. In the first group biomedicine and clinical medicine as well as biology represent a life-science focus of the scientific platform. This focus is especially clear-cut in Sweden, closely followed by Britain and other Northern European countries. The other cluster contains Japan and a number of countries in Western Central and Southern Europe. The focus of this cluster is on physics, chemistry or mathematics, i.e., a platform of high-tech industry in the non-life sciences.

The third cluster is dominated by sparsely populated countries like Australia and Canada. These countries tend to have their focus on a scientific platform dominated by geo-sciences and biology.

The US is not included in this table. It seems to be a country large enough to afford a non-specialized platform, exhibiting the same structure of science as is found in the OECD as a whole.

The table gives a clear indication of the degree to which Swedish scientific research is being channeled into the life sciences and especially into medicine, which is crucial for the research and development projects of the pharmaceutical and medical technology companies, which constitute a fast-growing sector in the Stockholm–Uppsala region.

Another measure than the one given in the table above is the Swedish and Stockholm share in the world production of scientific products. The average share of the world's production of scientific outputs is around 1.5 percent for Sweden as a whole and around 0.8 percent for the Stockholm–Uppsala region, while the world percentage share of published papers in the field of clinical medicine has as an average over a long time-period exceeded 3 percent for Sweden as a whole and 1.5 per cent for the Stockholm–Uppsala region.

The global impact of scientific production varies to a great extent between different OECD countries as measured by the average number of citations per article.

Table 19.9 Global impact of scientific research as measured by the average number of citations per article, 1980–89

Switzerland	8.7
USA	8.6
Sweden	7.4
Denmark	6.8
Netherlands	6.8
UK	6.5
Belgium	5.9
Germany	5.8
Norway	5.6
Finland	5.4
France	5.4
Japan	4.9
Italy	4.3
Austria	3.9
Spain	3.0
Portugal	2.0

Source: Inforsk, Umeå, Sweden, Bibliometric On Line Search.

As shown in Table 19.9, Sweden ranks among the three leading countries in terms of scientific impact (measured by the frequency of citations).

In terms of total production and scientific productivity, Sweden also belongs to a group of countries strongly oriented to generating comparative advantages based on a relatively large science platform. The most science-oriented countries in the world are currently Israel, Switzerland, Sweden, Canada, Britain, Denmark and the US, as illustrated by Table 19.10.

Table 19.10 Total scientific production, 1988–90 in different countries, measured as number of published articles in refereed journals (US: index value 100)

	Total number of articles	Articles per capita of population
USA	100	100
UK	24	106
Germany	20	63
Japan	19	39
Russia	16	14
France	15	65
Canada	12	117
Italy	8	33
India	6	2
Australia	6	85
Netherlands	6	93
Sweden	5	132
Spain	4	26
Switzerland	4	142
China	3	1
Taiwan	1	13
Israel	3	154
Denmark	2	105
New Zealand	1	94
Finland	2	87
Norway	1	76

Source: Inforsk, Umeå, Sweden, Bibliometric On Line Search.

A statistical test of the relation between total production and scientific productivity in terms of the production per capita shows that there is no statistically significant relation between the total size of production and the level of scientific productivity. There are of course economies of scale due to the publicness of scientific ideas, but these economies of scale have to be exploited within each scientific field and do not influence scientific productivity on the aggregate scale of scientific research and development.

Sweden ranks among the leading countries both in terms of scientific productivity and in terms of global impact. This is a consequence of the high priority given to research and development in general as well as a consequence of the high degree of specialization of scientific research in fields that are necessary for the creation of an infrastructural arena for producting medical, pharmaceutical and biotechnical products for the global market.

The Stockholm–Uppsala region has developed a relatively strong position as one of the five leading scientific gateways of Europe, which is clearly demonstrated in the chapter by Wichmann Matthiessen et al. (Chapter 2). It can be shown that the rank order of scientific regions of Europe has not changed to any substantial degree from the 1980s until the end of the 1990s. Both in terms of the publicness of science and the slow change in the positioning of scientific regions it is reasonable to regard the scientific position of a region as possibly the most important infrastructure determining the long-term development potential of the region.

THE RELATIVE IMPORTANCE OF INDUSTRIAL COMPLEXES IN THE ECONOMY OF THE STOCKHOLM REGION

The research and development oriented industry of the Stockholm region is dominated by a number of globally oriented large companies. The most important examples of such companies are ABB (electrical engineering products), Ericsson (communication equipment), Scania (trucks), AstraZeneca (pharmaceuticals), Pharmacia-Upjohn (pharmaceuticals) and Electrolux (household appliances).

All these firms allocate a large share of their revenues to research and development activities. The two pharmaceutical companies in particular have extensive cooperation programs with the Karolinska Institute and with the School of Medicine and Pharmacology at Uppsala University. Recently, with the growth of research efforts in biotechnology and medical production technology, this collaboration has also been expanding toward the Royal Institute of Technology, which is now launching a broadly based biotechnology research and higher education program.

A CHANGING STRUCTURE OF EXPORTS

The transformation of the Swedish economy from a classical industrial nation into a knowledge, communication and information economy has changed the structure of exports. Especially pronounced in this transformation is the reorientation from *volume* to *value* of exported products. The inflation-adjusted dollar value of Swedish exports to the European countries has risen by 3.3 percent annually from 1960 to 1997. This increase in the value per ton exported is a reflection of a changing sectoral composition of exports as well as an increased value per ton within each individual export sector.

The reasons for this transformation from volume to value of manufacturing and exported goods are twofold. One the one hand the accelerating growth of manufacturing in the newly industrialized countries is forcing Sweden and other OECD countries to shift production away from labor- and natural-resource-intensive commodity production to products intensive in the use of knowledge, information and communications. But also in the production within any given industrial sector there is a shift toward a higher level of product complexity. One example is the production of automobiles and trucks, which is becoming more complex regarding both the informational complexity of the production specifications and the inputs of information technology, the use of knowledge and the multitude of different inputs needed for the completion of the final product.

CONCLUSIONS

Traditionally, the Stockholm region has since the seventeenth century been a political and economic gateway to the sparsely populated parts of Northern and North-eastern Europe. This role was reinforced during the remarkably successful period of industrialization from 1870 to 1970, when Sweden's growth rate and rate of industrialization were the highest in the world, together with Japan. During this industrialization period the relative share of the Stockholm region in Swedish employment and population grew from less than one-tenth to more than one-fifth. However, the industrialization of Sweden, which was based on the exploitation of natural resources, preserved an already established historical role of Stockholm as a gateway to Nordic and north-eastern countries and regions.

With the transformation of Sweden and the other Scandinavian countries into post-industrial C-societies, based on creativity and research and development, the Stockholm region has grown regarding both the size and scope of its interaction with other regions.

The important factor of density contributes to both the external and internal increasing returns to scale, which are crucial to newly established industries. The density of economic activity is in general close to twenty times greater in the Stockholm functional region when compared to the average density of Sweden. The density of labor with post-graduate education is more than thirty times greater.

In the transformation into the new postindustrial C-society, with its reliance on research and development and other creative activities, regions with a high knowledge density and a large scientific potential have proven to be especially attractive to high-tech and other knowledge firms. The Stockholm region currently belongs to the five most successful scientific regions in Europe, whether measured as total production, quantitative scientific productivity or as the impact on other parts of the world in the scale and scope of its interactions.

REFERENCES

Andersson, Å.E., C. Anderstig and B. Hårsman (1990), 'Knowledge and communications infrastructure and regional economic change', *Regional Science and Urban Economics*, **20**, 359–76.

Andersson, Å.E. and B. Johansson (1998), 'A Schloss Laxenburg model of product cycle dynamics', in M.J. Beckmann et al. (eds), *Knowledge and Networks in a Dynamic Economy*, Berlin, Heidelberg and New York: Springer-Verlag, pp.181–219.

Henderson, (1974), 'The Sizes and Types of Cities', *American Economic Review*, **64**, 640–56.

Johansson, B., U. Strömquist and P. Åberg (1998), *Regioner, handel och tillväxt (Regions, Trade and Growth)*, The Regional Planning and Traffic Office, Stockholm.

Krugman, P. (1979), 'Increasing returns, monopolistic competition and international trade', *Journal of International Economics*, **9**, 469–79.

Nadiri, M.I. (1993), *Innovations and Technological Spillovers*, Cambridge, MA: National Bureau of Economic Research.

Ohlin, B. (1967), *Interregional and International Trade*, (revision of the 1933 original), Cambridge, MA: Harvard University Press.

Strömquist, U. (1999), *Företagsplats Stockholm – Analyst för tillväxtpolitik (A Host for Companies – An Analysis for growth policy)*, Stockholm: Temaplan.

Wichmann Matthiessen, C. and Å.E. Andersson (1993), *Öresundsregionen: Kreativitet, Integration, Vækst*, Copenhagen: Munksgaard-Rosinante.

20. The Role of Institutions and Self-Organizing Networks in the Economic History of Regions

David E. Andersson

A common belief is that the network character of the emerging globalized economy represents a new development, which is replacing hierarchical national economies. This belief is hardly justified, since market interactions have caused nodes of economic activity – and linkages between nodes – to arise ever since geographical specialization of production and interregional trade was first practiced. The Hanseatic League and the network of city states in northern Italy are examples of pre-industrial network economies (Snickars, 1993). The new network economy is thus not a manifestation of a new concept. Rather, it represents a dramatic expansion in the geographical extent and multiplicity of interactions, as well as the emergence of new and increasingly dense networks.

The belief that network economies are replacing nation-state economies disregards the interplay between the two predominant forces that have shaped economic development: the state and the market. The state has an intrinsic tendency to accumulate power over time and to centralize economic decision-making. Conversely, the market tends to decentralize economic power.

The 'capitalistic nation state' of the industrial era was an attempt to nationally delimit and guide the industrial network economy, so that the structure of urban nodes and transport linkages was best represented as an integrated national network. The natural geographical extent of a national economy was a consequence of the typical infrastructural organization of the industrial era: sparse and relatively slow networks of rail and sea transport (Andersson, 1993).

Consequently, the market agglomeration process which gives rise to a rank-size distribution of city size (Batten, 1999) also was best approximated by taking the nation state as the pertinent economic unit. In terms of the subject matter of this book, the gateway regions of industrial society served as gateways to a national or subnational economy, rather than to a continental or multinational region.

EVOLVING NETWORKS AND LOGISTICAL REVOLUTIONS

Andersson and Strömquist (1988) argue that the physical infrastructure – especially transportation and communication networks – is of crucial importance in explaining long-term economic growth and restructuring. They especially emphasize the role of investments in critical links and the creation of new networks.

When a link connects two regions with different resource bases, it is inevitable that gains from integration will arise. This is because the effect of joint resource exploitation generically exceeds the sum of the effects from two isolated resource bases. Andersson and Strömquist think of the evolution of ever-larger trade and production areas in terms of the marginal creation of links between pairs of regions. A critical link is a link that bridges two already established networks, and which results in a dramatic expansion to the extent of the market.

When non-critical links are added to existing networks, we will experience a slowly changing evolution of the economic system. When a critical link is added, however, a revolutionary restructuring of the entire economy will result. Andersson and Strömquist call such a restructuring a 'logistical revolution'.

Sometimes, however, the revolutionary trigger is not a critical space-bridging link, but a critical space-bridging technology. This is because the density, speed and flexibility of a network determine what kind of interactions it can support. The slow-speed transport networks that predominate in an industrial society are best suited for moving goods from their production sites to their markets. The economic theory of the industrial era was also influenced by the prevailing network conditions, conceptualizing an economic system of stationary stocks of labor and capital (i.e., a national or regional economy) and flows of goods between the stocks (i.e., trade). However, the superimposition of ever more comprehensive high-speed networks has expanded the scope for interactions. For example, the air transportation network makes possible regular face-to-face meetings even between people living at great distances from one another. The stock of labor can no longer be regarded as stationary by necessity, not even if conventional temporal constraints – such as a specific year or month – are imposed on our concept of an economy. This has led some economists to think of the post-industrial economy as a multi-layered network economy (Batten et al., 1988; Kobayashi, 1993).

Nonetheless, a logistical revolution does not imply that the preceding economic structure will disappear in its entirety. Rather, a new economic system is superimposed on the preceding system. The newer system will however be of greater importance in terms of its overall contribution to the economy, even if most people continue to work within the older system of economic behavior in the initial phase of the new stage of development.

An example of how a critical link caused a logistical revolution is the arrival of trade capitalism in thirteenth-century Europe. This was caused by the establishment of a new shipping route from the Mediterranean to the Baltic Sea – which new shipbuilding technology facilitated – and a new bridge linking Northern and Southern Europe (Pirenne, 1936). These two links together caused a transformation of the economy. Thousands of new cities appeared in the following one hundred years. An urban network economy was superimposed on the predominantly rural, feudal system. The new urban economies became centers of trade and culture, with workshops and manufactories for the production of goods to exchange with the agricultural surplus. Transactions were facilitated by means of specie money and middlemen. In this way, a new urban capitalism emerged.

THE GEOGRAPHICAL LOCATION OF GATEWAYS

The pre-industrial network economy also caused some cities to become important nodes. These nodes served both as gateways to their hinterlands and as saddle points between regions. The infrastructural technology of the period was a key determinant for the location of these gateways. In contrast to current conditions, the sea served as a bridge rather than as a barrier to interactions. This was because sea transport was faster than land transport, owing to the primitive state of road and road vehicle technology. It was no coincidence that the peripheral cities of the Hanseatic League were seaports. Nor was it any coincidence that the Danish–Swedish border went through the sparsely inhabited woodlands of present-day south central Sweden, rather than through Öresund, a sound connecting the North Atlantic with the Baltic Sea.

The predominant nodes of the pre-industrial economy were either seaports such as Venice or Lübeck, or towns connected to the sea through navigable rivers, for example Bruges, Florence or Antwerp. Because of the lack of good roads, these nodes had relatively small functional hinterlands. Indeed, it was common for these urban nodes to be organized as autonomous city-states.

Although most of the important towns had better-than-average natural endowments, the rise of some of them to predominant positions is an illustration of the so-called 'lock-in' effect of urban development (Batten, 1999). This is when an initial perceived geographical advantage leads to a major infrastructure investment, which then triggers a self-reinforcing process of additional investments and accumulation of capital, leaving other locations behind. The implication is that time-specific perceptions of geographical advantage may influence the future locations of gateway regions, even when subsequent technological developments change the factors determining geographical advantage. The spontaneous accumulation of economic interactions and infrastructure in large cities may account for the extraordinary durability of these cities, as opposed to both nation-states and the more specialized smaller towns.

Apart from good natural endowments, gateways also require a central location *vis-à-vis* major product markets. This constraint was especially important at the earlier stages of economic development, because of greater both transportation costs and the geographical concentration of economic progress. From the thirteenth to the eighteenth century, all major economic gateways were situated near the Atlantic or Mediterranean coasts of Western Europe. The friction of space precluded any major gateways from developing in places such as Russia, Southeast Asia, or the Americas. With the onset of industrialization, the 'feasibility space' of gateway regions expanded to include the east coast of the Americas and the interior parts of Europe. But it is only from the 1970s onwards that the combined effects of reduced spatial friction and newly developed markets have enabled any region to be a potential major gateway, save perhaps for Sub-Saharan Africa.

THE LOCATION OF MOBILE PRODUCTION FACTORS AND INSTITUTIONAL QUALITY

A von Thünen approach can be used to describe the spatial pattern of economic activity by mobile and immobile production factors (von Thünen, 1826). Von Thünen's model assumes that a central marketplace is located on a plane of uniform fertility. It is further assumed that the price of a good (i.e., a mobile good) is determined in the central marketplace. An implication of the theory is that the transport cost of moving the good from an outlying location to the marketplace has to be absorbed in some way. The way that this transport cost is absorbed – given uniform fertility, uniform institutions, and a free market system – is through compensating land prices. Therefore, the increasing transport costs are exactly compensated by reduced land prices. (A more complex application of the von Thünen model introduces the notion of several goods with different space intensities of production, leading to spatial separation of land uses – Alonso, 1964.)

Kasper (1994) has extended von Thünen's model to deal with the location of mobile production factors and the spatial differentiation of institutions. First, there is a distinction between unit rates of return to relatively mobile production factors (firms, skilled labor) and relatively immobile production factors (land, unskilled labor, government administration). Second, both internal and external institutions vary across space. Kasper argues that the mobile production factors will look for locations which have desirable institutional properties from their point of view. This is to say that the owners of the mobile production factors will look for locations with a favourable combination of the expected unit rate of return and expected risk, relative to other places.

Examples of internal institutions that facilitate high rates of return to the mobile production factors include an acceptance of low wages (relative to productivity), and a willingness to learn. Risk-reducing internal institutions include high and consistent levels of honesty and reliability. Favorable external institutions include reliable government administration, the rule of law, and constitutional constraints on politicians.

Another, classical, way of approaching the relocation decisions of firms is to view them as a search for the cost-minimizing location. Each firm attempts to minimize a weighted sum of production costs, transport costs and transaction costs.

The weights of the three types of cost vary between firms. For example, production costs tend to be the most important consideration for firms engaged in electronic assembly, while transport costs are more important for heavy industry and localized services. Transaction costs, meanwhile, are especially important for transportable services, which make up a large and growing share in post-industrial economies. Douglass North has estimated that transaction costs make up more than 55 percent of GDP in advanced economies (North, 1992). Thus most firms in developed countries have a strong incentive to choose locations that allow them to economize on transaction costs.

INSTITUTIONS AND TRANSACTION COSTS

It is transaction costs that are most influenced by the institutional setting. The transaction costs that firms face can be thought of as a function of the various internal and external institutions of the economic entity in which the firm operates. However, transaction costs are not limited to the continually recurring, variable costs described by Coase (1937). They also include the fixed transaction costs associated with investment, entrepreneurship and innovation.

Giersch (1979) distinguishes between the production of three types of goods: Heckscher–Ohlin goods (with the von Thünen assumption of a homogeneous plane and given knowledge), Ricardo goods (differences in climate and natural resource endowment), and Schumpeter goods. Schumpeter goods (after Schumpeter, 1912) differ from the first two types of good in that the production function is new, or that the preference for the good has not yet been revealed. Schumpeter goods are closely related to entrepreneurship and innovation, and their production is thus influenced by fixed transaction costs. According to Giersch:

> These goods, often referred to as product cycle goods, can be called Schumpeter goods. Being the result of innovation, they will be produced where human capital is abundant and where the social atmosphere and the institutional arrangements are attractive to firms and persons who are prepared to devote resources to R&D and to risky ventures in expectation of transitory monopoly gains. An innovative sector added to a von Thünen cone that transforms the cone into a volcano. Center–periphery trade now also includes the lava of knowledge (transfer of technology) incorporated in Schumpeter goods.

An implication of the relationship between fixed transaction costs and innovative production is that innovative firms and persons will be attracted to locations with favorable institutions for dynamic competition among entrepreneurs, as well as to locations with knowledge and accessibility advantages.

Hong Kong is a good example of how favorable institutions have attracted a sufficient number of firms and entrepreneurs to make it an innovation center in infrastructure, financial services, logistics and light manufacturing (Enright et al., 1997). Another implication is that innovative centers or nodes must continue to generate new knowledge and Schumpeter goods in order to retain their centrality.

Kasper argues that the economic ascendancy of the East Asian 'tigers' was due to a great extent to the effect of institutions that did not add too high (fixed and variable) transaction costs on the (initially) low production costs in manufacturing.

From a more dynamic perspective, the accumulation of mobile capital and productivity improvements in certain locations eventually leads to an expansion of domestic product markets. The peripheral position of the rapidly developing East Asian economies has in this way become less peripheral relative to world markets, as the East Asian economies have become important product markets for each other. Even in the absence of the dramatic reductions in transport and communication costs that have taken place in the postwar period, Asian economies would have become less peripheral.

Cities such as Hong Kong and Singapore have for this reason become gateways of global importance comparable to major European gateways such as Frankfurt or Milan.

THE IMPACT OF GLOBALIZATION AND INTERJURISDICTIONAL COMPETITION

The globalization of markets that has been occurring since the 1960s has been branded the '4th logistical revolution' by some economists (Andersson and Strömquist, 1988; Kobayashi, 1993). In this revolution, we are witnessing the effects of a critical space-bridging technology. The new globalized economy, which has been superimposed on national economies, has been made possible only through the emergence of a new integrated computing and communication technology. It is through this technology that the transaction costs associated with international financial flows have been brought down. It also has led to a globalization of the availability of knowledge and information.

In *The Rise and Decline of Nations*, Mancur Olson (1982) described how the accumulation of rent-seeking interest groups in stable democracies leads to an increasing diversion of resources from wealth-creating to redistributive activities, leading to institutional decay and higher transaction costs for innovative activities. Olson claimed that the only way to halt this process was either through destructive shocks to the system, such as a war, or through thoroughgoing reorganizations of the political and administrative structures. However, it is becoming increasingly evident that logistical shocks have a similar effect.

Globalization has not only decelerated the growth of official government spending, it has also globalized the informal economy. Moreover, the growing importance of interjurisdictional competition has made the effects of domestic rent-seeking more obvious (Streit, 1996) argues that interjurisdictional competition has had two roles. In addition to its role as a constraint on legislative power, it has also been a procedure for discovering efficient institutions.)

The current economic transformation is not the only example of how an external logistic shock rejuvenates the economy by halting the accumulation of political power. An early instance of a similar effect was the proliferation of towns in the thirteenth and fourteenth centuries. This had the effect of limiting the scope for feudal lords to exploit landless serfs, since the opportunities for 'rural flight' increased.

Thus there was a causal chain linking critical space-bridging links to urbanization to decentralization of economic power. The industrial revolution is yet another example, linking new transport links and technologies to the abolition of guilds, increased international trade, accelerated urbanization, and greater opportunities for entrepreneurship.

LOGISTICAL REVOLUTIONS AND THE ORGANIZATION OF NETWORKS

Logistical revolutions also have a profound effect on the character and hierarchical organization of infrastructural networks. In general, older networks have had more of the characteristics of a made order, whereas newer networks such as the Internet have much in common with the spontaneous order exhibited by market interactions (Hayek, 1982).

The effect of the industrial revolution was to establish networks between national gateways (or nodes), supplemented by regional nodes according to the hub-and-spoke principle. The long-distance links mainly conveyed goods and natural resources, as well as to some extent political (military and diplomatic) flows.

The character and organization of post-industrial networks are more complex. Perhaps most important is the heterogeneity of network organization, which makes it possible for different organizing principles to coexist. The shipping network has retained a decidedly industrial structure, with hub seaports serving as terminals for tradable goods. This network has however been in decline, with the notable exception of East Asian shipping (owing to the lack of overland links between the region's five most developed economies).

The rail network is in some ways similar, but the proliferation of high-speed linkages in the densely populated corridors of Western Europe and Japan has augmented its traditional role of transporting goods and commuters with the function of conveying irregular knowledge flows for the purpose of face-to-face meetings. This knowledge function is even more important to the air transport network, which is also organized according to the hub-and-spoke principle.

An interesting post-industrial network is the road network, which combines an industrial function (the transportation of goods and commuters) with a post-industrial organizing principle (a dense network of links with many hierarchical levels of nodes). The most revolutionizing network, however, is the integrated computer and communication network known as the Internet. This network has the thoroughly post-industrial function of transmitting disembodied knowledge and information, in addition to an absence of space-specific nodes or links.

Still, the near-universal availability of the Internet does not render location considerations irrelevant, since the disembodied knowledge that it transmits is typically a complement to the embodied knowledge communicated through face-to-face meetings.

THE INFRASTRUCTURE AND NETWORKING POSSIBILITIES

This last qualification alludes to a distinction between two levels of connectivity: (infrastructural) networks and networking (or activity networks), where the networks have the role of making networking possible and desirable. In classical industrial societies, the main networks encompassed railroads, sea-lanes and roads. These networks constituted the arena for networking in the shape of international and interregional trade in manufactured goods and natural resources. In post-industrial society, the air transportation network and the Internet are the main supplements to the 'industrial' infrastructure networks. The proliferation of networking is much more dramatic. As mentioned earlier, the air transportation network serves as the main conduit for embodied knowledge. The Internet, on the other hand, facilitates a great number of new activity networks requiring access to flows of disembodied knowledge and information such as long-distance retailing, financial services, scientific cooperation and coordination of logistical systems. The combined effects of the air and computer networks have also made possible the creation of decentralized, multinational firms.

The multi-layered character of post-industrialism makes it impossible to identify an unambiguous hierarchy of gateways. In industrial society, this problem was much more straightforward. New York was the unequivocal gateway to the United States, by virtue of being the main hub (and interchange) of the railroad and shipping networks, on which tangible goods were transported. Even in countries with a landlocked gateway, such as France, the primacy of one gateway was evident. Although Marseilles and Calais were the most important seaports, they did not function as national gateways. Goods had for the most part to be transported through Paris, the hub of the national rail network.

When looking at contemporary networks, the picture becomes much less clear-cut. In East Asia, for example, Hong Kong is the quantitatively most important air transportation and shipping node. The most important road and rail node, meanwhile, is Tokyo. When we shift the focus to find the quantitatively predominant global hub for infrastructure, the picture becomes even more diverse: Chicago (air transportation), Hong Kong (shipping) and Tokyo (rail). The same diversity applies to centers for networking: New York (stocks), London (currency transactions), Los Angeles (entertainment services), Seattle (book retailing). It is the purpose of this book to look at the diversity of global and regional gateways, from multifunctional gateways such as New York City to smaller regions with a gateway niche such as Miami, Vancouver or Stockholm.

GATEWAY FUNCTIONS

Some economists (e.g., Jacobs, 1969; Sassen, 1994) distinguish between three types of location with nodal functions (see also Chapter 15 by Koschatzky:

1. Export-oriented production zones
2. Offshore financial centers
3. Global cities

This trichotomy focuses on activities rather than the infrastructure, where global cities are both financial centers and export-oriented production zones. An exported-oriented production center functions mainly as a saddle point between a production-intensive hinterland and overseas markets. This was the typical nodal function of the gateway cities of the industrial era. Still, there are several cities in modern economies that have retained this function, and which are of global import in terms of infrastructure utilization. An export-oriented production center can be located in an economy that exports high-value-added goods and services (e.g., Milan). It can also be located in an economy based on low-tech manufacturing (e.g., Shanghai). In the latter case, the functional hinterland tends to be more populous, and production tends to rely more on establishing relationships with multinational corporations.

A pertinent feature of an offshore financial center is a high concentration of financial services – in the form of banks, business consulting firms, stock exchanges, etc. – in a geographically small area. This type of node often serves as the location for the regional headquarters of multinational corporations, owing to their need for frequent meetings with lenders, investors and consultants. Examples of offshore financial centers include Singapore (Southeast Asia), Frankfurt (Germany and Central Europe), and Stockholm (Scandinavia and the Baltic countries).

However, the emphasis on financial services as one of only two functions of a nodal region is too confining. Financial centers may instead represent the most visible special case of a more general class of knowledge centers, where a center for the production of knowledge may also specialize in, for instance, high-technology innovation, mass media, design or entertainment. This consideration leads to the following, revised, trichotomy:

1. Export-oriented production zones
2. Knowledge centers (creative or innovative production of transportable services)
3. Global city regions

Global city regions, finally, have nodal roles both as exporters of goods and services and as producers of knowledge. The region that first comes to mind as a global gateway is arguably New York, which is home to the world's most important stock exchange. But New York is also the premier gateway to the economy of the northeastern United States and its high-value-added production of goods and services, with an emphasis on knowledge services such as research and development and culture-for-export.

London and Tokyo are two other cities with similar combinations of being nodes in the global financial and intellectual networks and exporters of various goods and services. Los Angeles and Hong Kong represent a somewhat different type of a global city region. They have attained global status by means of socioeconomic segmentation (see Suarez-Villa, Chapter 5). In the Los Angele –San Diego–Tijuana region, a multinational corporation may take advantage of both the accumulation of knowledge (especially in the high-technology sector and in entertainment) on the US side of the border and the low labor costs on the Mexican side and among the less skilled immigrants in Los Angeles. This spatial concentration of complementary advantages is augmented by the strong cultural links to the Spanish-speaking and East Asian worlds. A similar phenomenon has arisen in Hong Kong, where the low-cost manufacturing sector in Guangdong complements the advanced service sector in Hong Kong. In addition, Hong Kong serves as a cultural bridge between Greater China, Southeast Asia and the English-speaking world.

ENTREPRENEURSHIP AND MOBILE PRODUCTION FACTORS

Another distinction is between cities that have attained nodal status through domestic entrepreneurialism and cities that have attained it by attracting mobile production factors. We find both types of cities at similar levels of development. Also, the mobile production factors are not only embodied in multinational corporations, but also in mobile entrepreneurial individuals.

Domestic entrepreneurialism has been the predominant factor in gateways with a high concentration of small and medium-sized companies and with a tradition of restrictions against flows of capital and labor. The best examples of this type of node among the case studies in this book are probably Taiwan's west coast and Milan.

Entrepreneurialism has also been an important factor in the growth of cities with a history of immigration, although in this case the entrepreneurs are often mobile production factors, which are attracted to amenable business environments. This type of mobile entrepreneurialism typifies North

American gateways, but is less common in the Old World (Hong Kong and London are exceptions).

Mobile production factors in the shape of multinational corporations and financial firms have been most important in nodes with a history of 'planned growth', such as Shanghai, Singapore and Stockholm. These cities have had a more regulated approach to business formation, which has discouraged domestic entrepreneurship. In the more successful 'planned nodes', however, low labor costs relative to productivity and good infrastructure provision has offset part of the regulatory impediments, especially for large established firms, which can afford higher start-up costs.

We noted earlier how truly global gateways combined the categories of export-oriented production with knowledge-intensive services. In the same vein, global cities are cities that have enabled domestic and 'imported' small-scale entrepreneurship, while attracting or retaining the headquarters of multinational corporations and banks.

GEOGRAPHY, INFRASTRUCTURE AND POLITICS

Geographical, infrastructural, and political factors[1] influence which cities become important nodes in the global network economy. Geographical factors refer to the accessibility advantage afforded to nodes with a central location *vis-à-vis* transport networks and product markets. Such nodes have a better initial position because the transport costs associated with spatial friction are lower. This also offers them some leeway regarding (intranodal) infrastructural and political deficiencies compared with more peripheral locations. In Europe, such a geographical advantage is supposed to exist within the corridor known as the 'European Banana', stretching from southeastern England to northern Italy via southwestern Germany and Switzerland.

SOFT AND HARD INFRASTRUCTURES

The infrastructural factors of a node include the soft infrastructure of the institutional framework and the hard infrastructure of the built environment. Institutions can be divided into internal and external institutions (Kasper, 1998). Internal institutions differ from their external counterparts in that they evolve spontaneously within a society, and in that the enforcement mechanism is not part of the political system. External institutions, by contrast, normally rely on politically administered sanctions. The political system of a community, as defined by a constitution, is part of the set of external institutions.

While the internal institutions of a society are frequently overlooked in economic analyses, they are crucial to the economic development potential of a region. Indeed, an adequate set of internal institutions seems to be a necessary condition for economic restructuring, whether in the shape of industrialization or globalization. Elusive terms such as 'enterpreneurial spirit' or 'work ethic' are common in discussions of the serviceability of the internal institutions of a regional economy. More fundamental serviceability features include a general acceptance of property rights (Hayek, 1988), and a sufficient level of trust in a society (Fukuyama, 1995).

The hard infrastructure includes both immobile assets such as dwellings and factories and the transport and communication networks that connect them. Though many infrastructure investments have occurred because of political decisions, they are better conceptualized as the result of a process that is different from the implementation of regular political decisions. This is due to the function and durability of the physical infrastructure. The function of the physical infrastructure is to be the arena for the interactions between individuals and firms. Also, the durability and slowly changing nature of this arena means that it is treated as an exogenous factor by economic actors (Andersson and Strömquist, 1988).

From a dynamic perspective, the evolution of infrastructure networks has had more in common with spontaneous market processes than with the attainment of accessibility-maximizing planning objectives. This is because the nature of the economy, with thousands of nodes and millions of economic actors, makes it impossible to optimize or predict the effects of a comprehensive network plan (Andersson, 1998). Network evolution is better understood as the accumulative effect of decentralized link creation – mostly by local jurisdictions – which sometimes leads to unexpected phase transitions of the network itself as well as of the economic activities supported by the network.

THE IMPACT OF POLITICAL INTERVENTIONS

Both geographical accessibility and the quality and external linkages of the local transport and communication infrastructures reflect the slowly changing transport costs derived from spatial friction, while the quality of the soft infrastructure reflects the general transaction-cost level. The political factors that influence the location of nodes reflect more discretionary and unstable transaction costs, such as the cost of regulation, taxation, and restrictions on interjurisdictional flows of production factors. Whereas the infrastructural factors often imply the desirability of certain forms of active governance, such as a functioning legal system and an adequate transport network, the desired political factors more often imply government inaction. Individual entrepreneurs and established firms are more likely to prosper in an environment that provides substantial economic freedom.

For entrepreneurs, in particular, political additions to the already high start-up costs (i.e., fixed transaction costs) of new businesses can make ultimately profitable investments infeasible. Apart from the familiar burdens of high taxation, regulated labor markets and trade barriers, the role of land-use regulations deserves special attention (Andersson, 1999). Zoning ordinances, minimum lot-size requirements and building codes all impede the entrepreneurial, experimental process of finding suitable locations for production or exchange.

Jane Jacobs (1961) explained the relationship between land-use regulations and entrepreneurship in great detail. New, high-quality buildings can only support established, standardized or subsidized businesses, because business start-ups cannot afford the high overheads, at least initially. Jacobs wrote:

> As for really new ideas of any kind – no matter how ultimately profitable or otherwise successful some of them might prove to be – there is no leeway for such chancy trial, error, and experimentation in the high-overhead economy of new construction. Old ideas can sometimes use new buildings. New ideas must use old buildings.

Perhaps it is no coincidence that gateway regions with a sizeable proportion of run-down old buildings – such as New York, Hong Kong, the Milan–Venice corridor, or western Taiwan – have proved more adept at spawning new businesses than regions with heavy-handed land-use regulations, for example Frankfurt, Singapore or Stockholm.

In the high-technology sector the start-up costs are even higher. In traditional (non-innovative) sectors, fixed transaction costs are mostly limited to the cost of regulation and the search costs associated with finding a profitable location. High-tech firms incur additional search costs because of the difficulty of finding profitable knowledge inputs. This is why agglomeration economies are so important to R&D-intensive firms (Varga, 1998). The high transaction costs also explain why special exemptions from general regulations are often needed to enable high-tech entrepreneurship to occur ('science park' regimes often incorporate tax exemptions and a lighter regulatory burden than do firms operating outside the park).

For gateway cities with a specialized function as centers for finance and multinational corporations, land-use regulations are less important. Because of the possibility of intra-firm cross-subsidization, start-up costs are more easily absorbed. Instead, the 'MNC criteria' of a low rate of return to local production factors, low corporate taxes and the free flow of capital become more important. Some gateways combine attractive MNC criteria with a less attractive environment for entrepreneurs (e.g., Singapore), while other gateways are better at accommodating entrepreneurs than at attracting multinational corporations (e.g., Taiwan) (Andersson, 1999). Truly global gateways, however, exhibit relatively free flows of production factors, non-punitive tax rates, as well as a spontaneous development of land-use patterns and land-use quality.

NOTE

1. In this context, infrastructural factors refer both to the hard (physical) and soft (institutional) infrastructures. Institutions refer to general rules of conduct (internal institutions) and the political and legal systems (external meta-institutions). Political factors refer to the laws and regulations ('micro-institutions') formulated within the framework of a politico-legal system. For example, a sales tax (a legislated institution) may be introduced within the meta-institutional framework of American constitutional democracy.

REFERENCES

Alonso, W. (1964), *Location and Land Use*, Cambridge: Harvard University Press.
Andersson, Å.E. (1993), 'Infrastructure and the transformation to the C-society', in Roland Thord (ed.), *The Future of Transportation and Communication*, Berlin: Springer-Verlag.
Andersson, Å.E. (1998), 'Increasing networking possibilities and global structural transformation', *Journal of Applied Regional Science*, 3, 1–8.
Andersson, D.E. (1999), 'Land-use controls and economic freedom: the diverging histories of Singapore and Taipei' in D.E. Andersson and J.P.H. Poon (eds), *Asia-Pacific Transitions*, London: Macmillan.
Andersson, Å.E. and U. Strömquist (1988), *K-Samhällets Framtid*, Värnamo: Prisma.
Batten, D.F. (1999), 'The complexity of self-organizing East-Asian networks', in D.E. Andersson and J.P.H. Poon (eds), *Asia-Pacific Transitions*, London: Macmillan.
Batten, D.F., K. Kobayashi and Å.E. Andersson (1988), 'Knowledge, nodes, and networks – an analytical perspective', in Å.E. Andersson, D.F. Batten and C. Karlsson (eds), *Knowledge and Industrial Organization*, Berlin: Springer-Verlag.
Coase, R.H. (1937), 'The nature of the firm', *Economica*, 4, 386–405.
Enright, M.J., E.E. Scott and D. Dodwell (1997), *The Hong Kong Advantage*, Hong Kong: Oxford University Press.
Fukuyama, F. (1995), *Trust: The Social Virtues and the Creation of Prosperity*, New York: The Free Press.
Giersch, H. (1979), 'Aspects of growth, structural change, and employment: A Schumpeterian Perspective', *Weltwirtschaftliches Archiv*, 115, 629–52.
Hayek, F.A. (1982), *Law, Legislation and Liberty*, London: Routledge.
Hayek, F.A. (1988), *The Fatal Conceit: The Errors of Socialism*, London: Routledge.

Jacobs, J. (1961), *The Death and Life of Great American Cities*, New York: Random House.

Jacobs, J. (1969), *The Economy of Cities*, New York: Random House.

Kasper, W. (1994), *Global Competition, Institutions, and the East-Asian Ascendancy*, San Francisco: ICS Press.

Kasper, W. (1998), *Property Rights and Competition: An Essay on the Constitution of Capitalism*, Smithfield: The Centre for Independent Studies.

Kobayashi, K. (1993), 'The emerging new arena of transportation and communication in Japan', in R. Thord (ed.), *The Future of Transportation and Communication*, Berlin: Springer-Verlag.

North, D.C. (1992), 'Transaction costs, institutions, and economic performance', Occasional Paper No. 30, San Francisco: International Center for Economic Growth.

Olson, M. (1982), *The Rise and Decline of Nations – Economic Growth, Stagflation, and Social Rigidities*, New Haven: Yale University Press.

Pirenne, H. (1936), *Economic and Social History of Medieval Europe*, London.

Sassen, S. (1994), *Cities in a Global Economy*, Thousand Oaks: Pine Forge Press.

Schumpeter, J.A. (1912), *Theorie der wirtschaftlichen Entwicklung*, Leipzig.

Snickars, F. (1993), 'A systems view of infrastructure planning', in Roland Thord (ed.), *The Future of Transportation and Communication*, Berlin: Springer-Verlag.

Streit, M.E. (1996), 'Competition among systems as a defense of liberty', in H. Bouillon (ed.), *Libertarians and Liberalism: Essays in Honour of Gerard Radnitzky*, Aldershot: Avebury.

Thünen, J.H. von (1826), *Der isolierte Staat in Beziehung auf Nationaloekonomie und Landwirtschaft*, Stuttgart.

Varga, A. (1998), 'Universities and regional economic development: does agglomeration matter?', unpublished paper.

Index

corridor, definition 313
corridor cities, networks and 313
Crahan, M.E. 51, 55–6
creative activities 13, 15
Cuban missile crisis (1962) 127
Cunard Shipping Company 5, 134
Curtiss, Glenn 131–2

Dallas 22, 243
Danish-Swedish border, location 367
Darmstadt 284–5, 347
decentralization 22, 52, 365, 371
Delhi 218
Deloitte & Touche Washington study 121
denationalization 52
Denmark 37, 301–2, 357–9, 361
Denver 22
deregulation 52, 306, 308
Detroit 22, 57, 131
Dhaka 218
Directory of National Experimental and Research Organizations 241
diversification 36, 43
division of labor 65, 67
Dominicans, Hispanic businesses and 63
Dortmund-Dusseldorf-Cologne 19, 24–6, 299
Drennen, M. 51, 56–7
Drucker, P. 68, 71
Dulles International Airport (Washington) 107, 110–11
Dunning, J.H. 171, 194
Düsseldorf 289, 299, 305, 336–7
Dutch shipbuilding technology 67
Duvalier 64
dynamic learning environments 53

'E' arteries, traffic flow 311, 318–22
e-mail 142
East Asia 208, 227, 370, 373, 375
East India Company 66, 212, 256
Eastern European countries, transport and 319
'economic advantage of backwardness' 12
economic conduct 14
economic space, definition 313
economies of scale 12, 16, 41, 171, 316
  accessibility and 320
  creative activities and 15

economies of scope and 54, 299, 308, 314, 326
  hub and 6
  ideas and 17, 362
  self-perpetuating 45
  Singapore and 200
  Stockholm 346, 350–51, 356
  transport costs and 318–19
Economist, The 92, 230
Ecudorian immigrants, Washington 109
Edinburgh-Glasgow, scientific papers 19, 24–6
education 13–14, 297, 327
efficiency equalization, markets and 43
electrical engineering 39
Electrolux 362
electronic media 15
Emilia Romagna 316–17, 347
England, common law 66, 71, 74–5, 349
Enright, M.J. 170–71, 370
entertainment industry 15
epistemic risks 36, 38–9, 41
Ericsson company 362
Erie Canal 58
Essen 218, 299
Ethopian refugees, Washington 109
Euro, the 37, 69, 293
Eurobond 68
Eurodollar 68
Europe 10, 16, 190
  air transport market development 306
  bankers and 31
  barriers of language and culture 308
  core and periphery structure 298
  economic specialization 298–9
  emergence of urban system 301–7, 308
  'feasibility space' and 368
  financial clusters 37
  firms in Asia-Pacific 172
  functional regions 347
  higher education industry 308–9
  international links within 23
  links with Vancouver 147, 160, 165
  medium-sized cities and integration 304
  MNCs with RHQs and ROs 176, 185
  northwestern part 21, 27
  OECD estimates of road freight 319
  offices in Hong Kong 177, 182–4
  research in 22, 48
  ROs in Singapore 196